TEACHERS' UNION

*The TUI and its Forerunners
in Irish Education 1899–1994*

Edited by John Logan

A. & A. Farmar

Published by
A. & A. Farmar
Beech House
78 Ranelagh Village
Dublin 6
Ireland

ISBN 1-899047-44-1

Copy-editor: Finbarr O'Shea
Index: Helen Litton
Cover: David Lilburn
Designed and typeset
by A. & A. Farmar
Printing and binding by βetaprint

TEACHERS' UNION

To the memory of
all past members of the teacher organisations
in technical and vocational education

Contents

List of Figures

List of Tables

Contributors

Kieran Byrne	*Professor of education, University of Limerick*
Frances Donoghue	*Research assistant, University College Dublin*
Brian Girvin	*Senior lecturer in modern history, University of Glasgow*
Áine Hyland	*Professor of education, University College Cork*
Mary Jones	*Social researcher and author*
J. J. Lee	*Professor of history, University College Cork*
John Logan	*Senior lecturer in history, University of Limerick*
Michael McGinley	*Lecturer in industrial relations, University College Dublin*
Emmet O'Connor	*Lecturer in politics, Magee College, University of Ulster*
Eilis Ward	*Research fellow, Trinity College Dublin*

Foreword

From the beginning of this century, the Teachers' Union of Ireland and its forerunners have had the twin goals of advocating education reform and negotiating improved working conditions for their members. Each organisation has sought to promote a system of education that is free, non-selective, multi-denominational, co-educational and managed locally through democratic, representative structures. As the century ends, members of the TUI can be satisfied that the contribution of their predecessors to debate and discussion has helped to decisively form the present shape of second and third level education.

For many teachers their union is the most immediate and effective means of ensuring that their working conditions are such as to satisfactorily support their work as educators. In the past there were critical moments when individual teachers felt compelled to turn to their professional organisation for advice and support and, if necessary, collective action on their behalf. The response of the union on those occasions proved vital to the forging of professional identity and solidarity.

This volume seeks to examine that history and its publication may be considered particularly appropriate at a time of reappraisal and of continuing debate on the future of our education system. *Teacher's Union*—a collaborative work by a group of distinguished scholars—is also a very fitting record of the idealism and effort by generations of teachers and of their role in the making of modern Ireland.

Joe Carolan
President, Teachers' Union of Ireland
March 1999

Acknowledgments

This volume originated in a decision by the executive committee of the Teachers' Union of Ireland to commission a history that would be of use to present and past members of the union as well as anyone interested in the history of Irish education. Many debts were accumulated during its preparation which are now a pleasure to acknowledge.

The first is to the project's steering committee which at one time or other included serving presidents of the union, Tony Deffely, Billy Fitzpatrick, Alice Prendergast and Ed Riordan. A former president of the union and now its general secretary, Jim Dorney, and two former presidents, Kevin McCarthy and Seán McCarthy, served on the committee for its duration and the eventual publication of this volume is due to their enthusiasm, interest and determined support. Until her retirement as education officer in 1994, Gráinne O'Flynn inspired and guided the project. Her successor Rose Malone saw it to its conclusion.

Historians taking on a commission may be forgiven for fearing an excess of help from patrons. In this instance members of the steering committee read successive drafts of individual chapters and while each was improved significantly by their criticisms and comments, at no time did the editor or any of the contributors meet obstruction or interference. The term 'steering committee' proved a fortunate misnomer. All decisions regarding content and emphasis were left to the editor and it is with him that responsibility for any remaining shortcomings remains.

Other members of the union including Hugh Campbell, Tom Creedon, Liam Donovan, Jarlath Duffy, Michael Farrell, Noel Kelly, Matt Kingston, Tom Moynihan, Donogh O'Brien, Matt Power, James Wrynn and the late Jim Hickey provided valuable material. Officers and staff at head office including Breda Hall, Peter MacMenamin, Mairín Ganly and Hilary O'Byrne were generous with their time, and special thanks are due to the founding chatelaine of Orwell Road, Anne Hanley.

The vicissitudes of record keeping, especially in the early days of the union and during the life of its forerunners, have left many gaps which retired or former members sought to fill; sadly, three former presidents, Tom Carney, Eileen Quinlan and Liam Trundle, each of whom supplied missing pieces of the jigsaw, did not live to see the results of their collaboration. The personal and inherited memories of the last general secretary of the Vocational Education Officers' Organisation, Billy McNamara, were especially helpful in filling significant gaps. The advice of Muriel McCarthy was particularly welcome. A former member of the union, Barney O'Reilly, facilitated the collection of data on vocational education committee membership from his fellow chief executive officers, almost all of whom are former members of the union and some of whom—Muireas Ó Ceallaigh, Bobby Buckley, Jim Lyons, Oliver Hynes and Seán Blunnie—graciously provided access to other materials in their care.

The custodian of the TUI papers at the Archives Department, University College Dublin, Seamus Halperty, and the director of the National Archives, David Craig, and his colleagues Ken Hannigan, Aideen Ireland and Caitríona Crowe were, as always, generous with their time, while Sarah Ward-Perkins shared her unrivalled knowledge of trade union records. John Coakley, Eoin Devereux, Dick Haslam, John Horgan, David Lilburn, Lillis Ó Laoire, Nick Rees, John Stapleton, Tom Shortt, Joe Wallace and Bernadette Whelan each helped the project in ways both practical and wise. Thérèse Farrell and Anne Logan, observing the workings of the union at one remove, supplied significant material.

Publishers Tony and Anna Farmar provided support that went far beyond their professional obligations, and thanks are also due to Finbarr O'Shea, a tireless and meticulous copy-editor.

Finally it is a special pleasure to thank each of the authors of the individual chapters.

John Logan
February 1999

Abbreviations

ACEOVEC	Association of Chief Executive Officers of Vocational Education Committees
AnCO	An Chomhairle Oiliúna
ASTI	Association of Secondary Teachers, Ireland
CMGO	Cumann Mhúinteoirí Gairm-Oideachais
DATI	Department of Agriculture and Technical Instruction
ETTUC	European Teachers' Trade Union Committee
ETUCE	European Trade Union Committee for Education
IATIOO	Irish Agriculture and Technical Instruction Officers' Organisation
ICA	Irish Countrywomen's Association
ICPSA	Irish Conference of Professional and Service Associations
ICTU	Irish Congress of Trade Unions
IDATU	Irish Distributive and Administrative Trades Union
IFFTU	International Federation of Free Trade Unions
IFUT	Irish Federation of University Teachers
INTO	Irish National Teachers' Organisation
ITEA	Irish Technical Education Association
ITIA	Irish Technical Instruction Association
ITUC	Irish Trade Union Congress
IVEA	Irish Vocational Education Association
NCEA	National Council for Educational Awards
NUI	National University of Ireland
NUTTI	Northern Union of Teachers in Technical Institutes
OECD	Organisation for Economic Co-operation and Development
RCO	Representative Council of Associations of Officers of Agriculture and Technical Instruction Committees in Ireland
TUI	Teachers' Union of Ireland
VEOO	Vocational Education Officers' Organisation
VTA	Vocational Teachers' Association
WCOTP	World Confederation of Organisations of the Teaching Profession
WUI	Workers' Union of Ireland

1. Technical Education and Change in Irish Society

J. J. Lee

The Teachers' Union of Ireland and its forerunners have a proud record of concern for technical education that is as old as the century. They also have a history of support for the underprivileged in Irish society. It is appropriate therefore that, at a time of unprecedented speed of technological change and at a time when the founding principles of the welfare state are coming under increasing assault, we should stand back for a moment and ponder some of the main implications of where we have come from, and where we might be going. Thus the union's role in commissioning a history—a preparedness to have its past subjected to scrutiny and analysis—must be lauded. This is not just so that its record will be preserved for the use of present and future members but as a means of aiding debate on the union's continuing role in the development of technical education and its role in the broader society.

The close, indeed inextricable, connection between economic development and technical education has become axiomatic for many commentators. There is in fact a long tradition of ascribing the economic backwardness of Ireland to a lack of technical education. In one of the most celebrated studies of the problems and prospects of Irish economic development, *The industrial resources of Ireland*,[1] published in 1844, Robert Kane laid particular stress on the lack of industrial knowledge as a cause of Irish economic retardation. Kane, a graduate of Trinity College Dublin, one of the most eminent of nineteenth-century Irish educationalists, was still only thirty-five at the time of publication. But he had already founded the *Dublin Journal of Medical Science* in 1832, had begun publishing his successful *Elements of Chemistry* in 1841, had been appointed secretary to the Royal Irish Academy in 1842, and held posts as professor of natural philosophy at the Royal Dublin Society and as professor of chemistry at the Apothecaries' Hall. He would shortly become first president of Queen's College Cork, as well as the founder director of the Museum of Irish Industry.

Kane therefore brought a formidable range of both expertise and

experience, to say nothing of energy, to his observations. A great be-
liever in 'practical knowledge', he insisted that 'the education necessary
for industrial pursuits is very generally underrated in this country, and
from this cause alone springs a great deal of our want of industrial
knowledge'.[2] Kane nursed high ambitions, and high hopes, for the
impact of industrial education on what today would be called competitiveness:

> This subject of industrial education is, as it appears to me, specially important
> to this country, as without it any available development of our industrial
> resources must be almost impossible. In every branch of manufacture England
> is already in possession of the field, and if we only learn from her, and are
> competent merely to follow her routine processes, we must remain always
> behind in the march of industrial improvement . . . To keep a market does not
> require at all as much exertion as to obtain one; and hence it is only by the
> most strenuous exertion and by the most perfect knowledge of his trade that an
> Irish manufacturer can have any chance of success. To succeed against his
> English competitor, he must know more than him. It is evident that we have
> much to change, yet it is not impossible.[3]

Although stressing that 'agricultural education is . . . the object on
which immediate attention should be concentrated in this country',[4]
he recognised that 'the schoolmasters have to learn the principles of
agriculture, before they can teach them'.[5] Improving agricultural standards was not, however, simply a matter of education. Kane reposed high,
and as it turned out, exaggerated, hopes on the idea of providing tuition for teachers on 'model farms', from whence they would return to
their national schools to act as agents 'of industrial progress, by whose
precepts and example, the seed of practical intelligence can be cultivated, and return hundredfold'.[6] In this respect, Kane was but one of a
long line of optimists who deluded themselves about the potential of
agricultural education, largely because they failed to incorporate the
prevailing social, cultural and political realities into their image of agriculture.

As far as manufacturing was concerned, Kane placed his hopes in
the Royal Dublin Society emulating the Central School of Arts and
Manufactures in Paris, and similar institutions in Prussia and Austria.
Thomas Davis, incidentally, whose thought is often caricatured as hope-
lessly romantic (and although it is true that he ascribed Irish economic
backwardness ultimately to the damage inflicted by British conquest),
welcomed Kane's analysis.[7] Even if his orientation was not precisely
Kane's, he too found 'our industrial and general education very inferior'.[8] And he too sought to learn from European experience, arguing

that 'the schools and galleries, museums and educational systems of Germany deserve the closest examination with reference to the knowledge and taste required in Ireland, and the means of giving them'.[9]

Kane had clear ideas on how industrial knowledge should be inculcated. 'Science should be taught especially with a view to the application of its principle', while 'practice should be followed with constant reference to the principles upon which it rests'.[10] Although he conceded that 'the practical part of education for industry must be effected in the factory', he argued that 'all that part which consists in general and special scientific discipline might be most efficiently carried on by means of institutions of a collegiate character'.[11] Kane clearly raised a host of issues which remain just as relevant today as 150 years ago. But little was done for more than a century afterwards to foster 'industrial' education. Why?

The failure was frequently attributed to the anti-materialism of Catholicism. It was indeed to be expected that, in a country riven by religious rancour, with a governing class distinguished above all by its religion, economic backwardness, once it came to be regarded as a criterion of character, would come to be blamed on the influence of the Catholic Church in general, and of the clergy in particular, by the type of mindset that found this assumption congenial. This became all the more likely as the north-east became the only part of Ireland to industrialise, and industrialisation soon came to be equated in much Protestant thinking with the moral superiority of the individual. The qualities that were peculiarly conducive to eternal salvation transpired to be those which, through a happy divine dispensation, were also peculiarly conducive to the maximisation of profit. Long before Max Weber penned his classic study of the Protestant ethic, the equation of economic superiority, and especially industrial superiority, with the superior religion had become a staple of Protestant thought.

Nor was this sentiment confined to sectarian bigots. Indeed, it was Horace Plunkett, whose judgement might be suspect but whose spirit and instincts were indisputably generous, who gave most publicised expression to it, leading to a celebrated confrontation with Fr Michael O'Riordan, then vice-rector of the Irish College in Rome, at the turn of the century. Plunkett attributed Irish backwardness mainly to the alleged lack of what we would today call an enterprise culture in Ireland, which in turn derived, in his estimation, from the sense of resignation to a divinely decreed earthly fate inculcated by Catholic teaching.[12]

Fr O'Riordan, in his robust response, *Catholicity and progress in Ireland,* was careful to stress that the Catholic Church did indeed value the spiritual above the material.[13] But he insisted that it did not denounce the material. 'Industrial progress is undoubtedly both a law and a duty for a people', he insisted, '. . . but it is not their highest law, nor their first duty'.[14] O'Riordan sought to escape from the polarisation of 'spiritual' and 'material' by arguing, in an interesting twist, that a culture which valued only materialism bore the seeds of internal decay:

> The will and the heart are the great motive forces in human activity, and if due attention is not given to the proper cultivation of those, the attempt to build a truly prosperous nation is as vain as the task of the fool in the gospel who tried to build his house on sand.[15]

Whatever one's response to Fr O'Riordan's reasoning in this respect—and the issue remains one of high contemporary relevance—he himself had no difficulty in incorporating what he called 'technical training' into the Catholic ethos. His concept of 'technical training' will appear rudimentary from today's perspective, but it reflected the thinking of his time. He devotes an entire chapter to 'nuns and technical training', in which he cites numerous instances of the industrial and technical work which convents had been doing—with, as might be expected, the work of Mother Bernard at the Foxford Woollen Mills taking pride of place. His conclusion that 'there is hardly a primary school in the country under the charge of nuns in which training of a practical or industrial nature has not always formed part of the education of the pupils'[16] may well have been an exaggeration, but it hardly reveals any ideological antipathy to technical training.

Fr O'Riordan felt, in fact, that the nuns were far more effective than the itinerant instructors of the Department of Agriculture and Technical Instruction, established under Horace Plunkett's secretaryship in 1900. However partisan his perspective—Fr O'Riordan could hardly be expected to forgo the opportunity of taking a dig at Plunkett's exaggerated rhetoric on behalf of his infant project—he did ask some key questions, which he felt 'the economists of the Department do not seem to have seriously considered whilst they have been dispersing itinerant technical teachers over the country'.[17] Above all, he asked 'What is to become of these children when they grow up and have learned all we will have taught them? Are time and money to be spent in training them for the benefit of the foreign countries whither they are sure to go for want of a way of living here?'[18]

These were crucial questions. Could technical instruction serve as an engine of economic development? Could it pull the economy in its train, or help kick-start an inherently sluggish economy? How far could technical education foster industrial development, as distinct from facilitate it? Did the market have to exist before the supply could make a difference? Was it possible to think of supply creating its own demand? The answer is debatable. My own view is that, as the economy in general has become much more technology driven in recent decades, it may well be the case today that, in a wide range of activities, supply can do much to create its own demand. But that was much less the case in the circumstances of the country at the time of the Plunkett-O'Riordan controversy.

This is not, however, as is frequently but mistakenly assumed, a question of a conflict between, on the one hand, academic, non-market-oriented education, and on the other, practical, relevant, market-oriented education. It is true that ideologies of the intrinsic superiority of 'academic' education did develop. But they were not the driving force behind the provision of the bulk of what is today called academic education at either second or third level. It is simply a mistake to assume that Irish education was so devoted to things of the spirit, or to the inherited values of a classical education, that it had no time for market criteria. The bulk of Irish education was always relentlessly market oriented, from the hedge schools to the universities, in accordance with parental perception of market opportunities. Whether it was practical or not may be a matter of opinion. But it was certainly deemed to be relevant. It is a vulgar confusion of our times to equate our concept of practical with relevant.

Relevant meant relevant to getting a job. There was little free education, at least after primary level. Parents no more relished the idea, then than now, of paying for their children to remain dependent on them for life. They sought to equip them with the education most relevant to the good jobs of the time. It just so happened that the good jobs were not, for the most part, in Irish industry. They were frequently in government service, where many an able Irish candidate—Michael Collins and Seán Lemass would be conspicuous examples (two highly 'practical' men incidentally)—succeeded handsomely in the entry examination. As new opportunities arose, conscientious parents sought to have their children equipped for jobs in public administration, teaching, the police, secretarial work and nursing.

But this was, for the most part, opportunity in the administrative and commercial sector rather than in the industrial manufacturing sector. Ireland developed, as tends to be the case with colonial countries in general, more as a trading than as a manufacturing economy, more engaged in exchange than in industrial production. The Belfast area formed a partial exception, but only a partial exception. It is normal to see it as enjoying a spectacularly successful industrial record compared with the rest of Ireland. And so it did. But the industrial record of east Ulster, much less of the counties that would constitute Northern Ireland, was actually a rather modest one by British and western European standards other than those of the rest of the country. In population terms, the performance was very ordinary compared with the rest of the United Kingdom, or of western Europe, from the mid-nineteenth century. The growth of Belfast itself, in so far as it depended on the shipbuilding industry, derived from a virtual accident of location by non-local investors. This is not for a moment to denigrate the achievement, but rather to remind us of the criteria of comparison which allow nineteenth-century Belfast to appear spectacularly successful—which few could claim twentieth-century Belfast has been, except for the spurts derived from wartime booms. In terms of per capita income it seems that the differences between North and South, or at the very least between the northern and southern halves of the eastern part of the country, were very small. The differences were exaggerated for polemical purposes by propagandists on both sides. Irish nationalist propagandists liked to attribute the industrialisation of east Ulster to the favoured treatment of the linen industry by the British government at an earlier period, while Ulster unionist propagandists naturally sought to maximise the alleged difference in economic performance between the 'Protestant' North and the incorrigibly retarded 'Catholic' South.

As it so happened, a disproportionate amount of such industry as there was in the South happened to be controlled by Protestants. Entry was not exactly by open examination, nor did canvassing disqualify. There was not much point in Catholics seeking positions with good promotion prospects in most banks or railways, two of the biggest sectoral employers. Nor did Belfast industry offer glowing management prospects for Catholics. Outside Belfast, in an economy dominated by small family firms, openings for outsiders, whether Protestant or Catholic, were few. It is possible to exaggerate the 'objective' economic difficulties confronting Irish industrial development. But it is equally pointless to deny that political-ideological circumstances significantly conditioned both the objective prospects and subjective mind-sets.

Middle-class and lower middle-class Catholic Ireland did not have its eyes lifted permanently to the heavens, obsessed with the joyous expectation of eternal salvation. It had them, at least for educational purposes, fixed very firmly on the ground, taking up emerging job opportunities and preparing its children assiduously for such openings as

did occur in public service and the professions. In a country ravaged—
and rationally ravaged, given its history—by a sense of insecurity, the
security of the permanent and pensionable post exerted a magnetic attraction for many of the ablest young minds in the country, almost
down to our own day. Where unemployment was high and prospects
poor, job security came to be prized as virtually an end in itself by many
a parent and many a child.

It is doubtless true that what were generally seen as better prospects
in the bureaucracy and in the professions, at however modest a level,
contributed to the inferior status then assigned to technical education.
This reinforced the aversion to 'trade' that filtered down from aristo-
cratic Protestant circles into the values of a rising Catholic middle class,
who sought to emulate the values of the aristocracy even while they
displaced them and then often purporting to despise them. There was
nothing peculiarly Catholic about this, however. Robert Kane himself
had railed against the superiority attached in Trinity College to education for the professions, insisting that 'industrial knowledge is much
more difficult to acquire, and much more extensive in its range, than
professional knowledge'.[19]

Kane's claim, although no doubt understandable in the light of slights
he himself presumably endured, is itself indicative of a besetting weakness of much educational thought; the need felt by advocates of any
particular perspective to denigrate all other perspectives. Human beings
can learn more, both about their subject and about themselves, from
further thought and practice. The moment denigrating the 'other' sur-
faces in educational debate—whether it be 'academic' denigrating 'practical' or 'applied' denigrating 'pure'—thinking has invariably moved
from educational concerns to issues of status and self-image. It might
be argued that it is only human nature to try to invest one's own area of
activity and interest with a status superior to that of others. But then,
education is supposed to enhance understanding of both oneself and
others. Indeed, if it does not do so, it is hard to see why it should be
deemed to be education at all.

That an inferior status was for long attributed to technical education reflected very poorly on the quality of mind inculcated by much of
the education available at secondary school and university. Much of the
teaching in these institutions did not, obviously, inculcate the breadth
of mind or the capaciousness of judgement characteristic of the truly
educated person. But this was not, it should be stressed, something
peculiar to Ireland. It was characteristic of most economies and societies in broadly similar circumstances. In Ireland's case, it was powerfully

reinforced by the intellectual and psychological consequences of English rule. For the English ruling class also purported to despise the technical—that may well be one reason for the long-term decline of Britain in the twentieth century.[20] Given that we took so much of our thinking from England, even while we professed to reject its influence—the anomaly Douglas Hyde identified in his 1892 lecture 'The necessity for de-Anglicising Ireland'—it would have been remarkable if this perspective had not infiltrated our own thinking also, apart from other reasons altogether.

However unjustifiable the combination of arrogance and ignorance revealed in the condescending attitude towards technical education and towards practical training, it must be stressed again that this did not derive fundamentally from an aversion to technical jobs. There was of course a certain amount of aversion, linked with self-images that developed among members of the bureaucracy and the professions as they fashioned a value system designed to inflate their sense of self-importance. But that could persist only because of long-term economic sluggishness. It was less an aversion to technical jobs than a lack of technical jobs that allowed the mind-set to flourish for so long. Had the jobs been available, it seems highly likely that parents would have revised their attitudes in the light of burgeoning economic opportunity. It is in fact difficult to identify any significant sector of Irish industry whose development can be plausibly claimed to have been blocked by sustained shortage of the requisite skills. There were, and are, specific difficulties at specific times. But there has been more frequently oversupply than shortage in most economic sectors. At times this led, inevitably, to substantial emigration on the one hand, or, amongst those staying at home, to the defensiveness reflected in mechanisms for controlling numbers of apprentices and entry to various crafts.

None of this justifies the inferior status long assigned to technical education. But it does warn against the assumption that if only legislation had been more 'progressive'—if the Vocational Education Act 1930, for instance, had adopted a more ambitious approach—or if only value systems had been more 'enlightened', the economy would have flourished thanks to the higher priority allocated to technical education. As Seán Lemass thrashed around after the end of the war to try to gear Irish industry for a less protectionist age through the agency of his proposed Industrial Efficiency and Prices Bill, he listed 'the extension of facilities for technical training of workers' as a priority, together with improvement in the design of both factories and products.[21] But Lemass was trying to force the pace in the face of only limited demand, and nothing much would happen until the economy began to pick up in earnest more than a decade later.

Once actual market demand emerged for technical skills, the official response was actually fairly prompt. There were of course some delays, and some of the inherited attitude towards technical education remained, as was reflected to some extent in a report of the Council of Education, as late as 1962.[22] But in a longer historical perspective, it is the speed of the response that followed the publication of T. K. Whitaker's *Economic development* in 1958 that is most striking. The following year An Cheard Chomhairle—a national apprenticeship board—was established, to be duly superseded in 1968 by AnCO, to be in turn superseded, in the merger with the National Manpower Agency and the Youth Employment Agency, by FÁS in 1987. Patrick Hillery, Minister for Education in the first Lemass cabinet, signalled the intention to found regional technical colleges in 1963. By 1969 five had opened. The two national institutes for higher education in Dublin and Limerick, each with a mission in the field of technological education, would follow shortly.

Given the previous pace of decision making in educational policy, this rate of activity was phenomenal. Unfortunately, some of the regional technical colleges were treated as second-class citizens, organisationally and architecturally, and an opportunity was missed to produce structures and facilities worthy of the enhanced significance and status now attached to the primarily technical sector—not, of course, that universities always displayed an appropriate sense of aesthetic responsibility either. The response of the existing universities to either the national institutes for higher education or the regional technical colleges was not always the most gracious. Any number of cross-currents concerning status and self-image, as well as genuine intellectual concerns, often muddied the waters. There were tensions, not only between humanities and social sciences on the one hand, and science and technology on the other, but between science and technology themselves, as indeed between humanities and social sciences. Tensions existed within as well as between each of these broad categories and cleavages occurred within institutions, and sectors, as well as between them.

The national institutes for higher education, now of course full universities in their own right, and the regional technical colleges, now institutes of technology, have made their mark handsomely since their establishment. Not only have they brought a whole new stream of activities within the higher education ambit, but they have enormously enhanced access to higher education, not least by their location, from Letterkenny to Tralee, and from Waterford to Dundalk. Nevertheless it is possible to detect a continuing sense of grievance overlapping, if not precisely coterminous with, this sector. As recently as 1996, the government white paper, *Science, technology and innovation*, lamented the failure of the state to provide 'a sustained commitment' to science and technology.[23] This can be readily accepted. What is more debatable is whether this lack of 'sustained commitment' is due, as was argued, to the fact that 'the national establishment culture was not supportive'.[24]

My own perspective is itself inevitably sectoral. I cannot write with the authority of a scientist or technologist, though I have tried to foster teaching and research in the history of both areas. What I am most conscious of is how derisory state support for research in any area has been. It is of course true that Ireland has a proud record of literary achievement. But that owes hardly anything to state support. Indeed, if one were to consider censorship a major obstacle to literary creativity—in practice it probably wasn't, but that's a different matter—one might say that much of the literary achievement has occurred despite the state, rather than because of it. In the socio-economic sphere, support for research was negligible at least until the founding of the Economic Research Institute (now the Economic and Social Research Institute) in 1960. And that body was founded only through initial support from the American-based Ford Foundation.

But surely, it must be assumed, we have lavished research support on historical inquiry. Are we not indeed a people obsessed with history? In fact, state support for historical research has been virtually non-existent. The cost of Neil Jordan's film, *Michael Collins*, has almost certainly exceeded the total amount of support for historical research since the foundation of the state. It is difficult to think of any other western European country which has devoted so little support to research into its own past. The long-term neglect of archives and of libraries has just begun to be remedied. But the condition of the National Library, for instance, is a matter of notoriety. The advertised salary of the director of the National Library is about half that of the secretary general of a government department. And it is certainly the case that no country in western Europe is as dependent on foreign researchers—and on the research support they receive from their own countries—to explore its history. If 'the national establishment culture' has been 'supportive' of historical inquiry, this has certainly not translated into actual support for research. At the crucial level of postgraduate research, support has indeed been poor for science and technology but it has, nevertheless, been far better in those areas than in the humanities or social sciences. This may be an undemanding criterion but it does suggest that the problem with 'the national establishment culture' is not that it has been hostile to research in the area of science and technology, but that it has been, at best, indifferent to research in any area.

The white paper threw down a gauntlet to the alleged 'national establishment culture' and indeed to the value system of the society at large. The dominant thrust of the document is not only the centrality of science and technology to economic growth, but the primacy of materialism as the core value of modern society. It is doubtful if any government document has ever proclaimed the materialistic interpretation of history in such uncompromising terms. Time and again the decisive criterion invoked to justify particular recommendations is their potential contribution to economic growth. There is, it is true, one sentence that does suggest that there might be other possible values involved: 'Apart from its intrinsic merits, science and technology is also increasingly bound up with huge moral and political/philosophical issues, for example, in the biological sciences and the development of the information society.'[25] But there is no development of this perspective in the rest of the white paper. However 'huge' the 'moral and political/ philosophical' issues may be, they are clearly deemed irrelevant in this context.

The document is full of penetrating observations and recommendations. It is surely right to stress the importance of regular retraining in an age of perpetual change. This of course has implications for the basic type of education at both second and third level. To go back to Kane, this must include inculcating a capacity for understanding general principles, as well as acquiring particular skills. It is sensible to teach courses 'linked to the needs of the economy and the likely sources of employment'.[26] But these needs are not written in stone. They are in course of rapid and sustained change. There is now a built-in obsolescence to many jobs. Unless the quality of education is good enough to equip young people to adapt to change and not solely to supply the immediate needs of employers, whose concern is for the most part inevitably and naturally with their short-term profits, then there may be a danger that many citizens will be left ill-equipped—many of them at a relatively young age—to cope with constant change. 'The skills with which workers start their working lives are now unlikely to see them through to the end of their careers.'[27] With roughly a forty-year working life, employees at all levels are likely to require reorientation on several occasions, and not merely as they enter the workforce. It is therefore essential that the foundations be soundly laid, to provide them with the basis for adapting to changing technical and organisational requirements.

That is one reason why, from a purely practical perspective, the polarisation of science and technology on the one hand, and humanities and social sciences on the other, should be deplored. Balance is crucial to an efficient as well as to a civilised society. A balanced education should encompass the teaching of techniques of thought and action that regard understanding of both the human and the technical as a continuum of a learning experience rather than as alternatives, or even polar opposites.

Science, technology and innovation embraces globalisation as the wave of the future. The primacy of the technological imperative governs the analysis. All we can do apparently is ride the surf. 'Long established industries and ways of life are disappearing',[28] we are told. But there is a fundamental difference between 'industries' and 'ways of life'. Industries disappear because they are rendered obsolete by market competition. They are out-competed in the economic market. 'Ways of life' are not inanimate objects like industrial products. They involve human beings, not products. They are a mixture of objective and subjective. They involve mind-sets and modes of thinking. Workers can be rendered redundant over their heads, through no decision of their own, indeed against their will. But a way of life becomes redundant only through a decision by those affected to abandon an old one and embrace the new.

There is nothing necessarily wrong with that. But the implication here seems to be that there is only one way of life compatible with globalisation, and that it will be technologically determined. This will be apparently the inescapable consequence of embracing the science-technology-innovation value system preached in the white paper. 'Public policy theorists argue that the logic of the rational calculus must, in the end, cut through the complicating layers of culture, conflict, compromise and history—as allegedly in private life.'[29] 'Public policy theorists' do not, however, parachute in from outer space. They are products overwhelmingly of a particular segment of American culture. Like most theorists devoid of historical perspective, they happen to equate the particular circumstances in which they find themselves with eternal truth. It may indeed be that that will be the case from now on. The juggernaut of technology may level all local distinctions. The big battalions are on its side. But if this is inevitable, the logic is that Ireland, or indeed Europe, or any distinctive entities, should cease to exist, at least culturally. If that is not the case, then there is no reason why Ireland, or anywhere else, need adopt this perspective, or at least adopt it uncritically, unless we choose to do so. 'The logic of the rational calculus' is, after all, simply a euphemism for a particular ideology.

If the world is being reshaped on a gigantic scale, it is for this purpose. All other values are apparently to be subordinated to this. There should be gender balance, for instance, we are told, in science and technology subjects, because 'the state and industry lose out if female science and technology graduates are not given equal opportunity to use their talents in the business sector'.[30] That is true. But it is not 'the state and industry' which lose out in the first instance. It is the female graduates themselves, if their aspirations and potential lie in that direction, and they are frustrated by gender conventions from pursuing them. It is rather ironic that 'the state' should receive such prominent mention here when the ideology of 'globalisation' logically dispenses with the state, except as the local agent for the ordering of global requirements.

It ought to be the glory of technological discovery to enhance the range of human choice. In this value system, however, technological progress seems to reduce choice, because the technological imperative steamrolls all societies in the same 'global' direction. The possibility of choice ought to make for a more complex world, not a more simple one. Where there is little choice, few 'moral and political/philosophical' decisions have to be made. Constraints limit choice, and it is precisely the possibility of choice opened up by technological advance that obliges human beings to ponder their value system. The challenge of the information revolution is not, ultimately, technological, essential though it be to keep fully abreast of it, or rather to be in the forefront of it, to remain competitive. The real questions are: what is this information for and what is the goal of competitiveness? The information revolution is not culturally neutral. It comes loaded with particular cultural assumptions, for better and for worse. The information revolution could prove enormously liberating for a people in our position. But it could also, unless we are fully alert to the implications, go far to reduce us to the level of clones of the more powerful cultures pioneering this revolution.

The Teachers' Union of Ireland and its forerunners have at critical moments made significant contributions to thinking about educational issues, and about the type of society we ought to have. It is particularly important that teachers' unions should address this issue, partly because their members are at the cutting edge, partly because they ought in any case to be among the most qualified in society to do so. And if they don't do it themselves, it will be done for them. Their ideology will be wished on them by the establishment culture. Irish government is not particularly ideological in a party political sense but it can be quite ideological in a value system sense, as the white paper itself demonstrates. And we are, of course, quite entitled to adopt that position if we so wish. But let us realise that there are decisions to be made, and that we should make those decisions consciously, rather than becoming the passive recipients of value systems determined elsewhere—which would indeed be an ironic, not to say incongruous, consequence of the embracing of an enterprise culture. 'Innovation' and 'enterprise' should extend to thinking about the human consequences of scientific, technological and organisational change as well as about the change itself. We are only beginning to contemplate these issues. It is important that as wide a range as possible of voices should contribute to the discussion. The science and technology community, whether in education, industry or elsewhere, have a right to engage in debate on policy and practical concerns and their impact on the issues of the day. But it would obviously be a rejection of its historic role if the Teachers' Union of Ireland, whose members now have so central a role to play in the vanguard of the information revolution, were not to play an equally prominent role in the forefront of this essential debate.

Notes

1 Robert Kane, *The industrial resources of Ireland* (Dublin, 1844).

2 *Ibid.*, p. 394.

3 *Ibid.*, pp. 401–2.

4 *Ibid.*, p. 404.

5 *Ibid.*, p. 405.

6 *Ibid.*

7 Arthur Griffith (ed.), *Thomas Davis: the thinker and teacher* (Dublin, 1914), p. 152.

8 *Ibid.*, p. 130.

9 *Ibid.*

10 Kane, *Industrial resources*, p. 399.

11 *Ibid.*, p. 402.

12 Horace Plunkett, *Ireland in the new century* (London, 1904; Kennikat Press reprint, London, 1970), *passim*, but especially pp. 101ff.

13 Michael O'Riordan, *Catholicity and progress in Ireland* (Dublin, 1905).

14 *Ibid.*, p. 61.

15 *Ibid.*, p. 62.

16 *Ibid.*, p. 419.

17 *Ibid.*, p. 407.

18 *Ibid.*, p. 419.

19 Kane, *Industrial resources*, p. 394.

20 Martin Wiener, *English culture and the decline of the industrial spirit 1850–1980* (Cambridge, 1981).

21 J. J. Lee, *Ireland 1912–1985: politics and society* (Cambridge, 1989), p. 292.

22 Department of Education, *Report of the Council of Education as presented to the Minister for Education: the curriculum of the secondary school* (Dublin, 1962).

23 *Science, technology and innovation: the white paper* (Dublin, 1996), p. ii.

24 *Ibid.*

25 *Ibid.*, p. 9.

26 *Ibid.*, p. 8.

27 *Ibid.*, p. 9.

28 *Ibid.*, p. 15.

29 *Ibid.*, p. 9.

30 *Ibid.*, p. 125.

2. Laying the Foundations: Voluntary and State Provision for Technical Education 1730–1930

Kieran Byrne

The campaign for a system of state-supported technical education in nineteenth-century Ireland was part of a wider demand increasingly voiced in Britain. The Irish demand for technical education was thrust forward on that more vigorous course and it benefited accordingly. Notwithstanding the claims by some administrators that industry in Britain had become less competitive due to deficiencies in its system of technical training, there was a growing expectation in Ireland that native industry might gain from imitating English initiatives, particularly those which had sought to align educational provision with industrial requirements.

For those who sought to secure industrial development in Ireland through educational means the past provided a chronicle of disappointment and frustration. For example, William Hickey, an advocate of an alignment of instruction with industrial demands, argued provocatively in the 1830s that the learning transmitted at the elementary schools was a 'bad education I would have you avoid . . . it makes a man think the handles of the plough or the business of the counter would disgrace him'.[1] Taking up the same theme a member of the Dublin Mechanics' Institute asserted in 1824 that Ireland had 'her Goldsmith, her Swift, her Burke and her Sheridan, but she had not an Arkwright, a Jameson or a Watt'.[2] Not surprisingly, the leading Irish utilitarian, Robert Kane, devoted his energy to these issues as well. In *The industrial resources of Ireland* he argued trenchantly that Ireland's advancement depended not only upon those who pursued liberal humanistic studies, but more importantly, upon those who could apply the results of scientific research to industrial development.[3] Persuasively presented though these arguments may have been, the task of conversion remained difficult, and a witness at the Royal Commission on Technical Instruction in 1883 complained that 'the general impression is that it is degrading to enter anything which smacks of trade or handiwork and great sacrifices are made to put children to college where they will get what is called a profession. A change in the habits and customs of the people is the first step towards altering that state of things and we can only do that by increased primary education and good sense.'[4]

During the course of the eighteenth and nineteenth centuries a series of initiatives by a diverse range of individuals and institutions sought to create an educational system more responsive to Ireland's industrial potential. It is the purpose of this chapter to trace those developments through six different phases. The first began in the early part of the eighteenth century with the establishment of the Dublin Society. The second phase followed from that initiative and saw the growth of scientific and technical institutions in a number of regional centres. These paved the way for a third phase which saw the emergence of the more popularly supported mechanics' institutes. Then followed a fourth phase in which two official bodies, the Commissioners for National Education and the Department of Science and Art, began a formal process of extending state support to manual and technical instruction. During a fifth phase, which stretched from the 1870s to the 1890s, increasingly cohesive and effective demands for a system of technical education were articulated. They led to a final phase which was inaugurated by the passing of the Agriculture and Technical Instruction (Ireland) Act in 1899. Its provisions led to substantially increased investment in technical education and the laying of the statutory and administrative foundations on which the modern system of vocational education was built.

Technical education and the Royal Dublin Society

The foundation of the Royal Society in London in 1660 with the aim of promoting a new spirit of inquiry in the sciences provided a prestigious exemplar which was followed over twenty years later in the foundation of the Dublin Philosophical Society in 1683.[5] Some of the founding members of the Dublin society were also members of the Royal Society and they hoped to replicate its impressive achievements in Ireland. The Dublin Philosophical Society proved much less successful than the Royal Society however. It eventually disbanded but some of its members helped to form a new body, the Dublin Society, at a meeting in Trinity College in 1731 for the purpose of 'improving husbandry, manufacture and useful arts'. Its members soon agreed that the promotion of the 'sciences' should be added to its original objectives and its constitution emphasised the primacy of experimentation and the empirical collection of data.[6]

The papers and findings of each scientific meeting of the society were printed and circulated amongst its members and in an attempt to stimulate enterprise and inventiveness funds were voted for a premium system. Soon awards were being made for exemplary hop and flax growing, earthenware manufacturing, distilling, lacemaking, agricultural innovation and 'instruments lately invented'.[7] Amongst its earliest initiatives was the establishment of drawing classes. Premises were acquired and fitted out in 1746 at Shaws' Court and a Mr West of Waterford was appointed first drawing master. Initially the main emphasis was placed on ornamental drawing for application in the decorative arts but the curriculum was soon extended to include figure drawing, architectural drawing and modelling in clay. Subsequently a second teacher was employed and a scheme of premiums and scholarships was introduced.[8] In 1749 the society obtained a charter of incorporation and was thereafter known as the Royal Dublin Society. By then it was receiving government grants amounting, on average, to £5,000 annually. In 1803 the grant increased to £10,000 and subsequently it fluctuated between £7,000 and £10,000.

The opening decades of the nineteenth century saw the Royal Dublin Society responding to the growth of scientific activity elsewhere. Thus in 1800 it appointed a committee to report on the direction and progress of newly established societies in Britain, particularly the innovative and highly successful London Institution. The committee argued that the Royal Dublin Society should be more active in the promotion of technical education, and as a result the society voted funds for the provision of facilities for a professor to lecture on hydraulics, mechanics and allied subjects. Between 1800 and 1804, £17,000 was expended in the renovation of teaching premises at Poolbeg Street. Funds were voted for visiting lectures. In 1810, Sir Humphrey Davy was appointed as guest lecturer and in 1812 the society appointed Professor Jameson of Edinburgh as professor of mineralogy and Richard Griffith as professor of mining. In 1834 Robert Kane was appointed as lecturer in natural philosophy; as subsequent events would prove, this was an inspired appointment, for Kane had become the country's leading advocate of technical education.[9] Such foundations ensured that during the course of the nineteenth century the work of the Royal Dublin Society would expand and prosper. Some of its institutions, for example its art school and its library, were transformed into great national institutions under the control of the state, while at the same time the society continued through exhibitions and competitions to promote the educational mission for which it had been founded, particularly in agriculture and industry.

Regional scientific institutions

While cultivating its own enterprise, the Royal Dublin Society actively fostered kindred institutions. Among the first to benefit from its help was the Cork Institution. It had been founded in 1799 by Thomas Dix Hinks, a graduate of the Dissenting Academy at Hackney, with the aim of creating an institute for scientific and technical instruction whose graduates would be able to apply their knowledge to agriculture and manufacturing.[10] With the financial support of other interested parties, a beginning was made with a course of lectures delivered by Hinks himself in 1802. The syllabus was remarkable for an inclusive content drawn from natural history, astronomy, electricity, hydrostatics and mechanics. The Cork Institution acquired premises which allowed the development of a library, a lecture room and a model room. The Royal Dublin Society gave support by donating books, equipment and specimens, and the institution followed its example and established a scheme of premiums for innovation in agriculture and industry. Samples were available on loan, inventions were explained and technological equipment was put on display. These strategies proved popular; the institute's report for 1813 proudly recorded a growing interest in new technologies and noted that 'the number of workmen who come to examine them and who may be often seen measuring the particular dimensions, so as to copy them, is very great'.[11] Parliament was petitioned for support and responded with an annual grant of between £2,000 and £2,500, and in 1807 the institution was incorporated as the Royal Cork Institution.[12]

Given Belfast's pivotal role in a rapidly industrialising region, it is not surprising that it developed technical education institutions. Central to this development was the founding of the Belfast Academical Institution in 1807. Its original plan provided for the creation of two departments. One of these, the school, devised a syllabus for a 'complete English and mercantile education' and 'classical literature'. The other department, the collegiate, taught mathematics, physics, logic, metaphysics, literature, moral philosophy, chemistry, botany and agriculture.[13] A public appeal for funds met with a generous response, to which was added an annual parliamentary grant of £1,500. Despite this, the institution was insufficiently endowed to realise its objectives. Soon other agencies emerged in Belfast to promote similar goals. In

1821 a Natural History Society was founded and an Art Society was founded in 1836.[14] Other provincial initiatives at the time included the Galway Amicable Society, which under the leadership of James Hardiman became the Royal Galway Institution in 1838.[15] It too sought to provide lectures, a library and a reading room. Similarly, the Limerick Institution founded by local business and landed interests promoted instruction in science, art and technology in the late 1830s and 1840s.[16] Each of these regional institutions had the potential for further development as centres of scientific and technical education. Not surprisingly, when the government proposed the establishment of the utilitarian 'provincial colleges' in the early 1840s, Belfast, Cork, Galway and Limerick were each considered as possible sites. Individuals who had been active in their local scientific and technical institutions pointed to past achievements and were eloquent in their efforts to have one of the new colleges sited in their city.[17]

The mechanics' institutes

The diffusion of a new initiative—the mechanics' institute—through a number of regional centres in the period from 1824 to 1860 was a significant element in the emergence of a system of technical education in the middle years of the nineteenth century. Mechanics' institutes aimed to instruct 'mechanics'—the term used at the time to describe a wide range of engineering and technical occupations—in the scientific principles underlying trade and industry. In that, the institutes were a radical departure from earlier initiatives which had tended to address the demands of proprietors rather than the needs of operatives. Irish initiatives were part of a movement that had started in London and spread quickly northwards through the industrial centres of England and Scotland. Within a year of the founding of the pioneering London Mechanics' Institution by George Birkbeck in 1823, a similar project was established at 15 Sackville Street in Dublin.[18] By 1825 institutes had been established in other urban centres, notably Armagh, Belfast, Cork, Galway, Limerick and Waterford.[19]

While rapid industrialisation in England might have proved a receptive environment for the movement, Ireland was clearly not so fertile. Yet, English industrialisation provided a vivid example of progress and encouraged the belief that Ireland should not be left behind. While an educated labour force was acknowledged elsewhere as a means by which industrial advancement might be sustained, in Ireland it was advocated as the means by which the country's industrial decline might be stemmed. Consequently, as the pace of industrialisation quickened in England, the potential for the application of technical education also assumed grander proportions. In Ireland, in contrast, the impetus to establish mechanics' institutes sprang more from economic ambition and aspiration than from existing demand.

The original aim of the mechanics' institutes was primarily directed to the industrial education of the artisan, but that utilitarianism was gradually extended to include education in literature and history. These goals might be realised through the provision of libraries, lecture halls and reading rooms. In some of the bigger institutes—and closely resembling what had been successfully developed at Liverpool—schools were also provided.[20] Thus the Cork Mechanics' Institute established a school whose syllabus included algebra and geometry and their applications to architecture, surveying and navigation.[21] An annual fee of ten shillings was payable in quarterly instalments and certificates of merit were awarded to pupils who, having attended for a year or more, satisfied a board of examiners. The school met a vigorous demand for instruction and by early 1826 more than ninety students were enrolled in classes in arithmetic, grammar and geography with smaller enrolments in Euclid, algebra, mensuration, surveying, sections, navigation, trigonometry, book-keeping, globes, drawing and French.[22] In the Dublin Mechanics' Institute class teaching was also used as a preparation for attendance at advanced lectures. The annual report for 1842 noted, for example, that close to 200 pupils had been given lessons in practical architecture, mechanical, ornamental and figure drawing, natural philosophy, writing, arithmetic, mathematics, grammar, music, French and dancing.[23] A mathematics night school was established at the Galway Mechanics' Institute as early as 1828 where instruction in arithmetic, geometry and algebra was available free of charge for the sons and apprentices of members.[24] At the Ennis Mechanics' Institute pupils were taught arithmetic, Euclid and grammar, while at the Waterford Mechanics' Institute classes were conducted in reading, writing, arithmetic, practical geometry, navigation, grammar, geography, book-keeping and drawing.[25] At the Clonmel Institute attendance at the evening school averaged twenty-four; its president proudly claiming that 'the proficiency attained by many of them in mathematical science would reflect credit on a much higher educational establishment' and in 1850 it opened a school of art.[26] Each institute augmented its efforts by drawing on the support of the Royal Dublin Society's scheme of providing visiting celebrity lecturers such as Robert Kane or Edmund Davy. Thus in 1844 twelve different lecturers addressed the institutes in Cork, Nenagh,

Carrick-on-Suir, Waterford, Galway, Killarney, Coleraine and Clonmel.[27]

The fortunes of the mechanics' institutes declined sharply in the second half of the nineteenth century. The hoped-for industrial expansion did not materialise and the contraction in employment in manufacturing led, inevitably, to a draining of the pool from which the institutes might draw their student members. The affairs of many of the institutes were wound up, their buildings sold and their assets distributed amongst surviving members. In some cases, an institute survived but on lines quite different from those set down by its founders. In Galway, for example, the local institute degenerated into a social and drinking club. Others, such as those at Belfast and Dundalk, retained some of their earlier educational idealism and combined their resources with those of local reading rooms and literary societies to meet the growing interest in reading. In Limerick it became a social club and headquarters for the trades council, an organisation of the city's employees and trade unionists.[28] By the end of the century the work of the mechanics' institutes as providers of technical education to the aristocracy of labour and its retainers had all but petered out.

The promotion of technical education by the state

The establishment of the Commissioners of National Education in 1831 was an attempt by the state to provide elementary education for the children of urban and rural manual workers. The core curriculum promoted in the new national schools consisted of elementary literacy, numeracy and religion. In addition, the commissioners followed the example of the providers of charity schooling and aimed to promote manual instruction, believing it an appropriate curriculum for the children of working people. Thus in 1832 they made grants to two agricultural schools, the following year they created a model farm at Glasnevin for the instruction of national teachers and in 1838 the Albert College opened in Glasnevin as a special agricultural school. Along with founding model agricultural schools, the commissioners promoted agricultural education as part of the general elementary curriculum of older boys and they also devised a special domestic curriculum for older girls. In the 1850s and 1860s they added drawing, navigation and mechanics to the curriculum and by the 1870s the national school curriculum included physics, chemistry, handicraft and electricity.[29] Few pupils were given the opportunity to study these technical subjects however. They were available only in the small number of schools that had qualified teachers and they were classified as extra subjects and thus outside the compulsory curriculum. Most importantly they were confined to the syllabus for higher classes and thus available only to the small minority of older pupils who spent more than four or five years at school. Schooling was not compulsory and the exigencies of the lives of most children ensured a brief period of schooling which was focused narrowly on the acquisition of elementary skills. It reflected a view of education and society encapsulated in the remark by Cardinal Cullen when giving evidence to the 1870 Commission on Primary Education: 'Too high an education would make the poor oftentimes discontented, unsuited to following the plough and for using the spade.'[30]

The establishment of the Department of Science and Art in London in 1853 marked the beginning of another ambitious attempt to promote scientific and technical education. Its principal purpose was to supplement the work of existing agencies by means of science museums, technical schools, state examinations and the payment of grants on the basis of examination results. The new system had to be largely self-supporting: local initiative and funding were prerequisites for any grant of state aid. Irish educationists responded to those challenges and a further advance was secured with the introduction of schools of design under the new Department of Practical Art in the 1850s. Art schools were established in Belfast, Cork and Dublin, and by 1860 there was a school in Waterford, another in Clonmel in association with its mechanics' institute and one in Limerick under the auspices of the recently established Athenaeum.[31] These schools provided a progressive context within which industrial art and design could be taught. Students were generally employees in local businesses, and the local promoters and their staff sought to align the syllabus to the industrial needs of the hinterland. The Belfast school, for example, in its report for 1850 recorded that 'The manufacture of "linen bands" and "headings" has very greatly increased probably threefold, since the establishment of the school; and the improvement of the quality of these articles in a still greater proportion is directly due to the pupils of the school.'[32]

The new initiative had obvious benefits for existing science and art schools but it was not without defects. The Department of Science and Art was regarded by some critics as less than helpful, and in 1864 in the evidence of various witnesses to the Select Committee on Schools of Art a murmuring discontent was clearly articulated. For example, James Brenan, headmaster of the Cork School of Art, was critical of a lack of support by the department's officials. That, he argued, was manifested most noticeably in the area of financial assistance, the state's grant being insignificant compared with the amount raised locally. Furthermore the strategy of making grant payments contingent in part on the results gained in examinations served only to promote cynicism as pupils observed their teachers confining their efforts to the content of the prescribed course. The policy was stoutly defended. Henry Cole, the secretary to the Department of Science and Art, argued that it had served Irish interests well and he drew attention to the expansion of art education in the country in the years following the department's foundation. He admitted however that the Belfast school had closed in the mid-1850s and when it was suggested that its failure was the fault of his department he argued that in allocating state funds the prevailing principle of 'self-help' had to be upheld. It would be better that the Belfast school should cease to exist, he argued, rather than be maintained upon the 'vicious' principle of subsidy from public taxation: 'If Belfast is not alive to its own interest', he declared, 'then we have nothing further to say about it.'[33]

By the 1860s, when constitutional nationalists were turning their attention towards the prospect of a greater degree of home government, an analogous campaign was under way for the establishment of a separate Department of Science and Art for Ireland. The initiative was stimulated by the inauguration of the Dublin Exhibition Palace and Winter Garden Company in 1862. The company aimed to establish a voluntary institution with goals similar to those of the great science and art institution at South Kensington, and with the support of Dublin's merchants and bankers and the general public a fund of £50,000 was raised for the project. By 1865, when the palace was formally inaugurated a total of £95,000 had been expended and the difference between initial capital and expenditure was easily offset by the profits from the exhibition. However, two years later the company recorded a loss of £42,000 and its pleas for further public subscription went unanswered. An appeal was made to the Treasury, and through memoranda, deputations and public meetings the company fought for survival. Its members argued that Irish science and art agencies should be placed under the control of a resident Irish board responsible to parliament through the Irish Office. A Dublin department would have functions analogous to that based in London: it would co-ordinate the work of all science and art institutions within its jurisdiction and its resources would be available to all of the country's schools and colleges. Links with the Department of Science and Art in London would then be superfluous.

By 1868 it seemed as if some of those demands might be conceded. On 27 March, *The Times* reported that the Chancellor of the Exchequer had given an undertaking that the government was prepared to give a separate science and art institution to Dublin which should be 'a sister to and not a subordinate of the English establishment'. A few months later a commission of inquiry on the Department of Science and Art was given a twofold brief. Firstly it should ascertain the best means by which a separate department might be established in Ireland and secondly it should consider how those Irish institutions currently grant aided by the department might be more effectively co-ordinated. However the commissioners made it clear that they were not in agreement with the decision to establish a separate Irish department and requested a more open-ended brief. Having been asked to report on the virtue of a separate department, the commission found against the proposal: the campaign to have a separate department established in Ireland had lost its first battle.[34]

Demands for a system of technical education

By the last quarter of the nineteenth century English manufacturing industry had been overtaken by foreign competition. The Paris Exhibition of 1867 revealed that Britain no longer enjoyed first place in the race for industrial prosperity. Lyon Playfair, a former secretary of the science division of the Department of Science and Art and a juror at the exhibition, admitted defeat and demanded an inquiry which would authoritatively reveal to the people of England the means 'by which the great states are attaining an intellectual pre-eminence among industrial classes' and how the results of such an inquiry 'might be brought to bear on the progress of their national industries'.[35] Such criticisms did not go unanswered and the government responded with a sequence of investigations including two select committees of inquiry and a royal commission. Of these, the Royal Commission on Technical Instruction set up in 1881 under the chairmanship of Bernard Samuelson, a member of parliament and a successful iron manufacturer, would have serious implications for Ireland.[36]

The commission was directed to make a comparative study of technical instruction in specified countries and that in the United Kingdom and to measure its effectiveness in promoting industrial efficiency. Within that frame of reference the commissioners decided to examine Ireland separately from the rest of the United Kingdom and they argued that Ireland, because of its industrially underdeveloped status, must be afforded state support commensurate with its unique conditions. The Department of Science and Art was again singled out for attack as a rigidly centralised institution whose failure to cope with the disparate demands of industrial Ireland was a persistent defect. The inadequacy of the national and intermediate schools as a preparation for technical instruction courses was also alleged. One after another, Irish industrialists had their dissatisfaction recorded as they related their belief that the dearth of adequately qualified artisans inhibited industrial development.

The commission made a number of recommendations which revealed an alertness to Irish needs. In particular it recommended a revision of the textbooks used in the teaching of industrial processes and rudimentary science in the national schools. It recommended instruction in the use of tools and manual work and proposed that national teachers be given appropriate courses at the central training institution. The commissioners believed that domestically located manufacturing and handicrafts would benefit from such reforms. Predictably, they advised that the Board of Intermediate Education take steps to provide for the practical teaching of science in the secondary schools and that the Royal College of Science be given a central role in the preparation of science teachers.

The immediate outcome of the findings and recommendations of the commission was the Technical Instruction Act 1889. Under its provisions local bodies were given authority to raise funds through local taxes in aid of technical instruction. The legislation would prove to be less than effective, however: some municipal authorities, notably Cork, Belfast, Limerick and Dublin, availed of its provisions and the building of schools at Kevin Street, Pembroke and Ringsend in Dublin were notable achievements but in jurisdictions under the control of the boards of guardians the funds raised for educational development proved inadequate.[37] Furthermore, the Act failed to address the concern that the Department of Science and Art was far too centralised and distant an institution to respond to the specific needs of diverse localities. By handing over the control of technical instruction to the Department of Science and Art its administration and leadership remained as remote as ever. For Ireland that policy had acute implications. The structure of the Irish industrial framework was diverse: few national industries existed and the country's industrial activity, such as it was, derived its sustenance from relatively small-scale local industries. A policy that failed to acknowledge that decentralisation should be an inherent component of its administrative structure could do little to meet Irish needs.

During the final decade of the century the lobby for an Irish system of technical education remained active. *The Irish Builder* was one of a number of publications that contributed to the debate, placing the issues before the public in a frank manner and delineating prevailing concepts of technical education. As spending on technical instruction declined in the 1890s there was growing concern that Ireland was falling behind Britain in obtaining its share of resources. Clearly, the urgent requirement was to displace adopted British policy with an adapted Irish one, and in 1893 a formidable coalition of landed, commercial, political and educational interests formed the Technical Education Association of Ireland. From 1902 its annual conferences became a major platform for the articulation of opinion on technical education, and its standing committee and those of its successor organisations became a powerful representative body for local technical and vocational education committees. In the political arena policy making became more accommodating as well. The strategy of 'coercion and conciliation' under Chief Secretary Arthur Balfour and the campaign of 'constructive unionism' combined to secure for Ireland a sequence of reforms, particularly in land tenure, local government and education.

It was perhaps Horace Plunkett who brought the most powerful and distinctive voice to bear on the educational questions of this period. He was from a well-connected ascendancy family and was converted to the creed of technical education and development by a spell ranching in Wyoming. Plunkett returned to Ireland and was elected member of parliament for South Dublin in 1892. In 1894 he founded the Irish Agricultural Organisation Society and in August 1895 he wrote to all Irish members of parliament and other interested parties inviting their participation in a conference to discuss economic issues. Its initial meetings were held during the parliamentary recess and from that it took its name, the Recess Committee. The committee's report, issued in July 1896, paralleled that of the 1881 Royal Commission on Technical Instruction.[38] It argued trenchantly for an educational system which, like that of some continental countries, would seek to align educational institutions with industrial needs. To that end it made the case for the reform of primary and secondary school curricula, the creation of special agricultural, industrial and art schools, the promotion of evening continuation schools, higher technical colleges of agriculture and the creation of professorships of agriculture and applied science in the universities. It criticised the allocation of responsibility for technical instruction between different controlling bodies and advocated an Irish department of agriculture and industries which would have authority to administer agricultural and scientific instruction—'a large department on new lines which would be free and able to give continuous and undivided attention to its work'.[39]

These proposals, widely supported by a range of nationalist and unionist opinion, presented the Conservative government with another opportunity to appease Irish educational interests. The proposals also found support in the findings of the reports of the 1897 Commission on Manual and Practical Instruction in Primary Schools and the 1899 Commission on Intermediate Education. At the same time the 1898 Local Government Act, which replaced the grand juries with elected county councils, had created a new administrative and fiscal infrastructure within which local education committees might operate. As these educational and political movements converged, the government withdrew a Bill designed to provide for the creation of a new administrative structure for agricultural development and replaced it with a broader proposal, the Agriculture and Technical Instruction (Ireland) Act 1899, which provided for the inauguration of a Department of Agriculture and Technical Instruction in Dublin on 1 April 1900. Thereby the bonds which kept Irish technical institutions subservient to a lofty and remote South Kensington were finally severed.

The Department of Agriculture and Technical Instruction

The new department was given three principal functions. First was the provision of courses through central institutions such as the Dublin Metropolitan School of Art, the Royal College of Science, the Albert College, the Munster Institute and through the provision of extension lectures. Second, it was given responsibility for funding scientific and technical instruction in secondary schools. Third, it was required to promote the founding of technical schools by granting aid directly to local authorities and by empowering them to raise funds through local rates. The department operated under a president, an honour given *ex officio* to the Chief Secretary as head of the Irish Office, a general council representative of a wide range of political opinion and advisory boards representative of agricultural and educational interests. Thus the Board of Technical Instruction consisted of the president and the vice-president, representatives of local authorities, chambers of commerce and trades councils, representatives of the Commissioners of National Education and of the Intermediate Education Board and four persons appointed by the department. Day-to-day administration was the responsibility of a vice-president and his staff. Horace Plunkett took up the post of vice-president on 2 November 1899 and though he lost his parliamentary seat in 1900 and was unsuccessful in an attempt to regain it at a by-election in 1901, he nonetheless continued to act as vice-president until 1907. He depended heavily on a group of brilliant administrators, notably T. P. Gill, who served as departmental secretary until 1922, and two assistant secretaries, Robert Blair and J. R. Campbell, appointed for technical instruction and agriculture respectively.[40]

The principle of devolution was exemplified in the formation of local technical instruction committees. Following the department's establishment, staff from the central office visited each local authority to advise on the formation of an appropriate local structure. The potential of technical education was greatest in the major urban centres and there the borough councils were urged to delegate responsibility to special technical instruction committees composed of public representatives and members drawn from 'existing educational institutions and other qualified persons'.[41] Soon committees were functioning in each of the county boroughs—Belfast, Cork, Derry, Dublin, Limerick, Waterford— and in seventeen smaller urban districts. Joint committees for agriculture and technical instruction were formed in seven counties and technical instruction committees were formed in twenty- two other counties where urban and county councils operated jointly.[42] The formation of local committees brought a significant element of democratic accountability to the administration of education for the first time and their successful operation and popularity provided a compelling argument for the inclusion of local committees as a central element in the new vocational education structures devised in 1930.

Each new committee was required to devise an appropriate scheme of technical instruction for its jurisdiction. Groups which might benefit from instruction, such as young people in employment, school leavers, artisans, managers and foremen, were identified. Primary and secondary teachers who might be able to teach technical and scientific subjects became a particular target, and the department's training courses for serving teachers at the central institutes and in the new technical institutes and schools did much to raise standards in science and technical instruction at all levels. The legislation empowered county and urban district councils to borrow capital from the Local Government Board, and magnificent new schools and institutes soon became the most obvious manifestation of the department's impact. If a committee felt unable to provide a new building it had the power to rent a premises and if sparse population resulted in low demand—a likelihood in rural districts—instruction was provided through itinerant teachers who gave short courses in temporary premises.[43]

The Department of Agriculture and Technical Instruction was founded at a time of significant social and economic change. Its officers established a powerful trajectory of growth and development by responding to increasingly enthusiastic calls for educational provision while initiating their own innovative projects. The department met a long-felt need during a period of profound political change, but few of those who participated in its establishment could have foreseen the political upheavals that would accompany its formative years and that would lead to its fragmentation in 1920 and ultimately to its demise in 1922.

Provision for technical education in the new Ireland

The Department of Agriculture and Technical Instruction had been established against a background of growing support for Home Rule. Attempts to legislate for a parliament in Dublin to which the Westminster parliament would devolve most of its functions in relation to Ireland had failed in 1886 and 1893, but a third Bill became law in 1914. It was reasonable to assume not only that the implementation of Home Rule would secure the future of the Department of Agriculture and Technical Instruction but that the department, as a highly successful innovation, would also serve as an appropriate model for other initiatives in administrative devolution. However, the outbreak of war in 1914 and growing opposition in Ulster to the terms of the Home Rule Act led to its implementation being postponed until after the war. Two years into the war the Easter Rising and the intensification of militant nationalist sentiment that followed the execution of its leaders and an attempt to introduce compulsory conscription served to mobilise support for Sinn Féin. By the end of the war in 1918, if not before, it had become clear that the government could not secure agreement to a Home Rule scheme as formulated in 1914. Nationalist opinion under the leadership of Sinn Féin now sought a much greater degree of political independence, while its opponents, under the increasingly effective leadership of the Ulster Unionist Council, were firmly united against a nationalist dominated devolution. In the face of such conflicting forces the government decided to impose Home Rule on Ireland, but with separate provision for North and South that would lead to the partition of the island and to the formation of two separate Irish states.

The contours of a southern Irish state began to emerge following the general election called at the ending of the War for 14 December 1918. Sinn Féin captured 73 out of 105 seats, most of them in the south and west. Thus strengthened, the party proceeded to implement its strategy of establishing national institutions as alternatives to those functioning under the United Kingdom parliament. Consequently it decided to absent itself from Westminster and to meet instead in Dublin, as Dáil

Éireann. It established a number of ministries, one of which, Agriculture, sought to replicate some of the functions of the Department of Agriculture and Technical Instruction, and when the Second Dáil convened following the general election of May 1921 it appointed a Minister for Education. Despite the optimism and confidence that prompted their foundation, the Dáil ministries could not replicate the extensive bureaucracy of the Department of Agriculture and Technical Instruction at its Merrion Street headquarters; more significantly, they were without the capacity to provide alternatives to the funds which flowed from the Treasury and on to the local committees and which underpinned most expenditure on technical education.[44] They could do little other than exist as symbols and portents of a changing order, as restless and idle limbs of an administration-in-waiting.

Home Rule came to the six north-eastern counties with the Government of Ireland Act 1920. It provided for the establishment of a devolved parliament in Belfast which began to function in May 1921. A new Department of Education was formally established in Belfast on 7 June 1921 and on 1 February 1922 responsibility for technical instruction in the six counties was transferred to it from the Dublin Department of Agriculture and Technical Instruction. The transition was eased considerably when senior members of the department availed of the opportunity to transfer to Belfast where they sought to continue the practices that had developed in Merrion Street over the previous two decades. They assumed responsibility for monitoring and regulating the schemes that had developed under the north-east's six county councils, two county boroughs—Belfast and Derry—and fourteen urban district councils. Subsequent legislation allowed the urban district councils to act as the local authority for technical education, schools in rural areas were placed under the control of regional education committees and those in the two county boroughs were placed under borough education committees. Within that structure technical education in Northern Ireland began a pattern of development whose trajectory would increasingly diverge from that in the rest of Ireland.[45]

During the period from January 1919 to July 1921 the mutual antagonism of Dáil Eireann and the government in London—bitterly manifested in the War of Independence—blocked any possibility of a political settlement for the twenty six counties. However, the calling of a truce on 9 July 1921 followed by negotiations which led to the signing of a treaty on 6 December and its acceptance by Dáil Éireann on 7 January 1922, cleared the way for the formation of a Provisional Government on 14 January; this functioned until the establishment of

Saorstát Éireann on 6 December 1922. Though the Provisional Government included a Minister for Education from 1 February 1922, responsibility for technical education passed, along with responsibility for agriculture, from the old Department of Agriculture and Technical Instruction to a Minister for Lands and Agriculture. When a Department of Education was created in April 1923 it assumed responsibility for technical instruction, gradually taking charge of various policy and administrative duties. The transfer of functions was completed in June 1924 when new legislation, the Ministers and Secretaries Act, formally established the Department of Education and transferred to it the technical instruction functions that from 1900 had been discharged by the Department of Agriculture and Technical Instruction.[46]

Table 2.1: Technical schools, students and teachers in Saorstát Éireann 1924–9

	Established technical schools	Students enrolled	Teachers	Other centres with recognised technical classes	Students enrolled
1924	65	21,808	1,035	380	10,295
1925	65	21,637	1,035	625	21,035
1926	67	22,336	1,058	1,248	41,417
1927	70	24,630	1,074	1,245	35,548
1928	70	28,900	1,087	1,314	40,037
1929	72	32,834	1,097	1,228	36,823

Source: Department of Education, *Annual reports*.

The new Department of Education centralised political responsibility for all aspects of education in its minister and gave administrative charge to a permanent secretary. The first minister to be appointed, Eoin MacNeill, served until the end of 1925. Politically conservative, he espoused a cautious role for his department. He had, as he told the Dáil, a 'horror of state-made education'[47] an attitude reinforced by the view of his colleagues that funds were scarce and that innovations or reforms, especially those requiring expenditure, should be strictly limited. Nonetheless a diverse range of interests were prepared to argue that the new state required, at the very least, a reconsideration of existing curricular policies. Their advocacy proved effective, and measures such as the Intermediate Act 1924 introduced a reform of the secondary school curriculum while the recommendations of a 1926 conference led to modification of the primary school curriculum.[48] Pressure for a review of technical school curriculum came from a number of interests, including the Labour Party and Trade Union Congress, industrialists and other employers, as well as from the technical teachers and officers in the department's technical branch. The outcome was an Executive Council decision in 1926 to establish a commission of inquiry into technical education consisting of representatives of the Dáil, officers of the Departments of Industry and Commerce, Finance, and Agriculture, overseas experts and teacher representatives. John Ingram, senior inspector of the Department of Education's technical branch, was appointed chairman.[49]

The Commission on Technical Education held its inaugural meeting on 6 October 1926 and in the months that followed established working groups and took submissions from interested individuals and organisations. It conscientiously reviewed practices elsewhere and visited a cross-section of the country's technical schools and institutes. The outcome of its work was a comprehensive review of existing provisions at each level of the education system as well as a lengthy list of recommendations for the future of technical education. Their scope was wide ranging and comprehensive. Thus, with the intention of raising standards generally, the commission proposed the introduction of a compulsory primary school leaving certificate and that the technical curriculum in primary schools should be augmented. Reviewing higher education, it argued that if the universities were not going to develop technological studies, a separate technological institute should be established for that purpose instead. The greater part of the commission's recommendations—and, in the light of subsequent developments, what would prove the most significant—dealt with provision for technical education at second level. The commission proposed the establishment of a country-wide network of continuation schools for pupils aged fourteen to sixteen following a curriculum based on manual and technical skills. The commissioners knew that the test of a proposal was the extent to which pupils availed of it. Their investigations had shown that participation rates for fourteen and fifteen-year-olds were low, especially amongst the social and occupational groups from whom the continuation school might draw its pupils, and they proposed that the issue might be dealt with by making provision for whole-time or part-time compulsory attendance. Underpinning all of the commission's proposals was the principle that any future development of technical education should be on the existing administrative foundation of democratic, accountable, locally appointed committees.[50]

When the report was presented to the newly appointed minister,

John Marcus O'Sullivan, on 5 October 1927 he remarked that its recommendations would require additional legislation to provide for developments over the 'next ten or twenty years'. At the time that perspective may have seemed realistic enough, but the legislation that followed in 1930 created an institutional framework that facilitated the comprehensive development of vocational and technical education at both second and third level over the half-century that followed. In the face of those achievements, the minister's assessment proved excessively modest.

Notes

1 J. J. Holland, *The Bannow farm school 1821–1827* (Dublin, 1932), pp. 19–20.

2 *Freeman's Journal*, 16 December 1824.

3 Robert Kane, *The industrial resources of Ireland* (Dublin, 1844); see also, Patrick Keating, 'Sir Robert Kane and the museum of Irish industry', in *Proceedings of the Educational Studies Association of Ireland Conference* (Dublin, 1979), pp. 276–86.

4 *Royal commission on technical instruction; further reports with evidence and appendix, 1884 c.* 3981 xxxi pt i, iv, q, 5230.

5 K. Theodore Hoppen, *The common scientist in the seventeenth century* (London, 1970), pp. 14–16.

6 *Report of the select committee appointed to inquire into the administration of the Royal Dublin Society with a view to the wider extension of the advantages of the annual parliamentary grant to that institution and to whom the return of the charter rules and regulation of the Dublin Society was referred*, H.C. 1836 (9445), xii, p. 335.

7 *Ibid.*, p. 338.

8 John Turpin, *A school of art in Dublin since the eighteenth century: a history of the National College of Art and Design* (Dublin, 1995), pp. 35–7.

9 W. H. Brayden (ed.), *Royal Dublin Society bi-centenary souvenir 1731–1931* (Dublin, 1931), p. 15.

10 *Ibid.*, p. 2.

11 Cork Institution, *Annual report* (Cork, 1813), p. 16; also *Seventh report of the commissioners of Irish education inquiry*, H.C. 1826–7 (443), xiii, p. 501.

12 *The charter and byelaws of the Cork Institution together with a list of the proprietors* (Cork, 1808); see also S. F. Pettit, 'The Royal Cork Institution: a reflection of the cultural life of a city', in *Journal of the Cork Historical and Archaeological Society*, lxxxi (1976), pp. 70–90.

13 William Gray, *Science and art in Belfast* (Belfast, 1904), p. 5.

14 *Ibid.*, pp. 12–13.

15 *Galway Weekly Advertiser*, 2 March 1839.

16 *Limerick Chronicle*, 21 May 1845.

17 T. W. Moody and J. C. Beckett, *Queen's, Belfast, 1845–1949: the history of a university*, i (London, 1959), pp. 23–5.

18 *Report of the proceedings of a general meeting of the friends and subscribers of the Dublin Mechanics' Institution 8th March 1826 with the Lord Mayor in the chair* (Dublin, 1826).

19 J. M. Huson, *The history of adult education* (London, 1851).

20 G. W. Roderick and Michael D. Stephens, 'Approaches to technical education in nineteenth-century England, part iv: the Liverpool Mechanics' Institution', in *Vocational Aspects of Education*, xxv (1973), pp. 100–1.

21 *Southern Reporter*, 5 January 1830.

22 *Cork Evening Herald*, 5 February 1836.

23 *Report of the board of directors of the Dublin Mechanics' Institution, 1842* (Dublin, 1842), p. 4.

24 *Connaught Journal*, 12 June 1828.

25 *Ennis Chronicle*, 6 May 1826; *Public Announcement of Waterford Mechanics' Institute*, 1846.

26 *Tipperary Free Press*, 24 July 1850.

27 National Archives, 'Royal Dublin Society: a detail of the expenditure of the sum of £500 granted by parliament, session 1844, for defraying the expenses of professors giving lectures in the provincial towns of Ireland, 14 February 1845' (CSO rp 919130).

28 R. G. Morton 'Mechanics' institutes and the attempted diffusion of useful knowledge in Ireland', in *Irish Booklore*, 2 (1972), pp. 67–9.

29 D. H. Akenson, *Irish education experiment: the national system of education in the nineteenth century* (London and Toronto, 1970), pp. 349–51.

30 *Royal commission, primary education* i, part i, *report of the commissioners*, [C 6] H.C. 1870, xxviii, pt i, p. 34.

31 *Report from the select committee on scientific institutions (Dublin); with the proceedings, minutes of evidence, appendix and index*, H.C. 1864 (495), xiii, 1.

32 *Reports and papers relating to the head and branch schools of design*, H.C. 1851 (1423), xliii, 419, p. 37.

33 *Report of the select committee appointed to inquire into the constitution and working and into the success of the schools of art*, H.C. 1864 (401), xlvi, 603.

34 *Report of the commission on the science and art department of Ireland*, i, H.C. 1868–9 (4103), xxiv, 1 and ii, *Minutes of evidence appendix and index*, H.C. 1868–9 (4103–1), xxiv, 43.

35 *Report of the schools inquiry commissioners relative to technical education*, H.C. 1867 (3898), xxiv, 261, p. 6.

36 *Royal commission on technical instruction, first report*, H.C. 1881 (3171), xxvii, 153.

37 Jim Cooke, *Technical education and the foundation of the Dublin United Trades Council 1886–1986* (Dublin, 1987), p. 50.

38 *Report of the Recess Committee on the establishment of a department of agriculture and industries for Ireland* (Dublin, 1896).

39 *Ibid.*, p. 4.

40 Susan M. Parkes, 'George Fletcher and technical education in Ireland 1900–1927', in *Irish Educational Studies*, 9, 1 (1990), pp. 13–29.

41 'Suggestions for the guidance of local authorities and others in preparing schemes of technical instruction for approval by the Department', in *Journal of the Department of Agriculture and Technical Instruction*, 1 (1900–1), p. 106.

42 Commission on Technical Education, *Report* (Dublin, 1927), pp. 168–9.

43 For general organisation see, *First annual general report of the Department of Agriculture and Technical Instruction (Ireland) 1900–1* [Cd 833] H.C. 1902, xx, 511; *Third annual general report of the Department of Agriculture and Technical Instruction for Ireland, 1902–3* [Cd 1509] H.C. 1904, xxi, 261.

44 Daniel Hoctor, *The department's story: a history of the Department of Agriculture* (Dublin, 1971), pp. 93–125.

45 D. H. Akenson, *Education and enmity: the control of schooling in Northern Ireland 1920–50* (Belfast, 1973), pp. 39–71.

46 *Report of the Department of Education for the school year 1924–5 and the financial and administrative years 1924–25–26* (Dublin, 1926), pp. 5–7; Ministers and Secretaries Act 1924, 1, v, Schedule; fourth part.

47 Dáil Éireann, *Debates*, ii (4 January 1923), col. 523.

48 Séamas Ó Buachalla, *Education policy in twentieth-century Ireland* (Dublin, 1988), pp. 60–1.

49 Commission on Technical Education, *Report*, p. 2.

50 *Ibid.*, pp. 141–60.

3. Dawn Chorus: The Origins of Trade Unionism in Vocational Education 1899–1930

Emmet O'Connor

During the nineteenth century, technical education in Ireland developed on an *ad hoc* basis, driven by voluntary effort primarily. Learned societies and private patrons played the major role in its promotion up to the 1880s. The Dublin Society, later the Royal Dublin Society, had established the Metropolitan School of Art in 1749 and helped to found the College of Science in 1867. The Royal Cork Institution founded a school of design in 1849, and the Athenaeum Society of Limerick built a school of art in 1855. Similar initiatives were taken in Belfast, Waterford, and Clonmel, where Charles Bianconi, of road transport fame, was a patron.[1] Mechanics' institutes, intended to offer scientific education for artisans, were introduced from 1825. This British concept had a chequered career in Ireland. Ironically, its translation to Ireland coincided with the onset of a relentless decline in native manufacture that was eventually to reduce most of the country to a state of near deindustrialisation. Though the institutes were supposed to be managed by tradesmen, many came under middle-class direction and understood their function to be the moral improvement of the working classes rather than technical instruction. Exclusive use of the English language acted as another barrier to mass appeal. Nonetheless, an estimated twenty-seven centres, mainly in the anglophone eastern half of the country, boasted a mechanics' institute at some time between 1825 and 1870.[2] The institutes provided the only instruction available for artisans up to the establishment of the City of Dublin Technical Schools at Kevin Street in 1887. Dublin corporation's financial commitment to the schools confirmed the emerging importance of local authorities in the advancement of technical education.[3] The provision of facilities was now a political issue, and urban authorities pressed for more state backing.

State support for technical teaching had begun on a general basis in the 1850s with the establishment of a government Department of Science and Art. The department made available 'South Kensington' grants (so called from the London location of the department office) to school managers, teachers, and students on a 'payment by results' basis. From 1859 onwards, the department also held qualifying exams for teachers of scientific instruction. By 1889, there were 14,000 students in classes connected with the department. As the system evolved, so too did dissatisfaction, in Britain as well as Ireland, over the inadequacy of facilities and the lack of direction. A Royal Commission on Technical Instruction was appointed in 1881, and its report inspired the Technical Instruction Act 1889, the first attempt to rationalise the provision of technical education. The key clauses of the Act empowered local authorities to strike a rate for technical instruction. Though Irish members of parliament supported the legislation, its impact in Ireland was disappointing. Industrial underdevelopment, underfunding, and an unsuitable local government structure outside the cities combined to ensure that few authorities other than the county borough councils applied the Act.[4]

The related field of agricultural education fared no better, despite state involvement from the outset. The Commissioners of National Education had included agriculture in their school curriculum and founded the Glasnevin Institute, later Albert College, in 1838, and the Munster Institute in 1853. Attempts at further development however, including the establishment of model farm schools and a faculty of agriculture in the College of Science, were not successful. After 1870, the model farm schools were sold off, the Munster Institute nearly closed, and the College of Science dispensed with its chair of agriculture.[5]

As spending on technical instruction declined in the 1890s, there was growing concern that Ireland was falling behind Britain in obtaining its share of state resources. Clearly, the urgent requirement was to displace adopted British policy with an adapted Irish one. To this end, an impressive caucus of landed, commercial, political, and educational interests formed the Technical Education Association of Ireland in 1893, and Horace Plunkett took the process a step further in 1895 when he convened a meeting during the parliamentary recess.[6] The Recess Committee, as it became known, aimed to inquire into the better administration of agriculture and technical instruction. Its report criticised the division of instruction between different controlling bodies, and attracted widespread enthusiasm for a proposed Irish Department of Agriculture and Industries which would have authority to administer agricultural and scientific instruction. True to its intent of 'killing Home Rule with kindness', the Conservative government gradually came round to accepting the implications of the report. The committee's recommendations were strengthened also by three other developments in 1898: the reports of the Commission on Manual and Practical Instruction in Primary Schools and the Commission on Intermediate Education, and the Local Government Act, which replaced the grand juries with elected county councils, fortuitously creating a more efficient infrastructure for local education committees in rural areas. In consequence of these timely interventions, the government withdrew a Bill confined to agriculture in favour of the Agriculture and Technical Instruction Act 1899. This Act provided that a Department of Agriculture and Technical Instruction (DATI) for Ireland should come into being on 1 April 1900. Horace Plunkett and T. P. Gill were appointed vice-president and secretary of the DATI respectively. Under their guidance, the development of agricultural and Technical education began in earnest.

The sectional associations

The educational work of the DATI was divided between two of its six branches, agriculture and technical instruction, and sprouted into a diverse empire. From the Commissioners of National Education, the department assumed certain responsibilities for Albert College, the Munster Institute, the Museum of Science and Art, the National Library, the Metropolitan School of Art, the Botanic Gardens, and the College of Science; from 'South Kensington', it took over functions in relation to grants for science, art, and technical instruction. Its field of operations would later include experimental farms and rural domestic economy schools. Conscious of having inherited a failed system from 'South Kensington', Plunkett and Gill determined to be 'missionary' and innovative. The DATI was soon to introduce new courses, overhaul teaching methods, and expand facilities to all parts of the country.[7]

Public goodwill was crucial to expansion, partly because Plunkett believed in the principle of self-help, and partly because the colonial regime wished to offset its undemocratic basis with extraparliamentary channels of political participation. To minimise resistance to a project identified with Plunkett, a unionist, and Tory deviousness about 'killing Home Rule with kindness', departmental machinery was linked to local government; its only connection with Dublin Castle was the titular position of the Chief Secretary as president *ex officio*. Local authorities were entitled to elect members to three advisory bodies, the Council of Agriculture, the Agricultural Board, and the Board of Technical

Instruction, which had the right to veto departmental expenditure. Also, in 1901, the Irish Technical Instruction Association (ITIA) was formed to co-ordinate local instruction schemes and act as a voluntary pressure group.[8] Moreover, the 1899 Act extended to the new county councils the powers already conferred on the urban authorities to levy rates for instruction, and stipulated that state aid could be given only in proportion to local spending. Cork and Mayo county councils refused initially to co-operate with the DATI for political reasons. But classes were soon afoot in all counties under local committees. Six-week courses, usually in manual instruction or domestic science, where the norm in rural areas, with afternoon classes for juveniles and evening sessions for adults. There were few manufactures to which instruction could be linked, though committees in poorer districts sometimes tried to promote cottage industries like knitting, lace-making, or crocheting. About thirty urban technical instruction schemes operated independently of county programmes, and in other cases county and urban authorities ran joint schemes.[9] Between 1902 and 1910, the number of students in classes connected with the DATI rose from 30,000 to 43,000 in the technical sector, and 7,000 to 15,000 in the secondary sector.[10] Typical of the DATI's broad-mindedness was the availability of Irish as an optional subject in technical classes from the earliest years. By 1914, the department was disbursing £3,000 annually to fifteen colleges of Irish.[11]

Having assured nationalists of its bona fides, the DATI learned to cope with the more dogged problems of shortages of suitable staff, finance, and facilities. Apart from a few agricultural specialists retained directly by the department to cover grouped counties, teachers were recruited and employed by local authorities.[12] A majority of the early intake were English or Scottish. Native disgruntlement was mollified somewhat as summer training courses for teachers got under way almost immediately. Attendance at these courses reached a peak of 848 in 1905, and subsequently the need abated.[13] Appointments of English and Scots to higher departmental posts continued to rankle, causing the ITIA to resolve in 1911 that the qualifications required for these jobs be stated precisely. Thereafter, Irish candidates were noticeably more successful.[14] Judged by examination results, the quality of teaching advanced steadily, and in 1913 the DATI dispensed with the exam system of the English Board of Education in favour of one of its own.[15]

Finance, inevitably, remained a perennial problem. However, the DATI substantially improved the revenue of technical instruction committees following the introduction of a new programme in 1906. The programme extended the provision for grants, given on the basis of attendance and an annual inspection, from science and art subjects to genuine technical disciplines, resulting in a significant expansion of teaching of manual instruction, domestic science, engineering, commerce, and trade subjects. Regulations were further liberalised in 1911.[16]

By 1914, most large towns had a technical school, but as the 1899 Act made no financial provision for the acquisition of accommodation, facilities were often deplorable. With typical frankness, George Fletcher, an assistant secretary for technical instruction in the department and a leading educationalist, told the ITIA:

> All classes of buildings were employed to meet the need. In one place a fever hospital, in another a disused jail, in others disused chapels were adapted, while in one case a technical school is to be found underneath a large water tank which supplies the town with water. In many cases private houses have been pressed into the service. In rural districts the case is worse still.[17]

Indeed, rural teachers would later recall the days of the 'barn' technical schools. Inspectors' reports regularly noted problems of dampness and of poor lighting, heating, ventilation, and equipment. The system of basing grants on attendance added to the strain by tempting teachers to enrol unjustifiably large classes. Worse off again were itinerant instructors, who could rarely last more than ten years of cycling out in all weathers without irreparable damage to their health.[18]

Staff organisation evolved gradually, on a sectional basis. The first of the so-called sectional associations was the Association of Principals of Institutions of Technical Instruction in Ireland, formed in 1903 to enable members to confer on matters of educational interest and to pool information on and experience of the administration of the technical instruction Acts.[19] By 1912, there were cognate associations existing for teachers in technical institutes, manual instructors, art masters, agricultural instructors, horticultural instructors, secretaries of agricultural and technical instruction committees, poultry and dairy instructresses, itinerant instructors, commerce teachers, chemistry teachers, and domestic economy teachers.[20] The sectional associations were part professional body and part trade union, though with an average of forty or so members scattered throughout the country they could scarcely be either with effect. Usually their formal aims were to promote efficiency through collegiality and making suggestions to the DATI, to foster technical education, and to defend members' interests.

Staff grievances focused on demands for tenure, salary scales, and pensions. Terms of employment were precarious. Officers were appointed from one year to the next and could be let go at any time, without explanation, at a month's notice, or when their annual appointment expired. Local authorities were not obliged to strike a rate for technical education under the 1899 Act, and the DATI could not make a grant to a scheme not in receipt of local authority subvention. Salaries were small, and scales non-existent. A school principal might earn £150 per annum, a teacher of engineering £100, and a domestic economy teacher (usually female) £80.[21] Increments had to be applied for personally to the local committees, and were subject to DATI approval. Complaints about wages were raised with the ITIA as early as 1905, as local committees encountered difficulty in finding suitable staff, especially for executive posts. Job advertisements sometimes went unanswered for up to a year. Officers were in turn unhappy with a perceived bias in recruitment by joint committees of agriculture and technical instruction, who were allegedly more concerned about a candidate's knowledge of farming than competence at teaching.[22]

The earliest known co-operation between the sectional associations arose out of the superannuation question. Local committees were entitled to award pensions and the first appointees assumed their posts to be pensionable, but appointments soon became so numerous that liabilities were seen to be beyond the cover of the monies available from the rates, and officers began to doubt their status. Pensions, if granted, were subject to annual renewal, and inadequate.[23] From 1908 onwards, sectional associations offered suggestions on how the problem might be resolved. Dissatisfied with progress on a sectional basis, they united in 1912 to form a Standing Committee on Superannuation for Teachers and Officers engaged under Agricultural and Technical Instruction Schemes in Ireland.[24] The objective was a national, state-backed, departmental scheme. The Scots had theirs, and one was promised for England and Wales.[25]

The standing committee attracted sufficient interest to encourage a closer co-ordination. A linchpin in this process was the indefatigable J. J. O'Connor, founder and secretary of the Manual Training Teachers' Association.[26] Working from the office of J. M. Buckley, secretary of the Joint Technical Instruction Committee for Cork, 'J. J.' made the Manual Teachers' one of the most dynamic of the sectional associations, even editing an association journal. This tacit collusion between administrator and teacher testified to a recognition that poor working conditions militated against good education.[27] The *Vocational Education Bulletin* later paid tribute to Buckley's role:

Although his secretarial duties tied him to his office, and he could rarely visit classes, he fully realised the shocking conditions under which his staff worked; cow sheds, barns, old chapels, flagged floors, derelict schools, paraffin oil lamps for illumination, etc.; three centres per week, cycling in all weathers day and night, under-paid, no scale of salary, miserable allowances, dismissal on a month's notice, no pensions; just enthusiasm and what smug people describe as the pioneer spirit! Well this is where J. M. Buckley came in with service, heart and soul.[28]

After four months gathering data on superannuation schemes, a committee of Buckley's staff convened a conference of representatives of whole-time officers of agriculture and technical instruction committees in Kevin Street Technical Schools, Dublin on 4 January 1913. Twenty-four delegates attended from eleven sectional associations. The conference appointed a standing council and appealed to affiliates for an initial contribution of thirty shillings each to finance a campaign. On 22 February, a deputation was received sympathetically by senior DATI officials. The department was at the time formulating a superannuation scheme, but officers were anxious that not more than 2.5 per cent per annum be deducted from salaries, with the balance coming from public funds. The deputation accepted advice to seek prominent political support for a lobby of the Chancellor of the Exchequer for a Treasury grant, and officers responded generously to an appeal for five shillings each to subvent expenses. The standing council's political canvass left nothing to chance. Its delegation to London was to include John Redmond, Sir Edward Carson, and William O'Brien, leader of the nationalist splinter group, the 'All for Ireland' League. In the event, the pressures of budgetary matters and the third Home Rule crisis caused David Lloyd George to cancel the meeting at the last moment. Nonetheless, a scheme was delivered to the Treasury, and the standing council was pleased with the degree of cohesion it had acquired from the experience.[29] The outbreak of war arrested progress in the short term; it would stimulate a greater militancy in the long run.

The RCO

The First World War created novel demands for the DATI, diverting the resources of its agricultural branch from educational work into a food production campaign, which trundled into action at once with meetings and other publicity. As the financial constraints prevented any increase in the number of agricultural officers, local committees of instruction simply retrenched. Winter classes were particularly affected. Teaching staffs were reduced too, through enlistment in the British army; about one hundred and twenty officers had joined the colours by November 1915, and another twenty-five would follow.[30] Beyond the Belfast region, attendance levels at technical classes remained high, but schemes had to be curtailed and building proposals deferred. Cut-backs in grants to local committees eventually threatened to plunge the whole system into crisis, until the DATI was rescued by a special government subvention in 1919.[31] One positive outcome of the stress on the home front was a new emphasis on apprenticeship training and calls for the introduction of day- and block-release courses. The immediate postwar period witnessed a growing demand for better educational facilities, especially in the north-east, and an unprecedented interest in educational reform.[32]

The war years were a trying time for all employees. While the needs of Britain's war economy brought higher prices and a profits boom for employers and farmers, the government pegged wage levels at 1914 rates in controlled sectors of employment. As there had been no inflation before the war, machinery for wage adjustment was often rudimentary or non-existent. Production demands and the growing labour shortage facilitated a big push on wages after 1916 and prompted increasing state intervention to top up controlled rates with cost-of-living bonuses. From 1916 to the onset of a slump in autumn 1920, wages rose faster than prices. But the pace of advance was uneven, with those of greatest importance to the war effort being the first to benefit.[33] Officers of committees of agriculture and technical instruction had direct experience of this inequity. The mobilisation of agriculture for the war effort, notably after the introduction of compulsory tillage in 1917, allowed employees on that side of the DATI's work to enjoy significantly better remuneration than their colleagues in technical instruction, who deeply resented the neglect of technical education in circumstances of increasing personal hardship and growing need for educational improvement.

Signs of a trade union recovery became evident in 1916, and over the next four years union membership in the country rocketed from under 100,000 to over 225,000. Against this background, the better organisation of agricultural and technical officers on a national basis took shape on 25 July 1917 when delegates of ten sectional associations met to establish a Representative Council of Associations of Officers of Agriculture and Technical Instruction Committees in Ireland, known for short as the RCO.[34] Like the pre-war standing committees, the RCO purported to speak for all whole-time officers of committees of agriculture and technical instruction, including secretaries and clerks, about five hundred men and women in total. In 1918, on foot of a membership application from the Agricultural Overseers' Association, the rules were amended to permit officers employed directly by the DATI to join.[35] However, the RCO was never a closed shop. Occasionally, a sectional association was not in affiliation, while others were poorly organised. An executive appointed by the representative council convened in turn on 6 October 1917 to begin the work of framing a constitution, forming advisory committees, and providing for finances. Rules were based mainly on those of the Manual Training Teachers' Association, reflecting the guiding influence of J. M. Buckley and J. J. O'Connor, now RCO honorary secretary. The RCO was very much a federal body, with the sectional associations retaining a say on rules and remaining vital to organisational work.[36] Given the communications technology of the time, co-ordinating ten or so voluntary groups required considerable dedication, especially where association secretaries were negligent or easy-going. O'Connor's first annual report was frankly critical of his colleagues. Revenue in particular was to become a headache, as the executive depended on the sectional secretaries to collect and forward affiliation fees and membership dues, which were set at five shillings each six months for whole-time officers and two shillings and six pence for part-timers.[37] In matters of policy, each sectional association continued to pursue its specific interests while the RCO took up issues of common concern. As affiliates wished to have terms of employment standardised on a national basis, they complied willingly with the tendency towards joint policy making at RCO level. Because of the RCO's bias towards education however, associations on the agricultural side retained a slightly more distinctive agenda.

The inaugural meeting of the RCO executive adopted a five-point programme dealing with salaries, tenure, superannuation, additional Treasury funds for the DATI, and friendly co-operation with all public bodies engaged with the promotion of agricultural and technical education.[38] With inflation eroding purchasing power, wage improvement was the immediate priority. On 4 January 1918 the RCO urged the DATI to pay war bonuses to all whole-time officers on the same scale as that adopted for civil servants. A temporary cost-of-living bonus along these lines was awarded in 1918, periodically renewed, and continued into Saorstát Éireann as a supplement to the basic salary levels for officers of committees of agriculture. If the executive took some justifiable pride in this breakthrough, it was given little time for complacency. Rates approved by the DATI were not necessarily paid by the committees, who had in any case to satisfy the department of their ability to pay. Agricultural officers expressed dissatisfaction with the increases awarded in some cases, and they had separate grievances over working conditions and delays in the payment of food production bonuses. In late 1919 the RCO raised its sights, demanding a minimum wage of £250 per annum for all officers, rising annually to a maximum of £500, automatic receipt of civil service bonuses, and better travelling and maintenance allowances and offices and residences for itinerant instructors.[39]

Though improvements were sanctioned in April 1920, the RCO was bitterly disappointed at the absence of any change in salaries for officers of technical instruction—facing into an uncertain political future, bonuses conferred scant security—and it was as much as the DATI could do to prevent a dangerously high level of resignations in the better paid agricultural branch. Agricultural instructors had seen their annual salary band revised from £150–300 in 1918 to £150–350 in 1920. Rates for cognate personnel tended to be lower. The equivalent bands for horticultural instructors, for example, were £100–200 in 1918 and £150–250 in 1920. By contrast, the band for technical teachers remained at the 1916 figure of £120–150 for men and £80–120 for women. This was supplemented with a yearly bonus of £107 for men and £76 for women, but the RCO claimed that whereas a male teacher's total remuneration had risen by 85 per cent on the pre-war level, and a female teacher's by 73 per cent, the cost of living had increased by 145 per cent over the same period. Frustration was made all the more acute by the fact that many officers had been at maximum salary levels for over ten years, and other workers were overtaking them. A pay award in May 1920 gave a head police constable £310–335 per annum, oven hands in Dublin bakeries earned £250 per annum, and an unskilled man in Henry Ford's plant at Cork started at £239 per annum. Despite a general conviction that terms of employment required a radical overhaul for the good of education—the ITIA called for salaries to be doubled—the DATI rejected any revision of pay levels in the absence of a Treasury grant for technical instruction.[40]

Similar problems affected part-time teachers, and their claim for a war bonus was taken up by the Association of Science and Engineering Technical Teachers. Matters threatened to come to a head in Cork in 1919, where a Part-Time Teachers' Association affiliated to Cork trades council and voted for strike action to secure a 50 per cent pay increase. The dispute persisted until August, when the DATI allowed that technical instruction committees might raise remuneration for part-timers by up to one-third in certain circumstances.[41]

On two of the 'three Fs'—fixity of tenure, fair salaries, and freedom from anxiety for old age—the RCO did make substantial progress in 1919. With the help of Ireland's few remaining Nationalist MPs and the National Union of Municipal Officers, a clause was inserted in the Local Government Bill providing for pensions and tenure for existing officers of committees of agriculture and technical instruction on a basis similar to that for local authority officers. Officers could not now be dismissed without pensions or due compensation, save for incapacity or misconduct. Though job security was still not absolute, as local authorities might refuse to strike a rate, this eventuality was made more remote (or so it seemed) by the fact that such authorities would be liable to compensation claims. The Local Government Act also allowed war bonuses to be added to salaries in determining gratuities or pensions.[42] The RCO's satisfaction with the Act was mitigated somewhat by its application to existing officers only. Those employed after it came into force in June 1919 would remain without tenure or pension rights. Nonetheless, the RCO had established a precedent for all technical teachers to be treated as public servants and a ground for further advance. The practical advantages of public servant status were obvious. Counterparts in secondary schools, for example, had received no war bonus, and in 1919 the average annual salary for lay teachers in Catholic schools was £139 for a man and £97 for a woman.[43] On the other hand, secondary teachers enjoyed a higher salary ceiling, better working conditions, and more socially convenient working hours.

By 1919, the RCO was beginning to think of itself as a trade union, and in January of that year the executive approached the Labour Party and Trade Union Congress regarding affiliation.[44] (From 1914 to 1930 the Party and Congress were one and the same.) Labour was at the time shedding its 'cloth cap' image. The Irish National Teachers' Organisation (INTO) had affiliated in 1918, and the Association of Secondary Teachers, Ireland (ASTI) was to do likewise in 1919.[45] Since the conscription crisis of 1918, Congress had become steadily more political and, as such, appeared to be a natural ally. If craft unions had sometimes voiced reservations about opening classes in trade subjects to all and sundry, labour generally gave sterling support to technical education.[46] In the heady postwar climate it seemed as if a Labour government must surely come. Now was the time to shape the future of education policy. The politicisation of Congress was not without controversy of course, especially as it was driven by nationalism as much as the burgeoning of trade union membership. Both the INTO and the ASTI lost members in consequence of joining Congress.[47] Grassroots opinion in the RCO was more coy. Though the sectional associations were urged repeatedly to conduct plebiscites on the question forthwith, and those held were mainly favourable, an underwhelming response frustrated hopes for a link with Congress.[48]

The 'trade unionisation' of the RCO continued regardless, spurred on by pride in its record of winning improvements in tenure, pensions, bonuses, subsistence allowances, and salaries for agricultural officers. In May 1920 there were threats of 'drastic action' and blacklisting of colleagues still outside their sectional associations. The Dublin city technical education committee resolved subsequently that all teachers in technical or trade classes should be members of their appropriate union.[49] The trade union mentality was deepened by contacts with other unions, notably the National Union of Municipal Officers (later the Irish Local Government Officials' Union), which assisted the RCO in lobbying to amend the 1919 Local Government Bill and coping with occasional wrangles over the administration of technical instruction. On educational issues, the RCO collaborated, as the need arose, with the INTO and the ASTI. Senior RCO figures were well-disposed to closer liaison with the latter body, and during the Cork secondary schools strike of 1920, Cork agricultural and technical instruction officers pledged full support and raised levies.[50]

While education had always been of concern to the sectional associations, these years witnessed a qualitative change in attitude. The concept of 'educational reconstruction' became a theme in RCO thinking. Central to this idea was the extension of agricultural and technical instruction into a national education system, and the acceptance of technical instruction as integral to a balanced education. In 1918, the RCO tried to lobby the Chief Secretary in Dublin Castle over the level of grant aid to the DATI. At its first annual general meeting on 9 July 1918, the RCO executive reported difficulties in securing a hearing, never mind recognition, from the Castle. The ITIA had also refused to include an RCO representative in a delegation to the Chief Secretary. It was then decided to promote a 'publicity scheme' through the press and meetings with politicians and civil servants, stressing that the RCO agenda was not restricted to the welfare of officers, but encompassed education and the public interest.[51]

The RCO demonstrated its civic commitment in May 1918 when it realised one of its first objectives in publishing a monthly paper, *Agricultural and Technical Education*. The introductory editorial made explicit that this was to be a journal of education primarily, open to all, and intended to 'awaken opinion on the vital need for organised education, and the establishment of a widely extended scheme of Agricultural and Technical Instruction'. Priced initially at two pence per copy, *A and TE* (as the editors liked to call it) became an ambitious miscellany of discussion papers on professional topics, information on agriculture, education notes on examinations and scholarships, snippets of current affairs, book reviews and cooking recipes, as well as news of the RCO and its sectional associations. The journal also publicised the activities of technical school students' unions, which sprang up around the country at this time to organise libraries, excursions, debates, concerts, and public lectures.[52] The editorial style was brisk: 'What are the Science and Engineering teachers doing? Their Association appears to be defunct. The Association of Commercial Instructors is taking things easy. Now, Mr Coakley, put some life into it.'[53] Articles, on the other hand, could be verbose.

The RCO's desire to stimulate a debate on education was neither exceptional nor entirely altruistic. Reflecting a broad desire for educational reorganisation as part of a wider social reconstruction for the postwar world, two viceregal committees on primary and secondary education were appointed in August 1918.[54] Their reports led to the introduction of an Education Bill in 1919, which proposed *inter alia* to transfer responsibility for technical instruction at central level from the DATI to a Department of Education, and at local authority level from the existing committees to joint education committees. The Bill also promised better salary scales, a superannuation scheme for technical teachers, and a big increase in state funding for education. An intense debate ensued. The RCO promptly appointed a parliamentary 'watchdog' committee on the Bill and subsequently joined a lobby to the Chief Secretary with colleagues from the INTO, the ASTI, and Congress. Teachers were generally sympathetic. The RCO welcomed the co-ordination of all three branches of education, while pressing too for representation of teachers on advisory committees to the proposed department and the establishment of Whitley Councils. Managerial interests, on the other hand, took a colder view. The Catholic bishops detected a threat to church control, while the ITIA wanted the DATI to retain its existing functions. In December 1919, the government withdrew the Bill.[55]

Meanwhile in swathes of the south and west, conditions for practical education varied from difficult to dangerous. The War of Independence seriously hampered technical instruction in rural districts, and classes were suspended in many unsettled parts. Tralee Technical School was occupied briefly by the British military in 1921.[56] A glimpse of the atmosphere is conveyed by Elizabeth Bloxham:

> I recall an evening in May 1920 when the roar of guns was heard in the remote country place where I was giving lessons in domestic economy. There was excitement and surprise in the faces of the few people I met on the lonely road. Many young men had been arrested and many more were 'on the run'. But the usual number of women and girls came to my class. Some had been held up and questioned by armed soldiers, whose lorries were tearing along the roads.[57]

The one growth area was Irish language teaching![58]

If the military conflict was troublesome, politics threatened to generate an impossible dilemma for the RCO. Under the first Republic, Dáil Eireann ran its own departments of government with the intention of dislodging the imperial state from routine contact with people. In view of its shoestring resources and the benign work of its rival, the Dáil Department of Agriculture thought it wise to maintain civil relations with the DATI, a line the latter was happy to reciprocate.[59] Nonetheless, some friction was virtually unavoidable, especially when Dublin Castle decreed that former political prisoners would not be eligible for public employment unless they dissociated themselves from armed rebellion. In compliance with this policy, the DATI refused to ratify the reappointment of Micheál de Lacy as head of Limerick School of Commerce in 1918. When Limerick technical instruction committee stood by de Lacy, its state grants were withdrawn. Limerick then continued its programme of technical education with a subvention from Dáil Eireann. This left the teaching staff in a quandary as to the legal implications for their status and pension rights. Eventually, the DATI allowed the staff to resign under the Local Government Act 1919. However, Limerick corporation severed relations with the DATI, recruited a new staff under the auspices of the Republic, and challenged the compensation claims brought against it under the 1919 Act. The case dragged on until 1923, when the Saorstát government agreed to award *ex gratia* payments. It was a thoroughly uncomfortable situation for the RCO, which acted to help the Limerick officers while stressing that its role and their work were strictly non-political.[60]

There was further consternation in 1919 when Cork county council decided not to strike a rate for agricultural and technical instruction in protest at the appointment of the prominent unionist Hugh T. Barrie as vice-president of the DATI. Appeals from teachers, trade unions, farming interests, and Conradh na Gaeilge, as well as members of Sinn Féin, secured a reversal of the council's decision. Had Cork persisted in its original wish it is likely that other councils would have followed suit. Longford county council refused to levy rates in 1919, and Limerick and Monaghan councils gave one year's notice of their intention to do

J. J. O'Connor, founding Honorary Secretary, in 1913, of the Representative Council of Officers of Agricultural and Technical Instruction Committees in Ireland, who retired as Honorary Treasurer of the Vocational Education Officers' Organisation in 1944; by Seán O'Sullivan 1942 (Crawford Art Gallery)

*Dressmaking and needlework class, Hastings Street Technical School, Belfast, 1903
(Ulster Museum)*

*Lettering and illumination class, Municipal Technical Institute, Belfast 1908
(Ulster Museum)*

Teachers attending a summer course in experimental science, Municipal Technical Institute, Belfast, 1908 (National Library of Ireland)

Teachers attending a summer course in plant physiology, Municipal Technical Institute, Kingstown, 1909 (National Library of Ireland)

Village hall set up for itinerant instruction in domestic economy, Clonaslee, 1911 (National Library of Ireland)

Domestic science instructress and students outside temporary classroom, Clonaslee, 1911 (National Library of Ireland)

Dundalk Technical School, 1905 (National Library of Ireland)

Day trades preparatory examination, Municipal Technical Institute, Belfast, 1910 (Ulster Museum)

Head master, School of Art, J. R. Shea, and students drawing from casts, Central Technical Institute, Waterford, 1908 (National Library of Ireland)

Teacher of typewriting and commercial subjects, Timothy McCormack, and students, Central Technical Institute, Waterford, 1908 (National Library of Ireland)

City of Waterford Technical Instruction Committee, 1910 (Noel Kelly)

Building the Municipal Technical Institute, Limerick, 1910 (University of Limerick)

Graduates of day trades preparatory class, Central Technical Institute, Waterford, 1916 (Tom Creedon)

Teaching staff at the Central Technical Institute, Waterford, 1923 (Noel Kelly)

likewise. The RCO was disturbed too at rumblings in Roscommon and Clonmel.[61] The war of nerves intensified in 1920 when Dáil Éireann directed local authorities to break off relations with the Local Government Board, and Dublin Castle ordered the DATI not to subvent authorities which declined to submit accounts for audit to the board. Grants were withheld from Longford, but the Dáil department avoided a general breach, opting instead to win Sinn Féin majorities on the DATI's advisory bodies at their next elections. In the event, these elections were never held. All changed with the creation of the Northern Ireland state and the Anglo-Irish truce in 1921.

The IATIOO

Although the DATI survived as a legal entity until 1931, the Government of Ireland Act 1920 began a whittling away of its functions. The Act gave to the Northern Ireland government authority for the department's services in the six counties and wound up its advisory bodies. Belfast then brought agricultural and technical instruction largely under its Ministry of Education, leaving practical training in agriculture with its Ministry of Agriculture. Yet the old DATI system still had some admirers. Lord Londonderry's Education Act 1923 sought to create an integrated non-denominational education system under the control of local education authorities, but made special provision for the continuance of Northern Ireland's fourteen urban committees of technical instruction.[62]

South of the border, the DATI's work was divided in 1923, with the Department of Education taking over the technical instruction branch and the Department of Lands and Agriculture inheriting agricultural instruction.[63] Given the hornet's nest stirred up by the 1919 Education Bill, the collection of the three main education branches under the one departmental roof drew surprisingly little protest. It did not in any case lead to the decompartmentalisation that some had hoped for. In the wake of the Civil War, which had again disrupted technical instruction, and facing more powerful managerial interests than its Northern Ireland counterpart, government policy on technical education remained unaltered for the time being, apart from a greater emphasis on the use of Irish.[64]

In keeping with the spirit of restructuring at large, the RCO asked its assistant general secretary, Frank McNamara, to devise a new representative organisation.[65] Activists were finding the RCO's umbrella format unsuited to the requirements of unity and efficiency. Activism was discouraged too by inadequate central funding; RCO rules, for example, forbade members to receive expenses other than the cheapest railway fares, so that those who sacrificed time and effort on behalf of their colleagues were sometimes out of pocket. Strengthening the sectional associations was clearly not an answer, as they were aligned on an occupational basis while the committees of agriculture and technical instruction were territorial. McNamara drew up the blueprint for a more conventional trade union body, the Irish Agriculture and Technical Instruction Officers' Organisation (IATIOO), which replaced the RCO in 1923. The IATIOO was administered by a central executive committee, elected by an annual congress. The executive in turn appointed a paid, part-time general secretary, who was required to be 'a whole-time employee of the Department', with the job going to McNamara. There was provision also for an honorary president, and this position was distinguished by George Russell (Æ) for several years. At ground level the IATIOO was organised in regional committees corresponding to the areas served by the committees of agriculture and technical instruction. The sectional associations survived until 1930—with the regional committees they were entitled to representation at annual congress—but in a much diminished role. Finances were improved. The membership subscription rate was set at ten shillings each per quarter, allowing executive members to meet regularly without personal loss and enabling delegates to annual congress to receive expenses for the first time.[66]

If better structured, the union was a smaller body than the old all-Ireland RCO. Cross-border colleagues formed their own Northern Union of Teachers in Technical Institutes (NUTTI).[67] To counter the problem of size, the IATIOO executive pursued a policy of alliance with larger kindred unions, federating initially with the INTO.[68] By far the biggest of the three teaching unions, the INTO had concluded a similar arrangement with the ASTI in 1919. Aside from organisational reasons, the link appealed to those who believed effective technical teaching to be impossible without improvements at primary level. Another benefit was the position of INTO general secretary, T. J. O'Connell, as a Labour deputy in Dáil Éireann, where he occasionally raised matters pertaining to IATIOO interests. Teachers' unity began to fray in 1927. The ASTI loosened its ties with the INTO, while the IATIOO ended its connection amidst some acrimony. In October, another federation was begun with the Irish Local Government Officials' Union, which also represented officers of technical instruction committees and in some cases had overlapping membership with the IATIOO. This amalgamation collapsed two years later in a nasty row over subscription fees. The IATIOO subsequently displayed a frosty attitude to appeals from the Local Government Officials' Union for co-operation over the 1930 Vocational Education Bill, though the Association of Principals of Technical Institutes took a friendlier line.[69] The IATIOO affiliated also to the Labour Party and Trade Union Congress, and contributed to the making of *Labour's policy on education.* Adopted in 1925, the document was the first attempt by any Saorstát political party to outline an education policy. In a minority report, Dr Robert MacDonald, the principal of Dún Laoghaire Technical Institute, agreed with its proposal to bring all branches of education under local public control, but argued for the retention of urban committees of technical instruction.[70]

The primary objective of the IATIOO was to unite all officers of agricultural and technical instruction in order to express their opinions and represent their interests on education. Thus, the wider concern of education was given symbolic pride of place. Other aims were to improve members' conditions, to advise and assist individual members on professional matters, to cultivate a fraternal spirit internally and links with kindred bodies at home and abroad, and to establish funds for legal assistance to members on questions of principle affecting them in their professional capacity and for relief of members unemployed or in sickness. A 'professional honour' code in the constitution defined behaviour unbecoming an officer and a trade unionist.[71]

Educational reform, tenure, pensions, marriage gratuities, compensation for dismissal, and fixed salary scales dominated the IATIOO agenda, and in a formative state the union enjoyed an exceptional opportunity to influence legislation. Its first challenge in this respect was to be the Local Government Act 1925. Here was a chance to revise the 1919 Local Government Act to have tenure and pension rights extended to all officers. However, the Department of Local Government regarded the inclusion of teachers under the 1919 Act as a mistake, on the ground that technical education was experimental and not yet a permanent feature of the public service. Would the new Act be regressive, progressive, or neutral? The initial draft of the Bill left the payment of pensions to the discretion of the competent local authority. After appeals to the minister by the IATIOO, and a conference on the Bill, the eventual Act guaranteed tenure and pensions to all officers with ten years' continual service; indeed, as local officers, they now enjoyed better pension rights than civil servants, though the gain was outweighed by a lower basic salary.[72] Women officers were still obliged to retire on marriage but were now entitled to a gratuity, Curiously the Act did not compel local authorities to pay their half of the gratuity and though it was rarely, if ever, withheld, local councillors objected occasionally to this 'wedding present' at the ratepayers' expense. For their part, the women resented having to suffer the embarrassment of public debate on their private lives.[73]

Educational reform slowly gathered pace in the Saorstát. On the agricultural side, changes had been recommended by the Drew Commission. Appointed in November 1922 to inquire into the options for state policy on agriculture, the commission emphasised the importance of education and advocated strengthening the position of agriculture as a subject at all three levels, together with the introduction of a system of continuing education. Some of its suggestions were taken up in 1926 when the government transferred Albert College and the College of Science to University College Dublin and established a dairy science faculty at University College Cork. The move drastically reduced the research complement of the Department of Agriculture, but the number of officers employed by local committees remained stable. Promotional opportunities for agricultural instructors were enhanced with the gradual replacement of the purely bureaucratic secretaryship of a committee of agriculture with a new post of chief agricultural officer, which combined technical and administrative duties. Working conditions and instructor mobility improved as push bikes gave way to motor bikes, and then motor cars.[74]

Saorstát Éireann's major initiative on technical instruction evolved between 1926 and 1930. The sector was then expanding at a steady pace. The number of technical schools in the state increased from sixty-four in 1924 to seventy-two in 1930. Over the same period, student enrolments rose from 22,000 to 33,000. However, whole-time classes were confined largely to Dublin, and attendance rates averaged a mere 50 per cent. In rural areas, where there were no permanent schools, itinerant instruction schemes were deplorably deficient. Due to the shortage of teachers, courses in subjects other than Irish, woodwork, commerce, and domestic economy were infrequent. Even in the schools, much of what passed for technical education was remarkably non-technical. When in 1926 a Department of Education survey on the work of its technical instruction branch revealed the extent of these problems, the Minister for Education, Professor John Marcus O'Sullivan, set up a Commission on Technical Education under the chairmanship of John Ingram, a senior inspector with the technical instruction branch. Its terms of reference were simple and open: 'To enquire into and advise upon the system of technical education in Saorstát Éireann in relation to the requirements of trade and industry.'[75]

Concerned with the quality of education, low pay, and bad conditions, the IATIOO had urged this move, and the organisation's honorary treasurer, J. J. O'Connor, was appointed to the commission. Through its submissions to the commission and negotiations with the Department of Education, the IATIOO set down markers for significant advances. In relation to pay, its chief demands were for the replacement of the cost-of-living bonus with fixed salary scales on equal terms with those in Northern Ireland. The department prescribed scales for manual instructors and domestic economy teachers only, and these were not compulsory. Other salaries were set by the local committees with departmental approval. In 1925 a science and engineering teacher earned an average total remuneration (salary plus cost-of-living bonus) of £333 per annum; a manual instructor, £393; a commerce teacher, £272; and a domestic economy instructress £203. By contrast, qualified colleagues in the North enjoyed a salary scale starting at £250 per annum and rising incrementally to £450. 'Those fortunate teachers', argued the IATIOO, 'would not wish for unity with the Free State where the cost of living is 10 per cent higher . . . and officers are kept in penury, discontent and slavery.' The IATIOO objected particularly to the practice of having to seek increments personally, often by soliciting the votes of committee members, and to the inadequacy of subsistence allowances for itinerant teachers.[76]

Ingram presented his report in October 1927, and called for radical changes to meet the demands of trade and industry, including the introduction of continuing education for fourteen to sixteen-year-olds.[77] Accepting that poor pay and conditions reduced efficiency and the number of good teachers, Ingram recommended definite salary scales, scales for travelling and subsistence allowances, automatic approval of annual increments on receipt of a satisfactory report from a departmental inspector, continued payment of cost-of-living bonuses for whole-time officers, and the introduction of standard conditions governing the appointment and duties of whole-time teachers. The commission advised also that whole-time officers should serve a two-year probation. The 1928 annual congress of the IATIOO expressed unqualified admiration for the commission's thoroughness, and urged immediate implementation of its findings.[78]

On 10 April 1930, a Bill embodying Ingram's principal proposals came before Dáil Éireann. The Vocational Education Act 1930 enlarged the scope of technical instruction to embrace continuing education, establishing a vocational school system at second level to 'supplement education provided in elementary schools' and to offer 'general and practical training in preparation for employment'. The ninety-six technical instruction committees were replaced by thirty-eight vocational education committees comprising representatives of local authorities and commercial, industrial, educational, and cultural interests.[79] Technical education retained its coeducational and non-denominational character, though in most cases the committees came to be chaired by a priest, and John Marcus O'Sullivan assured the bishops that the vocational system would not impinge on the domain of the denominational schools.[80] All officers of the technical instruction committees came under the new committees, with a guarantee that duties would not be adversely affected in the new dispensation and that posts would not be axed without compensation. Advances in conditions secured before 1930 were written into the Act, and teachers appointed subsequently would enjoy the same rights. The Act went a long way towards addressing the IATIOO's fundamental grievances. Training programmes were to be better regulated. The right to appoint technical teachers was vested in the committees, subject to the department's approval of the candidate's qualifications, and the standard qualification was to be a university degree. Salary scales were to be provided for two classes of teacher: permanent, whole-time staff in receipt of a definite salary, and temporary, part-timers paid on an hourly rate. Permanent staff were to receive a cost-of-living bonus on the same basis as civil servants, while part-time teachers were allowed a smaller bonus. When the Department of Education issued the first memorandum governing qualifications, pay, and conditions of employment in 1933, the salary scales were a disappointment to many teachers. But substantial points of principle had been met.[81]

With the introduction of the vocational schools, the IATIOO became the Vocational Education Officers' Organisation, representing about 450 of the 600 teachers in the system. Already, the union could reflect on a solid performance. Operating in a field but recently deemed experimental by the civil service, in a largely agricultural economy with minimal requirements of technical expertise, under first a colonial regime and then a government committed to maximising economic growth through cattle exports, and with a powerful clergy anxious to safeguard the interests of church schools, technical teachers had clocked up a better record in securing statutory improvements in conditions than their secondary school colleagues. Crucial to that achievement was their ambiguous position as both teachers and public servants under the 1899 Act. It was this which enabled a small, scattered and diverse profession to develop an organisational cohesion and take advantage of legislative change in 1899, 1925 and 1930. Not surprisingly, vocational teachers continued to emphasise their status as local authority officers into the middle years of the century.

Notes

1 John J. Carton, 'The development of technical education in Ireland 1889–1930' (M.Ed. thesis, Trinity College, Dublin, 1972), pp. 5–7.

2 Seamus S. Duffy, '"Treasures open to the wise": a survey of early mechanics' institutes and similar organisations', in *Saothar*, 15 (1990), pp. 39–47.

3 Carton, 'The development of technical education', p. 6.

4 *Ibid.*, pp. 8–27.

5 Patrick Kevin O'Leary, 'The development of post-primary education in Éire since 1922, with special reference to vocational education' (Ph.D. thesis, Queen's University, Belfast, 1962), pp. 197–206.

6 The Technical Education Association ceased to meet regularly after 1900 and was dissolved in March 1903. See James J. Cooke, 'The movement for a separate department for technical instruction in Ireland with particular reference to the role of Dublin corporation 1867–1902' (M.Litt. thesis, Trinity College, Dublin, 1982), pp. 263–6. For the Recess Committee and the origins of the DATI see D. Hoctor, *The department's story: a history of the Department of Agriculture* (Dublin, 1971), pp. 23–48.

7 Carton, 'The development of technical education', pp. 64–113.

8 O'Leary, 'The development of post-primary education', p. 24.

9 Carton, 'The development of technical education', pp. 81–4; Hoctor, *The department's story,* p. 88.

10 Carton, 'The development of technical education', p. 95.

11 Hoctor, *The department's story,* p. 89; Carton, 'The development of technical education', pp. 98, 105–6.

12 Hoctor, *The department's story,* p. 88.

13 Carton, 'The development of technical education', pp. 88, 101.

14 O'Leary, 'The development of post-primary education', p. 23.

15 Carton, 'The development of technical education', pp. 100–3.

16 O'Leary, 'The development of post-primary education', pp. 16–17; Carton, 'The development of technical education', p. 94.

17 *Journal of the Department of Agriculture and Technical Instruction for Ireland,* 12 (1911–12), pp. 307–8. See also Susan M. Parkes, 'George Fletcher and technical education in Ireland 1900–27', in *Irish Education Studies,* 9, 1 (1990), pp. 13–29.

18 'Statements of the RCO delegation to the DATI, 28 January 1921, National Archives (hereafter, NA), Department of Agriculture files, A 1922, AG1/7204/22.

19 *Irish Technical Journal,* August 1904.

20 Archives Department, University College, Dublin (hereafter, ADUCD), TUI papers, TU 30/28 (7). The sectional associations' exact titles were rarely cited, and some associations went through changes of composition. The following unusually formal list of affiliates to the RCO is dated 9 July 1918: Agricultural Instructors' Association, Art Masters' Association, Commercial Teachers' Association, Domestic Economy Instructresses' Association, Horticultural Instructors' Association, Manual Training Teachers' Association, Association of Principals of Technical Institutes, Science and Engineering Teachers' Association, Poultry and Dairy Teachers' Association.

21 *The Vocational Education Bulletin* (hereafter, *Bulletin*), 11 (July 1937), pp. 155–6.

22 ITIA Annual Congress, *Report*, 1919, pp. 73–8.

23 *Agricultural and Technical Education* (hereafter, *ATE*), July 1919, p. 242.

24 NA, Department of Agriculture files, A 1922, AG1/7204/22; *ATE*, May 1918, p. 21.

25 ADUCD, TUI papers, TU 30/28 (7).

26 J. J. O'Connor (1878–1952) was born in Cork and began his working life as a carpenter, later taking first class honours in all subjects of the building courses of the City and Guilds of London and the Department of Education; studied art at London University and woodcarving at Oberammergau; spent most of his teaching years at Mallow Technical School, where he served as principal until retirement in 1944; appointed director of training courses for manual instruction by the Department of Education in 1925 and served on the Commission on Technical Education; founder and secretary, Manual Training Teachers' Association; honorary secretary, Standing Council of Whole-Time Officers and RCO, 1913–20; honorary treasurer, IATIOO and VEOO, 1923–44, becoming an honorary life member of the latter on retirement; buried in Warrenpoint, County Down. See tributes in ADUCD, TUI papers, TU 30/28 (4).

27 Gerard A. Moriarty, 'Some aspects of the development of vocational teachers' organisations in Ireland 1913–59' (M.Ed. thesis, University College, Cork, 1984), p. 17.

28 *Bulletin*, 36 (December 1945).

29 ADUCD, TUI papers, TU 30/28 (7).

30 Hoctor, *The department's story*, pp. 98–106.

31 O'Leary, 'The development of post-primary education', p. 16.

32 Carton, 'The development of technical education', p. 103; O'Leary, 'The development of post-primary education' *story*, pp. 21–2.

33 For developments in the wider labour movement during these years see Emmet O'Connor, *Syndicalism in Ireland 1917–23* (Cork, 1989), pp. 21–4.

34 ADUCD, TUI papers, TU 30/28 (7); *ATE*, June 1918, pp. 32–3, July 1918, p. 60, July 1919, p. 242.

35 *ATE*, July 1918, p. 51.

36 Moriarty, 'Development of vocational teachers' organisations', pp. 18–20.

37 ADUCD, TUI papers, TU 30/28 (7).

38 ADUCD, TUI papers, TU 30/28 (7); *ATE*, June 1918, pp. 34–5.

39 *ATE*, May 1918, p.19, December 1919, p. 315, May 1920, pp. 374–6; ADUCD, TUI papers, TU 30/28 (4).

40 *ATE*, May 1918, pp. 58–9, May 1920, pp. 374–6, June 1920, p. 379; ITIA Annual Congress, *Report*, 1919, pp. 73–8. For the comparison of wage rates see John Coolahan, 'The ASTI and the secondary teachers' strike of 1920', in *Saothar*, 10 (1984), p. 44; *ATE*, June 1919, pp. 225–6, July 1919, pp. 241–4.

41 *ATE*, November 1918, p. 128, September 1919, p. 267.

42 Moriarty, 'Development of vocational teachers' organisations', pp. 25–6; *ATE*, June 1919, pp. 225–6, July 1919, pp. 241–4.

43 Coolahan, 'The ASTI and the secondary teachers' strike', p. 44.

44 *ATE*, November 1918, p. 128, September 1919, p. 267.

45 Coolahan, 'The ASTI and the secondary teachers' strike', p. 45.

46 O'Leary, 'The development of post-primary education', p. 18.

47 Coolahan, 'The ASTI and the secondary teachers' strike', p. 45. The INTO's links with Congress led Northern unionist members to form the breakaway Ulster Teachers' Union. See Richard Mapstone, 'Trade union and government relations: a case study of influence on the Stormont government', in *Saothar*, 12 (1987), pp. 35–46.

48 *ATE*, March 1919, pp. 174, 178, April 1919, pp. 195–8, July 1919, p. 240, December 1919, p. 319. An RCO delegation to the DATI on 28 January 1921 claimed that 'Technical officers had, despite insistent appeals, avoided an alliance with labour, not from self interest, but through an anxiety about a conflict with the Department's policy and schemes.' NA, Department of Agriculture files, A 1922, AG1/7204/22. Evidence from the *ATE* would suggest that the 'anxiety' lay with the membership rather than the leadership.

49 *ATE*, May 1920, p. 371, July 1920, p. 408.

50 *ATE*, September 1919, p. 273, October 1919, p. 289, May 1920, p. 362, June 1920, p. 390; for the ASTI strike see Coolahan, 'The ASTI and the secondary teachers' strike'.

51 Moriarty, 'Development of vocational teachers' organisations', pp. 21–2.

52 *ATE*, October 1918, p. 111, March 1919, p. 178, June 1919, p. 228, March 1920, p. 355.

53 *ATE*, June 1918, p. 355.

54 Coolahan, 'The ASTI and the secondary teachers' strike', pp. 43–4.

55 *ATE*, December 1919, pp. 315, 328; Coolahan, 'The ASTI and the secondary teachers' strike', pp. 44, 53–4. Whitley Councils, conceived by a parliamentary select committee on industrial relations under J. G. Whitley, were introduced into the imperial civil service in 1919 to allow staff and management to discuss matters affecting conditions of service.

56 Hoctor, *The department's story*, p. 106.

57 Quoted in *ibid*.

58 Carton, 'The development of technical education', pp. 105–6.

59 For relations between the Dáil department and the DATI see Hoctor, *The*

department's story, pp. 118–21.

60 *Ibid.,* pp. 118–19; *ATE,* September 1918, p. 91, October 1918, p. 115, July 1919, p. 244, September 1919, p. 276, October 1919, p. 294, March 1920, pp. 349–50; Dáil Éireann, *Minutes of proceedings,* 1919–21, pp. 149–50, 154–5; Dáil Éireann, *Debates,* iv (19 July 1923), p. 1087.

61 *ATE,* April 1919, pp. 193–4, July 1919, p. 241.

62 Northern Ireland parliamentary debates, *Senate,* i (21 September 1921), p. 53, (29 September 1921), p. 87; *House of Commons,* iii (17 April 1923), p. 354, (14 March 1923), p. 133.

63 Hoctor, *The department's story,* pp. 131–2, 138–48.

64 Carton, 'The development of technical education', pp. 106–8, 114–15.

65 Frank J. McNamara (1884–1954) was born in Limerick and educated at St Munchin's, Limerick Technical Schools and the Royal University; assistant secretary to Limerick technical instruction committee from 1904 to the dispute in 1919–20; commerce teacher in the Arklow Institute from 1920 and later principal teacher until retirement in 1949; made a fellow of the Royal Society of Arts in 1938 in recognition of his services to education; met J. J. O'Connor as a result of the Limerick dispute and became assistant secretary, RCO; general secretary, IATIOO and VEOO, 1923–52; buried in Limerick.

66 Moriarty, 'Development of vocational teachers' organisations', pp. 27–30; ADUCD, TUI papers, TU 30/28 (1), 'Rules and constitution of the IATIOO'.

67 There is no record of the NUTTI being registered as a trade union, though it is cited in a list of unions in *Trade Union Information,* 8, 43 (March 1953), pp. 1–6. See also ADUCD, TUI papers, TU 30/28 (4). Under its honorary secretaries S. G. Duckworth, Belfast College of Technology, and John T. Esdale, Portadown Technical College, the NUTTI maintained close links with the VEOO and the Vocational Teachers' Association. During the 1970s the NUTTI amalgamated with the (British) National Association of Teachers in Further and Higher Education. I am obliged for this information to Samuel Semple, Lisburn, president of the NUTTI, 1964–5.

68 The 'Rules and constituion of the IATIOO' adopted in January 1924 stipulated that the IATIOO should be affiliated to the INTO and Congress; see ADUCD, TUI papers, TU 30/28 (1).

69 *The Local Officer,* September 1928, p. 1, November 1928, pp. 9–10, May 1929, p. 17, September 1929, pp. 7–8, December 1929, p. 7, March 1930, p. 13, May 1930, p. 4.

70 *Labour's policy on education* (Dublin, 1925).

71 ADUCD, TUI papers, TU 30/28 (1), 'Rules and constitution of the IATIOO'.

72 Moriarty, 'Development of vocational teachers' organisations', pp. 32–4; ADUCD TUI papers, TU 30/28 (4).

73 Moriarty, 'Development of vocational teachers' organisations', pp. 34–5. The gratuity amounted to one-twelfth of the officer's yearly salary for each full year's service, or a year's salary, whichever was the lesser. Half the gratuity was to come from state funds, and half from the local authority rates.

74 Hoctor, *The department's story,* pp. 135–43.

75 O'Leary, 'The development of post-primary education', pp. 33, 36, 42, 60.

76 *The Local Officer*, August 1928, p. 9; Moriarty, 'Development of vocational teachers' organisations', pp. 40–1, 61. The quote is from ADUCD, TUI papers, TU 30/28 (6).

77 Carton, 'The development of technical education', pp. 120–1.

78 *The Local Officer*, August 1928, p. 9; Moriarty, 'Development of vocational teachers' organisations', pp. 40–1, 61.

79 Carton, 'The development of technical education', pp. 121–9.

80 J. H. Whyte, *Church and state in modern Ireland 1923–1979* (Dublin, 1980), pp. 37–8.

81 Moriarty, 'Development of vocational teachers' organisations', pp. 38–40, 56–60.

4. The State and Vocational Education 1922–1960

Brian Girvin

In 1922 the newly independent Irish state was at somewhat of a disadvantage in terms of its educational institutions. While the British legacy was extensive in many areas of public life including the economy, the legal system and the civil service, the new state had inherited few formalised state structures in the education sphere. Nonetheless it had to come to terms with a complex network of privately owned educational institutions, in many cases deeply embedded in the structures of society and for the most part flourishing. It was also a system which had been deeply influenced by what was perhaps the most powerful force in independent Ireland, the Roman Catholic Church. In the half-century following independence, the Irish state would on many occasions have to consider what might be its appropriate role in relation to educational provision. This was particularly so in the case of the vocational education sector and provides the subject-matter of this chapter.

New beginnings

The Catholic Church's special interest in education reflected its unswerving belief that Catholics should be educated in a Catholic environment under the direction of the church. Canon law and papal encyclicals made this explicit, as did various decrees from diocesan and episcopal synods.[1] The church's dominance in education reflected its wider influence in society. Consequently, the new state was in some ways ill-equipped to deal autonomously with educational issues. Most of the political élite accepted the traditional demands of the church, and as a consequence often confused religious ideals with national goals. Not surprisingly, most senior civil servants were products of church-run schools and, originating in a similar social milieu, they shared the assumptions and objectives of the new administrative, political and clerical élites. These factors contributed to the development of a close relationship between the hierarchy and the Department of Education. Furthermore, in the person of the first Minister for Education, Eoin

MacNeill, the department was led by an individual who identified closely with the church and its teaching, and that close relationship was continued by his successor John Marcus O'Sullivan. Yet the hierarchy was in many respects just another interest, albeit an especially strong one, seeking to protect what were considered to be its prerogatives. However church influence was deeper and more extensive than that of other interests such as business or agriculture: its unique strength lay precisely in its claim to be representative of the majority of citizens and in its insistence that it had a duty to provide clear direction on issues of faith and morals. Thus its moral authority was such that even on issues as self-interested as education, its advice was sought and accepted by the state. For the most part ministers and civil servants acted as if the church was a disinterested party in educational matters. One result of such convergence was the relatively low level of controversy on educational issues. Given the central role of the Catholic Church in society, there was a tendency to believe that what was good for the church would be good for society. Such a belief would inevitably constrain education policy makers.[2] A further constraint on policy making was the conservatism of post-independence society and the stability which underwrote this. It was a predominantly agricultural society and one which, while heavily dependent on one market, that of the United Kingdom, owed much of its economic success to its virtual monopoly access to that market. In a comparative context Irish agriculture was not particularly dynamic and, though it produced high levels of exports, much of the sector retained traditional values and norms, many of which were not particularly innovative or competitive.[3]

Any expansion of the educational sector would necessitate considerable expenditure, and during the 1920s the government pursued a policy which in fiscal terms can be described as restrictive. Effective control over expenditure was achieved by the Department of Finance, which followed a policy that remained cautious, if not conservative, throughout. Yet the Department of Finance was also in a dilemma. After 1924 the number of spending departments increased appreciably, leading to increased demands, and in response Finance had to insist proposals for expenditure should be fully justified. Thus, at a general level, fiscal restraint acted as an obstacle to any radical expansion of education, even if all other constraints were removed. In general the government's economic policy was supportive of low taxation, particularly of the agricultural sector: consequently, the tax base would remain narrow.[4] Nor did this restrictive approach change with the stabilisation of the Free State. If anything, between 1927 and 1932 the Department of Finance, reflecting élite and sectoral opinion, increased its influence over the public finances and therefore restricted possible initiatives. Despite these constraints, there were other reasons for the conservatism of educational policy. Irish literacy rates were high by European standards and its educational infrastructure was relatively strong, supplying not only domestic demand, but also 'high export quotas of clergy and doctors'.[5] Yet this was part of the difficulty: the educational system by 1927 was well equipped to provide the basic educational requirements for an agricultural economy, where most children never went beyond primary school, while the small and exclusive secondary and tertiary sectors provided the administrative and professional élite for the new state.

It may be that such an educational system had suited the requirements of a stable agricultural society within the British state. Once independence had been achieved priorities changed, and it could be questioned whether the existing educational system provided for those requirements. Prior to independence, educational policy and debate were dominated by demands for rights for Catholics and the recognition of the Irish language. By 1922 these demands had been largely met and, where not, the new state moved quickly to do so. After 1922 the context within which educational policy was formulated changed considerably, yet in many cases the demands of interested parties had not changed. The dilemma facing education reformers was that there was no strong constituency for reform. Eoin MacNeill was a conservative and, though as a university professor he was professionally concerned with education, his approach to schooling was cautious and inadequate to meet the needs of the newly independent state. This is not to claim that MacNeill was unconcerned by broader educational issues, only that he was unable to develop a ministerial style appropriate to the expectations which some educationists might have had.[6]

The main pressure in the Dáil for educational reform came from the Labour Party. Its spokesman on education was T. J. O'Connell. As a leading member of the Irish National Teachers' Organisation, he had a direct interest in promoting the interests of his fellow teachers, while his party had a strongly held belief that education was a factor in the improvement of the condition of the people and that education should be the right of all rather than the privilege of the few.[7] In 1924 the Irish Labour Party and Trade Union Congress established a committee to examine the education system. When it reported in 1925 it made a number of recommendations on the structure of the system itself and the content of the curriculum. One of the more enigmatic recommendations was that the Minister for Education should not be a member of the Executive Council, on the grounds that this was 'inappropriate'. Instead a council, representative of various educational interests, should be formed with the minister at its head. The report criticised the overlapping nature of the different types of schools, which it claimed led to duplication and confusion. It suggested that some of the time spent in secondary school should be compulsory but did not clearly indicate how this might be achieved. However, it did draw a distinction, within the secondary system, between an early and a later phase. In the first, beginning at age twelve and continuing to fifteen, education would be of a general nature and compulsory. In the later phase, the system would be divided into two, with one stream organised for those pursuing a professional career, while the other would be for technical training. Education would be free and it was strongly urged that working-class students should receive maintenance to allow them to continue at school after age twelve. From the report, it is clear that no special place was envisaged in the educational system for technical education though it warned that there should not be undue emphasis on professional qualifications from secondary school training. In a minority report, Robert MacDonald of the Dún Laoghaire Municipal Technical Institute and a leading member of the technical teachers' representative body, the Irish Agriculture and Technical Instruction Officers' Organisation, argued that technical education was weak, because of the low standard of primary education, which he asserted was due to low attendance at primary schools in Ireland when compared with those in England and Scotland. He proposed strong enforcement of school attendance laws on both parents and employers.[8]

As a general statement of aims for the improvement of education the document contained much of merit. However, its main recommendations were institutional and to an extent corporatist. It was also unrealistic in its failure to appreciate the need for a minister on the Executive Council rather than one who would be the representative of the corporate body of education. More remarkable, for a document published by the central body of the trade union movement, was the low emphasis placed on technical education. In view of these weaknesses it is doubtful whether this document had much influence in the debate concerning the possible reform of education over the following five years, though leading members of the Labour Party were strong in their support for the major reform of the period—the School Attendance Act in 1926— which made attendance compulsory for all between the ages of six and fourteen.

Of considerable significance was the policy review undertaken by the Department of Education for the government prior to the June 1927 general election.[9] It resulted in a memorandum which described the goals of the department: a reconstruction of the educational system, and the Gaelicisation and democratisation of education itself. It reported that 'a complete revolution' had been achieved in these objectives. In part, whether intentionally or not, this document adopted a similar approach to that of the Labour Party document. The Department of Education argued that prior to independence there had been no co-ordination between the various branches of education, but that following the establishment of the department in 1924 this had been achieved. While later historians of education have been sceptical concerning this claim, the department believed in 1927 that new foundations for progressive developments had been established and it confidently predicted that these provided the foundations upon which 'a completely new system of education is in progress of being erected not merely from the national but from the purely educational point of view'.[10]

The implications of this were radical from both an educational and a financial point of view. Nor did the department ignore this implication, for it recognised that second-level education would have to change and that there would have to be a clear distinction between non-vocational and vocational education. Non-vocational education was defined as an extension of the existing system of secondary schools, and it was insisted that the vocational sector, though different, would not involve 'differences in quality of education but only such as will arise out of the different needs of the class of pupils'.[11] To ensure compliance with these objectives, the department recommended that compulsory education be introduced for those not in employment between the ages of fourteen and sixteen. Part-time education would be provided for those in employment up to the ages of sixteen or eighteen. To achieve this the traditional approach to education would have to be jettisoned for one more open and flexible. If the state wanted all those over the age of fourteen to benefit from further educational opportunity, then the facilities would have to be available to attract them, and the memorandum stated explicitly that the aim of the department was to replace the old system in which post-primary education was a luxury for the children of the well-to-do with a 'democratic' system in which no distinction of class or means would be permitted.[12]

The department further recognised that the private secondary schools were an obstacle to this development and it sought a way out of the dilemma by recommending that the free primary schools develop a secondary department to which their pupils could progress. This would be facilitated by the Minister for Education utilising existing powers to make attendance at second-level courses in primary schools compulsory up to the age of sixteen. The department also believed that technical education could be transformed as part of this process and promised that once the recently appointed Commission on Technical Education reported it would act accordingly. It recognised the specific requirements of the agricultural sector and noted with satisfaction that rural science was being taught throughout the state, whereas previously relatively few areas had such courses.[13]

The memorandum therefore identified substantial areas for educational reform for the next two generations. It advocated democratic structures in education, an expanded secondary and technical system and that significant aid be provided to the poor to secure access. It also indirectly challenged the Catholic Church in its own preserve and hinted at the need for a more intrusive role by the state in both primary and secondary education. While it may be that the Department of Education was being unrealistic in its assessment of the context in which it operated and of the possible opportunities available to it, that such a memorandum was provided to the government prior to an election carries considerable significance in itself.

In 1927 there was considerable optimism and enthusiasm within the department concerning the possibility for serious and long-term change in Irish education. This memorandum in effect proposed the restructuring of the educational system to place it on a modern and expanding basis. Any such scheme would face a number of problems in any event. One was finance; the financial implications of the new compulsory education regulations were not addressed either in the document or elsewhere in the department at the time. It was also not clear that the political will would be available to push through the innovative schemes outlined. Given the condition of the education system at the end of the 1920s, the one area where the department might hope to achieve reforms was technical or vocational education. This was implicit in the memorandum and the basis for significant change was provided by the Commission on Technical Education which reported in 1927.

The Commission on Technical Education, 1927

The Minister for Education had appointed the Commission on Technical Education in 1926 as part of a government review of the main areas of public life to ascertain if reform was required. Though the government was conservative on a number of issues it did seek to establish the groundwork for policy making in a systematic fashion and it is clear that in most cases Cumann na nGaedheal's approach to policy formulation was not as ideologically motivated as that of its successor.[14] The commission's report was comprehensive and provided enough analysis and recommendations not only to transform technical education in the narrow sense of that term, but also to widen the vocational bias of education if this was what was required by the department. In tone and sentiment the report displayed considerable convergence with the departmental memorandum which preceded it.

At the heart of the report was a fierce criticism of the existing system of primary education. The commission found that many children left school before completing the primary cycle, and that the existing system did little to prepare them for technical or further education. It found that in many cases the standards were so poor that many of those who left school prior to completion of the primary cycle had only a minimum capacity to read or write, which effectively made them functionally illiterate.[15] This struck at the heart of the existing school system and challenged the education which it offered. The educational system provided some minimal education in the primary sector, but failed to prepare the majority of pupils either for employment or for entry to secondary education of any type, a failure highlighted in both the earlier Labour Party and Department of Education documents.

The report argued that if technical education was to contribute to the Irish economy then secure foundations had to be laid in the primary schools.[16] This led to three basic recommendations. The first recommended the institution of a system whereby every child in sixth class would be tested in an examination prescribed by the Department of Education and a school leaving certificate would be awarded. This would be complemented by the reorganisation of the secondary school curriculum to include such technical subjects as technical drawing and manual instruction. This change would have the objective of preparing young people to enter employment at sixteen. The second main recommendation was that a form of 'continuation education' should be introduced for fourteen to sixteen-year-olds. Continuation classes should be distinct from the technical classes and should have a distinct rural and urban character as appropriate. The third main recommendation sought to promote fuller attendance. In urban areas compulsion should be invoked for those between the ages of fourteen and sixteen not then in employment and those in 'approved employment' should have to attend classes for a minimum of 180 hours per year. In rural areas compulsion was not recommended, though everyone between the ages of fourteen and sixteen should have to attend classes for a minimum of 180 hours per year. The main aim of these recommendations was to provide urban and rural youth with an intensive preparation for entry to appropriate trades. To achieve this it was recommended that entry to trades and standards of proficiency should be based on the syllabus of the continuation schools.

The commission was also concerned to attract rural children to trades. It recommended that scholarships which were tenable at secondary schools should also be tenable at continuation schools. It advocated a reorganisation of the administration of the technical system and that an improved system of financing should be considered. It was recognised that the proposed reforms would require a major commitment on the part of the state and that everything could not be achieved in the short term; however, if caution had to be exercised, it should not be such as would impede the eventual implementation of a country-wide scheme.[17] Such realism did not disguise the radical intent of the report, for some of its central recommendations seriously challenged the existing structures and more importantly the vested interests within education. Its recommendations posited substantial intervention and investment by the state itself, and it is clear that there would be some, if not a significant, overlap between the areas of continuation education and secondary education. Not only was the commission urging the secondary schools to adopt a more technical curriculum, but it was also recommending that the primary curriculum should become the focus for training for admission to the continuation schools. These schools in turn would be the focus of a general education, but one with a significant 'practical' bias; only after this, that is from sixteen years of age, would technical education be attempted. Finally the commission urged the need to relate employment and economic requirements to the educational system in the belief that only by doing so could the economy be successfully expanded.[18]

In a reservation to the main report, John Good, a Dublin businessman and TD, took an even stronger line on the adequacy of primary education. He quite explicitly linked deficiencies in the primary level with weaknesses in the economy. He argued that there was a direct link between the high drop-out rate from primary schools in Dublin and the numbers registering at the labour exchange. Some 60 per cent of the boys had not got beyond fifth class, and he believed that the 9 per cent which had got only to third class could be considered illiterate. For girls the standard was a little higher, with the respective figures being 47 per cent and 9 per cent.[19]

It was clear from the report that a significant gap had opened up between the education provided by the primary school system and that provided by the church- controlled secondary schools, in particular because the latter provided teaching of a form which was neither technical nor addressed the requirements of a vocationally based system. The commission was concerned about the absence of a pool of competent workers which could provide the skills necessary for economic expansion and the modernisation of the economy. The report provided the basis for the Vocational Education Act 1930, which in turn became the central legislative framework for all policy implementation relating to technical education.

The Vocational Education Act 1930

The departure from the traditional education system facilitated by the Vocational Education Act involved three interrelated features. The first was the substantial degree of state control, which would operate through the new local vocational education committees. The legislation made such control explicit by giving the Minister for Education substantial powers over the functioning of the committees, which became increasingly dependent on the state for their income. That relationship also found telling expression in the legislative provisions that enabled a minister to dismiss a committee which was not fulfilling its duties under the Act.[20] A second departure was the emphasis on the vocational training of young people between the ages of twelve and sixteen. The Act stipulated that technical and continuation education would be provided by the local committee and it highlighted the need to acquire occupational skills in agriculture and industry. Thus a departmental memorandum to vocational education committees in 1942 highlighted the need to recognise the differences between vocational and other forms of education. Continuation education had 'to prepare boys and girls, who have to start early in life, for the occupations which are open to them'. These occupations, in general, required some sort of manual skill, and continuation courses had a corresponding practical bias.[21] At these two levels the state was moving beyond the traditionally accepted function of the state in education, though not necessarily in opposition to prevailing opinion. A third departure from the traditional education system heightened the possibility of difficulty here, and that concerned the non-denominational nature of the system being proposed. To all intents and purposes it seemed that the system would be secular, not only controlled by the state but staffed by lay teachers and controlled locally by a committee appointed by the local authority.[22]

Each of these factors posed a challenge to existing institutions and to none more so than the Catholic Church and the secondary schools. In a society heavily dependent on agriculture and with a high proportion of low-skilled manual workers in the towns, the attractions of vocational education were manifest. If successful in attracting large numbers of students the vocational system could offer a real alternative to the secondary school for those—the majority—who otherwise would leave school early and without recognisable skills to pursue employment. If this happened on an extensive scale the further danger to the church would be that finance and resources would be channelled into the vocational schools to the detriment of the secondary schools.

While the Catholic hierarchy did not openly criticise the Act, it was seriously concerned about its implications. On 12 October 1930 the Minister for Education John Marcus O'Sullivan met a delegation from the hierarchy. The delegation outlined episcopal concerns and highlighted its reservations on the sections of the Act dealing with students aged fourteen to sixteen. In response to this the minister wrote to David Keane, bishop of Limerick, outlining his understanding of the Act and how it affected the church. In virtually every detail the minister conceded to the hierarchy, and on the basis that the vocational schools would not offer 'general education' he explicitly denied there was any attempt to challenge the church's dominance in secondary education.[23] While insisting that there was no threat to the secondary system, O'Sullivan also argued that even when the state could afford a universal system of general education this would not be provided through the vocational schools. The tone of the letter suggests that the objectives of the 1927 memorandum, which advocated an expansion of educational opportunity, had been postponed indefinitely. Indeed, O'Sullivan insisted that one of the main difficulties he encountered when he introduced the Bill was pressure from those who wished to have a more general curriculum accompanying the vocational training. He believed that he had resisted this successfully, and he reassured the bishops that he had been careful the secure that 'no new principle of control in education should be introduced by this Act'. He maintained that the church authorities had no reason to feel uneasy about the Act, and denied that the traditional competence of the Catholic Church in the area of education would be in any way challenged:

> I strove to secure, with success, as I believe, that the Act should not run
> counter to established Catholic practice in this country, or to the spirit of the

Maynooth decrees governing these matters. This was one of the reasons why I insisted so strongly on the vocational character of the instruction to be provided under the Act.[24]

On two other issues O'Sullivan conceded to the bishops. The hierarchy had objected to coeducation and night classes, apparently on moral grounds. O'Sullivan's response was to advise the vocational education committees to schedule classes in such a way that the sexes would not attend on the same evening or at the same times; indeed it was his hope that night classes would be avoided altogether. The bishops also expressed concern about the provision of religious instruction in the new schools. This appears also to have been a point of concern for O'Sullivan. A commitment was made that the local clergy would provide the instruction within the school for those who required it, but that there would be no compulsion.

It is quite clear that O'Sullivan was concerned that the bishops would oppose the legislation and that consequently he would find himself in political difficulties. If his object was to save the Act, this was achieved. Though there was disquiet on the part of some bishops and sections of the teaching clergy, the hierarchy did not oppose the Act and the system was successfully introduced. O'Sullivan's assurances were accepted and turned out to be well founded. In addition, a distinction was drawn between teaching which had a practical or technical component and what was described as general education. The church accepted an element of multidenominationalism and state control in the former but not in the latter.

O'Sullivan's letter expressed far more conservative sentiments than those in the 1927 memorandum. Apart from his deference to the church, O'Sullivan also appeared to be pulling back from the earlier promise of radical change. Not only did he promote vocational education as an extension of existing technical programmes, but he was at pains to separate it from both the primary and the secondary system; vocational education would not be a competitor of either, but would rather have a distinct and separate function. Moreover, O'Sullivan now argued that any extension of compulsory attendance would be gradual and consequently he cut across the radical promise of earlier proposals. For whatever reasons the department, or in any event the minister, had clearly decided that conciliation of existing interests would be the preferred method for managing the education system. In such a context it would be difficult for a new section of the educational system to develop effectively or to expand.

Fianna Fáil in government

The change in government in 1932 did not transform the educational system in any fundamental way. Fianna Fáil may have proved to be innovative in other areas of policy, in industry for example, but its zeal does not appear to have extended to educational reform. Thus the Department of Education was able to report to Eamon de Valera, the President of the Executive Council, in May 1935 that no education legislation had been enacted since 1930. The department at this time seems to have been concerned mainly with the promotion of Irish and its expansion wherever possible.[25] This, of course, is not to imply that departmental officials were not seeking to develop innovative educational schemes. The secretary of the Department of Education, Seosamh Ó Néill, produced a memorandum for de Valera in July 1933 on the question of vocational education for rural areas. In it Ó Néill highlighted the failure to provide an education which would address the requirements of the economy and particularly those of the agricultural sector:

> Such an education, if it is to be effective must not only reach a certain standard in the necessary 'general' subjects but it must be such as will direct the minds and the interests of the people towards agricultural life and give them such a training that they will be able to deal successfully with the problems that arise from it. The fundamental weakness in our educational system to-day is that it does not fulfil either of the above purposes.[26]

While Ó Néill did not examine whether there was a constituency within rural Ireland for his proposals, his analysis is of considerable interest to the development of vocational education. He realistically concluded that any problems would have to be dealt with initially at the primary level. He recognised that few pupils entered the second level and that in any event the education provided there was not only inadequate to the needs of agriculture, but was designed to lead pupils away from the land. He argued that secondary education, by its nature, was organised to provide well-qualified candidates for the professions, the civil service and the clergy and that this was unlikely to change to any degree in either demand or provision. It would not be possible to transform the existing secondary structure, 'for obvious reasons', though he was reticent in making these explicit:

> Those schools are in general inaccessible to most rural pupils and even if they were accessible they have been set up and their educational work has been moulded, and must to a large extent continue to be moulded, by forces that make them unfitted for the education of rural pupils who intend to remain on the land.[27]

Consequently any changes would have to take place within the primary system. The alternatives, as he conceived them, were to reorganise the primary system or to develop continuing education in the vocational schools. His specific suggestion was to give an agricultural bias to the education of those aged eleven to twelve in primary schools. A junior school would be provided for the younger children and this would be followed by a senior school, which in addition to its normal function would serve as the continuation school for the pupils aged fourteen to sixteen and would thus be a secondary school 'completely suited' to the needs of an agricultural community. The immediate question for Ó Néill was which institutional arrangements could be devised to implement such a scheme. He believed that a number of options were available. The first was to retain the primary system as it existed but to utilise vocational education specifically in rural areas. This, he concluded, would be both ineffective and partial. Alternatively, it would be possible to transfer pupils to the existing vocational schools and to carry out the programme there. He recognised that this approach would encounter serious objections from the clerical managers and the teachers of the primary schools anxious to safeguard their prerogatives. He also doubted whether the vocational education committees would have the competence to oversee such an initiative.[28] The third possibility, and the one which Ó Néill clearly favoured, was that higher primary schools, involving a junior and a senior cycle, would be instituted. This would allow for the development to take place within the locality, provide a satisfactory response to possible clerical opposition but at the same time permit the introduction of a uniform curriculum for rural education.

Ó Néill recognised the difficulties associated with this scheme, but persevered with it in different guises over the next decade or so. The objective problem for any change was highlighted in 1934 after Ó Néill had recommended that higher primary schools should be provided in Gaeltacht districts, because such facilities were virtually absent there and no vested interest would be immediately challenged. After drafting a memorandum, Ó Néill wrote to the bishop of Galway concerning the proposals, apparently looking for the hierarchy's approval, prior to its consideration by either the Executive Council or the Department of Finance. In a note written at the same time, Ó Néill concluded that if the bishops were unfavourable to the scheme, it was not considered that it would be desirable to go further with it.[29]

The response from the bishops followed their general meeting on 9 October 1934. While they welcomed the scheme in general, in practice they were opposed to any innovation in this field. The two key issues for the bishops involved power and sexual morality: they believed that the proposals would lead to the erosion of clerical management through the further extension of state control and were also concerned about what was considered to be a moral danger 'for boys and girls from twelve to sixteen years coming long distances without any supervision'.[30] They added that if a scheme were introduced it should be part-time because of the demand for child labour in rural areas. Consequently, no decision was taken to proceed with the scheme, despite the fact that there were no secondary schools in most Gaeltacht areas.[31]

Very real limits had been set on a proposal that might have led to a significant change in educational provision. Even in its radical phase, Fianna Fáil would not seek to confront the significant influence of the church in education. De Valera had no wish to challenge the country's most important interest group, in part because he shared its ideological presuppositions. Yet, other views were present in the civil service and in this Ó Néill seems to have been more innovative in his thinking than some of his political superiors. It has been suggested that 'a Department of Education led by such a man as Ó Néill could not be regarded as a threat to the power of the church in the school system'.[32] Certainly Ó Néill did not seek to challenge the church, but he had clear ideas on how educational policy should be formulated to meet the needs of the new state. It is true that his innovative suggestions did not come to fruition, but this should not lead to the view that he simply acted as the voice of the hierarchy within the department. It may be that it was the politicians, in their refusal to confront the church on these issues, who inhibited change.

By 1936 de Valera was in the process of replacing the neutral and liberal-democratic constitution of the Free State with a new and specifically Catholic constitution which would meet a number of his ideological presuppositions. One involved the unification of the island, while another addressed the primacy of the Irish language in everyday life. But in addition to such specific objectives there is throughout the 1937 constitution a general ideological tone which might be characterised as Catholic. It is not surprising to find that de Valera consulted relatively few individuals on the articles in the constitution referring to religious and moral matters, while those he did consult were usually clergymen. Indeed it is now clear that the future archbishop of Dublin, John Charles McQuaid, played a crucial role in the formulation of a number of articles. While McQuaid and de Valera disagreed on some details, particularly concerning the place of non-Catholic churches within the constitution, in the main their views converged. Not only was the document suffused with Catholic sentiment, it gave constitutional expression to the Catholic position on a wide range of issues. The constitution limited the ability of the state to intervene in the education system. While ostensibly vesting power in the parents of a child, it provided no institutional focus for this. A consequence of the education provisions in the constitution, in conjunction with those on the family, was that the role of the state in education was reduced to negligible proportions while that of any agency which presumed to act on behalf of parents— chiefly the churches—was strengthened. That role was given additional strength in the provisions which guaranteed state funding for privately controlled schools.

Whether by accident or design, after the constitution was enacted the role and functioning of vocational education began to be questioned. When de Valera took the Education portfolio in 1939, he questioned the purpose of vocational education and suggested that the type of education given in the vocational schools could be better carried out within the primary school system. If implemented, such a change would have given the clerical managers of the primary school system direct control over vocational education.[33] In 1941 the professor of education in St Patrick's College, Maynooth, Father Martin Brenan, in an article in the *Irish Ecclesiastical Record* advocated a similar approach. He questioned the commitment of vocational teachers to religious teaching, arguing that recently voiced criticisms of vocational school students by employers were due to the failure of the vocational schools to create a Catholic moral climate. Brenan not only criticised what he saw as an absence of religion from the core of the teaching in the vocational schools, but complained that, despite claims to the contrary, boys and girls were attending school at the same time and even attending some of the same classes, a practice he considered to be undesirable and 'a form of naturalism that is not tolerated even in Nazi Germany'.[34]

The Vocational Education Officers' Organisation recognised that a defence of its members had to be made. The general secretary, Frank McNamara, offered a spirited rebuttal of most of the criticism levelled by Brenan and rhetorically asked if the vocational teachers, who had been educated in the church-controlled primary and secondary schools, were to be trusted with the moral and religious education of their students. McNamara clearly believed that his colleagues were to be trusted, but he recognised that Brenan did not believe this to be the case, though he could not say so directly. Brenan's criticisms were somewhat oblique, but their purpose, as McNamara highlighted them, was to promote the abolition of the vocational system by absorbing it into the existing primary system. In defence McNamara had to demonstrate that in reality there was no danger to the religious or moral character of the students who attended the vocational schools, and in so doing he cited a number of bishops and priests who had spoken positively about the system and pointed to the large number of clergymen serving on vocational education committees.[35] Nor was Brenan's attack an isolated incident. In 1938 another Maynooth professor and future bishop of Cork and Ross, Cornelius Lucey, argued that the Irish school system generally was not effectively Catholic and that a council of education, on guild or corporatist principles, was required to achieve such an end.[36]

Memorandum V 40

With vocational education under attack from such august and powerful interests it was no accident that in 1942 the Department of Education circulated Memorandum V 40 for the guidance of vocational education committees and their employees. It was a striking document and one which departed from any sense of ideological balance in clarifying the core values which the school might impart to its students. From the outset the religious purpose of vocational education was asserted. The ideals of the Christian home and nationality were stressed throughout the document and the principles contained therein were considered to be central to the very idea of vocational education: the nuance within it was directed towards bringing the underlying ethos as close as possible to that contained in the constitution. The impact of criticisms such as Brenan's was most evident in the section concluding the memorandum. It suggested that the role of the teacher did not conclude with the practical aspects of teaching, for the teacher must also

> safeguard the general purpose of the education which is to develop with the assistance of God's grace, the whole man with all his faculties, natural and supernatural, so that he may realise his duties and responsibilities as a member of society, that he may contribute effectively to the welfare of his fellow man, and by so doing, attain the end designed for him by his Creator.[37]

The section on religious instruction and social education reinforced these general exhortations. Religion was commended as essential in the vocational system and was to be incorporated into the normal teaching day through effective co-operation with the local clerical authorities, whose representatives were to be given the same status as the teaching staff. Not only would they give religious instruction at specific times but their colleagues, the lay teachers, would have to ensure that their subject-matter would be permeated with Christian values.[38] Social education, it urged, was closely associated with religious instruction. In terms of the creation of citizens the two served similar functions. Unlike religion, which it was assumed was deeply embedded in the collective consciousness, it is surprising to find that there are more problems with generating citizens. The claim was made that unlike more mature nations the Irish citizen was still enchanted by alien influences, and until the recent promulgation of a new constitution this operated as an obstacle to the true fulfilment of national identity and citizenship. The stable environment which usually underpinned the growth of a child to citizenship was not present, according to the writer, who in an instance dismissed the achievements of the first two decades of independence. If the memorandum bore the hallmark of Minister for Education Tomás Derrig's conservative republicanism it also advocated the mobilisation of the vocational school to the task of moulding the new state accordingly:

> a very determined effort is demanded of all those responsible for the training of the young if a right social order is to be established. They have not only to fight influences which are at variance with the correct social order but also to direct their pupils' thoughts into appropriate channels and train them in new habits. Instead of young people being moulded and fitted for the future by the very nature of the life about them, they must themselves form the pattern which is to be worked out by future generations.[39]

In reality, according to the memorandum, such circumstances existed in the past, and the restoration of the Irish language and a return to 'fundamental Christian truths' would re-establish what had been a viable tradition prior to the dominance of the alien influences.

Considerable emphasis was placed on the relationship between the vocational aspects of the training given and the value that this training would have for the individual outside the economic sphere. In addition, teachers in rural areas were encouraged to develop the spirit of agriculture as a focus for economic activity. The schools should strive to develop a genuine regard for manual work and should be formed on the 'high ideal' of rural life.[40] To reinforce all of this there was a special section on women in the home and the constitutional provisions concerning women were cited as the objective to be promoted. Vocational education could contribute to achieving this aim by teaching women how to manage the household budget and it implied that to do so properly was a patriotic duty. It is notable that it was only in this way that the memorandum made distinct proposals concerning the education of girls: most of them, it was assumed, would sooner or later become housewives or domestic servants.[41]

The viewpoints expressed in the memorandum contrasted in several respects with the evidence which the Department of Education prepared at the same time for the Commission on Vocational Organisation.[42] This appears to have been collected by the secretary of the department, Seosamh Ó Néill, and it contained a large section which was almost identical to his 1933 memorandum to de Valera on rural reconstruction. Even more remarkable is that, though the Commission on Vocational Organisation was established with the purpose of furthering a system of corporatism along Catholic lines, the concessions made to that ideology by the department were not strong and should be compared with Memorandum V 40. It may be that Ó Néill shared with many of his colleagues a strong opposition to the claims which the proponents of corporatism made against the bureaucracy of the civil service.[43] This might also mean that Ó Néill's influence was not particularly strong, and that in the context of vocational education at least, 'political considerations' took precedence over those of an administrative or a formal policy nature.

In its published report the Commission on Vocational Organisation was extremely critical of most aspects of government and certainly did not help its case by alienating most of the senior Fianna Fáil politicians. The section on vocational education was mainly concerned with the relationship between education and the economy, both agricultural and industrial. The evidence presented to the commission by the department focused on both of these and addressed the question whether the state was providing an education which could be considered vocational. Ó Néill pointed out that while some state concerns had availed of technical schools to train apprentices, most of the trades did not. Indeed, the scholarships available were normally taken up by entrants to one trade only, as all the others showed no interest. At this level alone the training of young people for skilled work remained outside the influence of the technical and vocational system. Ó Néill was also highly critical of the provision of educational facilities of a vocational nature in rural areas, though arguing that such facilities were fundamental to a progressive agricultural economy. He highlighted this problem in two ways. In the primary system less than 10 per cent of schools taught rural science and the proportion teaching domestic science had also fallen appreciably since compulsion was removed in 1934. This led to the second point, which entailed the social purpose of the vocational schools:

The main difficulty seems to be that the people look on vocational schools as a means of obtaining jobs for their children in towns and cities rather than as a means of bettering life and work on the land and that the young people tend on this account to neglect the rural science classes for attendance at classes in other subjects. I have been told that the boys who attend the schools are in a great number of cases not those who expect to inherit the farm but the younger sons who have to find jobs elsewhere and expect the schools to provide them with a means of doing so.[44]

Ó Néill then made a number of wide-ranging proposals to counter this problem and to increase the attractiveness of rural science for the farming sector. He suggested that compulsory education to the age of sixteen was an option, and he returned to his 1933 recommendations concerning the expansion of the primary school system to provide a form of senior cycle for those who remained in school after sixth class. Ó Néill's proposals did not differ in substance from his earlier ones, though he paid more attention to the obstacles and difficulties facing such a scheme. If realised, the reorganisation of the primary system into a junior and senior cycle would have diminished both the secondary and the vocational systems, and while Ó Néill does not appear to have shared the clerical distaste for vocational education it may be that he recognised that changes in this fashion might meet the criticism while at the same time promote the achievement of his own long-term goals.[45]

In a report prepared for de Valera in 1942 the Department of Education outlined some of its plans for the postwar period.[46] It proposed that vocational education policy should concentrate on extending full-time attendance at schools to sixteen years of age as soon as possible. This would expand the area of responsibility of vocational education and would have financial and social consequences. In particular, the department recognised that young people often contributed to the family income when they reached fourteen years of age and it strongly recommended that a system of family allowances should accompany any introduction of compulsory attendance at school up to sixteen years of age.[47] The difficulty with such a scheme was that it could not be restricted to students at vocational schools but would have to be extended to those attending other schools at a similar age and in similar circumstances. This would prove to be a very real financial burden on the state and one which the department recognised was a significant obstacle to any radical change. There were other problems as well. Opinion within the government was divided on the issue of family allowances, with conservatives such as Seán MacEntee worried that such an innovation would undermine traditional patriarchal values.[48]

In 1944 the Department of Education provided an analysis of the provision of education for those reaching fourteen years of age. It was estimated that 110,000 young people within the state were between fourteen and sixteen years of age; of these, approximately 58,000 were not attending any school while around 51,000 were attending schools. Of the former, some 33,000 were in employment, which left 25,000 young people neither at work nor at school. Of those attending school, 22,000 remained in the primary sector, while 17,000 were in secondary schools and 8,000 were in vocational schools. A further 1,500 were in part-time vocational education, and the remaining were in industrial schools or privately managed schools. Though the department acknowledged low participation as a problem with economic and social ramifications, its response had become relatively unambitious. It focused only on urban areas and advocated expanding the compulsory element 'when suitable opportunity' arose: in the interim any changes would have to be voluntary and compulsion would have to await a decision to raise the school-leaving age to sixteen.[49]

The end of the Second World War confirmed the triumph of social conservatism in Ireland. Nowhere was this more obvious than in the case of education where relatively few plans for educational reconstruction were devised even when the department of Education was pressurised by de Valera to do so. However, it would be mistaken to isolate the department as an obstacle to progress. Whatever about the changes in the United Kingdom and elsewhere in Europe, Ireland was ill-prepared economically and socially for the postwar years. Indeed a degree of smugness entered into cultural and social consciousness after 1945 based on a conviction that Irish values and Ireland's response to its social problems were superior to those of other, implicitly non-Christian, nations. This attitude, which displayed a lack of knowledge of other contemporary European states, was a symptom of a persistent malaise. It was generally accepted that Ireland had asserted its independence during the war and this reinforced a stronger sense of separatism than had existed previously. Relatively few policy initiatives emerged from the plethora of postwar planning proposals, and those that did, mainly authored by Seán Lemass, were neutralised by conservative forces in politics, the economy and society. The criticism made of postwar policy by Ó Buachalla—that it was based on 'a static vision of Irish society'[50]— though correct, fails to address the reality that most of the participants in Irish society accepted such a vision. The Catholic Church, the political parties, educated opinion and the mass of society appear to have shared a conception of social reality that not only favoured stability, but believed that to a large extent Ireland had achieved an optimal state which could be sustained indefinitely. In addition to this, and para-doxically in response to the actuality of social change, the rise of protest parties in the west of Ireland led the major parties to adopt political strategies which reinforced social conservatism rather than challenged it.[51]

The lack of innovation in educational policy can be specifically at-tributed to the growing insistence of the church that it should have effective control over all aspects of education policy. In his response to the charge by the Commission on Vocational Organisation that educa-tion was under state control and should be removed from this, the min-ister, Tomás Derrig, argued that not only was this not the case but that the state was firmly constrained by the influence of the church. It was not an unwelcome constraint however, and he argued that church con-trol provided a welcome and effective safeguard against any danger of totalitarianism.[52] The constraints on the state were quite specific. When in August 1946 a departmental committee on the educational system presented its interim report, it warned that while it was necessary to introduce some changes in the primary sector to attract those who would not proceed to secondary school, no changes could take place prior to consultation with the Catholic bishops. The report noted that only 12 per cent of those within the age group sixteen to eighteen were still at school, while 41 per cent of fourteen to sixteen-year-olds continued in education. The problem facing the committee was identified clearly:

> The pupils of less academic ability gain least under present conditions; and it is our opinion that all the older pupils who do not go to secondary or other schools would benefit greatly from a considerably widened curriculum, which, in addition to literary courses, would include practical subjects and activities. Such a curriculum would bring the work of the pupils more into relation with their environment, would stimulate their interest and call forth more effort because of its bearing on after-school life.[53]

One inference which can be drawn from this and other documents produced at this time is that the department was on the defensive. The proposals contained in the interim report echoed a number of policy options developed, by Ó Néill in particular, over the previous decade. However the obstacles to their realisation had become stronger rather than weaker. The idea of a second-level school which would be distinct from the existing secondary school and the vocational school came to nothing. In the first place the church viewed with suspicion any change which might challenge its dominance in the educational field, and more ecclesiastics expressed concern at what they believed to be state encroach-ment on areas of faith and morals. There were other vested interests also; teachers in vocational and primary schools viewed with suspicion changes which might undermine their status, if not their actual employment. Ó Buachalla reports that de Valera may have offered the control of vocational education to a religious order during the 1940s, and the circulation of Memorandum V 40 in 1942 also reflected the state of siege under which vocational education was then placed.[54]

That this was the case can be further seen in the extensive report by a departmental committee in June 1947. The committee reported in favour of raising the school-leaving age to fifteen and then to sixteen, but did not make a decisive statement to that effect. At the heart of this report was an assertion of continuity, with renewed emphasis on the primacy of Irish within the educational system. The report maintained that the revival of Irish should be at the centre of the system irrespective of what changes took place. It also acknowledged the importance of religion in the education system and in the life of the country, noting the recognition given to religion in the constitution:

> It is taken for granted, therefore, that the place of religion in the whole life of the school will be assured, however the system may be reorganised, and that the education of the child will be one single process embracing his religious and moral as well as his intellectual, physical and social training.[55]

Nor were these points simply rhetorical. The rest of the report reiterated these themes in a number of ways. In a supplement to the main report the authors provided an overview of education in Ireland from the coming of St Patrick until 1922, which articulated and buttressed the Catholic view of education throughout.

The report provided a succinct analysis of the development of vocational education. It showed that vocational schools were providing education for a significant minority of those aged fourteen to sixteen attending school. Some 7,400 attended vocational schools out of a total of 44,600; of the remainder, 20,800 attended primary school and 16,400 attended secondary school. The corresponding figures for the age group sixteen to eighteen were 3,500 in vocational school, 1,670 in primary school and 8,100 in secondary school. Thus the advantage gained by secondary schools in the fourteen to sixteen year age group had diminished somewhat in the older group. The relative importance of vocational schools can be further gauged by the expansion of the system from 65 technical schools in 1930 to 186 permanent vocational schools by 1944. This should be compared with the parallel expansion of the secondary system from 290 schools with 26,972 students in 1929 to

377 schools with 40,040 pupils in 1944. Clearly there was a demand for further education beyond the primary system, but it remained open as to how this would be satisfied.

The point at issue in this 1947 report and in discussions within the department was what would be the consequences of raising the school-leaving age. Up to the end of the war most pupils completed their education at primary school, at about the age of fourteen. If the leaving age was raised there would be a strong demand for a different type of system to deal with the extra students. The report concluded that while the majority of those aged twelve or older remained in a primary school, this had proved inadequate to their needs. However, if the system was to be changed 'the new system, however organised, should be subject to ecclesiastical sanction'. This self-denying ordinance appeared to exclude the vocational system from participation in any new process, and that prospect was explicitly addressed in the report. A completely new system of 'senior schools' was proposed which would provide the 'literary and practical' education required by older pupils after primary school. The advantage of this was that it would be under the control of the religious authorities.[56] The further attraction of such schools would follow from the church's unrelenting advocacy of sexually segregated schooling. The effect of this would be to make the vocational system redundant, and the report recognised this explicitly in its admission that the outcome of the introduction of such a system would place most of the teaching of those over twelve years of age in the hands of the religious.

The implications of these suggestions were not lost on one member of the committee, J. P. Hackett, who had chaired the earlier committee which led to the preparation and circulation of Memorandum V 40. Hackett maintained that the proposal for senior schools duplicated what was then being done in the ordinary continuation courses in the vocational schools. While noting that objection would be made to any new system which appeared to duplicate and make redundant one already in existence, he also noted that the proposals under review arose from a long-standing anomaly in Irish educational policy:

> They have their roots in the conflicting educational aims of the past, in the attempts at compromise, and in particular in the struggles of Catholics to maintain their own system of education in the face of determined efforts to establish two other systems. The objection to vocational education committees is that they tend to perpetuate the second of these systems—that they are in fact essentially undenominational education committees. Memorandum V 40

was an effort to effect a reconciliation by the denominationalisation of continuation education. I am now satisfied that no reconciliation is possible and that there is no real future for continuation education under vocational committees as at present constituted, notwithstanding the success of their day courses and the value of the work which has been done to date.[57]

Whatever about the relative success of the Vocational Education Act—and the committee illustrated that by including an account of its successful operation in a rural area—the impression remains that the system itself was under siege. Hackett recognised the threat, but was unwilling to defend the system on its merits, apparently concluding that the best way forward was to dismantle it at source. If a senior member of the vocational schools section of the Department of Education believed this, then it can be conjectured that serious consideration was given to curtailing it, if not actually abolishing it. Though such a radical step was not undertaken, this may be attributable more to inertia on the part of postwar governments than to any willingness to defend it. Thus Derrig's contribution to a debate on the issue in the Dáil in 1946 was lacklustre, presenting his view of vocational education in muted form and offering nothing to console or arm its supporters.[58]

In a later debate Derrig would claim that over £1 million had been spent on vocational school buildings between 1930 and 1945. Yet in the same debate another deputy pointed out that if the vocational sector currently received £577,000, the privately owned secondary system received £550,000 and the primary sector between £4 million and £5 million.[59] By this time policy priorities had been established by Fianna Fáil, and they were not to change. Vocational education was something they could do without, but if it was not going to evaporate in an uncontroversial way, then they would control its development and limit its expansion, thereby fulfilling the commitment made by the Minister for Education in 1930.

Coalition and consensus

The change in government in 1948 did not alter the direction of educational policy: as with much else, the broad outlines of education policy followed those which had been established by Fianna Fáil. A consensus had been established by the lengthy duration of Fianna Fáil rule, by the acceptance of the new constitution and by the stabilisation of society around a narrow set of norms mostly associated with nationalism, religion and the Irish language. In the person of Fine Gael's Richard Mulcahy this conservative consensus was maintained not only within the realm of education, but more generally within the new government. There was little innovation during the first inter-party government, and nowhere was this more evident than in education. Shortly before leaving office in 1951 Mulcahy addressed the annual convention of the Association of Secondary Teachers, Ireland in terms that not only reflected the consensus which prevailed on policy, but assumed a sense of cohesion and unity within the state which the conflict over the 'mother and child' health scheme had cast into doubt. Mulcahy extolled the central role of the religious in the Irish educational system and the subsidiary role of the state. He insisted rather incongruously that relations between church and state on education matters were well ordered, and that a 'sense of unity' reflected what he described as 'this happy relationship':

> Every day that passes increases my conviction that for all parties concerned in Irish education and its progress the bearings which guide and which will assure that progress are clearly marked and accepted: Christian idealism, with its humility, discipline and faith; a cultural conception of Irish nationality; the fact that we are an expanding and a missionary race.[60]

It can be inferred that the change in government in 1948 may have helped the vocational system, or at least prevented any radical change in education policy. The extent to which the incoming government continued the policy of Fianna Fáil is striking, and this combined with the subsequent political instability up to 1958 probably prevented any further erosion of the vocational sector. In so far as difficulties occurred after 1945, these were mainly associated with financing the vocational sector rather than with any fundamental changes in policy. The prevailing mood was one of satisfaction with existing structures. A special conference took place in April 1946 between departmental officials and the chief executive officers of the vocational education committees, at the latter's request. The meeting was called to discuss the state of vocational education and its future. Those present were of the unanimous opinion that the system was working well and could progress in a satisfactory fashion if more finance became available.[61] The prospect of change did not become apparent until the 1960s and then under very different circumstances.

What seems to be absent from the Department of Education for much of the postwar period was any suggestion of how vocational education could be developed in tandem with the requirements of the economy. This was recognised in principle by Minister for Education Richard Mulcahy in 1954. In response to the demand for cuts in expenditure, he noted that, while the vocational sector had grown since its inception, the needs of the country in regard to it were still very far from satisfied. Any effort to stem its growth, he suggested, would be likely to have very undesirable consequences. Though this might be construed as a case of special pleading in the face of potential cuts, Mulcahy added that low production levels in the economy could be accounted for chiefly by a lack of technical knowledge and skill on the part of industrial and agricultural workers.[62]

This problem had been noted earlier by the US representatives of the European Recovery Programme. After a meeting with one of the American officials, Dr Finlenden, a departmental official noted that the Americans were interested in devising ways by which Ireland could reduce its dollar spending, suggesting for example the expansion of tourism as one opportunity open to Ireland. There was considerable emphasis on the need to improve Irish productivity and technical precision. While the departmental official believed that the Americans would want Irish skilled workers in the event of a war with the Soviet Union, the criticism went deeper than this. Finlenden contrasted the state of technical training in Ireland with that in Germany. The latter, he noted, had a strong tradition in skilled technical work which it could develop without aid from the state. In contrast this tradition did not exist in Ireland and had to be encouraged by the state; such a tradition could only be generated through education.[63] Despite this recognition of the problem of relating technical education to the economy very little appears to have been achieved during the 1950s. This was a decade when the Irish economy fell well behind even the slowest of the western economies, apparently unable to share in the expansion which characterised much of western Europe. It is not until the crisis of the mid-1950s and its resolution during the early 1960s that a change in education was formulated and then it took a quite different form than one might have expected in the circumstances.

The decade of crisis increased the pressure on the state to reinforce traditional norms and processes. Even though a significant proportion of the population was emigrating, considerable time was given over by ministers, whether Fianna Fáil or Fine Gael, to furthering the denominational nature of the educational system. Thus, the reports of the Council of Education, though containing important insights into the educational system, served to secure the status quo. While one report commented favourably on science teaching, it was not prepared to sanction it as a compulsory subject due to a reluctance to extend compulsion in the educational system; the real reason however may have had more to do with expense and the prospect that that might lead to greater state control. More fundamentally, in its report on primary education the council recommended that the primary school system should be explicitly denominational. Another example of this concern can be seen in Richard Mulcahy's notes following a meeting with Brother White of the Christian Brothers' School in Dingle, who complained that the local vocational school was encroaching on its catchment area and, moreover, was providing grants to attract students from the Gaeltacht. The Christian Brothers had been opposed to the opening of the vocational school in the first place and had accepted it only when it was stated that it would offer only night classes. Two goals had been identified: first, any competition or even potential competition in the area of post-primary education should be firmly opposed, and second, a coeducational school, such as the vocational school would be, could not be tolerated.[64]

Perhaps the real reason for the obstacles to the further evolution of vocational education rested not on clerical opposition or even on some innate conservatism, but on a limited view of what role vocational education should play in economic and social formation. Most ministers praised the system and believed it served a useful function. But this function appears to have been social rather than economic or technical. Mulcahy could be extremely positive about the contribution of the system to the economy, but his own discussion of this matter never went beyond the general. He could note the improved status of education in rural areas because of farmer access to vocational schools, but realistic proposals for integrating technical education with the economic needs of the state or proposals for the specific application of continuation or technical education to the solution of economic problems were rare.

Conclusion

The absence of policy initiatives should not be surprising in the context of the 1950s. After all, most Irish politicians did not understand the changes which were already undermining the traditional economic and social system that had underpinned the state up to that time. It was only with the crisis that dominated the mid-1950s that Ireland began to evolve a strategy for economic development. Although the changes which took place did not at first have implications for vocational education, in the medium term economic modernisation required significant changes in how training and education might be fitted into the new consensus in favour of economic integration with the world market. It might have seemed that in this context vocational education would be well placed to expand and to offer a focus for a new type of education. But what occurred was quite different. Although *Investment in education*, the report on Irish education of an OECD survey team in the mid-1960s, would be critical of the secondary school, no attempt was made to radically restructure the educational system to meet the needs of the economy or to renegotiate the relationship between church and state. If anything, the state remained as cautious as before in its dealings with the hierarchy. It has been argued that the state became more assertive during the 1960s and laid claim to areas of competence which previously it had left by default to other agencies. That assertion was effectively challenged by the church, which was well placed, both ideologically and materially, to prevent change. In the event the changes in secondary schools, the Vocational Education (Amendment) Act 1970 and the development of comprehensive and community schools conceded much to the church and, if anything, enhanced the influence of the clergy in education at a time when its numbers and its cultural influence were on the wane. In effect, by the 1960s the state sector was weaker than at any time since 1930 and a new phase opened up which would further diminish the independence and autonomy of the vocational sector.[65]

Notes

1 Edward Rogan, *Synods and catechesis in Ireland, c. 445–1962* (Rome, 1987); J. H. Whyte, *Church and state in modern Ireland 1923–1970* (Dublin, 1971).

2 Brian Girvin, 'Social change and moral politics: the Irish constitutional referendum 1983', in *Political Studies*, 34.1 (1986), pp. 57–79.

3 Raymond Crotty, *Irish agricultural production* (Cork, 1966).

4 Ronan Fanning, *The Irish Department of Finance 1922–58* (Dublin, 1978), pp. 106, 59–119; Brian Girvin, *Between two worlds: politics and economy in independent Ireland* (Dublin, 1989), p. 46.

5 J. J. Lee, *Ireland 1912–1985: politics and society* (Cambridge, 1989), pp. 76, 90.

6 Séamas Ó Buachalla, *Education policy in twentieth-century Ireland* (Dublin, 1988), pp. 253–7.

7 Arthur Mitchell, *Labour in Irish politics, 1890–1930* (Dublin, 1974), pp. 181, 199–200.

8 Irish Labour Party and Trade Union Congress, *Labour's policy on education* (Dublin, 1925).

9 National Archives (hereafter, NA), Department of an Taoiseach, S. 5360/6, 'Review of the work of the Department of Education during the lifetime of the fourth Dáil Éireann', April 1927.

10 *Ibid.*

11 *Ibid.*

12 *Ibid.*

13 *Ibid.*

14 Lee, *Ireland*, pp. 94–140; Girvin, *Between two worlds*, pp. 17–46.

15 Commission on Technical Education, *Report* (Dublin, 1927), pp. 36–8.

16 *Ibid.*, p. 150.

17 *Ibid.*, p. 151.

18 *Ibid.*, pp. 151–2.

19 *Ibid.*, p. 153.

20 NA, Department of an Taoiseach, S. 2401, 'Vocational Education Act, 1930'; S. 7950, Vocational education committees amending legislation with reference to insurance, 4 July 1935; NA, Department of Finance, SO.18/0032/31, Department of Education to Finance with reference to dissolution of Mayo vocational education committee, 16 November 1931.

21 Department of Education, 'Organisation of whole time continuation courses in borough, urban and county areas' (Memorandum V 40) (1942).

22 Barney O'Reilly, 'Issues in the development of vocational education', in *Administration*, 37.2 (1990), pp. 152–70.

23 O'Sullivan to Keane, 31 October 1930, reprinted in Ó Buachalla, *Education policy*, pp. 399–403.

24 *Ibid.*

25 NA, Department of an Taoiseach, S. 2571/9, 'Memorandum by Department of Education, 31 May 1935'.

26 NA, Department of an Taoiseach, S. 9271, 'Educational reconstruction', Seosamh Ó Néill, 21 July 1933.

27 *Ibid.*

28 *Ibid.*

29 NA, Department of an Taoiseach, S. 9271, 'Higher primary schools in Irish speaking districts', 30 December 1933; Ó Néill to O'Doherty, 25 April 1934.

30 NA, Department of an Taoiseach, S. 9271, Copy of minutes of the meeting of the hierarchy, 9 October 1934, forwarded to Ó Néill.

31 NA, Department of an Taoiseach, S. 9271, Ó Néill to Roinn an Uachtaráin, 8 May 1936.

32 Brian E. Titley, *Church, state and the control of schooling in Ireland, 1900–44* (Toronto, 1983), p. 103.

33 Ó Buachalla, *Education policy*, pp. 268–9.

34 Martin Brenan, 'The vocational schools', in *Irish Ecclesiastical Record*, lvii (1941), pp. 13–27.

35 [McNamara] 'Reply to Dr Brenan's article by the general secretary', in *The Vocational Education Bulletin*, 22 (1941), pp. 3–7.

36 Cornelius Lucey, 'Making the school system of Ireland Catholic', in *Irish Ecclesiastical Record*, liv (1938), pp. 470–81.

37 Memorandum V 40, p. 22.

38 *Ibid.*, p. 22.

39 *Ibid.*

40 *Ibid.*, p. 15.

41 *Ibid.* The memorandum was drafted by J. P. Hackett, head of the technical instruction branch and chairman of the committee which compiled the memorandum (personal communication, James McDwyer, former inspector, technical branch).

42 NA, Department of an Taoiseach, S. 14392. The file is undated though a note states that it is no later than 1947. There is no statement that it was compiled for the commission but I have concluded that it was on the basis of a reading of the document and from other material which was prepared for this commission.

43 NA, Department of an Taoiseach, S. 13552, 'Commission on vocational organisation: departmental views on report', January to March 1945. For detailed criticism by the Department of Education see S. 12753 A/B.

44 NA, Department of an Taoiseach, S. 14392, 'Memorandum from the secretary of the Department of Education on the various functions of the Department of Education connected with vocational organisation', n.d.

45 *Ibid.*

46 NA, Department of an Taoiseach, S. 12891A, 'Postwar planning: education', 16 July 1942.

47 NA, Department of an Taoiseach, S 12891A, 'Memorandum on vocational education', 15 October 1942.

48 Lee, *Ireland*, pp. 283–6.

49 NA, Department of an Taoiseach, S. 12891A, 'Post-emergency policy for vocational education', 7 December 1944.

50 Ó Buachalla, *Education policy*, p. 265.

51 Girvin, *Between two worlds*, pp. 148–68.

52 Cited in Ó Buachalla, *Education policy*, p. 267; Lucey, 'Making the school system', had also criticised the lack of church control over education and complained of state intrusion.

53 NA, Department of an Taoiseach, S. 12891B, 'Interim report of the departmental committee to examine the educational system', 31 August 1946.

54 Ó Buachalla, *Education policy*, p. 269.

55 NA, Department of an Taoiseach, S. 12891B, 'Recommendations for the reorganisation of the educational system to meet a raising of the school leaving age', 27 June 1947.

56 *Ibid.*, para. 27, p. 13.

57 NA, Department of an Taoiseach, S. 12891B, J. P. Hackett, 'Note on continuation schools with special reference to paragraph 31', 18 July 1947.

58 Dáil Éireann, *Debates*, ciii (7 November 1946), cols 626–30.

59 Dáil Éireann, *Debates*, ciii (28 November 1946), col. 1643.

60 Archives Department, University College, Dublin (hereafter, ADUCD),

Mulcahy papers, P7/C/159, 27 March 1951.

61 ADUCD, Mulcahy papers, P7/C/158.

62 ADUCD, Mulcahy papers, P7/C/154, T.A. 444, 'Cost of public expenditure', 30 September 1954.

63 ADUCD, Mulcahy papers, P7/C/152, 'Memorandum', P. E. Ó Suilleabháin, 27 October 1949.

64 Statement by the Minister for Education on primary education: proposed changes, December 1956; NA, Department of an Taoiseach, S. 15015B/61, memorandum for government by Department of Education, 25 January 1961; ADUCD, Mulcahy papers, P7/C/154, Minister's note, 30 June 1954 and accompanying memorandum.

65 O'Reilly, 'Issues in the development of vocational education', pp. 162–4.

5. 'For the Youth of the Common People': The Vocational Education Officers' Organisation 1930–1954

Mary Jones

As part of the reform of technical education in 1930, the employees of the technical instruction committees were transferred to the new vocational education committees. The Irish Agriculture and Technical Instruction Officers' Organisation, which had represented the interests of the teachers and the senior administrative staff since 1923, responded by reforming itself in a new organisation, the Vocational Education Officers' Organisation, which became generally known as the VEOO and in Irish, Cumann na nOifigeach Gairm-Oideachais. It would continue to act as the sole representative organisation for teachers and salaried administrators in vocational education for the next twenty-three years. In 1953 a series of internal disputes would convulse the organisation, causing a large part of its membership to resign and to establish a rival body, Cumann Mhúinteoirí Gairm-Oideachais. Thus disabled, the VEOO would limp on, but in late 1954 it would agree to dissolve and to seek common cause with its competitor in a hybrid organisation, the Vocational Teachers' Association.

Organisation

On its foundation in 1930, the VEOO confined its membership to whole-time teachers and chief executive officers. The restriction to whole-time teachers was deemed necessary given the number of primary teachers employed part time to teach evening classes. Vocational teachers were themselves barred from taking part-time work; in 1934, the official organ of the VEOO, *The Vocational Education Bulletin*—generally known as the *Bulletin*—remarked, not entirely in jest, that 'the technical school as a happy hunting ground for people who have spare time from their main jobs to take up teaching as a side-line, is a bright thought'.[1] The VEOO's base broadened in 1933 when it agreed to extend membership to chief clerks of committees, though a resolution to include part-time teachers tabled for the 1935 congress was withdrawn following pressure by the executive. The ban on part-timers would remain throughout the organisation's history.

Those eligible to join did so through a regional committee, or branch. They were formed quickly in places such as Limerick and Waterford where technical education was well established, but progress elsewhere was slow. By 1936, however, the *Bulletin* was able to announce that with the formation of a committee in Kilkenny there was now a branch in every county but Clare.[2] Early the following year it triumphantly proclaimed that fifteen of the twenty teachers in Clare had at last joined and it appealed to the others, mainly peripatetic Irish teachers, to join.[3] At the same time the executive authorised the formation of a separate committee for Dublin city and in the next few years committees were formed in the other city and urban schemes.

Few details of the extent of the VEOO's membership over its quarter-century history have survived. The editor of the *Bulletin*—the general secretary Frank McNamara—rarely published membership data but would repeatedly state that the organisation included the greater number of those eligible to join, a proportion variously put at between 70 and 75 per cent. A generally optimistic tone was occasionally modified, as in 1936 when he reported that the number of non-members was 'considerable'.[4] Membership details submitted annually to the Irish Trade Union Congress (ITUC) suggested a steady and continuing increase, but the roundness of the figures—100 in 1930, 500 in 1940 and 600 in 1943—also suggested a rough and ready accounting system on the part of both the VEOO and the ITUC.[5]

More detailed data is available from 1946 onwards. That year the general secretary reported that the membership of 730 was equal to 77 per cent of the 946 teachers and officers whom he claimed were employed by vocational education committees.[6] Returns to the Department of Education for that year, however, reported 1,033 whole-time vocational teachers; these, along with approximately seventy administrators, serve as a realistic indicator of potential membership at that time. An unusually detailed membership tabulation at the end of December 1952 stated that the 'registered' vocational officers stood at 1,067, of whom 795 or 75 per cent were described as 'effective' members. However the total of whole-time teachers returned for that school year was 1,239, and if they and the administrative officers are taken as potential members, the proportion in membership would be nearer to 60 per cent. Shortly afterwards most members of the Dublin city and Cork city branches resigned, and over the next year and a half they were followed into a rival body by many others. By early 1954 the VEOO could only claim 465 members, of whom 331 were in good standing; when a vote on its future was taken in the summer of that year, only 296 participated. A more realistic assessment of strength may be derived from subscription income, something which becomes possible for the period from 1946 when financial statements were printed in the *Bulletin*. In that year subscriptions totalled £1,099, equivalent to 550 individual subscriptions at the annual rate of £2. By 1951 income had risen to £1,505, the highest in the VEOO's history, and in 1953, in the last available accounts, it was £1,380, equivalent to 460 members at the new rate of £3.

Figure 5.1: Vocational teachers and VEOO membership 1930–54

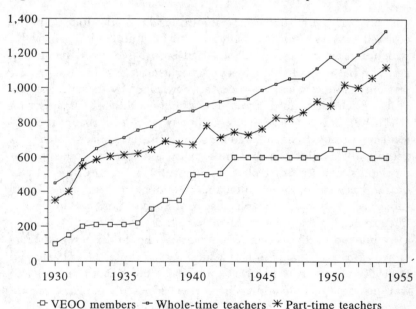

⊡ VEOO members ⊸ Whole-time teachers ✳ Part-time teachers

Source: Irish Trade Union Congress, *Annual reports*, 1930–54; Vocational Education Officers' Organisation, *Bulletin*, 1946–53; Department of Education, *Annual reports*, 1930–55.

Despite the uneven quality of the data it is clear that the VEOO never came close to reaching its goal of enrolling all potential members. Its claims of between 75 and 80 per cent membership now seem exaggerated: the more concrete subscription data of the late 1940s, at a time when its fortunes were at their best, suggests that effective membership then was nearer to 60 per cent. In the earlier years, and in the calamitous final years, it was much less. Its membership goal was in itself relatively limited, the organisation having throughout its history excluded part-time teachers. Some of these may have been members of other bodies, but a blanket ban suggests an unwillingness to address the needs of a large number of teachers who worked only in vocational education and a complacency which, in the long term, may have sapped its vitality. It did not, however, resort to a closed-shop policy: while its leaders often denounced those who benefited from the organisation's efforts while refusing to join it, successive congresses stopped short of adopting an exclusivist policy.[7]

Sectional interests

The original central body for technical teachers—the Representative Council of Associations of Officers of Agriculture and Technical Instruction Committees in Ireland—had been based, as its name suggests, on the autonomous subject teacher associations. The importance of subject interests had also been acknowledged by its successor, the Irish Agriculture and Technical Instruction Officers' Organisation (IATIOO), but as its role as a central body developed, that of the subject associations declined. Leading activists in the subject associations became office-holders in the central body and were assiduous in promoting its representative role. Thus with the founding of the VEOO on the basis of common rather than sectional interests, the original subject associations, in so far as they continued to exist, would be confined to dealing mainly with curricular issues.

While most activists transferred their energies to the new body, sustained activity by several subject associations during the late 1930s and the 1940s suggests that there were some teachers who felt that the VEOO was incapable of fully addressing their needs. Thus the rural science teachers revived their association in 1936 under the vigorous leadership of Fred Cronin, then headmaster at Mooncoin.[8] Woodwork teachers were similarly active, and the impact of these associations was such that in 1938 the executive decided to select from among rural science and woodwork teachers when making its customary co-options.[9] By the mid-1940s the executive had become less tolerant of what it now referred to as 'sectional' activity. In 1946 a request by the woodwork teachers' *cumann* for space in the *Bulletin* was refused on the basis that the executive 'did not feel that sectional associations generally were good for the Organisation, and that certain activities of the *cumann* in particular were detrimental'.[10] Such suspicion was inevitable, for less than a year after its foundation the woodworkers' *cumann* had over fifty members and was claiming, somewhat coyly, that its intention was 'to assist the VEOO in every way' in having unsatisfactory conditions removed. As the VEOO struggled to maintain its resources, the growth of another body able to claim the loyalty of its members had to be discouraged. The rural science teachers too were rebuffed and were informed by a huffed general secretary that, contrary to their claim, sectional interests had never been neglected by the executive.[11] When members of the Domestic Economy Instructresses Association indicated their discontent, the executive shifted from a position of benevolent if suspicious patronage to one of outright hostility: 'sectional associations are not recognised in the constitution of the VEOO!'[12]

The failure of the executive to establish an authoritative voice for such interests was a recurring grievance. It found expression at the 1950 congress when the Kerry branch tabled a resolution calling for the number of non-officer members of the executive to be increased to allow the formation of four panels which would represent constituencies formed from groups of school subjects. The executive threw its weight against the idea and congress accepted instead a resolution from Leitrim deploring the formation of 'splinter organisations'. The point was hammered home the following year by the adoption of a resolution from Kilkenny denouncing the formation of groups which it implied were sapping the VEOO's strength.[13]

Despite maintaining their rights as members of the VEOO, the chief executive officers had also formed their own association. Their strong separatist tendency was revealed in 1935 when they submitted a memorandum to the executive pointing out that their membership of the VEOO—alongside the teachers—might promote a perception of partiality on their part. They proposed the creation of a separate chief executives' section within the larger body which would obviate the need to participate in branch proceedings alongside their teacher colleagues. The proposal was rejected by an executive which had become increasingly protective of its claims.[14] Nonetheless the Chief Executive Officers' Association had its role as a separate representative body recognised by the Commission on Vocational Organisation. This was further acknowledged in 1947 when it was invited by the Department of Education to a major policy review and in 1952 when it negotiated a salary increase separately from the VEOO.

Significant gains by the chief executives undermined the VEOO's claim to be the representative body for all salaried vocational education officers and may have convinced some members that independent sectional action was more effective. In particular the undeniable advance in the negotiating status of the chief executives forced consideration of the extent to which the interests of teachers could be effectively served by a body which also aimed to represent their superior officers. It revealed a contradiction in its very structure, and few teachers were surprised and none would demur when, on the formation of a new representative body in 1954, it was proposed that chief executive officers be excluded from membership.

Centralised power

Having adapted the structures of its predecessor, the VEOO also retained its founding fathers. The honorary treasurer of the IATIOO, J. J. O'Connor, was appointed treasurer in 1930 and he would hold office, unopposed, until his retirement as headmaster at Mallow in 1944. On the proposal of the executive and with the approval of congress, he remained an honorary member of the executive until his death in 1952. Frank McNamara, the honorary secretary of the IATIOO, was appointed part-time general secretary in 1930 and when the *Bulletin* was founded as the organ of the VEOO in 1934, he became editor. He produced three to four issues a year in which he maintained a judicious balance between news and opinion on educational issues. His exceptional efforts were combined with his work as a commerce teacher, and later headmaster, in Arklow Technical School, from which he retired in 1948. Though then in failing health, he continued to act as general secretary and his continuing, if less frequent, presence at executive meetings, along with that of J. J. O'Connor, retained a tangible link with the earliest days of technical education.

As in all such bodies, however, the retention of control by a small group for a prolonged period, even if representative and retaining a mandate, may have served to promote an alternative locus of power. The structure of the central executive committee—comprising the general secretary, three honorary officers (chairman, treasurer and secretary), four members elected by the general body and two co-opted members—undoubtedly offered the executive the opportunity to develop a spirit of comradeship and common purpose. Throughout the VEOO's entire history, however, no more than forty individual members served at this level. Of these, seventeen were elected in the 1930s, thirteen were elected in the 1940s and ten were elected between 1950 and 1954. While this suggests a willingness to elect tried and trusted colleagues, it also reveals a dependence on a small circle which may have militated against the need to form an engaged membership.

Of the forty thus chosen, a much smaller number—fifteen in all—were elected at various times to one of the organisation's offices. Of these, twelve served as chairman, but in the other two positions turnover was almost imperceptible. Of four members who ever held the post of treasurer, one served for fourteen years and of the four who held the post of secretary, one did so for sixteen years. Disquiet became evident with the tabling of a resolution for the 1947 congress that no officer should serve for more than three years. This was ruled out of order, but was tabled again the following year.[15] Again, it was rejected, but further evidence of discontent was revealed in the demand that there be an annual meeting of branch secretaries with the executive with a view to improving communication. The sense of alienation was further revealed when the 1948 congress adopted a Dublin city resolution expressing dissatisfaction with the executive's remoteness and ineffectiveness.[16] By the end of its second decade the VEOO bore many of the hallmarks of an inward-looking and stagnating family business that had lost touch with its still numerous stakeholders.

Links with kindred organisations

In the mid-1920s the technical teachers, along with the secondary teachers, had been drawn into the ITUC under the umbrella of the primary teachers' body, the Irish National Teachers' Organisation (INTO). This relationship had been cemented through the work of a leading member of Congress, the INTO's general secretary, T. J. O'Connell. When the trade union movement split in 1945, the VEOO maintained its membership of Congress, though not without dissent. At the VEOO annual congress in 1947 two motions urging disaffiliation from Congress and another proposing affiliation to the rival Congress of Irish Unions were submitted but were ruled out of order by the executive. In 1950 four motions dealt with the split, one of which articulated a widely felt unease at the VEOO's lack of direction and suggested that, without firm leadership, the question of affiliation would continue to be a source of 'acrimony and distrust'.[17] Ambivalence and even complacency towards the central concerns of the trade union movement were pervasive however. It was exemplified in the executive's support in 1946 for the Irish Conference of Professional and Service Associations, whose claim to be the appropriate forum for the representation of salaried workers served to undermine the position claimed by the ITUC itself.[18]

Professional solidarity with the other teacher bodies, however, was seriously cultivated. Links with the INTO led to increased contacts with the secondary teachers' organisation, the Association of Secondary Teachers, Ireland (ASTI), and the first issue of the *Bulletin* in 1934 advocated a 'council of education' on which all teachers would be represented.[19] A resolution at the 1945 congress calling for a conference of the three teacher bodies resulted in a series of meetings which considered joint action for 'common purposes'.[20] A 1952 congress resolution proposed a union of the VEOO and the ASTI on the basis that similar salary scales had recently been granted to both. The VEOO also extended its own remit with the establishment of a benevolent fund in 1939 to assist the families of deceased members, and its 1945 constitution made provision for grants to cover expenses incurred in actions relating to professional duties as well as grants to dependants of deceased members, to members on sick leave and to members dismissed unfairly.[21]

In the period up to 1926 technical teachers could sit as members of technical instruction committees. That year, however, a provision in the Local Government Act prohibited employees from committee membership. Teachers were given the right to observe meetings however, and from 1930 the VEOO maintained that right. The committees, intent on establishing their prerogatives in the master–servant relationship, resisted such moves: teachers, in common with other members of the public, could read about proceedings in the local press.[22] Technical teachers also maintained the link formed by their predecessors with the Irish Technical Instruction Association (ITIA), which itself was renamed the Irish Technical Education Association (ITEA) in 1929 and underwent another name change to the Irish Vocational Education Association (IVEA) in 1944. Members of the VEOO attended the IVEA congress, either as fraternal delegates or as part of a vocational education committee delegation. In either case they were present as guests rather than as of right. As the IVEA itself grew in prestige as the central voice of vocational education, participation in its affairs brought the teachers close to the centre of a quasi-corporatist movement. Their status as committee employees, however, debarred them from participating on the basis of equality with committee members. That servile status was further underlined by a provision in the Seanad Election (Panel Members) Act 1947 whereby the VEOO, unlike the INTO and the ASTI, was prevented from nominating candidates in Seanad elections.

Education and society

The centralisation of decision making within the VEOO, proceeding in tandem with a consolidation of power by individual officers, raises questions related less to personal ambition and more to the difficulties encountered by a body caught on the cusp of change. The formulation by the VEOO of its own mission—as the representative of the main agents within a new system of education—was marked by the aspirations and the uncertainties of a society entering a period of social and economic development. Thus the members of the VEOO addressed the inadequacies of their own status and power within a context where ambivalence in relation to the vocational system itself was endemic. The context into which the system of vocational education was introduced was complex, and its effects on the agenda of the new organisation would be equally so.

The Commission on Technical Education had been set up in 1926 to examine the existing system of technical education in the country; it reported the following year. The Vocational Education Act followed in 1930, and while it was intended that the new schools would be the means of schooling the children of unskilled manual workers, the details of the relationship envisaged between the vocational schools and industry were left unspecified. Its central curriculum goal was clear, however: the provision of industrial training through the transmission of manual skills, in tandem with the effective social formation of future citizens. That Irish society was class based and would have a bipartite second-level school system was implicit in the Vocational Education Act. Under the Act education provision was devised for the children of manual workers which would seek to train them in manual skills, albeit in an environment intended as educational rather than instructional. That mission was acknowledged by the members of the VEOO who, as the *Bulletin* remarked, admitted that they were not dealing with 'selected types like the secondary schools, but with the masses who go to form the bulk of the community'.[23]

The place envisaged for technical education within the overall system had been indicated in the report of the Commission on Technical Education, with a proposed line of ascent from the primary school which was clearly differentiated by specific points of departure from that system. Those who entered the secondary school could proceed to the Leaving Certificate examination, which served as the main entry point to the various university faculties. None of the changes recommended by the commission, however, provided for a curriculum which would equip the youth of the common people to present for the Leaving Certificate, and the primacy of access for pupils of the secondary schools to the professions and thence to positions of social privilege would remain unchallenged. The vocational school would conserve rather than reform the social structures of the new state. Access to public service positions would also remain the preserve of the secondary sector through competitive examinations based on its curriculum. Although the ban was neither absolute nor official, the refusal of prominent public and private bodies to allow entry to those without a Leaving Certificate made an absurdity of the book-keeping, commerce, banking and typing of the vocational school curriculum.

In effect, the context into which the system of vocational education was thrust served to dictate the terms of the mission of the VEOO. A dictatorship—with prescribed outcomes for both teachers and taught—was, however, effectively resisted, an early indicator perhaps of the same collective impulse to oppose inherited privilege which would lead eventually to the break-up of the VEOO itself. In 1942, when the curricular parameters of vocational education were given greater elaboration in Memorandum V 40, the *Bulletin* offered sympathetic support for that brief and reflected upon the teacher's part in it. 'The vocational schools', it remarked, 'may help us to make our (always with us) hewers of wood and drawers of water—better, and more efficient, hewers and drawers.'[24] The irony was not misplaced. Officers and teachers were required, with scant resources, to school their charges with disquieting deference to a society where the new vocational schools were being used to conserve existing social and economic structures. Such accommodation was not unanimously accepted within the VEOO, however; among the critics was the general secretary, whose *Bulletin* articles waged an unrelenting campaign for equality of occupational opportunity for the vocational school graduate:

> The idea of creating a privileged class from amongst the students of secondary schools is unjust on the face of it: it is hateful to all who believe in equality of opportunity; by excluding the vast majority of students from competing, it is calculated to rob the public services of some of the best talent available; and it sets a high premium on social snobbery.[25]

Increasingly the VEOO would voice opposition to what it characterised as a 'ban' on vocational school graduates. In 1939 it successfully lobbied the Electricity Supply Board (ESB) to remove its requirement of a Leaving Certificate for recruitment to secretarial and clerical posts.[26] In 1943 its representations to the Department of Defence led to a reconsideration of the exclusion of vocational school graduates from competitions for sergeant pilots and that year also saw the Irish Tourist Association reformulate its recruitment policies.[27] This occasion, however, also prompted the claim by the general secretary that an attempt was being made to give secondary pupils a monopoly on entry to positions in the public service. He alleged that there was a conspiracy in official circles to make an informal ban more effective, and in support he cited a recent example of a government department requiring forty clerks each with a Leaving Certificate.[28]

The demand that vocational school courses be recognised as appropriate preparation for specific occupations led inevitably to demands for a nationally organised examination as a means through which the graduates of vocational schools would gain recognition. In a 1936 *Bulletin* editorial which purported to examine the case for and against, Frank McNamara left his readers in no doubt where he stood: every occupation had its assessments, he argued, and as examinations provided a widely accepted cornerstone for the secondary system it would be folly if the VEOO were to oppose their introduction. The examinations which many individual schools had devised should, he suggested, be developed and extended throughout the system.[29] At that year's congress he was supported by the chairman, Gus Weldon, who dismissed the argument that a national examination would undermine the autonomy of individual schools, a curricular principle implicit in the legislation and enthusiastically supported by senior figures within the ITEA. He further suggested that, if the VEOO itself were better financed, it could operate as an examining body.[30]

Pressure for the introduction of a national examination grew. In 1943 a former chairman of the VEOO, Barney O'Neill, by then chief executive officer in Carlow, found some support at the ITEA congress when he proposed that the Department of Education should introduce a national examination for continuation courses.[31] The ITEA then set up a subcommittee which, having considered the issue, proposed an examination for 'groups' of subjects, with commerce being nominated for the initial trial. At that year's VEOO congress the chairman, J. A. O'Donnell, added his voice to the growing consensus: a national examination, he suggested, would quickly gain the approval of pupils, parents, teachers and employers. He also predicted that the industrialists who insisted on an Intermediate Certificate would be well satisfied with a vocational school certificate, were it available.[32] He reported that in the absence of an appropriate examination some pupils were taking the apprenticeship examination and it was proving popular despite its exacting standard and high fees. The aloof attitude of the Department of Education was ridiculed, and O'Donnell was careful to remind delegates that the VEOO had always supported the principle of examinations, but as a progressive educational strategy rather than as a method of controlling teachers and pupils.[33] The campaign bore fruit, and at the 1945 congress the chairman Billy Cleary was able to welcome the department's decision that a new examination, the Day Vocational (Group) Certificate, would soon be in operation. He enthusiastically promised teacher support and asked that the VEOO be represented on a proposed syllabus committee.[34]

Ultimately, an effective challenge to the structural division in the second-level system would require the creation of a common curriculum and common pathways to occupations and to further education. The successful introduction of the Group Certificate in 1947 indicated the extent to which a national curriculum and examination might provide the basis for further development, and it was suggested that the vocational school might, in terms of the country's educational network, eventually occupy a position comparable to that of the secondary school. Such a possibility may have prompted a Tipperary branch resolution to the 1948 congress that the National University of Ireland (NUI) be asked to recognise a pass in specified subjects in the advanced technical examinations as sufficient to merit exemption in university entrance examinations. The executive put the proposal to the NUI which loftily dismissed the request, marking it as read.[35]

The 1950 congress saw further support for a broadening of the curriculum in the adoption of a resolution from the Leitrim branch calling for the introduction of history and another from Tipperary calling for the introduction of music. The following year Leitrim pressed to be informed of what steps had been taken to take the proposals a stage further but had to admit that such moves challenging the status quo would be firmly resisted. Thus when the standing council of the IVEA and members of the VEOO met Department of Education officers in February 1950 to press for the broadening of the curriculum, they were informed that the vocational schools should operate on the assumption that they were, by definition, different from the secondary schools. They were required to have a manual curriculum and should only deal with 'cultural' subjects in so far as they related to trade and industry, a view entirely consistent with the curricular principles laid down twenty years before.[36]

Social formation and degrees of resistance

The urge to exclude also extended to the ranks of the skilled manual workers, and while the vocational school was obliged to fashion its curriculum to the contours of industry, it would find the aspirations of its pupils curtailed by deeply rooted apprenticeship traditions. The Commission on Technical Education proposed separate statutory apprenticeship committees for each trade or craft, but when the Apprenticeship Act was introduced in 1931 it stopped short of making provision for mandatory committees. The designation of a particular trade or craft for regulation could only be effected following joint representation by employers and employees. While furniture-making, house-painting, hairdressing and the brush and broom trade were designated in 1933, there was no indication that the other trades would follow. The VEOO was concerned at the *laissez-faire* tone of the legislation, particularly the absence of provisions which might question what many in industry—both workers and employers—regarded as the divine right of admission to apprenticeship for the sons of tradesmen, irrespective of talent or technique. The legislation made provision for the introduction of statutory control of apprenticeship ratios in all new industries, but, until its implementation, access for the graduates of the vocational school to the 'aristocracy of labour' continued to be resisted from within.

The provision of apprenticeship courses at vocational schools was likeliest in the case of trades designated under the 1931 Act. Thus in September 1938 notice was served on registered apprentice hairdressers in Dublin to attend at the Kevin Street school and in 1940 courses in French polishing were organised for furniture apprentices at Bolton Street. Outside Dublin the shortage of facilities made such provision more difficult, but links with industry were developed, including some where trades had not been designated. By 1935 co-operation had been established with footwear factories in Carlow, Clonmel and Dundalk, the pottery in Arklow and the aluminium works in Nenagh. In Limerick the VEOO anticipated an 'interesting' relationship between the new Irish Wire Products factory and vocational students.[37] By 1943 apprenticeship schemes utilising school-based instruction had been introduced by the ESB, the Army Air Corps and the Society of Irish Motor Traders, all of whom, the VEOO noted with satisfaction, required prior training in a vocational school.[38] They were joined in 1947 by Córas Iompair Éireann, which in its new regulations stipulated a year's satisfactory progress at a vocational school as a condition for apprenticeship.[39] Despite such developments, however, the opportunities to obtain an apprenticeship remained limited and, as the *Bulletin* characterised it, would continue to be a telling example of occupational inequality:

> the principal qualification for securing apprenticeships is that the boy is the son of a tradesman; it does not seem to matter whether he has the suitable educational attainments or the natural aptitude for the calling. Every year we

have enrolled in our schools hundreds of boys ideally suited and desirous of entering these almost-closed occupations.[40]

Despite the limitations in the legislation, the VEOO could claim some achievements in this area, but given the wider trade union movement's urge to protect the privileges of its members, its criticism fell on deaf ears.[41]

If the opportunities afforded the sons of the common people were to be carefully stipulated, an idealised calling for their daughters was fostered with missionary zeal. The *Bulletin* spoke lyrically on the future of vocational schoolgirls, suggesting that 'a first class certificate in domestic economy would soon be recognised as a more useful possession in the matrimonial market than a modest fortune'.[42] Despite moderate industrial growth, employment opportunities for women remained low, and throughout the period from 1930 to 1950 the home would continue to be the principal workplace for those women who did not emigrate. At the 1937 congress, the chairman, Barney O'Neill, argued that, despite considerable difficulty in persuading young girls and their parents of the virtues of domestic service,

> it must be remembered that the function of such classes in our schools is not for this purpose alone, but rather to initiate every girl, no matter what her station in life may be, into the knowledge and accomplishment of her future duties as woman, wife, homemaker, mother and educator of children.[43]

The extent to which initiation in a domestic role would preclude equipping young women with the means of enjoying gainful employment may have been difficult to assess. Some agencies, for example the schools of domestic economy in the earlier part of the century, had presumed that the domestic work of a women could have a clear economic dimension. In preparing girls for employment in service, they provided a curriculum that embraced 'all the domestic duties of a country or farm house with the addition of dairying, poultry-keeping and gardening'.[44] The household occupation envisaged for the daughters of the common people reflected also the extent to which being a housewife, by definition, included domestic industry. For example, in the mid-1920s in Leitrim, eight centres provided training in home spinning and in Galway, 147 centres provided instruction in domestic economy, sprigging and knitting.[45] The social formation of young women, and the presumption of marriage and motherhood, did not necessarily exclude preparation for some economic activity.

By the 1930s, however, a perception of domestic economy as both social formation and preparation for productive work may have been receding. Referring to the national returns the Department of Education noted that women were 'very generally employed in commercial occupations', but added, perhaps ominously, that 'many of them remain in employment for a few years only'.[46] Nonetheless the opportunities for industrial employment for women were, at this time, increasing. National economic policy from the early 1930s resulted in a range of key industries being protected by the introduction of tariffs. Although many women continued to be employed in domestic service, a notable feature of new industries such as ready-made clothing, packaging and electrical goods manufacturing was the employers' apparent preference to employ women, generally at rates well below those paid to men. As male unemployment rose and as changing methods of production eroded traditional demarcation lines, calls by organised labour for restrictions on the employment of married women grew. For employers, there was a compelling attraction in technologies which undermined the negotiability of male skills and permitted the employment of lower paid labour. This, allied to the growing numbers of young women leaving family farms and searching for work, presented an overwhelming case for the employment of cheap female labour. The incursion by women into industrial employment prompted a memorandum from the Department of Industry and Commerce which indicated that the minister was convinced of the necessity for statutory prohibition, for without it 'women may rapidly be recruited for most classes of industry that are likely to be developed'.[47] He would limit by statute the choices open to women in contexts where the preferences of women—in terms of curriculum and their personal ambition—threatened the prevailing social ethos.

Against a background of a sometimes utopian vision of a modernising state, and with some recognition of their own ambivalence towards that, the vocational teachers began to articulate a degree of resistance to the restrictive terms of their assigned role. This was especially so where a crude instrumental relationship between childhood and industrial profit was posited. The need to do so became clear in 1936 on the publication of a departmental report on the proposal to raise the school-leaving age.[48] Its tone, cautiously urging that no change in existing provisions be contemplated lest it cause hardship on family farms or lead to a demand for maintenance grants for older pupils, disappointed many in the VEOO and they were not appeased by a recommendation for a limited form of compulsion for fourteen and fifteen-year-olds not yet employed.[49] The chairman, Gus Weldon, argued that while self-interest might lead a teacher to discourage further pressure on the system, the VEOO should take a wider view: both the cultural formation and the economic formation of future citizens was at stake. He declared that children were being combed out of town and countryside to supply industry with cheap labour, and he asked rhetorically whether factory economy was the only economy to be considered.[50] In 1943 a resolution from the executive calling for the compulsory attendance sections of the 1930 Act to be extended to the whole country was passed.[51] The following year the general secretary, speaking at the National Planning Conference, proposed an extension of compulsory schooling within a state-controlled school system. The privately controlled second-level education system excluded many children, he argued, while the absence of progressive legislation led to the abuse of child labour.[52] While the sectional interests of members of the organisation often militated against the building of an effective negotiating body, the VEOO, through the collective concerns of these teachers—be it examining the conditions of child labour, the reduction of education to utilitarian cost–benefit analysis or the disregard of non-certificated learning—sought to confront the injustices of the system as it had been constructed by their political masters.

Conditions of labour

The employees of the technical instruction committees acquired security of tenure and pension rights under the Local Government Act 1919. Those rights were affirmed by the Local Government Act 1925, which also made provision for protection against dismissal without compensation other than for incapacity or misconduct. The Vocational Education Act 1930 provided for the transfer of employees of technical instruction committees to the new vocational education committees and stipulated that while thus employed they should continue to enjoy conditions 'no less beneficial' than previously.[53] The Act also provided for similar conditions for teachers and officers appointed subsequently. Thus, committee employees inherited conditions which compared well with those of their counterparts in the primary and secondary schools: on many points they were better.

Relatively favourable conditions may account, in part, for the modest aims of the VEOO. In general these were to avoid disputes, to secure co-operation between a committee and its staff, and to negotiate for teachers 'reasonably good conditions of service so that they can give wholehearted service'.[54] Nonetheless it is clear that the VEOO was prepared to struggle, if necessary, for the rights and status of teachers. In the first issue of the *Bulletin* in May 1934 the editor referred to their predecessors as 'soldiers who had no army'.[55] In the new order, however, the *Bulletin* would work 'to dispel the prevailing ignorance about the work of the Organisation, to conquer apathy and to arouse a vigorous spirit of common endeavour'.[56] It would give voice to grievances and provide informed criticism: alert to the vulnerability of the lone critical voice, members were assured that 'if individuals must remain inarticulate, the *Bulletin* can speak'.[57]

Close links had existed between the employees of the technical instruction committees and the Department of Agriculture and Technical Instruction. They remained, in large part, as an expression of the personal friendship and trust between the VEOO's honorary treasurer, J. J. O'Connor, and the head of the technical instruction branch at the Department of Education, John Ingram. In 1931 the terms of employment and working conditions of vocational teachers were consolidated in a departmental document, Memorandum V 7, which was continually updated as the basic instrument of staff regulation by vocational education committees. Procedurally, the practice of having deputations received by senior officers in the department—generally Ingram—continued and these were reported on in the *Bulletin*. The informal foundation of such links were, with the help of the ITUC, formally consolidated in 1935.[58]

The Vocational Education Act shifted the balance of power within vocational education in favour of the local committees and of their representative body, the ITEA and later the IVEA. Industrially, this shift of power had considerable implications in terms of working conditions centrally agreed between the department and the VEOO. Implementation of agreements was uneven, as committees and individual chief executives began to exercise various discretionary rights granted under the Act. The VEOO argued that, as agents of a national service, the working conditions of teachers should not vary between counties. Where, in the event of a dispute, members were unable to attain satisfaction, the executive sent a delegation to address the offending committee.[59] Thus in October 1938 the executive travelled to Cavan where the committee claimed a right to vary conditions as promulgated by the department. In the wake of the meeting a committee member, Paddy Smith—then an ascending political star—was reported in the press as saying that he had never seen a more 'unruly or more disrespectful deputation' in his life. The executive placed a notice in the local newspaper which calmly and effectively rebuffed that attack.[60] Shortly afterwards, having received no satisfaction at Cavan, the VEOO appealed directly to the ITEA, and urged that its standing committee direct 'its constituent members to treat their staffs in accordance with an accepted code'.

Procedures for the appointment of officers and teachers would remain a contentious issue. Under the terms of the Local Authorities (Officers and Employees) Act 1926, the selection of chief executives could be made either by the Local Appointments Commission or, in the case of existing employees of committees, directly by the committee, with the approval of the minister. In 1934 the VEOO protested at what it believed to be an uneven application of that principle and noted the extent to which prevailing canvassing practices militated against the interests of some of its members.[61]

> The absurdity of stating in advertisements that canvassing will disqualify is beyond words. If the ban were really meant and could be enforced it would be highly desirable. But everybody except a simpleton knows that what disqualifies a candidate is not canvassing, but ineffective canvassing. The innocent who goes about to members saying: 'Please vote for me because I am well qualified and badly want the job' will no doubt be disqualified, but he who knows the hidden wires to pull, the buttons to press, and the subterranean ways to high places, he certainly will be placed in the race. Why not cut the cant?[62]

While Memorandum V 7 set general qualifications for positions within the system, it gave no guidance on selection procedures. The vacuum thus created led to difficulties. Consequently in 1936, the VEOO was forced to challenge what was, in effect, an undermining of professional status when a primary teacher was appointed headmaster of Marino Vocational School in Dublin over several qualified vocational teachers. The VEOO had sought to have the competition for this post confined to serving vocational teachers, arguing that the position required experience within the sector and that, since vocational teachers could not compete for posts in primary schools, the terms of the competition were inherently unjust. The VEOO appealed to the minister, Tomás Derrig, who argued that the principle of open competition had been accepted by the vocational education committee and he would not involve himself in its affairs. The general secretary, however, challenged Derrig's concept of open competition and argued that it should include a test whereby candidates would be expertly assessed. While the VEOO accepted that the committee had the legal right to make an appointment, it argued that since all posts were subject to the minister's approval, he should refuse to sanction an appointment resulting from unjust procedures.[63]

In response to pressure from members, the executive agreed in December 1936 to send a deputation to the Department of Education to press for an alteration of conditions of appointment to take account of experience and service within the sector.[64] Though unable to effect a formal change in conditions, the executive grew more confident of its position and the following year wrote to the Cork committee—then about to make a senior appointment at the School of Commerce—urging that a 'promotion' principle to advance a serving employee be applied. The request, while regarded as impertinent by one member, was accepted as legitimate by the chair and others. The teacher was eventually appointed to the post.[65] The mood within the VEOO was reflected with the unanimous adoption of a resolution by that year's congress that senior appointments be made from within the sector. A motion from Carlow took the principle further by proposing that five years' experience in the vocational sector be made a condition for any appointment as chief executive or headmaster.[66] Not surprisingly, when the promotion principle was not followed in Carlow in 1938 a protest was sent to the local committee and to the department.[67] The advertising of a chief executive post in Sligo, without stipulating a five-year requirement, resulted in more protests.[68]

The salaries payable in 1930 had been introduced for existing officers rather than as a right implicit in future appointments. The 1930 Act permitted the minister to prescribe salary scales by regulation and established that committees should not pay less than those scales. In practice the minister did not prescribe scales but indicated by circular the salary payments that would be authorised. Under the new system the vocational education committees, as employers, held significant discretionary power. However, while there is evidence that some committees may have

Table 5.1: Average annual salary levels 1925–32

	Average basic	Cost-of-living bonus	Average total
	£	£	£
Manual and building	176	117	293
Science and engineering	204	129	333
Commerce	161	111	272
Irish	133	99	232
Irish organiser	183	120	303
Art	169	114	283
Domestic economy	112	91	203
Home industries	66	59	125

Source: Teachers' Salaries Committee, *Reports and appendices presented to the Minister for Education, 29th July, 1960*, appendix i.

attempted to pay less than the minister would have been prepared to sanction, in general the ministerial scales seem to have been applied.[69]

A new salary scale was implemented from 1 October 1932. It provided for the ending of salaries specific to school subject and introduced, instead, incremental scales differentiated on the basis of sex, qualifications and experience. While the men's scale started at £130 and progressed by annual £10 increments to £200, that of women commenced at £120 and progressed to £170. Men, therefore, were paid approximately 15 per cent more than women, a differential which significantly narrowed the gap between rates paid to the majority of women teachers as teachers of domestic economy and home industry and the rates paid to the male teachers of science, engineering and building. Additional payments were available to teachers whose work took them to a number of schools, and for teaching through Irish. The regulations also provided for cost-of-living bonuses and for the promotion of teachers who had reached the top of the scale.

The progress of teachers without a training certificate was limited, and within the VEOO, as in many professional bodies, there was ambivalence in relation to the treatment of teachers with labour skills accredited within the hierarchy of labour compared to those with academically certified skills. In the wake of Memorandum V 7, manual instructors became ineligible for promotion past £150 without an instructor's certificate and were debarred from the higher scales without an honours qualification. The extended scale also served as a promotional mechanism. Sanction for progression would not be given unless the department was satisfied with performance.[70] The certification of knowledge, whether academic or experiential, was frequently discussed in the *Bulletin* and while the notion of a standard scale was widely welcomed, the conditions which would exclude a large number of experienced teachers from the higher reaches of the scales, or the possibility that it could be used as a mechanism to promote 'diligent service', became a focus of anger, some of which was directed at an executive whose effectiveness was now questioned.[71] From September 1934 it became compulsory for teachers of commerce, science, domestic economy and art to be able to speak Irish. In 1937 the VEOO negotiated special headmaster's allowances ranging from £20 to £50 a year and a special higher diploma in education increment of £10, while an honours degree allowance was negotiated in 1938. This form of developing the efficiency of the system—with competence and skill recognised through formal accreditation—was also reflected in the trend towards limiting key posts to those with higher qualifications. In effect, the concepts of diligence and conscientiousness, explicit in Memorandum V 7, were being equated with possession of a degree. Although the VEOO argued that an honours degree should be given recognition, it also believed that a scale of equivalence should be devised to reward teachers who did not have, or who historically could not have obtained, such qualifications.[72] Clearly the department and the VEOO held different views as to the most effective means of ensuring the success of vocational education. When the qualifications for commercial instructors were stipulated by the department in late 1939 their effect was to confine future appointments to those with a degree. The *Bulletin* was scathing in its contempt for the new regulation, commenting that the principle of 'the career open to talent' ought to have the words 'from the university only' added.[73] The official denial of the long-established contribution of the non-graduate teacher would serve to whet the appetite of the VEOO to move more effectively in its challenge to inequity.

When the VEOO turned its attention to the terms of the Local Government (Cost of Living) Bill in 1940, the mood of an army under siege was palpable. Its executive briefed members of Seanad Éireann, who then argued against the effective elimination of section 99 of the Vocational Education Act 1930 which had provided for the safeguarding of conditions of service for officers transferring to the new system. William Cummins, a primary teacher and a trade union member of the labour panel, argued that it was a 'serious thing to break statutory guarantees' while Robert Rowlette, a Dublin University member, put the case more strongly: 'I think it is always a mischievous principle, on the face of it, to interfere with a contract by legislation.'[74] Not all shared this view. The McGillycuddy of the Reeks declared that in the face of the privations of the Emergency, it was a reasonable economy to fix a previously adjustable figure by reference to the setting of the cost-of-living bonus.[75]

The impact of the cost-of-living bonus system on officers and teachers in the vocational sector was already immense. Through the *Bulletin*, officers were reminded of how much their conditions of service had worsened. In January 1940 the total annual income at the maximum of the normal scale was £320 and the *Bulletin* argued that a teacher at the same point in 1921 would have been paid £433 per annum.[76] After the passage of the Cost of Living Act, a report in the press indicated that the Minister for Education had suggested, further, that 'officers held office at the will of the local authority. That had been decided at a court case.' A deeply dispirited general secretary proclaimed to his battered corps: 'we have no contracts and can be sacked at will'.[77]

In the face of such pressures, the position taken by the VEOO in relation to the terms of the Trade Union Bill published on 30 April 1941 reflected the ambivalence of many in the wider trade union movement. This was expressed in a combination of extreme caution in relation to the capacity of the proposed legislation to restrict the activities of trade unions and a sense of the opportunity for the organisation to secure its own position as negotiator for all officers and teachers in vocational education. That position was not yet fully established and the reluctance of many teachers to commit themselves to membership of the VEOO may have reflected a sense that the organisation, as yet, lacked effective status. The general secretary, Frank McNamara, suggested to each regional committee that the proposed legislation would almost certainly lead to a 'restriction' in the activities of the organisation, a point made even more strongly in the *Bulletin*:

> Without discussing the general merits or demerits of the Bill (and its highly contentious nature is undeniable), it is clear, so far as the VEOO is concerned, that the absolute discretionary power given to the Minister for Education in regard to recognition of 'any organisation of teachers' as an 'excepted body' is drastic and indeed revolutionary.[78]

The *Bulletin* and the members of the regional committees were immediately harnessed to the cause of recruitment and armed with the plea that under the proposed legislation vocational teachers who were not members of the VEOO would have no lawful means of entering negotiations regarding salaries and terms of employment. To do so they would have to be members of an 'excepted body' or of a body holding a 'negotiation licence' for which a minimum deposit of £1,000 would have to be paid. The logic of such a position was self-evident, and the passage of the Bill made the task of recruitment easier. In a letter marked 'very urgent and important', McNamara wrote to each branch secretary:

> I trust that you will make the position known to all vocational education officers in your area, and take the necessary steps to have the paid up membership so effective that the Minister cannot refuse to give the organisation the recognition to enable it to continue its activities for the benefit of its members.[79]

Resistance to the proposals throughout the trade union movement was marked by ambivalence, not least because many shared the view of Seán Lemass, now Minister for Supplies, that the country had too many unions. In a society where industrial development was circumscribed by the constraints resulting from the war, however, the trade unions

Class for apprentices at Irish Wire Products, Municipal Technical Institute, Limerick, 1937 (Limerick VEC)

VEOO executive committee members (front) Mary Feeney, Frank McNamara, Patrick Tarpey, Nicholas Hartnett, Paddy Parfrey, Michael Ó hIceadha; (back) William McNamara, James A. McDonell, William Cleary, Michael J. Cryan, Seán Ó Tuama meeting at Parnell Square Technical School, Dublin, 1949 (Irish Times)

VEOO annual congress delegates, Parnell Square Technical School, Dublin, 1942 (Irish Times)

Special course for trainee hotel workers, St Anne's Vocational School, Limerick, 1953 (Conroy Photos)

Enrolment of first year carpentry and joinery apprentices, Municipal Technical Institute, Limerick 1953 (T. Dennehy)

VTA annual congress delegates, Wexford, 1957 (Wexford People)

VTA members Maura Egan, Nicholas Hartnett, Seamus Rossiter and Patrick Lane sign articles and memorandum of association, Urrús na nGairm-Mhuinteoirí Teoranta, 1964 (TUI)

Tom Carney 1955–7

Liam McGrenera 1957–9

John S. McDonald 1959–61

Thomas McDonnell 1961–3

Gerry Lovett 1963–5

Seamus Peyton 1965–7

Teacher Kitty Purtill and senior secretarial class, Municipal Technical Institute, Limerick, 1955 (Limerick Echo)

Teacher Noel Power and intermediate metalworkwork class, Municipal Technical Institute, Limerick 1955 (Limerick Echo)

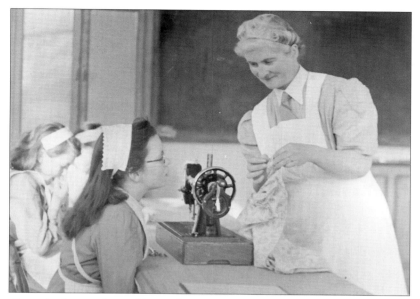

Domestic science teacher Kathleen Collins with pupils, Vocational School, Ennis, 1950 (David Browne)

Poultry management class, Vocational School, Newport, 1955 (TUI)

Tom Carney, founding member and president of VTA and principal of Ringsend Technical School, Dublin, outside temporary school premises, 1979 (Irish Times)

Administrator Anne Hanley at Head Office, 73 Orwell Road, Dublin, 1980 (Lensmen)

were increasingly aware of the potential to have their primary negotiating function effectively removed by the state. The parallel introduction of a 'Wages Standstill Emergency Order', at a time when the price of essential commodities was soaring, forced unions to devote a disproportionate amount of energy simply to ensure the maintenance of existing conditions. The VEOO interpreted this holding brief as a need to address the impact of the new legislation, and to mount, in response, a spring offensive. In continuing debate it was apparent that for members, the implications of a proposal to give the minister the right to change the requirements of office were ominous. The *Bulletin* spoke of its 'dangerous, if not sinister, character', and argued that other proposals would deprive officers of an existing right to a sworn enquiry. Through the medium of parliamentary questions and debate, notably in the Seanad, the implications of the Bill for vocational teachers were explored, and by the summer of 1941 a victory was claimed when the minister excluded the vocational education committees and the committees of agriculture from its provisions.

The difficulties experienced while securing rights for its members was, undoubtedly, an indicator of the lack of respect afforded the VEOO itself. It was also, however, a telling indicator of the prevailing political climate. For these public sector officers, conditions of employment could be changed by statute, in a period where in Ireland, as throughout Europe, the disposition towards centralised control of economic and social development was increasing. The Local Government Bill, which proposed in 1940 to take away existing statutory rights for public servants without consultation, affected some conditions of service for teachers. When the *Bulletin* charged that the process smacked of 'blitz-legislation', it was acutely aware that the Bill contained 'disturbing provisions', which included the reduction of pensions legally payable to the officers of vocational committees. A further, more fundamental, provision would give the Minister for Local Government arbitrary power to retire an officer 'irrespective of competency or age by imposing new qualifications even for an officer with long and efficient service'.[80]

The Vocational Education Amendment Bill, presented in 1943, added to the already considerable body of legislation which eroded the conditions of service set down in 1930. The Bill had four critical sections which together served to breach any contract that the Department of Education, by legislative or normative means, had ever entered into with vocational education officers. Section 6 made provision for the introduction of an age limit for officers in the service. Under the Local Government Act of 1925, retirement at sixty-five was not compulsory for those in good health. While opposition to a compulsory age of retirement might be interpreted as unwarranted protection of gerontocracy, the problem for the VEOO lay in the pension requirement of forty years' service in continuous whole-time employment. This presented a classic conundrum as many teachers had not been able to obtain the necessary qualifications for a position until after the age of twenty-five. The 1925 Act had recognised such a possibility and for the calculation of pension entitlement made provision for 'additional years' to be added to the actual number of years served.[81]

Section 7 gave both a committee and the minister power to suspend an officer summarily if they had reason to believe that the officer 'had done something deserving disciplinary action'. Suspensions could continue 'until so terminated'. In a similar vein section 8 empowered the minister to dismiss a teacher if of the opinion that a teacher was unfit or incompetent. It thus gave the minister what a succession of editorials in the *Bulletin* described as 'power of arbitrary dismissal', the effect being the loss of the right established in 1930, the right to lose office only on the result of a local inquiry, and then subject to appeal. To copper fasten such provisions, section 9 stated that merely being in office at the time of the passage of the legislation would not preclude such officers from having the previous sections applied, 'without prejudice'.

Such an assault upon established rights could not be interpreted as in any sense incidental to the intent of the proposed legislation. The VEOO argued that the 1930 Act had given adequate powers of dismissal to the local committees, subject to the minister's sanction, and that in any case the minister could act even without the advice of a committee. Either way, a local inquiry would first have to be held; the proposal to remove that requirement was a serious threat to the vocational teachers and would give the minister what the *Bulletin* described as 'a free hand for the most drastic action possible against an officer'.[82] Stung into action, the VEOO organised a campaign of lobbying members of the Oireachtas and the debates on the Bill revealed substantial pockets of support. Roddy Connolly, the Labour Dáil deputy for Louth, hammered home the point by asking why the minister required 'dictatorial powers'. Such action, he suggested, might be understandable in a service honeycombed with incompetence or dishonesty, or if some secret society aiming at disruption had got it in its grip. Such was not the case, he argued, but his pressure on the minister to clarify the reasons for introducing the Bill met with no success.[83] William Magennis, a Seanad nominee of the Taoiseach, concluded that section 9 of the Bill empowered the minister to commit a breach of contract in an 'open, naked and unashamed violation of the old tradition of sacredness of contract'. Senator T. J. O'Connell, a member of the culture and education panel, proposed the deletion of the sections increasing ministerial power. This was defeated by a narrow majority and the Bill, as presented by the minister, was passed. [84]

The Minister for Education Tomás Derrig gave tacit endorsement to the legislative denial of legal pension rights and to the reinterpretation of section 99 of the 1930 Act to remove protection of existing rights, and he suggested that 'officers of the vocational education committees have been especially favoured in various ways compared with other officers'. With oblique reference to a perceived air of 'inefficiency' and 'slacking', he served notice that 'a contrary policy' was now required.[85] On the agenda of the VEOO, a major battle threatened; locating the site for such battle, however, proved as difficult as ever.

For its own part the Department of Education maintained a significant distance from the VEOO and its agenda. A meeting of the executive in 1945 noted with a mixture of annoyance and regret that the department 'had not been represented at the congress in over twelve years'.[86] Then, like a David casting stones at some distant Goliath, the VEOO attacked the department's 'moth eaten scales' which, for twenty-five years without revision, had been offered as consolation for officers 'cycling along country roads' to bring education to the youth of the common people. The VEOO pointed to the threat of an exodus of teachers to other schools both at home and in Britain; it urged the government to ensure that economic duress would not drive teachers to seek employment elsewhere and to donate to the development of other countries an energy badly needed at home. The *Bulletin* raised a collective eyebrow at the claim of 'exceptionally favourable treatment' and countered that 'vocational education officers are getting weary of humbug'.[87] Few institutions, however, even those under siege, speak with one voice, and in 1946—in the first cautionary note it had ever felt obliged to sound—the *Bulletin* urged its readers to note that 'anything printed in the *Bulletin* does not necessarily represent the views of the executive committee or of the VEOO unless it is so expressly stated'.[88]

Under the presumed benign hand of the Minister for Local Government, the VEOO anticipated the introduction of the 'long promised Bill' which would revise the pension terms for local officers, including the principal reform sought by the VEOO—that of provision of a gratuity for dependants of officers who died in service. For those who continued in such service, however, common grievance did not suggest common consent as to a solution. Relations with the Department of

Education, despite discontent within the VEOO on questions of conditions of service, became, at least publicly, fulsomely deferential. In the pages of the *Bulletin*, the president told VEOO members of his 'very sincere appreciation of the courtesy and kindness extended to your officers by the Minister. His understanding of our work and difficulties is stimulating and encourages in our minds a feeling of confidence and hope.'[89] At the 1949 congress the presence of Minister for Education, Richard Mulcahy, was referred to as 'a source of pride and joy' and, despite his refusal to appoint a representative of the VEOO to the Council of Education, a realignment of departmental priorities was cautiously anticipated. Mulcahy, however, deftly retreated from the extravagance of the presidential address, by characteristically placing himself not, as his host had suggested, as 'the central figure in education', but rather as at one with the ranks of those assembled, 'because he was one of ourselves'. Any assumption of common cause would prove unfounded.

Women, married or single

The first issue of Memorandum V 7 stipulated that recruitment of married women to permanent posts was prohibited and that women teachers would have to retire on marriage. The impulse to restrict employment opportunities for women was further strengthened in 1936 when section 12 of the Conditions of Employment Act gave the Minister for Industry and Commerce the discretion to grant prior rights to male workers.[90] The enactment of Bunreacht na hÉireann the following year ensured that its apparent guarantee of fundamental rights would neither infringe nor threaten the traditionally prescribed role and duties of women.

Against a background of growing hostility to the notion that women should have equal access to the workplace and equal treatment within it, the VEOO adopted an equal-pay resolution at its 1938 congress. Nonetheless, as with all other aspects of the changing economic and social order, the VEOO would prove neither immune from ambivalence nor entirely disinterested in the cultivation of a special role for women generally and its women members in particular. The payment of marriage gratuities and the introduction of scales differentiated on the basis of marital status would reveal an ambivalence at the heart of both the VEOO and the wider vocational education system. The brief given to vocational education was inherently ambivalent: the task of establishing new formal procedures without challenging existing structures. And the VEOO, as an institution, developed a related ambivalence, undecided about whether its job was to train or to sustain, to develop as an industrial force or to survive as a family business which would safeguard the rights of only some of its members.

In 1949, the emergence of different needs and the recognition of specific grounds for 'sectional' grievance amongst the members of the VEOO found an unexpected vehicle for expression. At a Dublin city branch meeting on 5 February 1949, a resolution was passed 'protesting strongly against the discrimination against women teachers in regard to increases of pay'. The protest was a response to a departmental circular on scales: whole-time teachers could be granted, with effect from 29 May 1948, an increase up to 11s a week in the case of men aged twenty-one or over, and 5s 6d a week in the case of women and of men under twenty-one years of age.[91]

The VEOO, in its objections to certain sections of the Local Government Bill in 1940, had in effect already declared its opposition to such differentiation; in reference to the proposed new superannuation scheme for officers of local authorities, the executive had stated that 'no differences between the sexes should be made'.[92] On this occasion, however, protest from the executive at the department's plan to impose differentiated scales was muted. While many of the suggested provisions were, the executive noted, 'open to criticism', and while the salaries of principals 'are not all that they might be' and 'women teachers feel they are being discriminated against unduly', the scales were 'a distinct improvement on the past' and 'in some respects they set a standard for the future'.[93]

For the VEOO the past had been notable for common triumph, for common defeat and for statements of common aspiration. By April 1950, however, the *Bulletin* acknowledged an increasing level of dissent within the ranks. Dissatisfaction at the failure of the department to address salary claims was evident throughout the branches, and at the 1951 congress Paddy Parfrey's presidential address was brief and dealt only with salaries. He referred to 'seething discontent' and warned that the complications arising from a shortage of qualified entrants to the profession would have 'detrimental results' which 'may be made wider in scope and effect as a result of concerted action by legitimately disgruntled vocational education officers'.[94] Seeking to ease growing discontent, the *Bulletin* urged caution and pleaded that 'it would be a great mistake to place any blame for the delay on the shoulders of the central executive committee'.

By January 1952, communication between Marlborough Street and the general secretary's home in Arklow was marked by a consistent refrain: 'The Minister for Education regrets . . . ' By July, however, the salary question was being discussed in the Dáil. What had long been intimated was now made public—the minister favoured differentials: 'the pattern that applied to the married and unmarried men and women teachers of the secondary schools' was to be emulated for their poor relations in the vocational sector. In the context of the deterioration of relations between the VEOO and the department, the intimations of a struggle for power in the executive gathered force. A 'feeling of disappointment and almost despair' was noted by the *Bulletin* as having 'obsessed the minds of vocational education officers', as the long-simmering salary dispute took its toll.

Conceding to the department's introduction of scales differentiated on the basis of marital status had serious internal implications for the VEOO. By definition, differentiation would serve to focus attention on the formation of its conflicting agendas. Neither the membership nor the executive was prepared to present a united front, and the discord became the stuff of local headlines. An article in the *Nationalist and Leinster Times* claimed that members were questioning the value of an organisation 'which caters only for a section of its members'. Responding on behalf of the executive, the president, Paddy Parfrey, suggested that such public display of difficulties indicated 'disloyalty' and 'inconsistency'.[95] The latter was a reference to the executive's claim that, while specific members such as the chairman of the Laois branch might suggest the salaries were 'an insult' and had been rushed through congress, the majority of teachers were in favour of the scales.[96]

Departmental circular No. 16 of 1952 formally introduced new scales and allowances. All male entrants would henceforth start at £55 below the previous minimum and would take six years to reach the existing minimum. The starting salary of women would be reduced by £33, and they would take about five years to reach the existing minimum. In the case of women, the economies had further implications: given, for the majority, a shorter period of service, the savings in salaries would be significant and the marriage gratuity, based on a lower scale, would itself be lower. As pointed out by J. A. McDonell, executive committee member from Laois, the gains for married men had been achieved at the expense of others:

> It is worthwhile recording that the small chief executive officers organisation was able to negotiate a satisfactory settlement without sacrificing their single men. We now have non-differentiated scales for inspectors, chief executive officers and even caretakers. The scorpion of differentiation is reserved for the poor teachers.[97]

The adoption of an equal-pay policy in 1938 implied rejection of differentiation on the basis either of marital status or of sex. By 1949, however, such aspiration failed to quell the discontent of women teachers who could but view the organisation's lack of success in this area with dismay. The Dún Laoghaire branch, in a resolution tabled for the 1949 congress, referred to the discrimination shown against women in the filling of administrative posts in the service. For women members, discontent continued to be fuelled by the inconsistent position of the committees on marriage gratuities—a grievance shared, even if underpinned by a wide variety of motives, by the majority of the members. The function and agenda of the organisation were shaped by deference to their assumptions, and despite public statements on the right of women to equal pay, the VEOO reflected society's general ambivalence towards the position of women. The gaining for women members of statutory rights to a marriage gratuity, although reflecting an organisational aspiration to secure contractual rights for all teachers, also reflected the assumption that the national interest was best served by the regular despatch of women from their classrooms to the secure berths of their conjugal homes. The claim for automatic marriage gratuities, although argued by the VEOO as representing accumulated pension rights rather than 'a dowry at the expense of the public purse', had always been firmly stamped by pragmatism:

> To refuse payment of a marriage gratuity would be a violation of a contract backed by an act of parliament and would be an encouragement to women teachers to continue teaching until they became pensionable instead of marrying. Our low marriage rate is an admitted social evil. Those who would stop the marriage gratuities would be strengthening and perpetuating it.[98]

More specific formulations for addressing the grievances of women members—a grievance evident, for example, in the strong protest against discrimination in regard to pay increases to women teachers at the Dublin branch meeting in 1949—failed to provoke comment from either the executive or the membership. The protest had come in the wake of a series of articles in the *Bulletin* where differentiated scales had been defended against the claim that anomalies in the pay scales of members were contrary to the function of the organisation. In October 1949, however, the executive, in response to a questionnaire from the ITUC, publicly committed the VEOO to the principle of equal pay for men and women.[99]

Principles, in difficult times, defer to pragmatism. In the debate surrounding the introduction of differentiated scales reference was made to the 'question of late marriages' having become a national problem which a responsible government should take steps to resolve. Although the VEOO had on several occasions rejected differentiated scales, these had been introduced in both primary and secondary sectors. The publication in the *Bulletin* of comparative figures indicating that the salary of a married vocational teacher was less than that of a primary or secondary teacher had fuelled debate which revealed a divided organisation. Those who protested against allowances 'to their married colleagues' were urged to emulate their counterparts in the primary and secondary sectors. An article in the *Bulletin* replied to the suggestion that this would prompt the employment of single and cheaper labour in terms which championed the cause of social formation, rather than by addressing the legitimate industrial concern of its own members. While conceding that he spoke with the conviction born of 'limited statistical proof', the persuasive tones of Micheál Mac Giobuin gave further assurances that the elevation of the married male member would proceed unimpeded by the ambitions of the 'lady' teachers, 'over 90 per cent of whom, it would not be denied, regard marriage, rather than teaching, as their ultimate vocation'.[100] By the early 1950s the agenda of the executive was, in effect, being diverted from addressing the working conditions of its collective membership to a concern to satisfy the social agenda of society and the marital status of its men. The pages of the *Bulletin* were increasingly coloured by the spectre of desperation, but desperation of a specific, familial order:

> In the plainest of plain words, my family and I are in the direst of need. My salary of £530 is totally inadequate on which to live, and to maintain my wife and seven children. Were it not for the occasional few pounds I earn in literary and other pursuits, my family and I would die of starvation.[101]

At an executive meeting on 21 August 1952, the departmental memorandum on salaries was considered. It proposed that, although new entrants to the service would receive lower salaries, there would be increased allowances for those with an honours degree or an honours higher diploma in education. Allowances would also be given for other specific qualifications, and hence entrance to the profession itself would be more attractive to those with certified qualifications, and less so to those without. Rent and children's allowances would also be introduced. Payment for night work, a major feature of the sector, was not so readily addressed. The unevenness of the demand for such work had long been a source of discontent. In a lengthy *Bulletin* article in 1948, Billy Cleary, a former president, had made reference to a survey of a hundred teachers drawn from urban, borough and rural schemes. While there was a large disparity in the actual hours taught each week—from a minimum of twenty to a maximum of twenty-nine—the survey also indicated that those with the greatest number of teaching hours were also doing the most amount of night teaching. Of the sample, 4 per cent had no night work, while 26 per cent worked three nights each week.[102]

The department, however, refused to take account of the different working conditions implicit in the exclusively day schools of the primary and secondary sectors: it was deemed 'a separate issue', and deferred indefinitely. The executive met the minister on 22 August and conveyed to him 'the unconditional acceptance by the central executive committee of the offer made to them'. The announcement of the new scales was made from Radio Éireann, and in December the minister made reference to the 'new status in respect of salaries which the vocational teachers had acquired'. They would, in future, 'be treated as teachers and not as civil servants or local government employees'. It was, in the wake of such disruption, almost an aside: the acceptance of the scales was achieved in the absence of an alternative set of coherent proposals and the new status imposed by the Department of Education confirmed, for many, the ineffectiveness of their organisation.

Figure 5.2: Maximum point of salary scales 1931–51 (£ per year)

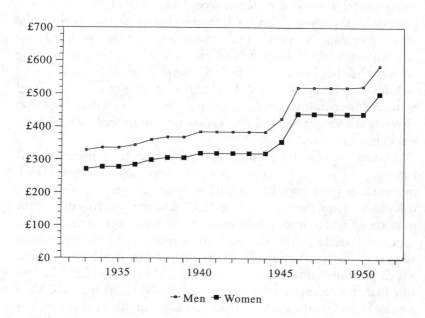

'The end of a chapter'

Despite Frank McNamara's lifetime of service at the heart of representative organisations, the incongruity of formulating a case from a room at his Arklow home with a view to engaging the ear of the Minister for Education was becoming obvious to a substantial section of the membership. As a consequence, by the late 1940s, the appetite for change at the top was increasing, if unfocused. Following McNamara's retirement from teaching, the executive appointed his son, William, to serve as his assistant. In 1947 the Cork city branch tabled a congress resolution that the constitution be amended so that this appointment would have to be approved by the annual congress. Another resolution, anticipating the general secretary's eventual retirement, sought to ensure that his replacement would be made not by the executive, but by congress, following a ballot. Both proposals were defeated, and another by the Cork branch demanding the resignation of William McNamara was withdrawn due to what its target would later report in the *Bulletin* as 'the overwhelming opposition of congress'.[103] The following year the proposal for the filling of the general secretaryship by ballot was again discussed and was again defeated.

From early 1950, William McNamara's position as 'assistant to the general secretary' became more difficult as illness kept his father from meetings and from participating in negotiations. The Dublin city branch pointed to the unsatisfactory salary negotiations as indicative of the intrinsic weakness of a body run by an ailing, part-time general secretary with the help of his son. Though a call to employ a whole-time secretary had been rejected by the 1951 congress on economic grounds, a Dublin city branch meeting on 8 December 1951 proposed a radical structural overhaul, including the appointment of a full-time general secretary and the placing of the VEOO under the umbrella of the Workers' Union of Ireland.[104]

During the following months many other branches expressed dissatisfaction with the salary negotiations and the executive was 'inundated' by demands from branches to hold a special congress to discuss the delay in resolving the issue. In May 1952, despite repeated requests, the minister refused to meet a delegation and by June a desperate executive appealed directly to the Taoiseach for a meeting. In his presidential address to that year's congress, Paddy Parfrey articulated the extent to which institutional structures and loyalty had been tested. While specific branches registered their discontent—Galway, Limerick and Laois among them[105]—there was a more pervasive rumble of disquiet. The acceptance of the scales had been followed by a raft of communications between Arklow and the branches which sought to convince a beleaguered leadership that there was a need to reassure the shaken confidence of members. Rather than addressing that reality, the executive took refuge by presenting an optimistic and ultimately blinkered interpretation of events. As it noted the 'resignation of three lady teachers from the Galway branch', it reassured itself that new teachers continued to join. In fact, resignations multiplied and the general secretary was forced to report that 'it is regrettable to see that so many old members have failed to keep themselves in good standing during the year'.[106]

In July 1952, criticism of William McNamara became louder when he failed to circulate to members a notice of the impending vacancy in the general secretaryship. His action was interpreted by some as an attempt to strengthen his own claim on the post, and he was duly censured by the executive.[107] Following the eventual resignation of McNamara's father, an executive member, Paddy Parfrey of the Cork city branch, proposed the recruitment of a 'professional' general secretary from outside the VEOO.[108] While the organisation considered this late move to recast its structures, it began to show the strains caused by the salary negotiation. In the absence of an authoritative voice which could reclaim their confidence, many members stopped paying their dues. The Galway and Limerick branches indicated their dissatisfaction at the failure of the executive to pursue 'a more vigorous publicity campaign to press the salary issue to a more successful conclusion' and it was urged to admit that it had been playing 'a weak hand'.[109] No concession was forthcoming, and the prevailing state of play was explained by reference to the 'regrettable' failure of successive ministers to bring negotiations on salary and conciliation procedures to a close.

In December 1952 the selection of William McNamara to replace his father as general secretary was marked by the resignation of four members of the executive, including the president. Pleas for loyalty followed, as did the painful exercise of healing wounds and seeking to fill depleted coffers.[110] Dissidents, meanwhile, moved swiftly to form a rival organisation, Cumann Mhúinteoirí Gairm-Oideachais. In March 1953 the executive responded to this move with a formal, and ineffectual, plea that 'unity in the ranks of workers' organisations is essential to the successful attainment of their ends'. The aspiration to unity, and a condemnation of the secessionists, formed the basis of a statement from the ITUC executive when it warned would-be secessionists 'that co-operation with the breakaway organisation is contrary to trade union policy and prejudicial to the interests of the trade union movement'.[111]

Such pleas found no resonance in a dispirited corps. The majority of the members of two of the largest branches—Dublin city and Cork city—resigned *en masse*, while other branches requested an early congress to discuss the resignations. Sligo town submitted a questionnaire to the executive requesting replies to various questions relating to the recent salary settlement and in an ominous postscript warned that 'the continuance of membership in Sligo town' depended upon the replies received.[112] In its final leading article, the *Bulletin* considered the fortunes and the failures of the organisation, and sounded its end note with a rhetorical, masculinist flourish cultivated over years of practice:

> What is needed at the moment is a virile movement to consolidate the work of the pioneers with the support in unity of the men of today towards the great new effort to satisfy the legitimate desires of the present generation.[113]

With grim understatement, and in a final consigning of those other than virile to the sidelines, the *Bulletin* was forced to admit that 'the fortunes of the VEOO have reached the end of a chapter'.[114] The aspiration to move collectively had, from its inception, been fraught with difficulty. That difficulty was, however, compounded by a social, economic and political context where ambivalence towards the new system was endemic, and where access for graduates of what Helena Moloney had once characterised as the 'university of the poor' to positions of parity and power would be systematically resisted. After almost a quarter of a century of conscientious effort, the VEOO, in effect, had become ideologically 'caught' on the cusp of change, ill-equipped to impinge upon the larger agenda of an emerging modern state and, hence, unable to develop a sufficiently authoritative voice to effectively service the demands of either teachers or taught.

The final congress of the VEOO was convened on 1 May 1953. Despite the protests of leading dissidents, it confirmed the appointment of William McNamara as general secretary. In June the president, Liam Trundle, attended the annual congress of the IVEA in Cork and sought a peacemaker in its ranks. Liam Ó Buachalla emerged as honest broker and convened a series of negotiating meetings in the spring and summer of 1954. He proposed the dissolution of both bodies and the coalition of their respective memberships in a new entity. Article 17 of the 1945 constitution, requiring the consent of five-sixths of the members, provided for such dissolution. In November 1954 a ballot was held and 296 members voted, of whom 276 voted for dissolution, 11 voted against and 9 spoiled their votes. On 1 December, a new body—Eagraíocht na nGairm-Mhúinteoirí—was formed. The last president of the VEOO, Liam Trundle, along with Eileen Quinlan, the president of Cumann Mhúinteoirí Gairm-Oideachais, became joint presidents, while members of both executives formed the committee of the new body.[115]

Notes

1 VEOO, *The Vocational Education Bulletin* (hereafter, *Bulletin*), 1 (May 1934), p. 2.

2 *Bulletin*, 8 (July 1936), p. 110.

3 *Bulletin*, 10 (March 1937), p. 148.

4 *Bulletin*, 8 (July 1936), p. 110.

5 ITUC, *Annual reports*, 1930–53.

6 Archives Department, University College, Dublin (hereafter, ADUCD), TUI papers, TU 30/28 (2), 'Report of honorary auditors, 31 May 1946'.

7 For examples see, *Bulletin*, 11 (March 1938), pp. 195–6, and 33 (November 1944), p. 667.

8 *Bulletin*, 10 (March 1937), p. 145.

9 *Bulletin*, 15 (November 1938), p. 248.

10 *Bulletin*, 38 (July 1946), p. 801.

11 *Bulletin*, 44 (July 1948), p. 1029.

12 *Ibid.*

13 *Bulletin*, 53 (July 1951), p. 1196.

14 *Bulletin*, 5 (July 1935), p. 59.

15 ADUCD, TUI papers, TU 30/28 (2), 'General secretary's annual report, 1947'.

16 *Ibid.*

17 ADUCD, TUI papers, TU 30/28 (3), 'Resolution from Dublin Branch to Annual Congress, July 19 and 20, 1950'.

18 *Bulletin*, 38 (July 1946), p. 799.

19 *Bulletin*, 1 (May 1934), p. 4.

20 *Bulletin*, 38 (July 1946), p. 799.

21 VEOO, *Constitution* (1945), pp. 10–11.

22 *Bulletin*, 38 (July 1946), p. 797.

23 *Bulletin*, 4 (March 1935), p. 43.

24 *Bulletin*, 26 (July 1942), pp. 494–5.

25 *Bulletin*, 25 (April 1942), p. 486.

26 *Bulletin*, 16 (March 1939), p. 263.

27 *Bulletin*, 30 (December 1943), p. 613.

28 *Ibid.*

29 *Bulletin*, 7 (April 1936), p. 79.

30 *Bulletin*, 9 (November 1936), p. 121.

31 ITEA Annual Congress, *Report,* 1943, p. 79.

32 *Bulletin,* 30 (December 1943), p. 614.

33 *Bulletin,* 31 (May 1944), p. 631.

34 *Bulletin,* 38 (July 1946), p. 799.

35 *Bulletin,* 44 (July 1948), p. 1033.

36 IVEA Annual Congress, *Report,* 1950, p. 52.

37 *Bulletin,* 14 (July 1938), p. 172.

38 *Bulletin,* 30 (December 1943), p. 598.

39 *Bulletin,* 40 (May 1947), p. 849.

40 *Bulletin,* 45 (November 1948), p. 1070.

41 *Ibid.*

42 *Bulletin,* 9 (November 1936), p. 126.

43 *Bulletin,* 12 (November 1937), pp. 172–3.

44 Department of Education, *Annual report,* 1925–7, p. 65.

45 *Ibid.*

46 *Ibid.,* p. 108.

47 Memorandum, Department of Industry and Commerce, September 1933, Conditions of Employment Bill.

48 *Report of the inter-departmental committee on the raising of the school leaving age* (Dublin, 1936).

49 *Bulletin,* 8 (July 1936), p. 109.

50 *Bulletin,* 11 (July 1937), p. 158.

51 *Bulletin,* 30 (December 1943), p. 602.

52 National Planning Conference, *Proceedings* (Dublin, 1943), p. 25.

53 Vocational Education Act 1930, section 99, subsection 2.

54 *Bulletin,* 15 (November 1938), p. 251.

55 *Bulletin,* 1 (May 1934), p. 2.

56 *Ibid.,* p. 3.

57 *Bulletin,* 2 (July 1934), p. 19.

58 *Bulletin,* 5 (July 1935), p. 63.

59 *Bulletin,* 15 (November 1938), p. 251.

60 *The Anglo-Celt,* 28 October 1938.

61 *Bulletin,* 1 (May 1934), p. 11.

62 *Bulletin,* 2 (July 1934), p. 22.

63 *Bulletin,* 9 (November 1936), p. 125.

64 *Bulletin,* 10 (March 1937), p. 147.

65 *Bulletin,* 11 (October 1937), p. 178.

66 *Bulletin,* 13 (March 1938), p. 194.

67 *Ibid.,* p. 198.

68 *Bulletin*, 15 (November 1938), p. 249.

69 *Bulletin*, 8 (July 1936), p. 108.

70 Memorandum V 7 (April 1933), section 13.

71 *Bulletin*, 3 (October 1934), pp. 33–8.

72 *Bulletin*, 17 (July 1939), p. 296.

73 *Bulletin*, 18 (November 1939), p. 320.

74 Seanad Éireann, *Debates*, xxiv (12 November 1940), col. 983.

75 *Ibid.*

76 *Bulletin*, 20 (July 1940), p. 375.

77 *Ibid.*, p. 383.

78 *Bulletin*, 23 (July 1941), p. 440.

79 ADUCD, TUI papers, TU 30/28 (5), 'General secretary to honorary secretaries, regional committees, 13 May 1941'.

80 *Bulletin*, 20 (July 1940), p. 371.

81 Department of Education, circular G, 15477/25.

82 *Bulletin*, 31 (May 1944), p. 617.

83 Dáil Éireann, *Debates*, xcii (14 December 1943), col. 801.

84 Seanad Éireann, *Debates,* xxviii (9 March 1944), cols 1033–96.

85 *Bulletin*, 31 (May 1944), p. 628.

86 ADUCD, TUI papers, TU 30/28 (4), 'Central executive committee minutes, 29 June 1945'.

87 *Bulletin*, 31 (May 1944), p. 629.

88 *Bulletin*, 38 (July 1946), p. 774.

89 *Bulletin*, 45 (November 1948), p. 1070.

90 See, ITUC Annual Congress, *Report*, 1935; Mary Jones, *These obstreperous lassies* (Dublin, 1988).

91 Department of Education, 'Revision of remuneration of staffs of vocational education committees', memorandum (1948).

92 ADUCD, TUI papers, TU 30/28 (5), 'Objections to certain sections of the Local Government Bill of 1940, Section ix'.

93 *Bulletin*, 38 (July 1946), p. 776.

94 *Bulletin*, 54 (November 1951), p. 1211.

95 *Bulletin*, 55 (March 1952), p. 1262.

96 *Ibid.*

97 *Bulletin*, 42 (November 1947), p. 936.

98 *Bulletin*, 21 (November 1940), p. 390.

99 ADUCD, TUI papers, TU 30/28 (4), 'Central executive committee minutes, 27 October 1949'.

100 *Bulletin,* 43 (March 1948), p. 984.

101 *Bulletin,* 55 (March 1952), p. 1250.

102 *Bulletin*, 44 (July 1948), p. 1030.

103 *Bulletin*, 41 (July 1947), p. 893.

104 *Bulletin*, 55 (March 1952), p. 1242.

105 *Bulletin*, 57 (November 1952), p. 1302.

106 *Bulletin*, 56 (July 1952), p. 1287.

107 ADUCD, TUI papers, TU 30/28 (4), 'Central executive committee minutes, 15 July 1952'.

108 *Bulletin*, 58 (April 1953), p. 1335.

109 *Bulletin*, 56 (July 1952), p. 1283.

110 *Bulletin*, 58 (April 1953), pp. 1335–7.

111 ITUC, 'Statement adopted 27 March 1953 concerning breakaway from Vocational Education Officers' Organisation', *Bulletin*, 58 (April 1953), p. 1357.

112 *Bulletin*, 58 (April 1953), p. 1339.

113 *Ibid.*, p. 1333.

114 *Ibid.*

115 ADUCD, TUI papers, TU 30/38 (1).

6. The Curriculum of Vocational Education 1930–1966

Áine Hyland

During its first two decades the essence of the vocational curriculum was its variability from school to school and the freedom given to each school to develop courses suitable for its pupils and responsive to the local labour market. The Department of Education laid down principles and goals but made no attempt to prescribe course content. The framers of vocational education believed that if they stipulated detailed programmes they would promote standardised instruction not always suited to local needs. In the late 1940s a national examination, the Day Vocational (Group) Certificate, was introduced and with it a centrally designed syllabus. Together these reduced the autonomy of individual teachers but in comparison with the secondary sector the vocational school still retained a greater degree of freedom to develop a distinctive curriculum. The reforms of the 1960s led to a decline in emphasis on the Group Certificate and the intensification of a process that saw the vocational curriculum absorbed into a more general second-level curriculum. Other reforms would lead to the rapid development of the technical curriculum, but in a new institution, the regional technical college.

Inquiry and reform, 1925–30

The new state was confident and optimistic as it formulated a role which technical and vocational education might play in industrial development and in promoting economic well-being. Self-government had brought the freedom to plan new structures and to reform inherited institutions and in 1926 the state appointed a commission 'to inquire into and advise upon the system of technical education in Saorstát Éireann in relation to the requirements of trade and industry'.[1] When the Commission on Technical Education completed its analysis it was critical of the limited development of whole-time technical instruction in the period since the passing of the Agriculture and Technical Instruction Act in 1899. It found that only 250 to 300 young people enrolled annually in the technical schools and that their mainly evening courses were undeveloped, largely because the schools were not sufficiently 'in touch' with industry and were unable to provide specialised training for those in employment. It ascribed the great decline in the numbers of skilled workers to the lack of a general appreciation of the value of technical education and to the failure to develop the systematic technical training which other countries regarded as essential to industrial success. A central goal—that of providing continuation and technical education in rural areas—had not yet been faced. One of the difficulties facing technical schools was the standard of elementary education of many incoming students and it put forward a strong case that rural science and drawing should be obligatory in primary schools.[2]

In their analysis of the curriculum, the commissioners adverted to the fact that science and handicraft, the two subjects that they considered should form its backbone, accounted for only 23 per cent of the curriculum of technical schools. Commerce accounted for about 40 per cent and domestic economy about 24 per cent. Many of those taking courses in commerce did so because they hoped to improve their proficiency in arithmetic or English and not because they intended pursuing a business career. The commissioners decided that sixteen years of age was the appropriate age to begin technical and agricultural education and so they recommended the provision of additional facilities for both whole-time and part-time education for students aged between fourteen and sixteen. Thus they recommended a radical reform of the system and the establishment of continuation classes and schools, the programme of which would be distinct from that of technical schools and classes.[3]

In setting out guidelines for the organisation and content of continuation courses the commissioners operated on the assumption that reforms should be based on principles that took account of prevailing economic and social structures. The goal of sexually segregated education was reflected in the proposal that a part-time scheme for boys in rural schools might be conducted between 9.30 a.m. and 12.30 p.m., while girls might attend in the afternoon from 2.00 p.m. to 5.00 p.m. They suggested a curriculum that might include practical mathematics, rural science, drawing, woodwork, cookery, sewing, laundry, Irish and Irish music, composition, letter writing and reading, commercial and agricultural geography, local and national history, and civics. Full-time courses should be the norm in urban schools but not in rural areas where children would have to move more quickly into adulthood and the workplace. Urban continuation schools should provide technical, domestic and commercial courses suitable for future manual and craft workers and where appropriate might include Irish, English, geography, industrial history, science, manual instruction, domestic economy, book-keeping, civics, mathematics, drawing, business and physical culture. The commissioners did not favour a didactic approach to teaching and, like the Belmore commissioners some thirty years before, they recommended that 'the object of the teacher should be to encourage observation, initiative, and self-reliance, rather than to impart information and enforce rules'.[4]

Not everyone supported the view that the continuation school should be pedagogically and administratively different from the national school. In his evidence to the commission, Fr Timothy Corcoran, the professor of education at University College Dublin, argued that the continuation school, like most other schools, should be under the control of the churches.[5] His view was developed in a series of articles published in *The Irish Monthly* in 1930 in which he warned that without clerical management the proposed schools might promote coeducation and neglect religious instruction.[6] Despite such warnings the 1930 Vocational Education Act provided for democratically appointed local committees to administer and manage the system, subject only to the authority of the Minister for Education. Each committee was given the power to establish and maintain continuation schools in its area and to establish and maintain courses of instruction in continuation education. The new schools would continue and supplement education provided in the primary schools, but they would also include general and practical training in preparation for employment in trade and industry.[7]

During the debate on the Bill, the Minister for Education, John Marcus O'Sullivan, was eager to emphasise the distinctiveness of the new schools. He stressed that they would be more suited to adults than children and hoped that the practical bias of the curriculum would promote more positive attitudes towards manual work.[8] While making some provision for rural science the Bill did not propose provision for general schemes of agricultural education. Such would remain with the Department of Agriculture, a decision that would subsequently lead to much criticism. O'Sullivan may have hoped that the 'practical bias' of the curriculum would allay any fears that the Catholic hierarchy might have about the new continuation courses. The carefully worded exposition of the proposals which he made in the Dáil may not have been sufficient to allay episcopal concerns however, and in October 1930

David Keane, the bishop of Limerick, met O'Sullivan to discuss those aspects of his proposals in which he and his fellow bishops were particularly interested. Shortly afterwards O'Sullivan wrote to Keane making it clear that vocational and technical education was the sole concern of the Act. He assured the bishops that general education, either before or after the age of fourteen, would continue to be given in primary and in secondary schools and that if a system of general education was ever made available for all children at second level it would not be through the conduit of the new schools. He could assure the bishops that he had resisted pressure 'from both inside and outside the Oireachtas' to widen the scope of the Bill and to make larger provision for general and cultural education.[9]

Constructing a vocational curriculum 1930–42

The Department of Education issued an explanatory memorandum in 1931 setting out the framework within which each vocational education committee should devise its curriculum.[10] It effectively reiterated the points that had been made by the minister in the Dáil and in his letter to the bishop of Limerick. The memorandum drew attention to the comprehensive nature of the definition of continuation education in the legislation and indicated that this would allow the committees to develop a system of education specially suited to the particular needs of their respective areas. It also pointed out that the main purpose of a scheme of continuation education was to provide vocational instruction for fourteen to sixteen-year-olds who had left primary or secondary school. Its curriculum would be of a general vocational character, though with a bias towards the local economy. The memorandum was unequivocal that the vocational schools should have a pronounced technical content and an appropriate pedagogy:

> The mode of conducting such schools and classes and the methods of instruction employed should differ radically from those of the primary and secondary school. A definite break both as to subject matter and its treatment is needed all through the vocational course. What subjects of the ordinary school curriculum are included, they should be treated with a view to their direct utilisation in employment.[11]

The memorandum referred to the existing trade preparatory schools as a good example of what continuation courses were intended to provide. These schools, it suggested, provided 'typical continuation work', and it pointed out that, while half of their instruction time was devoted to subjects such as woodwork, metalwork, practical science and drawing, the other half was given over to general subjects that should be taught in such a way as to be of direct service to the pupils in their future occupations. The trade subjects were listed before the general subjects and in dealing with them the memorandum emphasised their vocational application. It suggested that for organisational purposes each county might be divided into a number of areas and that a school might be built in the principal town of each. Every school should offer full-time courses to boys and girls who intended staying on the land. The boys' course should include woodwork, metalwork, commercial geography, practical mathematics, drawing and rural science, and the girls' course should include needlework, cookery, household management and other subjects that might be useful to the life of a woman in the country. Courses in commercial subjects should be made available to those who for economic reasons would not be able to stay on the land.[12]

In 1941 Fr Martin Brenan, the professor of education at St Patrick's College, Maynooth, launched a determined attack against the vocational schools.[13] They were, he suggested, deficient as educational agencies primarily because they lacked a religious basis. In response the Irish Technical Education Association called on the Department of Education to issue a memorandum clarifying the aims of continuation education. As a result, Memorandum V 40, providing a comprehensive statement of aims, was issued in July 1942.[14] The memorandum was intended 'not only to place on record what is of permanent value in the experience gained so far but also to define clearly the fundamental aims of continuation education'.[15] It stated that the provision of continuation education entailed not only the organisation of practical instruction but also the further development of the training that the pupils received at home and in primary school. However, the memorandum went further than the 1931 explanatory memorandum by specifying the type of education that should be provided and proposing a comprehensive curricular framework for all continuation courses. It stated that it would not be possible to lay down conditions for the organisation of continuation courses that would suit all urban areas because of wide variations in their occupational structures. Instead, each should gradually develop the type of continuation education most suited to its circumstances. Three forms of continuation courses might be provided in urban areas: 'preparatory' for children over primary school age but not yet qualified for entrance to a normal continuation course; 'selective', which would prepare pupils for any one of a group of allied occupations; and 'specialised', which would by closely linked to a particular trade offering reasonable employment prospects. Sample timetables, as set out in Table 6.1 and Table 6.2, were circulated.

Table 6.1: Proposed preparatory continuation courses for borough schools 1942

Boys		Girls	
Subject	*Hours per week*	*Subject*	*Hours per week*
Manual instruction	8	Domestic economy	8
Drawing and craft work	2	Drawing and craft work	3
Mathematics	4	Arithmetic	3
Irish	3	Irish	3
English	3	English	3
Physical training	1	Physical training	1
Religion and other subjects	7	Religion and other subjects	7
Total	28	Total	28

Source: Department of Education, Memorandum V 40 (1942).

The memorandum specified that in rural areas the curriculum should be practical and all pupils should learn to work with their hands. Boys should learn to use tools and execute procedures that might gain them work as carpenters or builders, while girls should learn to use domestic equipment and acquire a reasonable skill in the practical processes of cookery, laundry and needlework. All pupils should gain practical experience of horticulture in the school garden.

Table 6.2: Proposed preparatory rural continuation courses for rural schools 1942

Boys		Girls	
Subject	*Hours per week*	*Subject*	*Hours per week*
Manual instruction, drawing	8	Domestic economy	10
Rural science and surveying	5	Household science, gardening	3
Practical mathematics	4	Commercial arithmetic, business	4
Religion, Irish, other subjects	8	Religion, Irish, other subjects	8
Total	25	Total	25

Source: Department of Education, Memorandum V 40 (1942).

The Department of Education, no less than the vocational education committees, had been stung by Professor Brenan's attack and, guided by its senior inspector J. P. Hackett, it defended its position by offering an explicit statement of the place of religion in the vocational school. Hackett's directives to the school authorities were drafted with the intention of dispelling any notion that the schools might be at variance with the prevailing religious ethos:

Continuation education must be in keeping with the Irish tradition and should reflect in the schools the loyalty to our Divine Lord that is expressed in the prologue and articles of the Constitution. In all schools it is essential that religious instruction be continued and that interest in the Irish language and other distinctive features of the national life be carefully fostered. The integration of these elements with one another and with the body of the curriculum is a task calling for the co-operative efforts of all teachers.[16]

Having unambiguously committed the vocational schools to faith and fatherland, the memorandum went on to clarify that 'the immediate purpose of continuation education is the preparation of boys and girls who have to start work early in life for the occupations which are open to them'. Lest however anyone might think that the role of the continuation school was unduly limited, it stressed that these were not the only factors to be considered. The memorandum conceded that the bulk of the continuation course should be allotted to practical subjects 'because of the urgency of the economic end for the young', but went on to state that this made it all the more necessary to safeguard the general, ultimately religious, aim of education. To this end the memorandum echoed the state's 1937 constitution and stipulated that it was essential that all pupils 'with due regard to the rights of parents' should receive instruction in the fundamental truths of the Christian faith. Vocational education committees were thus required to provide facilities for religious instruction and required to incorporate it in the timetable of their schools. But it would not be sufficient merely to provide facilities and time for religious instruction. Every subject on the syllabus should be 'permeated with Christian charity' and the whole organisation of the school 'whether in work or recreation' should reflect the same spirit.[17]

The memorandum also argued that Irish had a 'pre-eminent value as an instrument of social education'. It characterised it as standing alone, 'as a natural link with the national civilisation of the past' and as a unique influence which might be used to 'mould the conduct of the young people into conformity with the traditional pattern'. It stated that for those reasons not only should Irish have a special place as a subject but the language should also play a prominent part in general civic training.

The final section of the memorandum dealt with 'women in the home'. This put forward an ideal of marriage and motherhood, but also the notion that women, through their domestic labour, were a major contributor to the economic life of the nation. It sought to measure the contribution that a 'capable' housewife might make to the national economy, suggesting that the 'capable' as opposed to the 'careless' housewife could save the nation £14,000,000 yearly through prudent management. Here too, in both language and emphasis, the memorandum was strikingly redolent of the clauses dealing with women in Bunreacht na hÉireann:

> Women dealing with home duties are concerned not only with practical affairs, but with the most intimate of all human relationships and the most capable housekeeping in the world cannot produce good homes unless those at the head of them are inspired by some higher ideal than economic efficiency . . . The state recognises the family as the natural, primary and fundamental unit group of society . . . By her life within the home the woman gives to the state a support without which the common good cannot be achieved.[18]

The memorandum concluded by stipulating that continuation courses for girls should be conducted on the assumption that soon they would be responsible for the care of a home and a family and for the early education of the children who would carry on the national tradition.

During this period there was a widespread belief that the education of boys and girls should be different and separate. Girls at vocational school were to be educated for domestic service or to work in commerce and business, positions regarded as temporary, prior to marriage and the domestic duties highlighted in Memorandum V 40. Boys should be educated for manual work and to a lesser extent for positions in business. The strictures of the Catholic Church on separated education as a prelude to separate adult spheres as enunciated in a 1929 papal encyclical had been accepted unequivocally by the education policy makers. In 1946, at the opening of the vocational school in Cabra, Archbishop John Charles McQuaid praised the Dublin city vocational education committee for building separate schools for boys and for girls, stating that 'not merely for moral discipline is this important but I consider it marks an advance in educational practice. I am proud that Dublin in particular and vocational schools in general have been the most convinced opponents of mixed education.'[19]

Both the 1931 and 1942 curriculum directives have been criticised for their emphasis on education as a preparation for employment and for a neglect of broader educational goals. Paul Dolan, for example, has argued that the 1931 policy was particularly remiss in this respect and that only when dealing with the organisation of continuation education in county areas did the 1942 policy seek to bring out the educational value of continuation education.[20] However, it is clear that the emphasis on occupational training was conscious and deliberate and was motivated largely by the concern of the government not to antagonise the Catholic Church. Successive ministers were well aware that the provision of general education in schools other than those controlled by religious institutions would not be accepted by the bishops. To achieve acceptance, the state had to reassure them that vocational education, by definition, excluded general education.

The state also had to reassure the bishops that religious instruction in the schools was not being neglected. Following the circulation of Memorandum V 40 the annual reports of the Department of Education would invariably contain a paragraph praising the way in which the vocational schools provided for religious education. The report for 1943/4, for example, noted the systematic courses in religious instruction in all schemes, the celebration of masses at the opening of the school year, school retreats and the positive reports on religious teaching from the church-appointed examiners.[21]

The Irish language was also selected for special attention. Thus in 1944/5 it was reported that in several centres valuable assistance in the formation of classes in vocational schools was given by Comhdháil Náisiúnta na Gaeilge. In Bray, for example, the classes were stimulated by linking classroom instruction with the 'Listen and Learn' broadcasts by Radio Éireann, while in Drogheda large audiences were attracted by lectures in Irish given by experts on subjects such as farming, music, films and censorship. The reports also noted a steady development in social activities through Irish. Debates and 'question-time' were proving popular while concerts and ceilithe were well patronised. Drama too had its enthusiasts and there was scarcely a centre in which at least one Irish play was not produced during the session. In the county boroughs and larger urban centres pupils were entered for feiseanna and drama festivals. In the great majority of schools a cumann Gaelach was organised, and school magazines printed an increasing number of articles in Irish. Scholarships to the Gaeltacht were offered by most committees and as a result nearly 600 students were able to take a course there in the summer of 1945. Successive reports urged the integration of Irish into social events centred in a school and praised those teachers who adopted a non-academic approach to the teaching of the language.[22]

The years of the Second World War brought new problems for vocational schools. The earlier trend of growing enrolments, particularly at part-time courses, slowed and declined. Older children were enticed away by the promise of war work in Britain and Northern Ireland and younger pupils were kept at home on family farms while fathers and older children moved away. A shortage of building materials led to the postponement of school building and refurbishment. Classwork too was hampered by the shortage of materials and equipment. However, the vocational schools would find a new and valued wartime role through helping the population to cope with food shortages. Thus in April 1941 a circular dealing with the prevailing shortage of wheaten flour was sent to committees proposing that special lectures and demonstrations should be given by domestic economy teachers on the use of potatoes and oatmeal as flour substitutes.[23] The wartime diet of infants and invalids, food preservation and cooking in a time of fuel shortage were also taught. Special lectures and demonstrations were held and it was estimated that during the spring of 1941 no less than 120,000 people attended. The following year however, it was reported that the rationing of materials and other emergency measures were having an adverse effect on attendance, though on the other hand rationing of manufactured textiles had given a new impetus to classes in spinning and dyeing.[24] During 1943 it was reported that owing to the reduced bus services and the great difficulty in securing bicycle tyres, attendance of country students was worsening. Many of the vocational schools that normally served an area with a radius of ten to twelve miles were reduced to serving pupils within a walking distance of three to four miles.[25]

The vocational school and rural life

The debate on vocational education during the 1930s and 1940s revealed a conflict between declared policies and the curricular brief which the state gave the rural vocational school. The rural economy in the late 1920s and early 1930s was depressed. By 1931 the prices for agricultural products had fallen and unemployment had risen by 50 per cent. More and more people were leaving the land for the towns and cities and many would leave the country altogether. The government declared a commitment to keep the people on the land and to improve living conditions and it reasoned that the new vocational schools could revitalise rural areas. However, separate government departments for agriculture and education had been established and the Department of Agriculture was assiduous in arguing that it alone had the right to organise agricultural education, a demarcation that was made explicit in the provisions of the Vocational Education Act 1930. The inability of the Department of Education to include a comprehensive programme of agriculture within the vocational school may have encouraged pupils and their parents to regard the school as a means of acquiring the skills which would be a passport to the town. Only a very small proportion of students ever enrolled in rural science courses.

This tendency was deplored by the Department of Education and by teachers on a number of occasions and in 1937, the chairman of the VEOO, Barney O'Neill, took advantage of its annual congress to criticise the direction of popular demand:

> Obviously there must be a direct bias to the main industry of the country—agriculture—in the whole-time day courses which it provides for young people between the ages of fourteen and sixteen years of age drawn from a radius of roughly six miles from the school centre. I must not be taken as suggesting that the aim of such schools is to teach agriculture to these young people but rather to lay a foundation of knowledge which will enable the rural population the better to appreciate the many advantages of life in the country as compared with life in the town. It is easy to state this as the ideal to be aimed at . . . the greatest obstacle is the attitude of parents in rural areas—an attitude quite understandable—which looks on education not leading directly to a position in a town or a city as obviously something not worth troubling about.[26]

Similarly in 1938, at the opening of a new vocational school at Ferbane, the chairman of the Offaly vocational education committee cautioned the pupils in his audience not to enrol if they thought the school would be a 'stepping-stone to a job in some town where you can bang away at a typewriter'. A year later, at the annual congress of the VEOO, the chairman, Michael Cryan, hammered home the point that the rural school should be 'based on the work and needs of the people'.[27] Such aspirations faced complex difficulties. As Memorandum V 40 noted, it would be hard to secure enrolment and regular attendance while the demand for cheap labour on family farms drew children away. Interest was maintained with difficulty and in some instances it was not possible to organise a second-year course. For many young countrywomen the main chance of advancement lay in gaining a clerical position in a town. They looked to the schools to provide a stepping-stone, as did those who hoped to gain employment in urban Britain.

The reluctance of the state to promote the full integration of agricultural education within the school system drew special criticism from the Commission on Vocational Organisation in 1943. It pointed out that the two departments of the state which had most to do with the vocational needs of the country—agriculture, and industry and commerce—had only indirect and relatively restricted functions in regard to vocational education. The Department of Education funded a network of schools that reached into every parish and town, yet its schools, especially the vocational schools, were not empowered to teach agriculture. They offered the occasional course in horticulture and bee-keeping and day courses in rural science but nothing of a practical nature that would be immediately applicable in farming. It urged that the temptation to provide courses merely to secure pupils should be resisted by committees, especially if it led to the provision of commercial courses and an implicit rejection of rural values.[28]

The development of technical education

The 1930 Act defined technical education as subjects pertaining to trades, manufactures, commerce or other industrial pursuits including the occupation of women in the household, as well as education in science, art, music and physical training.[29] The Act also stated that the minister could extend the definition by order to 'include instruction in such subjects connected with such pursuits, employment and occupations (other than agriculture) as may be specified in such order'. Notwithstanding the hopes expressed in the legislation, the twenty years which followed saw little enough development in technical education. By 1950 whole-time technical education was available only in the large urban centres of Dublin, Cork, Limerick and Waterford and in County Clare: in all, 514 students were enrolled. The relatively high capital cost of technical instruction may have inhibited growth but it is likely that the relatively low demand for the type of expertise it created was the main reason why technical education was not more widely provided.[30]

There was, however, a strong demand for instruction in part-time and evening technical courses. In 1947 these included, for example, courses as diverse as cooking for chefs, hairdressing, mechanical engineering for the shipbuilding and railway trades, glass technology, textile technology and radio operation. A special course for those bringing electricity to the countryside was organised at Naas Vocational School in 1948. The following year the Department of Education reported that it was not possible to meet the demand for all such classes and waiting-lists were being used. Apart from the standard courses in engineering, building and domestic economy in urban centres and courses in woodwork and domestic economy in rural areas, classes were also formed to meet special needs. Thus in Gorey a class was established to provide preliminary training for employees in a newly established engineering factory. At Schull a two-week course in the maintenance of marine engines was provided for local fishermen, while the Galway committee organised a six-week course in net-making for the fishermen of Inis Meáin. At St Mary's College of Domestic Science in Dublin courses were organised in conjunction with the Irish Tourist Association for the training of hotel cooks and at Bolton Street a special course in oxy-acetylene and electric welding was provided for eighty-six tradesmen to serve developments in vehicle construction. In some places classes were formed in conjunction with a local branch of the Irish Countrywomen's Association, where along with the more usual cookery and needlework, instruction was given in rushwork, in the spinning and dyeing of wool and in the curing of skins. Evening discussion groups for farmers and farm labourers became a regular feature of many rural schools. In July 1949 the Department of Education issued a circular to committees dealing with instruction in building in rural areas and as a result rural building courses were developed. There were four centres in Kerry, three each in Cork and Leitrim and at least one in each of eleven other county schemes. Poultry houses were the most popular project: eight were built in Leitrim, twelve in Mayo and twelve in Limerick, each to accommodate between fifty and a hundred birds, while in Cork projects included the making of farm gates, pig troughs and chicken runs. In most cases the joinery work and the concrete building blocks were made in the school. All these projects qualified for grant aid from the Department of Agriculture. From the 1930s onwards the Department of Education set examinations in a wide range of technical subjects. By 1935 trade tests (junior and senior) and technological certificate examinations were provided in carpentry and joinery, plumbing, plastering, cabinet making, brickwork, painting and decorating, motor car engineering, mechanical engineering and electrical engineering.

The Commission on Technical Education had argued that there was

Table 6.3: Apprenticeship courses in vocational schools 1954/5

Trade	Location	Duration (weeks)	Attendance
Electrical engineering	Dublin	13	191
Electrical engineering	Dublin	13	26
Mechanical engineering	Dublin	13	32
Mechanical engineering	Portlaoise	4	24
Blacksmith	Kells	6	10
Blacksmith	Dungarvan	6	9
Blacksmith	Letterkenny	6	10
Building	Banagher	8	12
Building	Mohill	8	12
Building	Tubbercurry	8	16
Fishing	Cill Rónáin	8	18

Source: Department of Education, *Annual report*, 1954/5.

a need for the effective regulation of apprenticeship and the provision of appropriate training courses. The Apprenticeship Act 1931 envisaged that vocational education committees would play a significant role in the education of apprentices but it did not ensure that committees would always provide such courses. Thus it has been argued that the legislation was almost a complete failure. From the beginning it was evident that its success would depend to a large extent on the co-operation of the trades and employers and that such a partnership could only be formed with difficulty. Even as late as 1954, the number of trades and employers that had been designated under the Act was minute and there were less than 500 apprentices attending vocational schools, their number and nature a reflection of a region's economic development.

The industrial expansion which the state actively promoted through the 1950s led to an increased demand for skilled labour and improved training provision. An attempt was made to reform the regulation of

Figure 6.1: Total enrolled on technical and apprenticeship courses 1953–66

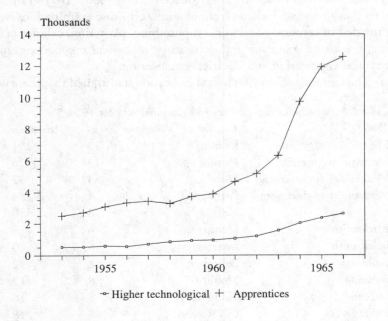

Higher technological + Apprentices

Source: Department of Education, *Annual reports,* 1953–64 and *Statistical report,* 1965/6.

apprenticeship through the Apprenticeship Act 1959. One consequence was the formation of a national apprenticeship board, An Cheard Chomhairle, in 1959. In an effort to improve entry standards to apprenticeships An Cheard Chomhairle decided that a pass certificate in the Day Vocational (Group) Certificate examination should be the entrance level qualification. Soon various schemes were put into operation and the curriculum began to develop under the control of a range of local and national committees.

Proposals for reconstruction

By the early 1940s the future of continuation education was under threat. A memorandum prepared in 1942 by the secretary of the Department of Education for submission to the Commission on Vocational Organisation argued that the vocational system had failed to contribute to the building up of a progressive agricultural economy. It suggested that the blame for this lay with the vocational education committees, though it failed to acknowledge that the Vocational Education Act excluded agricultural education from their remit. While arguing for a radical restructuring of rural education it also assumed that the secondary schools, 'whose pupils are intended for the church, the professions, the civil service or similar callings', had no role in rural education.[31] The proposed solution was radical: the reorganisation of primary schooling into two distinct sectors, a junior sector for pupils up to eleven or twelve years serving the same purpose as the existing system and a senior sector for pupils from eleven or twelve upwards. The senior school would provide second-level instruction for a substantial area, such as a parish, and would supply the needs of the pupils who graduated from the area's primary schools. It would also serve as the whole-time second-level school for the pupils from fourteen to sixteen with a curriculum suited to an agricultural economy. It would have a unified curriculum planned for a four-year course with proper co-ordination of the practical and literary side of the work and appropriate equipment. It would, if properly organised, 'supply a social centre for young people in rural areas and would be a focus from which direction and stimulation of thought on agricultural life and problems might naturally be expected to give the proper bent to the rising generation'.[32]

Despite the existence of the vocational education committees, the department argued that the new schools should be under the same management as primary schools. It went further and proposed that the senior schools should be staffed by primary teachers 'who have been selected for advanced work and have received special training in agricultural and craft subjects by means of intensive courses or otherwise'.[33] This was redolent of the proposal made to the Commission on Technical Education by Fr Corcoran that continuation education should be provided only within the primary school under church management by teachers trained in denominational colleges.[34] In considering the provision of a comprehensive system of rural education under the control of vocational education committees as an alternative to the 'ideal', the memorandum concluded that a system which would

> retain the existing primary school organisation and supply agricultural direction by the provision of continuation education in the rural districts under the powers granted by the Vocational Act of 1930 . . . would be a partial and ineffective method since the Act applies only to pupils of fourteen years and over . . . and the vital problem of the education of the rural pupils between eleven or twelve and fourteen would still remain unsolved.[35]

The alternative would be the transfer of pupils at the age of twelve from primary schools to the continuation schools under vocational education committees. This possibility was summarily dismissed in one sentence: 'Apart from the opposition which such a solution would be certain to meet with, it could not, it is felt, be recommended on educational grounds.' The anticipated 'opposition' was presumably a reference to how the church might react to such a proposal. A little more than ten years before, John Marcus O'Sullivan had reassured the Catholic bishops that if secondary education was ever extended, it would not be through the vocational school.[36]

A further threat to the continuation schools came in the report of an internal departmental committee which was established in March 1945 and reported in June 1947. This committee was chaired by Labhrás Ó Muirthe and its secretary was Dominic Ó Laoghaire, both of whom would subsequently become secretaries of the department. The committee had 'to examine the education system and to make recommendations as to what changes and reforms, if any, are necessary to raise the standard of education generally and to provide greater educational facilities for our people'.[37]

There are many similarities between the recommendations of this committee and the proposals of the 1942 memorandum to the Commission on Vocational Organisation. The committee recommended that generally pupils should be transferred from primary school at the age of twelve and that the commonly used term 'national school' should be replaced with that of 'junior school'. It went on to ask what would be the best way to cater for children up to the age of sixteen under a system of compulsory attendance. Here again the answer was very similar to the solution proposed in the 1942 memorandum. The children should transfer from the junior schools around the age of twelve to a new type of school, a senior school. In the early stages its curriculum should provide mainly for continuation work in the subjects taught in the junior school but it should include also manual training and general science or rural science for boys and craft work and domestic science for girls. In the later stages the emphasis should be laid increasingly on practical subjects. The report stated categorically that 'the principle of separate provision for boys and girls in senior schools should be recognised'. It indicated that the application of this principle would present no difficulty where large numbers of pupils were concerned, but that special provision might be made if the number of pupils was small, though in such cases separate accommodation would have to be provided for instruction in practical subjects.[38]

The issue of the control and management of the proposed new senior schools was not considered in the report other than in one ambiguous sentence: 'The general educational process is . . . essentially reli-

Table 6.4: Allocation of hours per subject for the proposed senior schools 1947

	Boys Year				Girls Year		
Subject	*I*	*II*	*III*	*Subject*	*I*	*II*	*III*
Irish	5.0	4.0	3.0	Irish	5.0	4.0	4.0
English	5.0	3.0	2.0	English	5.0	4.0	3.0
History and geography	2.0	2.0	2.0	History and geography	2.0	2.0	2.0
Mathematics	5.0	4.0	4.0	Arithmetic	5.0	3.0	2.0
Drawing	2.0	2.0	2.0	Drawing, crafts	2.0	3.0	3.0
Singing	1.0	–	–	Singing	1.0	1.0	1.0
Physical education	2.0	2.0	2.0	Physical education	2.0	2.0	2.0
Manual training	3.0	4.0	6.0	Domestic science	3.0	6.0	8.0
Science	–	4.0	4.0				
Religion	2.5	2.5	2.5	Religion	2.5	2.5	2.5
Total	27.5	27.5	27.5	Total	27.5	27.5	27.5

Source: Report of the departmental committee on educational provision (1947).

gious and the new system, however organised, should be subject to ecclesiastical sanction.' There was little enthusiasm for using the existing vocational education committees to manage the new senior schools:

> Vocational school buildings under existing control cannot however be used as senior schools and even if they could would provide accommodation for only a fraction of the pupils concerned. It may therefore be necessary either to transfer pupils under fifteen or sixteen years of age following whole-time continuation courses to other buildings or to arrange conditions under which the vocational school buildings may be legitimately used as senior schools.[39]

The authors of the report did not explain what would constitute a 'legitimate' use of vocational school buildings. But since the terms of the 1930 Act did not in any way preclude the use of vocational schools for purposes such as those of the proposed senior schools it is likely that the committee's concern related to the approval or sanction of the Catholic Church, rather than legitimacy under the Act.

The justification for the new senior schools was based, in part, on the perceived success of the continuation vocational school. That had been recently endorsed in Memorandum V 40 but its author, J. P. Hackett, felt obliged, as a member of the committee, to make clear his inability to support the use of continuation schools as senior schools. He characterised them as undenominational and said that their existence compromised attempts by the Catholic Church to fashion a system under its control. Memorandum V 40 was an attempt to reconcile the contradiction but Hackett's experience of reactions to it and the fate of other experiments led him to conclude that there was 'no real future' for continuation education as constituted under the vocational committees.[40]

The report pointed out that the existing continuation courses in the vocational schools differed in important respects from what was proposed for the senior schools. In the vocational schools, manual subjects were the main subjects while the literary were subsidiary. This would have to be reversed in the proposed senior schools, for the first two years at any rate, where the main subjects would be literary and the subsidiary subjects manual. That principle underpinned a proposed prototype curriculum, as set out in Table 6.4.

The report had come at a pivotal time in education. Following the Second World War many European countries had introduced radical reform of their education systems. In 1944 free second-level education for all was introduced in England and Wales and in 1947 Northern Ireland followed suit. There was growing criticism of the educational system in the South—criticism which was perhaps best articulated by the primary teachers through their union, the Irish National Teachers' Organisation (INTO), in its 1947 policy proposals, *A plan for education*. It condemned the lack of educational opportunity which it alleged was 'denied to the majority of our people' and it argued that education had leaned too heavily towards the academic and intellectual with a consequent neglect of the practical. The result, it suggested, was a rush for the 'white collar' jobs and an inversion of social values: the artisan, the craftsman, the producer were being regarded as inferior to the lawyer and the civil servant. The INTO recommended that secondary and vocational education should be placed on an equal footing, that one should not be regarded as intellectually or socially superior to the other. It also suggested that equality would be hastened if the curricula of secondary and vocational schools had more in common. The report supported the contention—made on a number of occasions by teachers and officers within the vocational sector—that public examination programmes, as well as the requirements demanded of candidates seeking employment in commercial and government organisations, constituted a noticeable and 'irrational' bias against the vocational school pupil.[41]

However, a radical reform of Irish education was not in prospect and the recommendations of the departmental committee and of the INTO *Plan for education* made little impact. The departure of Fianna Fáil from government in 1948 was no doubt an important factor in the equation. One of the first acts of the new minister, Richard Mulcahy, was to set up a Council of Education. It would become engrossed in a slow-moving and ultimately complacent analysis of education whose continuing deliberations became a recurring excuse for inaction. Ironically, this may have served the interests of the vocational sector. Given the tone and recommendations of the 1942 memorandum and the 1947 report, it was likely that any subsequent reforms would have increased the pressure to remove continuation education from the control of the vocational education committees.

The Day Vocational (Group) Certificate examination 1947

One of the curricular strengths of the vocational school was its commercial and secretarial courses. Students completing these were well placed to take up positions as clerks and secretaries in public and private offices. However, recruitment to most public service positions was increasingly based on results at the Intermediate and Leaving Certificate examinations of the secondary schools and these could not be taken by vocational school pupils. This anomaly was pointed out by the Vocational Education Officers' Organisation (VEOO) on a number of occasions in the late 1930s. In 1939, its organ, *The Vocational Education Bulletin*, reported that its executive committee had made representations to various bodies with a view to securing reforms that would enable vocational and technical students to compete for appointments equally with secondary school pupils. The following year the *Bulletin* demanded that the 'ostracism of qualified students of vocational schools from appointments in services paid for out of public money' should be ended.[42]

The Department of Education was initially opposed to the notion of a national examination for pupils of continuation courses. A national examination would, by definition, imply a national curriculum and one of the fundamental aims of the 1930 Act had been to provide structures whereby schools could provide courses which would reflect local needs. The department reasoned that external examinations could not take into account the differences between one scheme and another.

Figure 6.2: Entries to various groups in the Day Vocational (Group) Certificate examination 1947–67

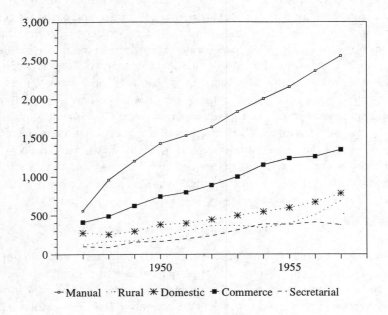

Source: Department of Education, *Annual reports*, 1946/7–1963/4 and *Statistical reports*, 1964/5–1966/7.

Instead, an end-of-year test, properly administered, could provide a guide to the standard of achievement in each school while allowing for an 'assessment of the personal equation' which could not be made by an external examining body.[43]

As a result of representations by the VEOO, the department conducted special country-wide inspections of whole-time day courses. The inspectors found that satisfactory progress was being made in the teaching of individual subjects, especially woodwork, metalwork, cookery, needlework and laundry; the efficiency of rural science was improving and commercial subjects were satisfactory. However it was suggested that teachers should pay more attention to the integration of the in-

Table 6.5: Grouping of subjects in the Day Vocational (Group) Certificate examinations

Group	Compulsory subjects	Optional subjects
Commerce (general)	Book-keeping	Commercial geography
	Commercial arithmetic	Retail practice
	Commerce	Shorthand and typing
		Irish
		English
Commerce (secretarial)	Shorthand and typing	Book-keeping
	Commerce	Commercial geography
		Retail practice
		Shorthand and typing
		Irish
		English
Domestic science	Practical cookery	Drawing and design
	Needlework	Business methods
	Laundry and household management	Book-keeping
	Domestic science (written)	Household science
		Irish
		English
Manual training	Mechanical drawing	Mathematics, mechanics and heat
	Woodwork or metalwork	Magnetism and electricity
		Drawing and design
		Irish
		English
Rural science	Rural science	Mathematics, mechanics and heat
	Woodwork or metalwork	Magnetism and electricity
		Mechanical drawing
		Irish
		English

Source: *Final report of the committee on the form and function of the Intermediate Certificate Examination* (Dublin, 1975), p. 39.

struction being given in the schools to provide for a better general education.[44] Despite generally satisfactory reports the vocational education committees remained uneasy. At the 1942 congress of the Irish Technical Education Association delegates agreed that the time had come for a national examination for vocational schools.[45] The underlying reason, it was argued, was the need to improve the employment prospects of pupils. If a uniform national system of examinations were instituted, successful students could compete on equal terms with students holding other certificates. The association set up a subcommittee to consider the issue and included on it representatives of the Chief Executive Officers' Association and of the VEOO, while the Minister for Education nominated three inspectors as advisers.[46]

When the committee reported to the 1943 congress, it recommended a national examination for continuation education. It suggested an examination for four groups of associated subjects: rural science, domestic economy, trades and commerce. Candidates would be examined in a number of compulsory subjects and in two chosen from a range of options.[47] Trial examinations were organised by the Department of Education in 1945 and the first country-wide Day Vocational (Group) Certificate examination was held in June 1947. The establishment of what generally became known as the Group Certificate removed much of the flexibility that had previously existed in the system, though the introduction of a system of centrally set examinations may have afforded an opportunity to improve standards of instruction and to meet the demand of parents and employers for a uniform standard.

The results of those who sat for the Group Certificate in its initial years disappointed its promoters. Between one-third and one-half of candidates failed. The highest failure rate was in the general commerce group, where less than half of candidates passed. The most successful were those in the rural science group where almost 70 per cent passed. Vocational school students, drawn predominately from families with

Table 6.6: Results of the Day Vocational (Group) Certificate examinations 1949

Group	Candidates	Passed	Pass rate (%)
Commerce (general)	642	313	48.8
Commerce (secretarial)	160	87	54.4
Domestic science	295	184	62.4
Manual training	1,200	776	64.7
Rural science	173	120	69.4
Total	2,470	1,480	59.9

Source: Department of Education, *Annual report*, 1948/9.

relatively low incomes, were under pressure to enter employment as soon as an appropriate position became available. Thus many successful and gifted students gained employment before the end of their second year and their departure from successive examination cohorts may have deflated pass rates. Table 6.6 shows the results of the Group Certificate examinations in 1949.

Further analysis of the results of the examinations in that year revealed that most candidates presented for one or two subjects in addition to the compulsory subjects in their group. The most popular optional subjects were English and Irish: of a total of 2,470 candidates, 1,674 took English and 1,515 took Irish. The optional subjects presented a range of attainment: 76 per cent passed in English, 56 per cent passed in Irish and over 90 per cent passed in cookery, household management, business methods and commerce. Over 80 per cent were successful in rural science, needlework and metalwork. Candidates were weakest in heat and mechanics in which 46 per cent passed, commercial arithmetic in which 44 per cent passed, and electricity and magnetism in which only 23 per cent passed.[48]

The numbers taking the examination increased almost fourfold in the ten years following its introduction. The most popular groups were manual training for boys and general commercial for girls. Rural science for boys and domestic science for girls continued to be less popular, notwithstanding the ubiquituousness of the vocational school in the rural landscape. Figure 6.2 shows the number of entries to the various groups of subjects in the period from 1947 to 1967.

Winds of change

During its first thirty years the academic attainment of entrants to the vocational schools was often low. The *Investment in education* report found that almost a quarter of those who entered vocational schools in 1963 had not obtained a Primary Certificate. The report also showed that a child who started in a vocational school was very unlikely to enter another sector of education or indeed to reach the higher levels of technical education. Against that background, the report stated 'it is unlikely that these schools attract their proper share of the better pupils and these handicaps must be borne in mind in any assessment of the work of the vocational schools'.[49]

A report prepared within the Department of Education and submitted to the minister in December 1962 referred to other factors which militated against a fuller and more successful development of vocational education. It referred, on the one hand, to the 'perhaps unduly academic bias of the secondary school programme' but argued that the vocational school erred in the other direction and responded too willingly to the dictates of the economy, resulting in utilitarian programmes which lacked 'liberality in approach' and neglected social and personal development.[50] This was not intended as a criticism of the vocational school but rather as indicating the limits which had been placed on it in 1930. The report went on to recognise that many defects had been offset in rural schools by the activities of voluntary organisations. Nevertheless, it maintained that it was generally true to say 'that the vocational school pupil, while fully conscious of the world of work, emerges from school with too narrow and restricted a preparation for life'. The committee studied vocational school timetables and found that history was not taught at all, geography to a very limited extent and while art was a subject in a minority of larger schools, it was not provided in most of the rural schools. It found that languages and religion generally occupied about seven and a half hours each week and that the remaining twenty or so hours were devoted to manual instruction. The authors of the report were conscious that an important factor influencing these programmes was the requirements of many apprenticeship committees, both statutory and voluntary, and of a number of other bodies recruiting workers and trainees in various categories. They argued that a notable defect in the vocational system was the absence of instruction in civics and of properly organised physical education, though these weaknesses were not unique to vocational schools. They identified the necessity for a review of the vocational sector and stated that 'present industrial trends provide the basis for a new meaning for skill, and the emergence of a technician as a major requirement for industry would appear to indicate that the time has arrived when vocational school patterns also should be subject to review'. The report went on: 'it is in this mood that we approach an elaboration of the faults we see within our existing post-primary system—in a frame of mind constructively rather than destructively critical—so that the recommendations that we make in this report will appear as clear remedies to the defects which we will candidly discuss'.[51]

Within a few months the *Investment in education* team was able to conduct a major investigation of the structures and social contexts of vocational education. It uncovered developments and trends that suggested that many vocational schools were successfully subverting the constrictions stipulated in 1930 and within a year Minister for Education, Patrick Hillery, would signpost the way to a future where the work of the vocational school would be fundamentally transformed.

Notes

1 Commission on Technical Education, *Report* (Dublin, 1927), p. vii.

2 *Ibid.*, p. 145.

3 *Ibid.*

4 *Ibid.*, p. 48.

5 Commission on Technical Education, 'Minutes of evidence', i, pp. 11–22.

6 Past Master, 'Continuation schools, iii', in *The Irish Monthly*, lviii (1930), pp. 276–80.

7 Vocational Education Act 1930, section 3.

8 Dáil Éireann, *Debates*, xxxv (13 May 1930), col. 1739.

9 John Marcus O'Sullivan to David Keane, 31 October 1930, as printed in Séamas Ó Buachalla, *Education policy in twentieth-century Ireland* (Dublin, 1988), p. 401.

10 Department of Education, 'Vocational continuation schools and classes: memorandum for the information of committees' (1931).

11 *Ibid.*, p. 2.

12 *Ibid.*, p. 3.

13 Martin Brenan, 'The vocational schools', in *Irish Ecclesiastical Record*, lvii (1941), pp. 13–27.

14 'Organisation of whole-time continuation courses in borough, urban and county areas' (Memorandum V 40) (1942), p. 2.

15 *Ibid.*, p. 3.

16 *Ibid.*, pp. 3–4

17 *Ibid.*, p. 4.

18 *Ibid.*, p. 5.

19 As quoted in John Feeney, *John Charles McQuaid: the man and the mask* (Cork, 1974), p. 24.

20 Paul Dolan, 'The origins of vocational education in Ireland and changing conceptions of the system from 1930 to 1978' (MEd thesis, University College, Dublin, 1979).

21 Department of Education, *Annual report* (hereafter, *Report*), 1943/4, pp. 29–31.

22 *Report*, 1946/7, pp. 29–30.

23 *Report*, 1940/1, p. 30.

24 *Report*, 1941/2, p. 28.

25 *Report*, 1942/3, pp. 25–6.

26 *The Vocational Education Bulletin* (hereafter, *Bulletin*), 12 (October 1937), p. 171.

27 *Bulletin*, 18 (November 1939), p. 323.

28 Commission on Vocational Organisation, *Report* (Dublin, 1944) especially paras 351–2.

29 Vocational Education Act 1930, section 4.

30 Kieran A. Kennedy, Thomas Giblin and Deirdre McHugh, *The economic development of Ireland in the twentieth century* (London, 1988), pp. 152–4.

31 National Archives (hereafter, NA), Department of the Taoiseach, S. 14392.

32 *Ibid.*

33 *Ibid.*

34 Commission on Technical Education, 'Minutes of evidence', i, pp. 11–22.

35 NA, Department of the Taoiseach, S. 14392.

36 O'Sullivan to Keane, as printed in Ó Buachalla, *Education policy*, p. 401.

37 'Report of the departmental committee on educational provision, June 1947', para. 1.

38 *Ibid.*, para. 28.

39 *Ibid.*, para. 31.

40 J. P. Hackett, 'Note on continuation schools with special reference to paragraph 31', printed as an appendix to 'Report of the departmental committee on educational provision, June 1947'.

41 INTO, *A plan for education* (Dublin, 1947).

42 *Bulletin*, 20 (July 1940), p. 371.

43 *Report*, 1939/40, p. 70.

44 *Report*, 1943/4, p. 43.

45 ITEA Annual Congress, *Report*, 1942, p. 67.

46 *Report*, 1941/2, p. 25.

47 ITEA Annual Congress, *Report*, 1943, pp. 57–8.

48 *Report*, 1948/9, p. 112.

49 *Investment in education: report of the survey team appointed by the Minister for Education in October 1962* (Dublin, 1966), p. 133.

50 Department of Education, 'Tuarascáil shealadach ón choiste a chuireadh i mbun scrúdú a dhéanamh ar oideachas iarbhunscoile', para. 15.

51 *Ibid.*

7. The Making of a Modern Union: The Vocational Teachers' Association 1954–1973

John Logan

On 24 November 1951, the Dublin city branch of the Vocational Education Officers' Organisation (VEOO) met to debate whether or not the teachers in the organisation should, as a group, seek to join the Workers' Union of Ireland (WUI).[1] The meeting had come about through the efforts of Tom Carney, a teacher of English in Ringsend Technical Institute, and Jim Noonan, a science teacher in Bolton Street Technical Institute. They argued that by joining the WUI they would gain in bargaining power and the use of a permanent head office. Taken together, their arguments were a provocative criticism of the leadership of the VEOO. The meeting also heard that the WUI was communist, with 'Moscow affiliation', and that association with it would necessarily involve members in a militancy that would ill-serve their interests. The meeting adjourned to get a 'ruling' on these issues from Fr Kavanagh, the director of Catholic Action in the Dublin archdiocese, and from Fr Aloysius, a Capuchin active as a trade union chaplain. The priests ruled that the teachers need have no scruples: involvement with the WUI would not, in itself, pose a spiritual or a moral danger.[2]

The meeting reconvened on 8 December 1951 under the branch chairman, Liam Trundle. The proposal to secede from the VEOO, as put by Tom Carney and seconded by Jim Noonan, was easily carried; however, to take the issue further would need a special congress and to convene it would require the support of two-thirds of the branches. Years later, Carney recorded that he realised the immensity of that task and that his efforts might be futile. Nonetheless, it was something worth trying, for whatever the immediate outcome of his initiative, he felt that a debate on the role of the VEOO was long overdue. Thus Carney submitted a memo to the executive on 19 December which included a report of the Dublin meeting and restated the arguments for reform. The executive unanimously rejected his proposals.[3]

For the time being Carney remained in the VEOO and in July 1952 he contested the election for honorary secretary, opposing Michael Hickey who had held the post since 1938. Carney was defeated, though his twenty-one votes to Hickey's thirty-one suggested that he had substantial support and that the pre-eminence of the members who had backed Hickey could no longer be assumed.[4] Then in December Carney offered himself for the vacant general secretaryship. On this occasion he had three opponents: William O'Brien-Crowley who taught commerce at Clonmel Technical School, Tom Brady who taught commerce in Dún Laoghaire Technical School and Billy McNamara, also a commerce teacher, who taught in Arklow. Of these, McNamara was the most formidable opponent. His father Frank had been secretary of the successive representative organisations since 1917 and as his health deteriorated, Billy had taken over many of his duties. In 1947 he was appointed 'assistant to the general secretary' by the executive and when his father resigned at the 1952 congress, Billy was appointed acting general secretary.

The executive met in Jury's Hotel Dublin on 8 December 1952 to select a new general secretary. Each of the four candidates was proposed, thus making a vote necessary. It resulted in five votes for McNamara, three for O'Brien-Crowley, two for Carney and one for Brady. On the second vote, Brady's supporter, M. J. Lee, voted for McNamara, while the other electors voted as before. Unable to attract any additional votes, Carney was eliminated. On the third vote, McNamara got six votes and O'Brien-Crowley, now being backed by Carney's erstwhile supporters, got five. The president Gerry Lovett then declared McNamara elected.[5]

The result precipitated the resignation from the executive of Carney's two supporters, Billy Cleary and Pat Taaffe. They were followed by Paddy Parfrey, who throughout the contest had supported O'Brien-Crowley. Lovett, who had also voted for O'Brien-Crowley at each stage, appealed to the others not to resign and stated that as president he could only resign at congress. Nonetheless within a fortnight he too would be gone. For the time being, the rule of the old guard within the VEOO had prevailed, but the closeness of the vote and the resignation of four of the eleven members of the executive revealed a seriously wounded body.

At an emergency executive meeting on 22 December Liam Trundle was appointed acting president. Realising the extent to which the organisation had been damaged by the resignations, he proposed to invite the dissidents to rejoin the executive and he drew satisfaction from reports of meetings in Longford and Donegal condemning the resignations. However when it met on 20 February the executive heard that 100 members of the Dublin branch had resigned. Fifty-five members remained registered but only twenty of these had attended a special meeting called to discuss the crisis. Deeply disturbed by such a haemorrhage, and hearing that a new organisation was being formed, the executive concluded that any approach to the dissidents would be futile.[6]

In a gesture designed to draw a line between itself and those who had dominated the affairs of the VEOO, the new organisation titled itself Cumann Mhúinteoirí Gairm-Oideachais and became generally known as CMGO. By now it had a committee and had appointed Tom Carney to draft a constitution. Its growing support, particularly amongst teachers who had been members of the Dublin and Cork city branches of the VEOO, prompted the April editorial of the *Bulletin* to characterise the crisis as a city versus country movement, and it called on the country branches—'the backbone'—to rally against a minority 'intent on destroying the organisation'.[7] The Irish Trade Union Congress (ITUC) joined the attack, characterising the CMGO as a 'secession or breakaway', and in a statement of 15 April 1953 it declared that any co-operation with the new organisation would be contrary to trade union policy.[8]

In May two of the leading members of the CMGO, Paddy Parfrey and Billy Cleary—each a former president of the VEOO—were invited to address the annual congress of the VEOO, ostensibly on the issue of the general secretary's appointment, but also in the hope that they and their followers might be coaxed back. Despite their spirited argument that the organisation needed a full-time general secretary, congress affirmed its confidence in the executive and approved McNamara's appointment. It then proceeded to a debate on what it chose to refer to as a split. The realisation that its claim to be the sole representative body was no longer sustainable gave the proceedings a conciliatory air, and in contrast with its earlier manoeuvres the organisation now moved cautiously. Deeply divided, the delegates agreed, for the time being, not to vote on a 'reunification' resolution. Winding up the discussion, Liam Trundle promised that the executive would explore any opportunity for a resolution. In three weeks' time he would travel to Cork to attend the congress of the Irish Vocational Education Association, or IVEA—the umbrella organisation of the vocational education committees—and he promised that he would intimate to the delegates there that the executive of the VEOO was willing to negotiate a settlement with its newly born rival.[9]

The IVEA had been founded in 1902 to act as a national forum for technical and agricultural instruction committees. It established itself as an authoritative body, but as the central employer organisation in vocational education its congress may not have seemed the most appropriate forum in which to examine the internal affairs of the VEOO, let alone mend a division in its ranks. However, the IVEA was much more than a meeting of employers: its congress, attended by committee members, public servants, trade unionists, clergymen, politicians and teachers, functioned as a quasi-corporatist body for everyone who was anyone in vocational education. Thus the Cork congress would be attended by all chief executive officers, most of them members of the VEOO, who as managers were anxious to see peace amongst the ranks of teachers. There was also the possibility that it might be attended by teachers and chief executives sympathetic to the cause of reform, including some who had by now joined the CMGO.

During the opening session Liam Trundle stated that he had been requested by the VEOO executive to seek the assistance of the IVEA in healing the split and to that end would be pleased to accept the services of a 'neutral chairman'.[10] He was followed by Paddy Parfrey, attending as a member of the Cork city vocational education committee delegation. As a former president of the VEOO he startled many in the audience when he declared that he was now on the executive of its rival, but he gave an assurance that it would listen sympathetically to any representations made by the VEOO. Among those in the audience was a University College Galway professor, Liam Ó Buachalla, there as a delegate from the Galway county committee. During the congress he would emerge as the honest broker sought by both sides. His pre-eminence within the IVEA and his national stature as a respected cathaoirleach of Seanad Éireann gave him the qualities necessary in a peacemaker.

During the winter of 1953 Ó Buachalla held a series of meetings at Leinster House with representatives of the rival bodies, and by the summer of 1954 he was able to propose the dissolution of both and 'the coalition of the respective members in a new entity'. The proposal formed the basis for an agreement reached in a meeting on 18 August in which each body was represented by five members; most significantly, the meeting agreed that Billy McNamara should be granted a testimonial 'in consideration of his relinquishing his post as General Secretary'. On 11 October the VEOO informed the ITUC that it had negotiated an agreement with 'another organisation of vocational teachers'.[11] In November 1954 both organisations balloted their members on the proposal to form a new body to be titled Eagraíocht na nGairm-Mhúinteoirí. Of the 296 VEOO members who voted, 276 accepted the proposal, 11 were against and 9 spoiled their ballot papers.[12]

The first meeting of Eagraíocht na nGairm-Mhúinteoirí was convened on 1 December 1954. Under the terms of the negotiated agreement the committee members of the rival bodies formed the executive of the new organisation under the joint presidency of the president of the VEOO, Liam Trundle, and the president of CMGO, Eileen Quinlan. Henry Sexton, a Dublin solicitor who had acted as adviser to Tom Carney, was appointed part-time general secretary. Soon he was arranging insurance cover for the 251 paid-up members, processing claims for the reimbursement of medical expenses and making representations to committees and to the Department of Education.[13] He convened the first executive committee meeting on 17 January 1955 when it was decided that the honour of taking the chair would fall to Eileen Quinlan. That position, it was then agreed, should be held in rotation with the other joint president, Liam Trundle. When arrangements were made for convening the inaugural congress of the new body at the Molesworth Hall in Dublin on 30 June 1955 a drawing of lots gave Trundle the honour of giving the presidential address, while Quinlan would preside the following day and hand over to the incoming president, Tom Carney. On the eve of congress the executive met for a dinner at which Liam Ó Buachalla was guest of honour. He was presented with a silver salver as a token of gratitude for his peacemaking. Shortly afterwards he presented a presidential chain of office for the use of the new body. When congress met its first decision was to replace 'Eagraíocht' in its title with 'Cumann', and from then until the 1973 congress it was known as Cumann na nGairm-Mhúinteoirí, or the Vocational Teachers' Association, but more generally as the VTA.[14]

Internal organisation and external links

The VTA adopted the structures of its precursors. Thus, for most members, the school committee, consisting of the members in a particular school, and the branch, formed from the members in each vocational education committee area, provided the immediate link to the wider body. The most tangible manifestation of membership was the monthly subscription, and regular payment was necessary if a member was to remain 'in benefit'. Subscriptions were the only source of income, financing the activities of the central organisation and its various benevolent funds. The inaugural congress established a capital fund, and a committee appointed by the 1959 congress recommended that it be reorganised as a security fund and registered as a friendly society. Provision was then made for the security fund committee members to act as directors of Urrús na nGairm-Mhúinteoirí, the company which would hold the assets. The VTA also established a provident fund to contribute to medical expenses, and in 1957 it negotiated the integration of its scheme with that of the newly founded Voluntary Health Insurance Board.[15] The association also sponsored personal accident and liability insurance, a legal advice scheme and a contingency fund for use in local disputes.[16]

Between congresses, a central executive committee, formed of delegates directly elected by the members along with the honorary officers and the general secretary, met regularly to ensure implementation of congress decisions and to respond to other issues as they arose. It delegated a subcommittee to oversee finance and from time to time appointed committees on specific issues. Their range indicates the changing contexts of the association's work: rural science (1956–63), headmasters (1956), technical education (1956–7), women teachers (1959–61), higher technological education (1960–3), apprenticeship (1961–3), tenure of married women (1963), education reform (1963–4), Irish (1963–4), technical sector salaries (1964–5), junior cycle syllabus (1965), education policy (1966–7), metalwork (1966–7), woodwork (1966–7), housing (1967–8) and link courses (1972–3).

Among the issues within the VEOO which had alienated Tom Carney and his supporters was what they perceived as the lack of an 'efficient secretariat', and to meet that need Henry Sexton was retained as part-time general secretary. Whatever hopes were vested in him would not be realised, for he resigned after the inaugural congress to be replaced by Tom Donaghy, an accountant at Albert College, Glasnevin. Within a few months, he too would resign. Breaking with previous practice, the executive then advertised the post and it drew an impressive thirty-four applicants, of whom eleven were interviewed in February 1956. The selection committee was unanimous in its choice of Charles McCarthy, a thirty-two-year-old barrister and member of the Radio Éireann Repertory Players. McCarthy would continue in a part-time capacity until becoming full-time general secretary in 1959. He served until taking study leave in 1972, which would lead eventually to his departure from the organisation and later an appointment as professor of industrial relations in Trinity College.

The new administrative practices too were a sharp break with the past. A typist was appointed in July 1955 and voted a weekly wage of £2, and another was recruited in 1957. The number had grown to six by 1973 when the finance committee, responding to pressure from congress to reduce costs, recommended a reduction to four. Initially the staff were located in offices rented at 144 Baggot Street, Dublin but moved in 1957 to 22 North Frederick Street. In 1966 they moved to a house at 73 Orwell Road which was purchased for £15,000 borrowed from the security fund. The move was conceived partly as an investment, for the house was much larger than the business of head office required: the association would pay a rent to the security fund for the use of one floor and it was planned that the other two would be let to suitable organisations.[17]

The VTA supported a number of autonomous organisations for the benefit of present and past members. Thus from 1961 it sent representatives to a recently formed Retired Officers' Association, and in 1967, when a group of teachers in Kevin Street Technical School formed a credit union, they got an office at headquarters. It opened membership to all in the association and in 1968, with ninety-seven members, became a registered company. That year also saw the foundation of the Vocational Teachers' Building Group to build houses close to the planned regional technical colleges.[18] The demand was less than hoped for, however, and most of the houses were eventually disposed of on the open market. A secondary objective, the provision of bridging loans, then became its main activity.[19]

In 1956, an attempt to form a separate organisation for headmasters was successfully opposed by the executive, which countered what it viewed as a dangerous fragmentation by setting up a headmasters' subcommittee.[20] Another organisation, Cumann Ard Mhaistrí Éireann, was founded in 1969. It requested the executive to send a representative to its meetings and on 11 October 1969, the executive's delegate, Kevin McCarthy, informed the new group that it could operate within the VTA but only if its rules were approved.[21] On that understanding the executive granted recognition to the association, by then named the Irish Association of Principals in Vocational Schools.[22] Subject associations, redolent of the groups of a half-century before, were also formed. These included the Engineering Teachers' Association and the Rural Science Teachers' Association, both recognised as panels within the VTA in 1972. Other groups were proposed, but their high running costs and the belief that effective subject groups would have to draw members from all second-level schools precluded the development of subject organisations exclusive to members of the VTA.[23]

The association continued to affiliate to the Irish Conference of Professional and Service Associations, or ICPSA, which had been founded in 1946 to represent non-trade union organisations, mainly on tax matters. That relationship was eclipsed, however, as the VTA strengthened its links with the ITUC and after 1959 with its successor organisation, the Irish Congress of Trade Unions (ICTU). The VTA continued to send delegates to ICPSA conferences but in early 1965, when it became clear that ICPSA would not support the principle of national wage agreements, the executive decided to disaffiliate.[24] The relationship with the trade union movement was copper fastened when ICTU elected Charles McCarthy to its executive in 1959, to its vice-presidency in 1962 and its presidency in 1963.[25] McCarthy's intense loyalty to ICTU, his sustained involvement in its affairs and his impressive performance as its president became a powerful expression of the association's development as a modern union.

Representation on official bodies would also further the association's interests. It was successful in having a member appointed to An Cheard Chomhairle (1959) and the Commission on Higher Education (1960) but it failed to gain representation on the Council of Education. By the mid-1960s its role was better recognised and it accepted an invitation to nominate members to the Intermediate Certificate syllabus committees; in 1966 it was given two places on the steering committee for the planned regional technical colleges and in 1972 a place on the Council for Correspondence Courses. On the other hand, despite repeated representations it was denied a place on the Registration Council for Intermediate Schoolteachers, the statutory registration authority for secondary schoolteachers until 1974.

The process of placing members where they might be able to further the association's aims extended to voluntary organisations. Nominations were made to the councils of Gorta and Macra na Tuaithe, and the association sent delegates to meetings of the Irish Red Cross Society, Macra na Feirme, UNICEF, the Social Study Conference, the European Teachers' Association and the Irish National Association for Mentally Handicapped. In 1957 it affiliated to the World Confederation of Organisations of the Teaching Profession and in 1973 it affiliated to the European branch of the International Federation of Free Trade Unions.[26]

Such activity did not gain full approval. A resolution submitted to the 1963 congress expressed concern at the 'increasing tendency' of the executive to deal with educational problems which, it suggested, were more properly the responsibility of the Department of Education.[27] The resolution was lost, but the following year a resolution that the association confine its activities to negotiating salaries and conditions was carried. The criticisms continued, and in 1967 congress accepted that there was 'serious anxiety and misgivings' concerning the conduct of the association's business. It established a special committee from which it pointedly excluded members of the executive. The committee homed in on the weak relationship between the branches and the executive and on what appeared as a lack of accountability, but in examining the general secretary's participation in outside bodies, it was forced to note that he did so in accordance with association policy. An 'amendment' submitted by Dublin city branch and included as part of the report took a more critical line: the general secretary, it argued, should be more answerable to the executive and should resign from external bodies, and the president, to whom the general secretary should be fully accountable, should be a full-time officer. It proposed that if foreign travel were planned, details should be submitted beforehand to the branches and that the executive should then act in accordance with the wishes of the majority.[28]

The report was evidence that many members felt weakened by what could be characterised, all too easily, as a remote and autocratic head office, and when the special committee submitted its report to the executive, the general secretary reported that the executive accepted 'all its recommendations'. However, a few weeks later, when some branches objected to the president attending a conference in Vancouver, they were curtly rebuffed by the executive.[29] For its own part, head office understood the potential for misunderstanding. The association was essentially a voluntary organisation, and the actions of its executive were mediated to the membership through local representatives. As a result its behaviour could be easily misunderstood. Thus, in his 1965 report, McCarthy pointed out that some of the branches had done nothing to establish consultative machinery locally, despite his efforts to promote this nationally.[30] If the national officers and officials appeared less than effective, they would enter the traditional plea: the organisation could only be as good as its members.

Vocational teachers and chief executive officers as employees of vocational education committees had shared membership of the VEOO, an information conduit which was severed by the VTA's decision to confine membership to teachers. An attempt to promote better communication was made in June 1956 when the executive asked the committees to set up joint consultative boards.[31] Some committees referred the proposal to the IVEA, which recommend rejection. Nonetheless, the Kildare committee set up a board in April 1957 and the Kilkenny committee established a board in 1959, and by 1967 others were operating in Cork, Carlow and Dublin.[32] Such initiatives prepared the ground for the acceptance of VTA members as observers, and later as full members, of vocational education committees. As employees they had been precluded from membership of committees by a provision of the Local Government Act 1925. To get round that, in February 1962 the association requested the IVEA to allow local branches nominate people who were not teachers to serve on committees. The proposal was rejected.[33] The pressure was sustained, with resolutions demanding representation being tabled at six of the ten congresses between 1963 and 1972.[34] These demands met with uncompromising resistance from interests unwilling to allocate a cherished committee place to an outsider and from those who shrank from the prospect of scrutiny more acute than anything successive generations of press reporters had ever managed. Nonetheless, by 1972 reports were being received that some committees were inviting association representatives to observe meetings.[35]

The association's counterparts in the primary and secondary schools, the Irish National Teachers' Organisation (INTO) and the Association of Secondary Teachers, Ireland (ASTI), had each accepted invitations to attend the inaugural congress in 1955, a practice which was reciprocated and repeated annually. At the inaugural congress the ASTI president stated that he looked forward to the day that all second-level teachers would be in the same organisation. The VTA response was politely welcoming but few of those present believed that it could be anything other than a friendly gesture. The desire for a closer relationship was revealed in a 1963 congress resolution tabled by Donegal which advocated the formation of a united teacher organisation.[36] An amendment tabled by Kildare advocated common action rather than amalgamation, while a resolution by Sligo county, proposing a joint council of the three organisations, was lost.[37] Such resolutions indicated, if not a desire for a full merger, at least support for a closer working relationship, and during 1966 a number of meetings between the VTA and the ASTI were held. Despite a decision to have further meetings, these did not take place due to 'pressure of work'.[38]

Against the background of a policy process which sought to introduce a common salary structure for all teachers a resolution from Leitrim at the 1968 congress called for the 'amalgamation' of all the teacher organisations, an amendment by Kildare sought an 'association' while a resolution from Roscommon sought 'collaboration'.[39] Congress adopted the more cautious route of co-operation, and the following year the general secretary reported that the executive would continue its policy of co-operation.[40] During February 1971 joint meetings of the three organisations were held under the auspices of ICTU which resulted in a joint document on an allowance dispute.[41] A resolution supporting a single second-level union was tabled at the 1972 congress, while an amendment sought to include all teacher organisations within its scope.[42] The process was repeated the following year when three resolutions supporting a merger of the two second-level teacher organisations and two others seeking a merger of all teacher organisations were tabled.[43] Whether such resolutions could be translated into action was far from certain at a time when ongoing school reform and the rapid expansion of third-level education left many issues unresolved and future prospects unclear.

Membership

None who attended the inaugural congress of the VTA needed reminding of the strife-filled circumstances of its birth. If the past had bequeathed a bitter legacy, the future was uncertain and the president revealed that while there were at most 700 members, the total number of whole-time vocational teachers was close to twice that. Central to a strategy for revitalisation was a series of meetings in each committee area addressed by members of the executive.[44] By March 1956 all but two possible branches, Sligo town and Waterford county, had been reorganised; then on 5 May 1956 the Waterford teachers formed a branch and on 23 February 1957 a branch was formed in Sligo. Soon the executive was receiving reports that some branches had achieved full membership.

The 1959 congress decided to open membership to part-time teachers thus ending a prohibition introduced in 1934, and by the end of the year ninety-one had joined. Like many part-time workers, they could prove difficult to organise and while the association continued to welcome them, in practice it did little to recruit them.[45] In 1960 trainee teachers were also deemed eligible for associate membership. In 1962 full membership was extended to teachers in the Irish Nautical College at Dún Laoghaire and in the domestic science teacher colleges.[46] Numerically the new recruits may have added little to the ranks of the association but their arrival was significant because it extended membership outside the employees of vocational education committees for the first time.

That process was extended in 1966 following the foundation of the state's first comprehensive schools as prototypes for a reformed second-level school system in which the characteristic elements of the vocational manual curriculum and the secondary literary curriculum might be fused. Their teachers were granted independent status at the Tribunal on Teachers' Salaries and some of them formed the Association of Comprehensive School Teachers. One of the new schools, Cootehill, replaced an existing vocational school, and when its teachers were transferred to the comprehensive the VTA retained them in membership in a separate branch.[47] Other comprehensive schools replaced both a secondary and a vocational school, while others were entirely new foundations. In such cases the VTA was in competition with the ASTI. When the first community schools opened at Tallaght and Blanchardstown in September 1972 the general secretary urged the teachers there who had been in the VTA to remain in membership and that there be full cooperation with their colleagues in the ASTI.[48] Other groups of comprehensive teachers met with the executive on 15 March 1973 and agreed conditions under which they would join the VTA.

Most employees of vocational education committees were teaching second-level courses, though a few—not more than 4 or 5 per cent—were teaching in city technical colleges and were in receipt of higher scales. Their number would increase greatly in the late 1960s with the foundation of the new regional technical colleges. Many of the foundation staff in the new colleges were long-serving committee employees and consequently were veteran members of the VTA. The association thus established its negotiating status in the colleges at their foundation, and to accommodate that development separate college branches were established in 1973. It proved to be an important and necessary stage in the association's development: in 1963 technical teachers at higher grades had constituted 5 per cent of the membership but by 1973 they accounted for 20 per cent.

Throughout its first two decades the VTA was relatively successful in achieving its aim of organising all whole-time vocational teachers: in 1958 91 per cent of all eligible teachers were members, in 1963, 87 per cent were members and in 1973, 89 per cent. Some members were dissatisfied with less than 100 per cent membership, however, and called for action to ensure it.[49] As a result, in 1968 the executive decided that it should seek an arrangement whereby retrospective payments resulting from any negotiation by the association would not apply to non-members, a position which was endorsed by the Public Services Committee of ICTU.[50] The proposal had a stern logic for members whose pursuit of better conditions entailed sacrifice, but there were many on the executive—not least its lawyer general secretary—who knew that as equal-pay policies gained legal underpinning, such proposals had little chance of implementation. Two resolutions tabled at the 1972 congress

Figure 7.1: VTA membership and total number of vocational teachers 1955–73

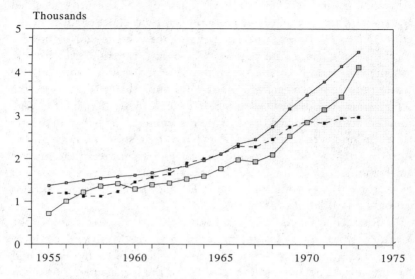

Source: Vocational Teachers' Association, General Secretary's annual reports, 1955/6–1973/4; Department of Education, Annual reports, 1954/5–1963/4 and Statistical reports, 1964/5–1973/4.

advocated compulsory membership of the association for all vocational teachers, while an amendment proposed that membership of any trade union would be sufficient. The following year a resolution advocating non-co-operation with teachers not in a union was tabled.[51] Despite such heady rhetoric the association stopped far short of adopting any policy that would lead to a 'closed shop'.

Salary

In his presidential address to the 1955 congress, Tom Carney reminded members that a progressive deterioration in salary had brought their real income below its 1938 level and that the absence of a conciliation and arbitration board exacerbated that unfortunate status.[52] In his reply, the Minister for Education, Richard Mulcahy, assured congress that he was indeed considering the setting up of a board for vocational teachers, similar to those established for both primary and secondary teachers in 1951. Eventually, on 16 February 1956 a draft scheme was received by the association and despite reservations at the heavy weighting of the 'employer' side—both the department and the vocational education committees were to be represented—the executive accepted it, arguing that it would have an opportunity to effect changes in the course of its operation. The adoption of the scheme still required a formal signing and on 3 January 1957—over a year and a half after the scheme had been promised—both the Minister for Education and the Minister for Finance declared that even though they wished to see the scheme introduced, they feared that it might lead to a demand for wage increases, which if spread to other sectors would create hardship during the continuing economic crisis. They asked that, should the scheme be introduced, it would be used only to deal with 'minor rectifications and small anomalies'. With that understanding it was accepted and adopted by its three parties—the VTA, the IVEA and the Department of Education—on 10 January 1957.[53]

The conciliation council would consist of two representatives of the VTA, two from the IVEA, a representative of the Minister for Education and a representative of the Minister for Finance. Both sides would have its own secretary, and the secretary of the Department of Education would take the chair. If an issue could not be resolved at conciliation, it would be referred to an arbitrator whose decisions, binding on both parties, would be submitted to the Dáil, where only a majority vote could overturn it. These became the mechanisms within which the association would negotiate the pay of its members until replaced in 1969 by a common scheme of conciliation and arbitration in which primary and vocational teachers would participate, to be joined by the secondary teachers in 1973.

The day the scheme was adopted also saw the award of a substantial salary increase to secondary teachers, thereby breaking the parity with vocational teachers that had been reached in 1952. The VTA executive informed the department that it understood parity to have been accepted as a basis for the vocational teachers' scale in 1952, and at its meeting on 16 February 1957 the executive agreed that it had no option but to submit a comprehensive claim. In so doing it argued that it was not going against the spirit of the agreement as the claim was not based on cost-of-living increases but rather on the structure of the salary and its several grades. The department, fearful that the claim would be treated as part of a national, government-sponsored cost-of-living negotiation, which if granted would influence the developing trends, resisted all attempts to have a meeting. Following a draft agreement between the national trade union organisation—the Provisional United Trade Union Organisation—and the Federated Union of Employers on a pattern of national wage increases, the Minister for Education Jack Lynch eventually agreed to meet the association on 21 September 1957.[54]

The minister argued that the agreement implied that an increase would be granted only if extra productivity could be obtained and that since that was not possible in the case of teachers, they should withdraw the claim. The association restated its position: the claim was for a restoration of parity, consequently it would not breach the original agreement. The minister resisted on the basis of the country's weak economic situation, and formally stated his position in a letter on 9 December 1957: not only would he continue to reject the claim, but even if it was submitted to arbitration and found in favour of, he would recommend its rejection in Dáil Éireann.[55] An irate executive then decided to submit two further claims to conciliation. One sought an adjustment to the difference in application of an earlier negotiated increase to vocational teachers and other salaried groups, while the other sought compensation for recent increases in the cost of living. In each claim, as with the general claims submitted by the primary and secondary teachers, the setting of pay levels relative to those of other teachers was a recurring and contentious issue. In response, the minister established a Teachers' Salaries Committee in December 1958 to identify principles which might help 'in determining the relationship between the remuneration' of teachers in the three sectors.[56] The fifteen committee members were representative of school managers, business interests, the government and the teachers. The VTA was represented by the president, Liam McGrenera, and the general secretary, Charles McCarthy.

When the committee concluded its work in May 1960 it recommended a 'basic school scale' which would take account of the nature of the work and promotion opportunities characteristic of the various sectors—in effect, three separate scales. None of the three teacher organisations was happy with this outcome. In reservations appended to the main report, the VTA set out its traditional objections to a differential between the two second-level sectors while the secondary teachers argued that since they entered the profession later than the others, they merited a higher starting salary.[57] Those reservations, cautiously expressed, were mild compared to the response of the primary teachers. In a carefully argued and sometimes bitterly phrased minority report, they rejected what they perceived as an implicit characterisation of their schools as lesser institutions and the implication that primary teachers were inferior in both quality and qualification. Rejecting a 'school' or 'sector' scale, they argued instead for one based on the intrinsic value of teaching as a vocation to be remunerated irrespective of the age, social class or intellectual capability of pupils.[58]

The committee had also recommended common conciliation and arbitration. The VTA accepted this in principle, though it wanted the right to place any sectoral claim before it and, if necessary, have it brought to arbitration. In contrast, the secondary teachers were opposed to a common scheme, fearing that it might lead eventually to a common salary. Five years earlier, the ASTI convention had formally adopted a policy which reaffirmed its atavistic belief in the exclusivity of its sector: secondary teachers, it argued, taught complex material of a higher standard to children at a higher stage of development. Accordingly the best graduates had to be attracted to secondary schools and retained there. That superior status, it submitted, was reflected in a rigorous set of registration regulations and made for a training of higher cost than that required of other teachers. It also argued that the absence of promotional prospects for secondary teachers, such as existed in primary and vocational schools, should be compensated by a higher salary.[59]

The VTA, like the ASTI, believed in sectoral distinction, and acting on a resolution of the 1963 congress, submitted a major claim based on the 'status' of its sector. Following an unsuccessful conciliation conference the claim was submitted to arbitration and settled there on 10 March 1964. That award, along with a national pay increase of 12 per cent, resulted in an overall increase, at the maximum, of 23 per cent. This substantially narrowed the gap between the vocational and the secondary teachers, though without restoring the parity which existed between 1952 and 1957. The ASTI now felt frustrated in its negotiations, and fearing that its relative advantage could be easily lost, decided to withdraw services at that year's examinations. The school managers attempted to placate the ASTI with a secretly negotiated increase of 12 per cent which would give its members approximately £200 a year more than the vocational teachers. The managers and their teachers both argued that as private institutions the secondary schools were entitled to make any additional payments that they felt the teachers deserved.[60]

When the secret deal became known to the VTA it reacted angrily. It was viewed not only as a further slip but as a sly attempt by both the secondary teachers and their employers to maintain a spurious 'exclusivity'. Furthermore, it seemed that the department, if not actively promoting the deal, had done nothing to prevent it. Consequently the conditions under which the 1965 arbitration hearing were conducted were less than favourable, and it ended unsuccessfully and with much recrimination.[61] Throughout 1965 and 1966 the VTA considered the means whereby it might regain the position lost through the secret award. If the secondary teachers were irritated by this, so too were the primary teachers, and they blocked the appointment of an arbitrator for the vocational teachers. At the same time they stepped up their political campaign for the introduction of a common scale. This served to increase the anxiety among the vocational teachers, which was revealed in the militant mood of the 1967 congress. By October of that year the executive had agreed that, if necessary, strike action would be taken.[62]

Meanwhile the Minister for Education, George Colley, continued to push for a common scale and when he met representatives of the teacher organisations in early 1966 he asked for their views on a common scale with provision for a set of qualification allowances. If he could succeed in getting agreement, he might be able to dispel the sense of grievance which both the primary and the vocational teachers had harboured for some time, while also further preparing the ground for the formation of a homogeneous teaching corps in a unified second-level sector. On the other hand, he was fully aware that any plan for a common system would provoke strong opposition from secondary teachers intent on maintaining their prerogatives. While tenaciously promoting the principle of a common scale, Colley was unsure of the form it should take or how, in an increasingly tense atmosphere, it could be introduced; so he sought to calm the atmosphere by the traditional device of appointing a tribunal. The previous salary committee had been a large representative grouping, but on this occasion a much smaller group, reflecting common employer and common employee interests but without separate sectoral representation, was proposed by Colley's successor, Donogh O'Malley, as a more appropriate device for setting the salary of a unitary occupational group. Agreement on committee structure was eventually reached, and the tribunal was constituted on 15 December 1967 with Louden Ryan, a professor of economics at Trinity College, as its chairman.

The Ryan tribunal was asked 'to recommend a common basic scale of salary' and 'to recommend what appropriate additions might be made in respect of qualifications, length of training, nature of duties'.[63] Clearly the principles on which the 1960 committee operated had been discarded: it was no longer a question of whether a common scale should be introduced, but of the mechanisms through which such a scale might be formulated and applied. Realising this the secondary teachers made a last-ditch attempt to have their case dealt with independently. Their plea was rejected but they got some reassurance from a promise by the minister that their conditions would not worsen and that if on the conclusion of the tribunal's work they remained dissatisfied, they could go back to using the existing conciliation machinery.[64]

At its first meeting with the Ryan tribunal the VTA argued that since all second-level schools were now offering a common course, their teachers should be on a common scale. Mobility between the sectors should be encouraged, but if one sector had a lower salary, 'seepage' from it to the other would rapidly follow. A salary increase was also necessary to ensure a constant flow of young blood into the sector. While the VTA's primary goal was the elimination of the difference between the secondary and the vocational teachers, it would no longer object to the primary teachers being brought to the same level. In conclusion it argued for a common scale though with appropriate allowances for qualifications and, somewhat inconsistently given its support for a common scale, a special second-level allowance.[65] In their submission, the primary teachers repeated their traditional objection to sectoral differentiation and argued for a substantial increase on the basis of recent increases in gross national product.[66] The secondary teachers then argued for qualification allowances knowing that a postgraduate higher diploma in education was not required of teachers in either the primary or vocational sector. If their claim for allowances could not be conceded, they argued, they would feel poorly rewarded for an extra year of required training while studying for the higher diploma.[67]

The Department of Finance supported the principle of a common scale and argued that it should be set at the level of the primary scale. In arguing against the VTA's case for setting the scale at a higher level, it submitted that there was no shortage of teachers. Furthermore the extent to which vocational teachers were being recruited from other services suggested that many of them found the salary attractive. It pointed out that vocational teachers had the opportunity to attain a principalship, something not open to most secondary school teachers. It also submitted that the payment to secondary teachers affected only the smaller non-pensionable portion of their salary paid by the school. In reply, the VTA referred to the state's own *Investment in education* report which had documented the extent of undersupply. In this it was supported by the chief executives and by the IVEA who vouched for the difficulty which committees experienced in filling posts. The arguments for parity made by the vocational teachers, the chief executive officers and the IVEA converged: each knew the problems that would confront the vocational school if its teachers were drawn to other schools or if they came to be characterised as less qualified, or their work as less demanding.[68]

The Ryan tribunal then convened joint meetings with the three teacher organisations. It soon became clear that on the issue of a common scale both the primary and the vocational teachers had moved to agreement. They also agreed on an initial point of entry based on a basic two years' training while additional years of training, research or experience would result in a higher entry point. The secondary teachers now had to accept those points, however reluctantly; but in a desperate attempt to maintain their superior salary and the prestige that flowed from it, they also argued that special allowances, additional to the common scale, should be payable for a pass degree and for the higher diploma in education. Together, the INTO and the VTA responded by arguing that a primary degree should not draw an allowance as it was the basic training qualification of secondary teachers. In making its case the ASTI said that in Northern Ireland and in England teachers were entitled to a primary degree and diploma allowance. It pointed out that the basic training for primary and vocational teachers was two years, whereas a secondary teacher with a degree and a higher diploma in education would have been in training for four years; extra increments would not be sufficient compensation for the costs of this training or for the loss of earnings during training. In a detailed submission, which also cited examples from Northern Ireland and England, the VTA argued for special allowances for the level of teaching and for posts of responsibility such as principal or vice-principal. It was supported in this by the ASTI, which argued that other posts in the school—librarian, careers and class teachers—should also attract allowances.[69]

The Department of Education responded by using labour market 'supply and demand' arguments. There was no shortage of teachers at primary level, it suggested, and the limited problem at second level was not a reason for rejecting a common scale. Backed strongly by the Department of Finance, it argued for a maximum salary set somewhat less than currently prevailed. The VTA reacted sharply against the ASTI case, arguing that the degree allowance would create two tiers of school and two tiers within a school. More importantly, it would bring teachers to the maximum very quickly and they would remain there for the greater part of their working life. The ASTI used civil service comparisons, and rhetorically asked if the department was less concerned about the schools than were the school owners who had 'justly' awarded the 12 per cent. On the basis of comparisons with Northern Ireland, the amounts offered were not enough. However, the ASTI suggestion that the second-level school should draw a special allowance—a development of the VTA's advocacy of special payments for 'higher' teaching—

was also rejected by the department as undermining the principle of a common scale.

The Ryan tribunal reported on 23 April 1968. As expected, its recommendations were built on the principle of a common scale, common that is to all women and to all single men, while married men would have a separate higher scale. Each scale would have seventeen increments: that for women and single men would start at £750 and go to £1,350 and that for married men would go from £950 to £1,700. The tribunal recommended that two years be adopted as the minimum training period. Thus, primary teachers having followed a two-year course should enter the scale at its first point and teachers whose training took three or four years should enter the scale at the second or third point respectively. Since two years was the usual length of primary training and four years the period most secondary teachers spent in university, the proposed entry points were sector specific. The report also proposed special additional allowances for various degrees and diplomas. Practically all secondary teachers would be eligible for such payments, and since the diplomas awarded by the primary and vocational training colleges would not count for qualification allowances, the differential between the sectors would be reinforced.[70]

The financial cost of bringing both vocational teachers and primary teachers on to a common scale set at the level of secondary teachers would be high. But such a solution would also leave the secondary teachers aggrieved. The department took a middle course and offered parity at a lower level, approximately that of the vocational teachers. This would be a victory for the primary teachers and might also be acceptable to the vocational teachers, while the secondary teachers might be coaxed into acceptance by the introduction of payments to holders of 'posts of responsibility' and a scheme of qualification allowances of immediate benefit to most of them. These payments would also benefit some vocational teachers, but at the cost of introducing a differential into their ranks which would reinforce the division between graduates and non-graduates. Not surprisingly, the device was viewed as an 'absolute outrage' by the VTA executive, and while it was debating the proposals it emerged that the department was proposing to offer payment of a degree allowance to all serving teachers. The VTA executive became suspicious when it emerged that the offer was conditional on acceptance of special 'responsibility' payments within the secondary sector. The proposal was leaked to the INTO, whose executive feared that a tendency towards making concessions to the secondary and vocational teachers would reinforce the existing division between first and second-level teachers.[71]

The Ryan tribunal report was not a negotiated document but an independent body's recommended principles on which future scales might be based. The omens for their adoption were not good, however, not least because of the perception amongst many teachers that the civil servants who would have to translate principles into practice were unsympathetic to their fears and the pervasive feeling that the proposed scales were too low.[72] Thus there was an inevitability in the initial rejection of the recommendations by the VTA delegates—sixty-four to eighteen—at a special congress on 15 June 1968.[73] The summer intervened, however, and the mood was softened by the satisfactory progress of the national wage negotiations. Following a ballot the VTA accepted the tribunal recommendations, having been assured that the fixing of the exact levels of the qualification allowances, including the equalising of degree and diploma allowances, could be decided subsequently.[74] The secondary teachers were determined not to accept and believed that they might maintain their existing advantage by continuing to use existing conciliation and arbitration machinery to negotiate separately. Consistent with government policy, the tribunal had recommended common arbitration, but the secondary teachers, knowing that existing schemes could continue until terminated by the minister and then only following six months' notice, held firm. They were playing for time, but if they appeared not to notice, the exclusivist position which they hoped to build on and which they assumed would be upheld by the minister had already been well lost. On 15 April 1969 the minister, Brian Lenihan, gave notice that he would terminate their separate conciliation and arbitration scheme.

The ASTI chose the posts of responsibility issue as a final battlefield. It argued for a rejection of post allowances, which it characterised as a sop for conceding parity with the other sectors. Such payments, it asserted, might be attractive to the vocational teachers long used to holding managerial and administrative roles, but not so in the secondary school where the religious were still in most cases the majority of the staff and formed its managerial cadre. The teachers, not surprisingly, had the full support of the school owners in this. On 1 February 1969 the ASTI went on strike and the school owners, sympathetic and themselves suspicious of the department, closed the schools. After a fortnight Lenihan made proposals that were accepted, thus ending the strike.[75]

The separate negotiation further alienated the primary and vocational teachers and convinced many of them that the department was insincere in its advocacy of common conditions and arbitration. The payments for posts, as recommended by the Ryan tribunal, were abandoned and, instead, lump sums of £300 after ten years' service and on the maximum for 'nominal' responsibilities were offered. It was made quite clear that virtually every secondary teacher would be paid the lump sum: what now appeared as a salary increase was being awarded.[76] This might not have been too upsetting to the VTA if the department had moved on the creation of posts of responsibility in vocational schools, but it had not. The association increased its pressure by making a counterclaim and holding a strike at all schools on 26 and 27 May.[77]

The department was now viewed suspiciously by all parties. It seemed as if it had been caught in its own trap and was attempting to free itself by reneging on what had been agreed with the secondary teachers. In the autumn of 1969 it withheld a very small general increase, but managed to placate the ASTI by keeping faith on the £300 ten years' service payment. This continued to cause great dissatisfaction with the VTA however, whose members began to think that the promise of parity, long a central strand in departmental rhetoric, was a fiction. The association decided on a campaign of strikes for January and February 1970 and showed its lack of faith in the negotiating machinery by publicly demanding an inquiry into the department's personnel division. To avert a crisis Seán O'Connor, an assistant secretary known to be sympathetic to the vocational sector, took over the personnel division of the department. His first action was to request Dermot McDermott of the Department of Labour to chair a conciliation conference, a move which soon led to the suspension of strike action.[78]

McDermott's talks, arranged for 28 January 1970, were in trouble from the beginning. The ASTI insisted that it could not be party to common negotiations and became enraged when it emerged that the promised £300 would not be paid to future entrants to the sector. The talks broke down but not before it became clear that they had opened up a new possibility: the ASTI had indicated that it might agree to setting aside some aspects of the separate 1969 agreement and might accept in their place 'compensation' in the form of extra increments. O'Connor saw this as offering some hope and the minister, Padraig Faulkner, then proceeded to take a role, announcing that he would implement what he considered to be an equitable solution. This he did in July 1970.[79]

The ASTI dismissed Faulkner's proposals and called a strike for 15 February 1971. The school managers, despite having closed their schools during the earlier strike, indicated that on this occasion they would stay open. By now the vocational school was able to offer the secondary

Scoil na gCeard, Kells, 1969 (Irish Times)

Minister for Education Brian Lenihan and VTA General Secretary Charles McCarthy at meeting of VTA executive committee, Athlone, 1969 (Pat's Photo Studio)

Minister for Labour Patrick Hillery and members of Clare Vocational Education Committee at the opening of the extension to the Vocational School, Miltown Milbay, 1968 (Clare VEC)

Seán Cooney 1967–9

Maurice Holly 1969–71

Kevin McCarthy 1971–3

Padraig Ó Conghaile 1973–5

Billy Webb 1975–7

Joe Rooney 1977–9

VTA General Secretary Charles McCarthy, VTA Vice President Patricia Hurley, Minister for Education Pádraig Faulkner, VTA President Kevin McCarthy and Chairman of VTA Building Group Liam Trundle at the opening of the teachers' housing scheme, Dundalk, 1971 (Byrnes' Photo Service)

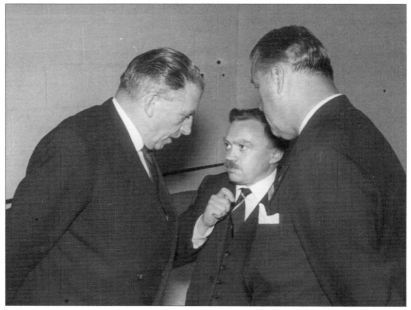

Taoiseach Seán Lemass and VTA General Secretary Charles McCarthy, 1965 (TUI)

Strike-bound classroom, College of Commerce, Rathmines, 1969 (Irish Times)

*VTA members Tony Dempsey, Sue O'Shea, Dave Caffrey and Maura Brennan on picket
duty at Vocational School, Enniscorthy, 1972* (Enniscorthy Echo)

VTA General Secretary Charles McCarthy at Head Office, 73 Orwell Road, Dublin, 1971 (TUI)

school curriculum, and for the first time in its history the ASTI had to consider the implications of coexisting with another sector which in certain circumstances might be able to accommodate pupils that it had long regarded as being exclusively its own. On this occasion the secondary teachers had overreached their bargaining capacity. Maurice Cosgrove, the ICTU president, intervened; he asked for a deferral of action and for all three unions, each equally a member of the ICTU, to join him in discussions. This was not necessarily a dispute between unions, he suggested, and while members of all three bodies were opposed to joining such 'negotiations' an agreement was reached which resulted in a lump-sum compensation for the secondary teachers. Within a week the department agreed to that proposal.[80] Cheered perhaps by this small gain, the ASTI reasserted its opposition to the principle of a common conciliation scheme; from January 1972, however, it had officers present at the common scheme as observers. Gradually a more trusting relationship evolved, and the ASTI—perhaps realising that no alternative was realistically feasible—accepted the common scheme in March 1973. A joint public statement by the three unions in September signalled their intention to campaign together against high income taxation and on other issues. The fires which in the past had indicated an intense rivalry and sometimes a barely concealed hostility were beginning to abate.

While the greater part of the VTA's negotiations was on behalf of its second-level teachers, from the late 1960s an increasing amount of time was spent on conditions in the expanding technological sector. Arrangements for staffing and pay in the new regional technical colleges had emerged in an *ad hoc* manner, and were for the most part based on the higher technical posts in the Dublin, Cork and Limerick technical colleges. Many of these posts had developed from second-level posts and a series of agreements negotiated through the 1940s and 1950s resulted in the creation of six separate technical grades: class II, class I, specialist, higher technological grade III, higher technological grade II and higher technological grade I.[81] The new colleges were developing rapidly but were in danger of being inhibited by archaic managerial and academic structures and it soon became impossible to equate the existing grades with new and emerging responsibilities. Consequently, many early claims arose out of difficulties regarding grading and allocation of posts, the sanctioning of new middle-level academic management posts, and in some cases the allocation of teaching duties between second-level and third-level courses.[82]

An initial claim, dealt with at conciliation in 1968, resulted in an offer which was accepted by the association in January 1969, and further claims for increases for the various grades and the creation of managerial positions led to protracted negotiations on a composite claim in 1970.[83] Little progress was made however, and the association was forced to impose a 'work to rule' at the end of May 1971. The rapid expansion of the regional technical colleges brought urgency to the ensuing discussions, but when the department's proposals were put to ballot in October they were rejected by members angry at a bureaucracy that appeared indifferent to the strains within the new sector. Negotiations were resumed against a background of discussions that would result in the introduction of university grades to the recently established National Institute for Higher Education in Limerick, but when new conditions were put in April 1972 they were rejected by one vote. Further negotiations resulted in an increase in the proportion of higher posts being created, the assimilation of the specialist and class II grades to an assistant lecturer scale, the assimilation of higher technological III to a lecturer I scale, and the assimilation of higher technological II posts to a lecturer II scale. At the same time conditions for new principal and senior lecturer posts were formulated. When put to ballot in June the new structures were accepted. A further claim for a 10 per cent increase on the basis of recent awards to university teachers was agreed in January 1973.[84] Establishing direct links between regional technical college scales and those in the university sector would prove to be an important stage in the convergence of higher education institutions.[85]

Men and women, married and single

Until 1946 each of the three sectors had separate salary scales for men and women. In that year women at the top of the scale in the secondary sector received 73 per cent of the salary paid to their male counterparts, in the primary sector they received 79 per cent, while in the vocational sector they received 83 per cent. In 1946 separate scales for married male teachers in both primary and secondary schools were introduced; these scales created a gap between the pay of married men and that of single men, and widened further the gap between the salary of male teachers and that of women. These three scales were reduced to two in 1950: the scale for married men was retained, while the separate scales for single men and women were merged; that structure was extended to the vocational sector in 1952. At their highest point, the new scales set the pay of single men and women teachers at approximately 80 per cent of that paid to their married male colleagues.

The notion of equal pay for equal work had been incorporated into the Universal Declaration of Human Rights adopted by the United Nations in 1948. The International Labour Organisation adopted a similar convention in 1951. The Treaty of Rome also incorporated an 'equal pay' provision, and in 1961 the Council of the EEC adopted a timetable for the implementation of regulations which would underpin the establishment of equal pay. In responding to questions as to why Ireland had not adopted such resolutions nor sought to develop its own strategies for equalising pay, ministers would state, somewhat disingenuously, that in Ireland wages were normally negotiated through free collective bargaining, a mechanism which in itself did not make it impossible to achieve equal pay.[86]

The first systematic examination by the VTA of the equal pay issue was facilitated by the executive's decision to establish a women teachers' committee in May 1959. It consisted of four unmarried women and a widow. In its first report it affirmed a commitment to the principle of equal pay for equal work and suggested that it might be effected by placing all teachers on the married men's scale. However it also suggested that the argument usually employed in wage bargaining—that marriage brought additional responsibilities and therefore merited higher wages—should also be applied in the case of single women, for they too were rarely without family responsibilities. The committee argued that widows returning to work should not be placed on the single scale and argued instead for special family allowances of 'a generous nature' for married men and widows with dependants. That such differentiation might undermine the principle of equal pay does not seem to have occurred to the committee.[87]

The committee's recommendations on equal pay were submitted by the executive as a resolution to the 1960 congress.[88] Congress also received three branch resolutions demanding the abolition of separate scales: each was worded in the language of marital status rather than sex, and they thus incorporated the large number of single men in the association within their scope. A fifth resolution accepted the principle of separate scales but argued for a reduction of the gap between the two. By executive recommendation, each of the resolutions was deemed to be encompassed in its resolution which called for the scale for married men to be extended to all teachers, irrespective of marital status or sex, and for 'generous' family allowances to be paid to married men and widowed women.[89] That resolution was passed and the executive then forwarded it to ICPSA with a request that it be dealt with as part of its ongoing negotiations on behalf of public sector workers. Thereafter it progressed slowly and the general secretary reminded delegates to the

1961 congress that of the fourteen organisations affiliated to ICPSA, only six seemed to be wholeheartedly in favour of equal pay, one was against it and seven had no policy on the matter.[90] The following two congresses would each hear a similarly gloomy tale: the issue was being dealt with, but by a body whose enthusiasm for pay equality was much less than that of the VTA.

Despite its adoption of an equal pay policy in 1960, the association continued to submit salary claims on the basis of the two existing scales, thereby leaving itself open to the charge that it was colluding with the opponents of equal pay. It justified its position on the basis that to claim a single scale would imply the introduction of a new principle and therefore would not meet the agreed criteria for arbitration. Thus the issue drifted, and its absence from the agenda of executive meetings and congresses during 1964 and 1965 seemed to suggest that it had been quietly dropped. That quiescence was challenged, however, by the tabling of four resolutions on equal pay at the 1967 congress.[91]

In its submission to the Ryan tribunal in January 1968, the VTA had argued that sex discrimination was not compatible with the notion of a common scale. It was supported in this by the secondary school managers who, quoting the UN convention, argued that salary scales should be free from discrimination on the grounds of sex or marital status: for the large number of teaching religious and clergymen, the point had a particular significance. Despite those arguments, the tribunal's recommendation of two separate scales—one for married men and one for single men and all women—indicated that the advocates of equity would have to wait. When it rejected the tribunal report at a special congress in June 1968, the association listed amongst its reasons the fact that the tribunal had not conceded the principle of equal pay. Not surprisingly, the 1969 congress had ten equal pay resolutions.[92]

The swell of protest had little apparent impact and there was nothing to indicate the possibility of change until the government, mindful of unfavourable comparison between Ireland and its would-be European partners, appointed a Commission on the Status of Women in March 1970. Its brief required it to make recommendations on how the participation of women in political, social, cultural and economic life 'on equal terms' could be ensured. Two months later, the Minister for Finance asked the commission to prepare an interim report on equal pay, with particular reference to the public sector. At the same time, the VTA executive—stirred into action by the disquiet of delegates at the 1969 congress—was preparing a claim for equal pay; this was submitted to the conciliation council on 19 October 1970 and then incorporated in a composite claim discussed by the council on 24 February 1972. Meanwhile the rank and file maintained momentum with five equal pay resolutions at the 1973 congress. Then, in 1974, congress had the satisfaction of hearing the general secretary report that the government had decided to introduce legislation which would implement EEC equal pay directives. The Anti-Discrimination (Pay) Act of July 1974 set 31 December 1975 as the date by which equal pay would have to be fully applied. A salary scale, common to men and women and without any marital status qualification, would be payable from 1 January 1975.

Though inextricably tied to the issue of equality, the official bar on the permanent employment of married women teachers and the requirement that a woman should resign on marriage occupied a much lower place on the association's agenda. The restrictions were included in the first issue of Memorandum V 7 in 1930 and similar requirements were extended to primary teachers in October 1933. The Department of Education did not immediately apply the regulation to secondary teachers, whose working conditions were to a much greater extent negotiated between the teachers and individual schools or one of the managerial organisations. The bar reflected the view, widely held at the time, that the proper activities for a married woman were to create a home, to serve her husband and to rear their children. In was also argued that in times of less than full employment, priority should be given to men, and that if women had to be employed, priority should be given to single women who as yet were without a husband to support them. If a woman was widowed then she became the principal provider for her children. In such circumstances she could resume employment, but while she was eligible for additions to her salary for each of her dependent children, her basic scale remained that of a single woman.[93]

The VTA was slow to argue the case for ending the marriage bar. In 1960 its all-female women teachers' advisory committee had recommended that 'for social reasons' and in view of the 'practical demands' of vocational education, the marriage bar should remain.[94] The bar was debated at the 1962 congress with many delegates—opposing the position of the women's committee—arguing that it should be removed, if only to ensure equity in the profession: it had been removed in the primary sector in 1948. Congress was divided, and on the executive's recommendation agreed to refer the question to the executive with the request that it should submit a full examination of the issue to the next congress.

The division amongst members was reflected in the two resolutions on the issue tabled at the 1963 congress: that from Wexford town urged that the bar be retained while another from Monaghan sought its removal. The executive presented a lengthy paper summarising a set of arguments for and against the removal of the bar. Having done so, it revealed its position by cautiously arguing for the status quo. It urged that in the filling of posts preference should always be given to single women over married women, arguing that only single women would be able to devote themselves fully to teaching, but somewhat confusingly conceding that consideration might be given to a married women if she was in economic difficulties. In such cases, it was suggested, she should be able to apply to the minister for a certificate giving her exemption from the existing regulation. 'The only grounds for the issue of such a certificate', it reasoned, 'should be economic hardship.' In other words, the economically stretched married woman should seek to be treated as a widow. In using the concept of economic necessity, the executive revealed a belief that the husband should be the primary wage-earner and only when that was not the case should his wife take on that role.[95] When the issue was discussed with department officials in November 1963, they resisted the proposal that the minister should be asked to adjudicate on individual cases of economic necessity. The executive conceded the point, and it struggled to find some identifiable criterion which might indicate necessity, such as a medical certificate of a husband's disability. In March the following year congress debated and defeated a motion calling for the removal of the bar, and another similarly phrased motion was then withdrawn.[96]

Despite these apparently clear signals in favour of the status quo, the tide of opinion may have been turning, for the 1965 congress considered five resolutions arguing for a removal of the bar while there were none in favour of its retention.[97] The 1967 congress too had five resolutions seeking an end to the bar, and none in favour. Shortly afterwards, at a meeting to discuss Memorandum V 7, the VTA pressed strongly for removal, a view that was supported by the department.[98] The IVEA however remained cautious: having debated the bar at its 1967 congress it did not wish to take a decision and referred the issue to the 1968 congress. Nonetheless the pressure for change was sustained and in its final recommendations the Ryan tribunal noted the abolition of the retirement at marriage regulation in primary and secondary schools and the consequent anomalous position of married women in vocational schools. It recommended that the department should rectify the anomaly as soon as possible. On 26 July 1968 the department issued a circular setting out the conditions for the employment of married women teachers in the vocational sector. It involved a cumbersome device—resignation on marriage and immediate reappointment—in order to create the alternative options of either the grant of a marriage gratuity or full pension rights.[99]

The VTA's relatively slow conversion to the cause of equal treatment for married women contrasts with its sustained support for a common salary scale. It campaigned for a common scale on the assumption that it would be achieved by bringing the lower paid single men and women to the scale long enjoyed by married men. A large section of the association would benefit from such a move if it was achieved. In contrast, the removal of the bar on married women would be of immediate benefit only to the few married women who had managed to obtain temporary work and who might then become eligible for a permanent post. Most women teaching were either single or widowed, and the ending of the bar would bring increased competition for whatever posts were available to them. The number of such posts was in decline: in 1926 40 per cent of vocational school teachers were women but by 1964 the proportion had dropped to 31 per cent. In a sector where employment opportunities for women were contracting, married women holding temporary posts would get only the mildest of sympathy from their single sisters. Doubtless, many of those single women contemplated the possibility that they too might eventually marry. If some hoped to combine marriage with a teaching career, drawing the benefits that permanent employment might bring, they remained silent for the moment. The goal of combining a career with married life would be something that the next generation of VTA members would pursue.

Working conditions

During the 1950s and 1960s, the VTA increasingly exercised its right to negotiate on behalf of members and to establish their right to due process and to equitable conditions. The basis of a teacher's contractual obligations were set out in Memorandum V 7, first issued by the Department of Education in 1930 and at intervals thereafter in revised form. In April 1956 the VTA followed the practice of its predecessor and submitted recommendations for a revision, but the six years that followed were a frustrating period of postponed and cancelled meetings in which official promises of a revised draft were repeatedly broken.[100] Eventually in June 1962 the association obtained a meeting with the Minister for Education. Joint conferences of department officials, the

IVEA, the chief executive officers and the VTA followed and resulted in a draft being placed before the 1963 congress. Such sluggishness on the part of the department can be compared with that of some committees, notably Westmeath, in delaying the payment of increases awarded at arbitration in 1958 and again in 1960, and that of the Waterford committee in delaying the payment of honours degree allowances.[101]

Sluggishness was not a quality entirely lacking in the chief executive of the Wexford county committee, P. B. Walsh. In the summer of 1956 he withheld salary due to seven teachers because, he maintained, they had not submitted schemes for the next session.[102] Following that, all but one teacher, Tom Powell, complied with the request. Though he had prepared a scheme, he refused to submit it, upholding the principle that a chief executive officer had no right to withhold a salary in order to discipline a teacher. On 16 August the general secretary, Charles McCarthy, and two members of the executive travelled to Wexford to meet Walsh. He would see only McCarthy, who agreed to that condition under protest. The committee chairman, Fr Butler, was prepared to meet the executive members and he conveyed an impression that he was in sympathy with their views. Within a week, however, he wrote to the general secretary stating that he believed that Walsh's action was 'legal and justified'. Members of the VTA executive met officials from the department on 24 August, submitted copies of the correspondence and asked that the minister be informed. McCarthy then advised Powell to submit schemes and at the same time sent a bluntly worded explanatory circular to vocational education committee members. His position was unequivocal: the legislation stated that salary could be withheld only if a teacher was suspended—something only a committee or the minister was empowered to do—and that a suspension had to be followed immediately by an inquiry.[103]

The Wexford committee's legal advice seemed to echo the association's view. When reporting to the committee's September meeting, Walsh admitted that he had been guilty of a 'technical error', but a report of the meeting in the local press also gave the impression that the committee believed Powell to be inefficient and recalcitrant. It also stated that he had tried to cause unrest and that if the chief executive officer had been mistaken in his actions, he had at least revealed the unsatisfactory state of affairs at the New Ross vocational school. Walsh had asserted that the 'tempo of work in the school was low', that it had lost public confidence and that consequently he had decided to transfer Powell to another school.

It was clear to McCarthy that Powell was being treated unfairly, and in view of the role of the local press in forming public opinion—a responsibility he felt it had discharged in a partial manner—he obtained from it an undertaking that in future it would state the association's views as well as those of the committee. Noting that the posts of woodwork and metalwork teachers had been recently advertised by the Wexford committee, McCarthy also placed an advertisement asking potential candidates to contact him first. Walsh then circularised all the teachers in the county, brusquely requesting that they inform him within four days whether or not they were satisfied with their working conditions. He thereby extended the scope of the conflict and precipitated the calling of an emergency meeting of all the Wexford teachers for 15 November. It emerged that some teachers, especially those on probation or holding temporary positions, feeling themselves under intense pressure, had already replied to Walsh. Nonetheless a resolution declaring dissatisfaction with conditions in the county and calling for an inquiry was adopted.[104]

Though hoping for a ministerial inquiry, the Wexford branch was content to accept the committee's invitation to make its views heard at a special meeting. McCarthy assiduously set about preparing for the meeting, documenting not only Powell's case but also that of other teachers who he believed had suffered as a result of Walsh's distinctive managerial style. However, neither his submission nor a petition by New Ross townspeople in support of Powell served to alter the committee's position.[105] Despite further meetings between McCarthy and the secretary of the department and urgent phone calls between Marlborough Street and Wexford, the committee stood firm. Against it, Powell seemed defenceless, and despite access to the minister, widespread public sympathy and supportive colleagues, he took the full consequences of its displeasure. Notwithstanding its forcefully stated resolve to take action, the association seemed powerless. Tom Powell received formal notice of his transfer to the school at Adamstown, fifteen miles from New Ross, on 23 March 1957 and was still teaching there when he died, aged sixty-two, during the summer vacation of 1965.[106]

If the incident had seemed little more than a clash of strong personalities, it produced a lingering sense of grievance, and as Walsh continued to enjoy a long reign nothing could convince the Wexford branch that an injustice had not occurred. Conditions in the county deteriorated in late 1971, and in his general secretary's report to the 1972 congress Charles McCarthy expressed disquiet at the committee's refusal to employ married women whole-time and at recurring breaches of an agreement on working hours.[107] Congress then passed a resolu-

tion calling for a ministerial inquiry and endorsed the executive's decision to support the branch's call for appropriate action. As a consequence, the Wexford members went on strike on 19, 26 and 27 April.
The Department of Education then agreed to meet the association and
to investigate conditions in the county. Following meetings with the
Wexford committee and the VTA, the department's representative, assistant secretary Seán O'Connor, drew up a fifteen-point agreement
which he hoped would provide a framework within which amicable
working relations might develop. It proposed a survey of conditions in
each school, regular meetings between the VTA and the committee,
VTA observers at committee meetings, removal of restrictions on married women and an appeals system. The agreement was accepted by
both sides on 19 June, but five weeks later the department informed the
association that the committee had decided to rescind the sections of
the agreement that affirmed the employment rights of married women
and it soon emerged that other parts of the agreement were also being
dishonoured. An incensed executive asked the minister to suspend both
the committee and the chief executive officer and to order a sworn inquiry into their conduct.

As the schools reopened in September 1972 feelings were running
high and the Wexford county branch pressed the executive to sanction
another strike. A special congress at Liberty Hall in Dublin on 31 September unanimously supported an executive proposal to withdraw all
Wexford members from 10 October. On the eve of the planned strike,
in what then appeared as a desperate and disingenuous gesture, Wexford vocational education committee declared its commitment to the
fifteen-point agreement. Neither the branch nor the executive was convinced of the committee's sincerity and the strike went ahead. The department then asked for a joint meeting of the executive and the committee. The executive agreed to attend, though making it clear that it
would do so, not for the purpose of negotiation, but merely to have the
association's position clarified and recorded. At the same time the department proposed that both parties should again formally ratify the
fifteen-point agreement and that the minister would appoint an officer
who, in conjunction with the Wexford chief executive, would make
recommendations as to how the fifteen points could be implemented.
The executive restated what it believed experience had shown: the proposals could not, in themselves, provide an adequate safeguard that
satisfactory working conditions would be established. In such circumstances few on the executive felt inclined to accept that further negotiations could prove fruitful, but following sustained intervention by the

IVEA and the Association of Chief Executive Officers of Vocational Education Committees (ACEOVEC), it agreed to attend a meeting in the Department of Education on 2 November, to be chaired by the secretary of the department.

The meeting quickly agreed that the fifteen points, along with the proposal for a special representative, would be formally ratified by the department, the VTA and the Wexford committee, and that both the IVEA and the ACEOVEC would act as its guarantors. The department announced that assistant secretary Seán O'Connor would carry out the promised survey and that the secretary of the department would chair the first of regular meetings between the Wexford committee and the VTA. Going further, the IVEA president suggested that an officer of the department should chair all subsequent meetings of joint consultation and that this officer would have the right to attend all meetings of the committee and the right to see the agenda and to discuss it beforehand with the chief executive to 'ensure that the minister's point of view was put clearly'. In a gesture of goodwill the department undertook to ensure that the strike period would not lessen pension entitlement and that there would be no victimisation of strikers. Then, when the ACEOVEC undertook to talk to its Wexford member and tell him that he should desist from his usual methods of inspection, it was clear to all present, if not to Walsh himself, that he was now fully isolated, even from his peers and erstwhile supporters.

A joint meeting to discuss the fifteen-point plan took place between the VTA and the Wexford committee on 5 December and was followed in January by meetings between the association's president, Kevin McCarthy, and the committee chairman, J. J. Bowe. Meanwhile, Seán O'Connor had conducted the promised survey and, having submitted it to the Wexford committee, recommended that the principal at Enniscorthy be removed. The committee felt unable to do so, and the minister, Richard Burke, then suspended him and ordered an inquiry into his conduct as principal.[108] Relationships deteriorated further when Walsh took proceedings against Kevin McCarthy because of a remark made in a radio interview. Any hope that Wexford had been pacified faded, and the sense of gloom deepened in September 1973, when on the reopening of the schools it emerged that two teachers in the county—one in Shielbeggan and another in Gorey—had not been reappointed by the Wexford committee. The executive decided that both teachers should appeal to the committee and, using procedures in the fifteen-point agreement, through it to the minister. The executive argued that pending the hearing of the appeal the teachers should continue working, but when they reported to their schools on 11 September they were refused admission. Their colleagues then withdrew their labour in support, while the committee confirmed its decision not to reappoint them. Richard Burke met the executive on 5 October and on the following Monday decided that while one of the teachers should be reinstated the other should not. At the urging of the executive the branch accepted the minister's decision, as did the committee, and the two schools involved reopened on Tuesday 16 October.[109]

An uneasy peace seemed to pervade Wexford until on 19 December three teachers at the Gorey school, without warning, were summoned to a committee meeting. Their solicitor asked for an agenda, and subsequently a letter from the chief executive stated that they would each be given an opportunity of hearing and replying to allegations made against them. Each case concerned their treatment of another teacher. The three asked for a postponement which was refused: meeting in their absence, the committee suspended them. This led inevitably to a full strike by branch members. On 17 January 1974 the minister requested an assistant secretary in his department, Tomás Ó Floinn, to conduct an inquiry into the suspensions. His report to the minister on 19 March formed the basis of proposals to both sides. The most significant was that each school in the county would have a board consisting of four vocational education committee members, two parents and the principal as secretary, and it would have full responsibility for the management of the school. The minister would nominate an officer to oversee the new system for at least a year and he would arbitrate on all disputes within the terms of the original fifteen points. Either side could appeal, and an inspector with sole inspection rights would be appointed to the county. This was accepted and members were instructed to return to work, having first agreed to take extra classes to help pupils make up for lost time. The schools reopened on 25 March, and an agreement was signed by all parties on 5 April.[110]

When the Wexford county branch challenged the right of P. B. Walsh to suspend Tom Powell in 1956, the VTA had been unsure of its strength and, without the funds that might underwrite a withdrawal of labour, was forced to accept defeat at the hands of an unbending committee. By the early 1970s much had changed. In the intervening years the association had grown greatly in size and acquired strong financial foundations. At the same time it had emerged as a body whose place in ICTU could command respect, not only from other trade unions but also from the wider public. Its role in the educational debates of the late 1960s was constructive and progressive, and the respect which its general secretary commanded gave him a credible authority in any negotiation. In 1967 the results of a ministerial inquiry into the Limerick city committee's conduct of recruitment and promotions had served to weaken the general standing of committees, and its subsequent sacking by the minister revealed an unsuspected vulnerability while vindicating the representative role of the VTA. Around the same time the right of the association to negotiate on behalf of members had been denied in the Galway county committee by the chief executive officer, Seán Ó Dochartaigh. As the association initiated court proceedings against him and his committee, a deeply embarrassed department intervened to affirm the negotiating rights of teachers.[111] By the early 1970s it had become clear that aberrant and dictatorial behaviour, whether by a committee or a chief executive, was something that a department intent on forging an alliance with teachers to promote its project of reform could neither afford nor tolerate. Progress was greatly aided by good personal relations between the VTA's officers and successive ministers and civil servants. The basis of a respectful trust was being laid down on both sides, and it was clear to many in Marlborough Street that far from being mischievous, the VTA's officers wanted no more than the fair application of agreed procedures.

Such progress was frequently achieved at substantial personal cost, most cruelly in the case of vice-president, Patricia Hurley, accidentally killed while on association business in Wexford in November 1972. Selfless and exemplary behaviour, the power of collective action and the decisive leadership of a succession of dynamic presidents had provided a compelling lesson for many, not least the hundreds of young teachers who were flocking into a rapidly expanding sector. If the aim in Wexford or Galway had been to break the power of the association and to leave the ordinary teacher vulnerable to the will of an autocratic employer, its effect, ironically, was the reverse. In the forging of collective consciousness, such events had once more proved to be a powerful flame.

Educational and social policies

Notwithstanding the ongoing need to strengthen basic negotiation rights and working conditions, the VTA, like its predecessor, continued to concern itself with issues of education policy. Thus in the late 1950s it became increasingly preoccupied with the injustices inherent in a divided and unequal second-level system. The 1959 congress adopted resolutions that continuation vocational education should be extended upwards into a senior cycle for the age group fifteen to seventeen and that the universities should admit vocational school graduates.[112] In his presidential address Liam McGrenera used progressive equal opportunity arguments when proposing the raising of the school-leaving age to fifteen and the introduction of a comprehensive grant scheme to replace the narrowly conceived scholarship system.[113] These points were repeated in a submission in 1965 to the Commission on Higher Education and the submission went on to argue that two streams within vocational schools should be established. The first, for students with a capacity for higher education, would consist of an extended continuation course of five years from which pupils could progress into regional technical colleges or into 'the more demanding' apprenticeships. The second stream would be for 'less able' pupils who would complete their schooling in two years and then enter 'less demanding' apprenticeships or industrial occupations.[114]

The reform of second-level education in the 1960s was widely welcomed within the VTA as an opportunity to create greater educational equality. How that would be achieved was less clear, and as the state's restructuring of the school system proceeded, vocational school teachers were faced with many dilemmas. For some, such as presidents Tom Carney and William O'Brien-Crowley, it was an opportunity for the vocational school to develop as a full secondary school which, while having the traditional technical subjects, would now lay at least equal emphasis on the secondary school subjects.[115] The Group Certificate should be abolished, they argued, and vocational teachers should take every opportunity to guide their pupils through a full secondary course and into higher education. For others, such as Liam McGrenera and the general secretary Charles McCarthy, the sector's glory was its technological curriculum whose inherent merits were a compelling justification for its development as the basis of an integrated system of second and third-level technological education. It should not be regarded as inferior, they argued, nor should it become a pale imitation of the secondary school. Instead, vocational school pupils should progress through a properly funded school to take a specially designed technical Leaving Certificate which would provide the path to higher education for the élite of an expanded technological sector.[116]

While a clear consensus on these issues had not formed, the association took a relatively conservative approach to reform, arguing that the cherished characteristics of its curriculum should be retained in any reorganisation. Such principles underpinned its response in May 1963 to Minister for Education Patrick Hillery's proposal to promote a comprehensive second-level system. While admitting that the continuation course had its defects, chief of which was its termination after two years without any obvious further stage, the association did not feel that the Intermediate Certificate course, as then constituted, would suit the needs of vocational school pupils and it argued strongly for the retention of a 'flexible' curriculum. In particular the association objected to proposals to extend Intermediate Certificate mathematics, English and Irish to become the common core of a reformed second-level system. Soon after, in an article in the VTA's journal *Gairm* provocatively entitled 'Abolish the Group Cert!', Tom Carney argued that it would be counterproductive to have pupils do both Group and Intermediate Certificate examinations, and that since there was a need to lengthen the period in school, the Intermediate Certificate should become the common terminal examination of the junior cycle.[117] Charles McCarthy—perhaps closer to majority feeling in the association—argued that the Group Certificate was more flexible than the Intermediate Certificate, though he agreed that the course should be extended to three years. He saw the difficulty of introducing a comprehensive curriculum in the smaller schools where, he warned, the Intermediate Certificate would dominate and eventually squeeze out the Group Certificate. A possible solution, he suggested, might be the introduction of co-operation between schools and, by extension, a more flexible examination system.[118] A similarly cautious approach was evident when the 1965 congress considered the proposal to introduce a 'technical' Leaving Certificate. The Dublin city branch proposed that it should be exclusive to the vocational school while amendments from Galway and Wicklow supported the plan and sought to reduce differences between a 'technical' Leaving Certificate and the existing examinations, in effect supporting the idea of a common examination. The amendments were rejected and the resolution, as originally put, was passed.[119]

The development of a hybrid second-level curriculum and schooling necessitated a reform in school management structures. The foundation of comprehensive schools in Cootehill, Carraroe and Shannon in 1966 was welcomed, and while the association was not to know that a secretly agreed deed of trust vested the new schools in church nominees, the appointment of a lay principal in each school and boards of management composed of an episcopal nominee, a committee chief executive officer and a department inspector gave the impression of a reasonable balance of public and private interests. The combination of an increasing demand for second-level places and a need for a systematic approach to provision was acutely felt by the state, the churches and the vocational sector and it soon resulted in a proposal to radically expand provision through community schools, formed either by amal-

gamating existing schools or as completely new foundations. Though
the text of a departmental document outlining new structures had been
published in the newspapers in November 1970, the association was
not officially given details until the following April. Without stipulating the number of members, the document stated that the board would
consist of representatives of the secondary school managers and of the
local vocational education committee and that the chairman would be
the bishop of the diocese or another person by agreement; it added that
it 'might prove possible' to include a parent or industrial representative
as a nominee of the main interests. Each school's trustees would be
nominated following agreement by the diocese and committee involved.
It was clear to the association that the structures had already been agreed
between the department and the bishops.[120]

Since the new development promised significant investment in buildings and equipment, the possibility that competition between schools
might lessen and the opportunity to be part of a major state-sponsored
initiative, it was welcomed by many in the executive. For others, however, it represented a radical and unwelcome shift in the balance between public and private control. Many vocational schools, it seemed,
would be swallowed up in new schools whose ethos might be expected
to replicate that of the private secondary schools. When the department
issued further details in May 1971, those fears were confirmed. They
stipulated three trustees, two of whom would be nominated by the local
bishop and the third chosen by him from a panel submitted by the
vocational education committee. The board of management would have
four members nominated by the secondary school authorities and two
by the vocational education committee. In a bid to gain allies amongst
the public and lessen the impression of episcopal domination, the document stipulated that two of the church nominees would be parents. At
a special congress on 4 June the association took the view that the proposals would bring fundamental alterations in the governance of institutions in which many of its members would work and that consequently they should be considered, at the very least, in a government
white paper. The association argued that the vocational school was open
to all children irrespective of creed and that any school hoping to build
in part on that structure should be the same. As hybrids, hoping to
absorb the best of two different traditions, the new schools should, in
their trustees and management, reflect vocational school and secondary
school interests equally. Parental and teacher members of boards should
be elected rather than selected, and the principal should be appointed
independently as a full member of the board.[121]

The VTA sent its proposals to the minister on 8 June, but a month later, when he announced details of new schools at Blanchardstown and Tallaght, it was clear that he had rejected them. The executive was incensed, especially since the establishment of the two new community schools would result in the closure of long-established vocational schools. Furthermore, because there was no secondary school involved in either development, it was unimpressed with an apparently disingenuous plea that in each case a religious order had been 'making arrangements' to set one up. Over the following two years the executive continued to press for changes, including provision for the selection of a principal by the Local Appointments Commission, management meetings open in the manner of vocational education committee meetings, places for the principal and an association representative on the board, and the removal of a new condition of employment—a 'faith and morals' clause— which, it argued, implied a lack of trust and confidence in its members. Then, in September 1973, the Blanchardstown school opened, and to its teachers who had transferred from the old vocational school it seemed to offer a significant improvement in their working conditions. Morale improved and the anxieties of the previous few years receded. The policy document of 1 October 1973 indicated progress on parity of representation for vocational education and religious interests and the election of parents to school boards, but as yet no provision for community or teacher representation, something that would not be conceded until 1980.[122]

Far from being secularist or antagonistic towards religious institutions, the VTA tended to reflect, more or less, the prevailing religious mood in the country. That was certainly the case in May 1957 when the executive agreed to commence its meetings with a prayer and in 1959 when, following the practice of similar groups, it agreed that the association should be consecrated to the Blessed Lady.[123] The decision was duly implemented at a mass celebrated by the archbishop of Dublin, John Charles McQuaid, despite a protest by a member from South Tipperary who pleaded that the position held by Mary in the Protestant tradition was such as to make the decision inappropriate in a non-confessional body.[124] By the early 1970s, however, the executive had ceased to pray formally—though its presidential chain would still carry the inscription 'For the greater glory of God'—and in 1973 the association may have been influenced by the prevailing ecumenical mood when it added a Protestant service to the congress agenda alongside the traditional congress mass. The following year both were replaced by a common prayer service.

In issues of national politics it also tended to take a middle route. In 21 June 1957 the Leitrim branch wrote to the executive looking for support for Ruairí Ó Brádaigh, a leading member of Sinn Féin who had been dismissed from his teaching post in Roscommon. This was not forthcoming. The 1972 congress considered fifteen resolutions relating to the upheavals in Northern Ireland. The president, Kevin McCarthy, proposed to the executive that it might support a scheme whereby Northern children caught up in the conflict could be placed with families in the South and attend local vocational schools. The executive endorsed this and advertised the scheme in Northern papers though it proved less popular than many expected.[125] More popular were a scheme whereby the association was able to give holidays to 1,300 Northern children in the summer of 1972 and another which distributed food and clothing through the North that Christmas.[126] In 1973 congress considered three resolutions on the North but none in 1974.

Throughout the 1950s, the greater part of the association's activity was concerned with second-level education. Nonetheless, as the body representative of teachers with responsibility for apprenticeship and higher technical education, it could not be unconcerned with the educational and training requirements that would stem from industrial expansion. Membership of international organisations gave officers an opportunity to observe developments elsewhere, and the tenets of the economics of education, a rapidly developing academic subdiscipline which sought to align the educational system more closely with the economy, soon found an echo on congress platforms.[127] Thus, when it was reported in 1956 that existing apprenticeship legislation might be amended, the executive commissioned a study of existing provisions and of developments elsewhere. Its recommendations sternly reflected the traditional view of the association: existing statutory provisions, lacking the power to make apprenticeship education and training compulsory, were inadequate; the general absence of goodwill by employers towards proper schemes of apprenticeship training served the needs of neither industry nor labour; the educational standard of entrants to apprenticeship was too low. The report led to a series of meetings with the Department of Industry and Commerce which provided the opportunity to make specific proposals, particularly on how compulsory day-release courses might be organised, and in late 1958 the association formed a joint committee with employer organisations to address the question of mandatory training.[128] As with similar initiatives in the past, this attempt at bilateralism produced disappointing results and led the association to pin its hopes on the impending legislation. The passing of the Apprenticeship Act 1959 provided for the formation of a new regulatory body, An Cheard Chomhairle. Central regulation by a body that could set standards and determine curriculum content had long been a demand of vocational teachers and there were hopes that An Cheard Chomhairle, representative of education, employers, labour and the public service, might facilitate much needed reform.

Following representations by the VTA, the association's president, John McDonald, was appointed to the new body, while several other members were asked to serve on its various subcommittees.[129] Together they constituted the association's committee on apprenticeship but its reports to successive congresses revealed that while An Cheard Chomhairle could act as a pressure group and be effective in formulating appropriate standards, it was unable to force either apprentices or employers to take advantage of an increasing number of courses. Another attempt to address the issue was undertaken in 1967 when the Industrial Training Act led to the establishment of a statutory training agency, An Chomhairle Oiliúna. Its formation marked a radical shift in policy. AnCO, as it was generally known, was given the power and the means to establish its own training facilities and that decision marked the beginning of a long process which would see vocational education committees become less involved in the provision of training courses.

Similarly, the association kept informed of and involved in the reform of higher technical education provision. Thus a resolution of the 1957 congress led to the setting up of a committee, on the financing and planning of technical education.[130] Liam McGrenera was a dynamic member of the committee, and in a wise and prophetic presidential address to the 1959 congress, he advocated the founding of regional technological colleges.[131] The executive then established a special subcommittee on higher technical education and took steps to ensure that it was represented on the government committee on the training of technicians. In 1960 Labhrás Ó Gotharaigh, an executive member, was appointed to the Commission on Higher Education, and in 1966 the general secretary was appointed to the Steering Committee on Technical Education where he played a significant role in formulating plans for the proposed regional technical colleges.[132] In setting out the foundations for the future form of technical education institutions, the decade from 1957 to 1967 proved decisive, and at each stage the association articulated its views through a succession of outstanding officers. The reforms of that period would lead to unprecedented growth in the number of students, teachers and institutions, and, in the following decades, a major alteration in the composition of the association's membership.

The end of an era

The VTA's recruitment of teachers from the privately owned colleges of higher education in 1962 broke a pattern established in 1917 when an association was formed to represent, exclusively, the employees of agricultural and technical instruction committees. In the late 1960s and early 1970s, the scope of the association broadened further with the recruitment of comprehensive and community school teachers. In deciding not to confine itself to the vocational sector, the VTA demonstrated trade unionism's tendency towards expansion and its own sensitivity to the general movement towards a unified and integrated school system. The process was formalised when a special congress on 3 February 1973 voted to extend the association to include, if required, teachers in all second-level, higher and further education institutions. A change in name became inevitable, and two months later a congress resolution submitted by the Sligo town branch sought to have the association renamed 'Irish Union of Teachers—Aontas Múinteoirí Éireann', while a Cork city branch resolution sought a change to 'Teachers' Union of Ireland'.[133] The latter resolution was adopted and immediately implemented.

The person who had overseen the transition, Charles McCarthy, had been granted leave of absence from the general secretaryship for two years from August 1972 to take up a research fellowship in Trinity College Dublin. As his leave came to an end he sought a further year but he also indicated that if granted that he would probably take up a different position at the end of the year. Though keen to facilitate McCarthy, the executive was reluctant to let the general secretaryship become the subject of continuing uncertainty. Leave was granted but on condition that McCarthy would vacate his post which would then be advertised. If McCarthy's hoped-for position failed to materialise he would be given the option of taking a half-time post with full pension rights.[134]

McCarthy had came to the association as it struggled to find its feet after a bitter upheaval in the ranks of vocational teachers. He found a small, impoverished body whose traditions of negotiation had been formed in the days of a leisurely and convivial corporatism. His sense of fair play and an instinctive desire to protect the rights of the weak were firmly anchored on his legal training and reinforced the strongly held belief of presidents such as Tom Carney, Liam McGrenera and Kevin

McCarthy that the VTA's fundamental duty was to resist any encroach-ment on the rights of its members. Charles McCarthy was intensely ambitious, in both a personal and a professional sense: he wanted to become a leading figure in the trade union movement of a modernising society and he also wanted to see his organisation become a fearless and efficient force on behalf of its members. In his own mind the progress of both became inextricably entwined. Because he was not always willing to delay change or to wait for a consensus he could appear impatient and even aloof, and thus he guided, encouraged and sometimes forced the transition from quasi-professional association to trade union. McCarthy believed that the VTA could be both an educational force and a fighting union. He was compassionate and humane and he had a strong social, if not socialist, vision. He rejected the ingrained paternal-ism of the vocational education committees and the unrelenting centralism of the Department of Education: if teachers had a role it would be as professionals and leaders as well as practitioners and hired employees. In either role they should have the full support of their col-leagues and progressive labour legislation. After nearly two decades much had been achieved by the union and its general secretary, and it was now time for both to move on.

Notes

1 T. J. Carney, 'Fifteen years after', in Cumann na nGairm-Mhúinteoirí, *Comhdháil bhliantuil* (Carrick-on-Shannon, 1967), p. 35.

2 *The Vocational Education Bulletin* (hereafter, *Bulletin*), 55 (March 1952), p. 1252.

3 *Ibid.*, p. 1261.

4 *Bulletin*, 57 (November 1952), p. 1314.

5 *Bulletin*, 58 (April 1953), pp. 1335–6.

6 *Ibid.*, p. 1339.

7 *Ibid.*, p. 1333.

8 ITUC, *Fifty-ninth general-secretary's report* (Dublin, 1953), pp. 31–2.

9 Archives Department, University College, Dublin (hereafter, ADUCD), TUI papers, TU 30/28 (5), 'Draft minutes of VEOO executive committee'.

10 IVEA Annual Congress, *Report*, 1953, p. 72.

11 ITUC, *Sixty-first general-secretary's report* (Dublin, 1955), pp. 27–8; ADUCD, TUI papers, TU 30/38 (7), 'Cumann Mhúinteoirí Gairm-Oideachais, minutes 16 August 1954'.

12 ADUCD, TUI papers, TU 30/38 (10), 'Eagraíocht na nGairm-Mhúinteoirí, Minutes of foundation committee'.

13 ADUCD, TUI papers, TU 30/38 (10, 9), 'Eagraíocht na nGairm-Mhúinteoirí,

insurance and miscellaneous'.

14 ADUCD, TUI papers, TU 30/1, 'Vocational Teacher's Association, Executive committee minute book' (hereafter, 'Minutes'), 20 June 1955.

15 'General secretary's report' (hereafter, 'Report'), in *Gairm*, 1, 10 (1958), p. 36.

16 ADUCD, TUI papers, TU 30/1 (1), 'Minutes', 21 June 1957.

17 'Report', in Cumann na nGairm-Mhúinteoirí, *Annual Congress: Gairm* (hereafter, 'Report'), 1967, p. 4.

18 Liam Trundle, 'Building group', in Vocational Teachers' Association, *Annual congress* (Kinsale, 1969), p. 23.

19 Aontas Múinteoirí Éireann, *1976 Handbook*, pp. 14–15.

20 'Report', in *Gairm*, 1, 6 (1957), p. 31.

21 ADUCD, TUI papers, TU 30/5 (1), 'Minutes', 24 October 1969.

22 'Report', 1971, pp. 66–70.

23 'Report', 1972, p. 24.

24 'Report', 1965, p. 23.

25 'Report', in *Gairm*, 2, 4 (1961), p. 39.

26 'Report', in *Gairm*, 1, 10 (1958), p. 35.

27 Vocational Teachers' Association, *Annual congress agenda* (hereafter, *Agenda*), 1963, p. 37.

28 'Report and recommendations to the executive committee and to congress of the special committee established by congress, 1967', printed as appendix 1 in *Agenda*, 1968, pp. 40–7.

29 'Report', 1968, p. 8.

30 'Report', 1965, p. 1.

31 ADUCD, TUI papers, TU 30/1 (1), 'Minutes', 7 October 1955.

32 'Report', in *Gairm*, 1, 6 (1957), p. 32; 'Report', in *Gairm*, 1, 19 (1960), p. 37; Marie Brady, 'Joint consultation: how it works in Dublin', in Cumann na nGairm-Mhúinteoirí *Annual congress* (Dublin, 1968), pp. 51–2.

33 'Report', in *Gairm*, 3, 4 (1962), p. 24.

34 *Agenda*, 1973, p. 54.

35 'Report', 1972, p. 15.

36 *Agenda*, 1963, p. 38.

37 'Report', 1964, p. 15.

38 'Report', 1967, p. 14.

39 *Agenda*, 1968, p. 28.

40 *Agenda*, 1969, p. 30.

41 ADUCD, TUI papers, TU 30/5 (2), 'Minutes', 1 July 1971.

42 *Agenda*, 1972, p. 49.

43 *Agenda*, 1973, p. 50.

44 ADUCD, TUI papers, TU 30/1 (1), 'Minutes', 7 October 1955.

45 'Report', 1973, p. 10.

46 'Report', in *Gairm*, 4, 3 (1963), p. 23.

47 'Report', 1968, p. 7.

48 'Report', 1973, p. 9.

49 'Report', 1968, p. 24.

50 'Report', 1969, p. 20.

51 *Agenda*, 1972, p. 48; *Agenda*, 1973, p. 50.

52 ADUCD, TUI papers, TU 30/1 (1), 'Minutes', 7 October 1955.

53 'Report', in *Gairm*, 1, 6 (1957), p. 24.

54 'Report', in *Gairm*, 1, 10 (1958), p. 29.

55 ADUCD, TUI papers, TU 30/39 (3), 'Department of Education to General Secretary, 9 December 1957'.

56 Teachers' Salaries Committee, *Reports and appendices presented to the Minister for Education* (Dublin, 1960), p. 4; ADUCD, TUI papers, TU 30/38 (7), 'Teachers' Salaries Committee file'.

57 Teachers' Salaries Committee, *Reports and appendices*, pp. 29–32.

58 *Ibid.*, pp. 22–36.

59 *Ibid.*, p. 11.

60 John Coolahan, *The ASTI and post-primary education in Ireland 1909–1984* (Dublin, 1984), pp. 237–8.

61 Charles McCarthy, *Decade of upheaval* (Dublin, 1973), p. 204.

62 ADUCD, TUI papers, TU 30/4 (2), 'Minutes', 14 October 1967.

63 Tribunal on Teacher Salaries, *Report presented to the Minister for Education* (1968), p. 5.

64 Coolahan, *The ASTI*, p. 274.

65 Tribunal on Teacher Salaries, *Report*, p. 24.

66 *Ibid.*, p. 21.

67 *Ibid.*, pp. 25–8.

68 *Ibid.*, pp. 46–8, 50–1.

69 *Ibid.*, pp. 51–4.

70 *Ibid.*, pp. 9–18.

71 McCarthy, *Decade of upheaval*, p. 208.

72 *Ibid.*, p. 206; ADUCD, TUI papers, TU 30/64 (4), 'Salary negotiations; posts of responsibility'.

73 'Report of special congress', appendix I to 'Report', 1969, pp. 31–2.

74 'Report', 1969, pp. 5–16.

75 Coolahan, *The ASTI*, pp. 281–5.

76 'Report', 1969, p. 1.

77 'Report', 1970, p. 18.

78 ADUCD, TUI papers, TU 30/66 (1), 'Narrative of dispute with Department of Education arising from Ryan Report', pp. 7–12.

79 *Ibid.*, p. 18.

80 'Report', 1971, pp. 12–14.

81 For details see, Teachers' Salaries Committee, *Reports and appendices*, pp. 80–1.

82 ADUCD, TUI papers, TU 30/74 (1), 'Posts of responsibility in colleges'.

83 'Report', 1969, p. 18.

84 ADUCD, TUI papers, TU 30/32 (3), 'Conciliation council for teachers: agreed reports 5/72 and 7/72'.

85 'Report', 1973, p. 4.

86 Commission on the Status of Women, *Report to the Minister for Finance* (Dublin, 1972*)*, pp. 16–19.

87 ADUCD, TUI papers, TU 30/2 (2), 'Women's advisory committee, minutes, 27 February, 1960'.

88 'Report', in *Gairm*, 1, 19 (1960), pp. 39–40.

89 *Agenda*, 1960, p. 18.

90 'Report', in *Gairm*, 3, 4 (1962), p. 16.

91 *Agenda*, 1967, p. 39.

92 *Agenda*, 1969, p. 30.

93 Eoin O'Leary, 'The Irish National Teachers' Organisation and the marriage bar of women national teachers 1933–1958', in *Saothar*, 12 (1987), pp. 47–53.

94 'Report', in *Gairm*, 1, 19 (1960), pp. 39–40.

95 'Report', in *Gairm*, 4, 3 (1963), p. 53.

96 *Agenda*, 1964, p. 34; 'Report', 1965, p. 14.

97 *Agenda*, 1965, pp. 34–5.

98 *Agenda*, 1967, pp. 50–1.

99 'Report', 1969, p. 4.

100 'Report', in *Gairm*, 3, 4 (1962), p. 19.

101 'Report', in *Gairm*, 1, 19 (1960), p. 37; *Gairm*, 2, 4 (1961), pp. 28–9.

102 ADUCD, TUI papers, TU 30/1 (1), 'Minutes', 16 February 1957.

103 Charles McCarthy, 'Vindication', in *Gairm*, 1, 4 (1957), p. 17.

104 ADUCD, TUI papers, TU 30/40 (2), 'Wexford dispute notes'.

105 *Ibid.*

106 'Report', in *Gairm*, 1, 10 (1958), p. 37.

107 'Report', 1972, p. 24; ADUCD, TUI papers, TU 30/40 (3), 'Wexford dispute notes'.

108 ADUCD, TUI papers, TU 30/88 (9), 'Memorandum of evidence at vocational teacher's inquiry in Wexford from the 13 to 16 February inclusive'.

109 'Report', 1974, p.14.

110 *Ibid.*, pp. 14–16.

111 *Gairm*, 7, 2 (1965), p. 31; *Gairm*, 6, 1 (1967).

112 'Report', in *Gairm*, 1, 19 (1960), pp. 41–3.

113 Liam McGrenera, 'Presidential address', in *Gairm*, 1, 13 (1959), p. 12.

114 Charles McCarthy, 'What our members think', in *Gairm*, 6, 4 (1965), p. 13.

115 William O'Brien-Crowley, 'Equal opportunities', in *Gairm*, 1, 16 (1960), pp. 27–8.

116 McCarthy, 'What our members think', p. 13.

117 Tom Carney, 'Abolish the Group', in *Gairm*, 6, 4 (1965), p. 9.

118 McCarthy, 'What our members think', p. 13.

119 'Report', in *Gairm*, 7, 2 (1965), p. 8.

120 'Report', 1969, pp. 24–6; 'Report', 1970, pp. 18–22.

121 'Report', 1972, p. 29.

122 Teachers' Union of Ireland, 'Community schools policy document', printed as appendix iii, in 'Report', 1974, pp. 24–5.

123 ADUCD, TUI papers, TU 30/1 (1), 'Minutes', 21 June 1957; 'Report', in *Gairm*, 1, 19 (1960), p. 41.

124 *Gairm*, 2, 6 (1961), p. 61.

125 'Report', 1972, p. 26.

126 'Report', 1973, p. 19.

127 For examples see, 'Report', in *Gairm*, 1, 10 (1958), pp. 34–7; *Gairm*, 1, 19 (1960), pp. 37–44.

128 'Report', in *Gairm*, 1, 6 (1957), pp. 32–3.

129 'Report', in *Gairm*, 1, 19 (1960), p. 44.

130 'Report', in *Gairm*, 1, 10 (1958), pp. 35–8.

131 'Report', in *Gairm*, 1, 19 (1960), p. 38.

132 ADUCD, TUI papers, TU 30/61 (1, 2), 'Steering Committee on Technical Education'; also, Steering Committee on Technical Education, *Report to the Minister for Education on regional technical colleges* (Dublin, 1967).

133 *Agenda*, 1973, p. 51.

134 'Report', 1974, p. 4.

8. 'Clergy, Politicians and Mutual Friends': The Vocational Education Committee 1930–1992

Eilis Ward

The governance of vocational schools sets them apart from most other Irish schools for two important reasons. First, they are publicly owned and managed by representatives appointed by the local authorities. Second, they are, in principle, non-denominational. Though a number of technical schools established in pre-independent Ireland had been owned by local committees and had promoted a non-denominational ethos, the Vocational Education Act 1930 became the means whereby a major expansion of public educational provision was attained. By indicating that the new state would not automatically leave the control and ownership of schooling to private, generally church-owned and managed, institutions, the legislation revealed a degree of independence on the part of the state and a willingness to challenge deeply rooted assumptions. At the same time the traditions and practices of the churches had given them a more-than-passing interest in the technical school and that interest would be brought to bear on the affairs of its successor. Thus the history of vocational education provides an opportunity to examine the exercise of local secular power for educational ends and its interaction with other agencies that have an interest in education. It is with this level of operation—the politics of local co-operation and conflict over resources—that this chapter is concerned.

The Vocational Education Act 1930

The 1930 Act handed responsibility for the development of the vocational sector to committees in specified local government jurisdictions. In giving local authorities that power the Act was adhering to the principle of local democratic control introduced in the Agriculture and Technical Instruction Act in 1899. However, unlike other committees of the local authority the vocational education committee had autonomous legislation, so that once formed, it would operate as a 'body corporate' independently of its parent body with power 'to acquire and hold land for the purposes of its powers and duties'.[1] The Act required that a committee set up schools to be funded by a combination of a compulsory local rate and grants from the national exchequer. The committee would be distinct from other local government committees in other non-formal ways. Many councillors would regard it as the most important forum after the council itself, and the social prestige attached to sitting on a committee dealing with education should not be discounted. It bestowed on members the power to allocate jobs and promotions within the school system. Its members operated in a sphere that generated a great deal of local interest and consequent press coverage, something that no public representative would have spurned.

Demographic changes and redrawing of local government jurisdictions would give an evolving profile to the committees. The legislation provided for the organisation of vocational education in thirty-eight jurisdictions: five cities (Cork, Dublin, Galway, Limerick and Waterford); six towns (Bray, Drogheda, Dún Laoghaire, Sligo, Tralee and Wexford) and twenty-seven counties—Tipperary, with its north and south ridings, constituting two. A new committee would be appointed following each local election and its period of office would coincide with that of its parent authority. In the period up to 1953, an election was provided for every third year, and the Local Elections Act of 1953 made provision for an election every fifth year. However, legislative reforms, the need to avoid clashes with general elections and the exigencies of political life have meant that, in practice, local government elections and the subsequent formation of committees have been frequently postponed: of the twelve elections due between 1928 and 1991, eight were postponed.

The size of each committee has been determined by the status of the local authority concerned. A city or town committee has fourteen members, not less than five and not more than eight of whom have to be elected members of its parent council. A county committee is similarly constituted, with provision for the addition of two members for any urban district council within the county, up to a maximum of four councils, and for counties with more than four urban district councils, an addition of one member to represent each council. These latter nominees may or may not be elected members of their nominating councils. In selecting members who are not elected councillors, a council is expected to name individuals to represent the local business and commercial sectors, trade unions and education. Such members are formally referred to as 'added members', and their purpose is to extend the democratic control of the new schools through the local population. While fourteen is the lower number of committee members, there is in theory no upper limit. The Cork county committee is the largest with twenty-three members, made up of the fourteen nominated by Cork county council and one from each of the county's nine urban district councils.

Thus the constitution of committees has allowed for a sizeable number of non-councillor, or added members. The proportion could vary from 43 per cent to 64 per cent of its members in the case of a city or town committee and from 26 per cent to 78 per cent in the case of a county committee. In practice, however, parent councils have tended to take up their maximum allocation of councillor seats and councillors have always formed a majority on the various committees. The terms of the legislation have ensured that county committees have had a much larger membership than city committees. This highlights a general feature of local government— inequitable ratios of representation between city and country. The Dublin city committee, with the largest budget and the greatest number of schools in the country, would have had great difficulty achieving a balanced representative spread in its committee of fourteen. In sharp contrast, both Sligo town and Wexford town—with but one school each—have always had a committee similar in size and constitution to that of Dublin.

For most of their history, the political complexion of committees has reflected that of the dominant political group on the parent council. When the Cork county council met in late September 1930 to appoint a committee the members agreed that they would allocate eight places to council members, the maximum allowed under the legislation, and that the councillors thus chosen would each represent one of the county's eight electoral districts. Having considered whether the eight seats should be allocated equally amongst the four parties on the council or in proportion to party strength, the chairman ruled that the councillors from each electoral district would together choose a representative. Five were elected unanimously and three following a poll: all were from Fianna Fáil, the party controlling the council.[2] In Limerick county, each of the councils elected from 1928 to 1955 had a Fianna Fáil majority and that complexion was reflected in the political profile of the subsequent vocational education committees. In Leitrim, Fianna Fáil controlled the council between 1942 and 1960, and during that period between six and eight of its councillors were appointed to the committee with a single seat being given on occasion to a Clann na Poblachta or an independent councillor. Following the 1960 election Fianna Fáil was still the largest party, but a coalition of the other parties saw the chair of the council and the majority of committee places pass to Fine Gael, a pattern that was repeated in 1967 and 1972.

In choosing non-councillors for the added places, political affiliation, whether demonstrated or assumed, was generally taken into account. For example, in Clare during the 1960s and 1970s a meeting of the Fianna Fáil Comhairle Dáil Ceantair prior to the inaugural meeting of a new council would decide the party's nominations for the chair and the various committees, including the vocational education committee, and in selecting non-councillors as added members, party membership and support remained a prime consideration.[3] In Kerry following the 1979 election the Fianna Fáil councillors organised a similar 'grand slam' and defended their action with the traditional justification that other councils 'had done the same thing'.[4] Public ownership may have been an originating notion of vocational education, but the everyday reality was marked by political partisanship.

Such monolithic reproduction of dominant parties characterised vocational education committees until the Local Government (Reorganisation) Act 1985 made provision for the allocation of committee membership in proportion to party strength on the parent council. Subsequently the ratio of councillors to committee places would determine the number who would combine to vote. For example, on a council of thirty-two members each group of four would nominate one of the eight councillor members of a committee. Thus a party with four members on a council would have one representative, a party with twelve would have three, while groupings of independents and parties with very few members could combine to elect a proportionate number of representatives. Though the legislation is discretionary, it has meant that minority parties can invoke it in their favour.

The 1930 Act did not, in contrast, leave much room for local manoeuvring for the position of a committee's chief executive officer, who would be selected by the Local Appointments Commission. The job could be described loosely as being to 'propose schemes and implement policy'.[5] While the management functions of the position were clearly specified, it was clear also that as long as the committee members did not act outside the terms of the legislation, or outside any regulations and requirements imposed by the Minister for Education, a chief executive officer's control over the members would be circumscribed by the nature of a committee. In particular, unlike other local government chief executives such as county managers, the chief executive officer in vocational education has no 'reserved functions' enabling action independent of a committee. Furthermore, while the state has allocated executive functions in financial matters to the office, it has not been given absolute responsibility for expenditure. Though chief executive officers generally have been recruited from the ranks of senior teaching staff, their function has always been to operate procedures drawn up by the state, and in that sense to act as its representative.

The committees and the churches

The principle of local democratic control of education directly challenged the assumption that religious authorities were the appropriate managers of the school system. As a consequence, the Catholic Church articulated its interest and sought to obtain assurances that what it viewed as its prerogatives would not be diminished. The manner in which the state deferred to the Catholic Church in the formulation of regulations for vocational education is documented in chapter 4 and it will be argued here that the ease with which the churches seemed to accept vocational education may have been a function of the extent to which clergymen were able to occupy a substantial portion of committee seats and the extent to which they were appointed chairmen.

One quarter of the members appointed to the inaugural committees in 1930 were clergymen.[6] Successive elections saw the proportion gradually reduce, and in 1970 it stood at one-fifth of the total. Given that councillors generally took the maximum number of seats allowed—anywhere between 57 per cent and 73 per cent of the total—the size of the clerical presence is even more significant; indeed on some committees most, if not all, the added or non-councillor members were clergymen. In Cork county, for example, six of the eight added members appointed in 1930 were clergymen, by 1942 all the added members were clergymen, in 1952 ten out of eleven were clergymen and in 1962 all the added members were clergymen. In Leitrim, all the added members appointed in 1930 were clergymen. In Longford, six out of nine added members of the committee appointed in 1930 were clergymen, in 1952 seven of eight added were clergymen and in 1962 all the added members were clergymen. In Limerick county, four of the six added members were clergy throughout the period from 1930 to 1950. In Roscommon, four out of six added members appointed in 1930 were clergymen and on each committee from 1934 to 1967 all the added members were clergy. In such counties it would have been easy for the clerical members to dominate proceedings and for the committee to operate almost as a quasi-religious body. In Galway county, during the ten-year period from 1949 to 1959, for example, clerics were in a majority at over half of all meetings of the committee.[7] At the other end of the spectrum, but somewhat exceptionally, lay Dublin, which alone of all committees did not have a single clergyman member between 1930 and 1950. The pattern was broken in that year when following representation by Archbishop McQuaid, Canon John Fitzpatrick was unanimously elected chairman of the committee and to all twelve of its local subcommittees.[8]

In 1930, twenty-five of the thirty-eight committees elected a clergyman to the chair. The number rose to a peak in 1950 when thirty chairmen were clergymen. In 1960 twenty-five clergymen were thus elected, and each subsequent election saw further reductions in the number of clergy being elected to the chair. In 1991 clergymen were elected to the chair in only three committees, Cork county, Louth and Waterford city, thereby maintaining an unbroken tradition of clerical occupancy of the chair in those committees since 1930. The Cork county committee elected Fr Florence McCarthy to the chair in 1930 and he continued to hold that position unopposed until he resigned in 1961. Following the appointment of the vice-chairman, Monsignor Sheedy, as his successor, the committee unanimously decided that in future the choice of chairman would be left to the clergy, stating that it was the committee's desire that the chair should always be occupied by a clergyman.[9] The clergy, in turn, initiated the custom of selecting the senior Catholic clergyman amongst them. Galway county committee elected an t-Athair M. Mac Branain in 1931 and continued to return him unopposed until he retired in 1967. Clare elected an 85-year-old priest to chair its first committee because of his 'ripe experience', and from 1932 until his death in 1961 unanimously returned Canon P. J. Vaughan to that position.[10] The Clare case also throws up an example of the extent to which deference to the clergy could mute real political differences: the committee was almost entirely Fianna Fáil during this period, while Canon Vaughan was an ardent and well-known Fine Gael supporter. Against the general trend in this period, four committees— Limerick county, Limerick city, Wexford town and Dublin county—never had a clerical chairman. While uncontested long-term occupancy of the chair by a clergyman was normal in many committees, it was not exclusively so. In Limerick city an independent city councillor P. J. Donnellan—who had first joined the technical instruction committee in 1919—was elected to the chair of the vocational education committee in 1930, and his occupancy continued without contest until he was dismissed along with his fellow committee members following a ministerial inquiry into their conduct in 1967.

The equation of chairman with clergyman rarely extended to include one who was not Roman Catholic. The only exception was in Bray, where between 1930 and 1950 a Protestant clergyman held the chair. The marked absence of Protestant clerical chairmen reflected the low number of non-Catholic clergy appointed to the committees. Twenty-two Protestant clergymen were appointed in 1930; the number declined gradually thereafter, until 1960 when sixteen were appointed. The 1967 election saw the number again reach twenty-two and on the formation of the committees after the 1991 election the number had again declined to sixteen. Thus most committees have not had a Protestant clergyman member for the greater part of their history and eight have never had one. Louth, Monaghan and Kildare reflect an aberration in the national pattern, having had two Protestant clergymen in office simultaneously. As counties with higher numbers of non-Catholic students, the record of Monaghan and Louth is not surprising, though it was not repeated in other areas with similar denominational profiles such as Cavan and Donegal. If there was a Protestant clerical presence on a committee, it was usually in the form of a single token member, and by that measure, the Protestant churches achieved their greatest extent of representation during the eighteen-year period from 1967 to 1985 with a clergyman on twenty-one of the thirty-eight committees.

The primacy of the Catholic priest in the governance of vocational education reflected a deep-rooted cultural trait. The national ethos in the formative years of the state would ensure that his church's leadership, morally and otherwise, would be generally sought and rarely ques-

Table 8.1: Lay and clerical membership of vocational education committees 1932–92

	1932	*1942*	*1952*	*1962*	*1972*	*1982*	*1992*
Catholic clergy	132	126	115	118	100	50	35
Protestant clergy	22	17	19	16	22	21	16
Total clergy	154	43	134	134	122	71	51
Total lay	467	478	487	487	499	550	570
Lay proportion	75%	77%	78%	78%	80%	89%	92%
Committees with:							
– Catholic clergy	36	35	36	37	38	30	26
– Protestant clergy	21	16	18	16	21	21	16
– Neither	0	1	0	0	0	7	11
– Clerical chairperson	26	27	31	26	18	14	3
– Lay chairperson	12	11	7	12	20	24	35

Source: Table is based on data extracted from membership lists supplied by the respective committees and chief executive officers.

tioned. Such precedence was reflected and given legal expression in the 'special position' accorded to the Catholic Church in the 1937 constitution, and in the case of vocational education explains the ease with which successive Ministers for Education were able to defer to episcopal demands. In such circumstances it is easy to understand how councillor members, unwilling to share membership of the committee with those of a different party, had no difficulty in forming a partnership with and even relinquishing their power to clerical members. Clergymen were widely regarded as the appropriate representatives of local educational interests, sometimes to the exclusion of all other interests. As in the case of the Galway county committee, it could be said that councillors willingly eschewed their democratic responsibility to attend meetings in the belief that the clergy would competently discharge the work of the committee.

The committees formed in 1967 saw a significant decrease in the number of clergymen appointed and each subsequent election saw a further decrease. Seven of the committees formed in 1979 were without clergymen and by 1991 the number had risen to eleven. Of the remaining committees, eight had but one clerical member, eleven had two and seven had three; Cork county—a striking deviation from the general trend—had five. There was nothing in the pattern of earlier decades to hint at such a sudden change. It occurred just as vocational education entered a period of expansion and at what might have seemed an inopportune time for the clergy to relinquish their surveillance of a substantial segment of education. It may not have been entirely within their power to maintain their previous level of membership, however, for if the governance of education had been important for the churches it was also of growing importance for an increasing number of lay citizens eager to hold a committee place. The educational reforms of the 1960s caught the attention of many; schooling had attained a heightened significance for parents and its importance was not lost either on a teaching force that was better organised and gaining a more acute sense of its professional status, or on those local political interests whose role up to that point had been relatively passive. In such circumstances a challenge to established patterns was not entirely surprising.

One such case was Cork county council, which had taken a decision in the 1940s to allocate all of its six added places to clergymen nominated by bishops whose dioceses lay in the county. Thus for the formation of successive committees the council sought two nominations from the Catholic bishop of Cork and Ross, two from the Catholic bishop of Cloyne, one from the Catholic bishop of Kerry and one from the Church of Ireland bishop of Cork, Cloyne and Ross. In 1991, in response to ministerial pressure to nominate a parent and a teacher representative to the committee, the councillors, having considered the option of allocating two places held by themselves, decided instead to reduce the number of episcopal nominees from six to four.

In Limerick the custom of electing clergy unopposed and of returning the sitting clerical members had been established during the first two decades of vocational education. Thus in 1956 on the death of Canon James Wall his nephew Fr Tom Wall was nominated to fill his place. However, because certain 'undertakings' had been given to the Irish Countrywomen's Association (ICA), the county council postponed the appointment until the position could be explained to the women.[11] The subsequent meeting was informed that Fr Wall would not be a candidate and the ICA nominee was duly elected.[12] When a clerical vacancy occurred in 1961, a councillor urged that the nomination of clergymen to vacancies should, as a matter of course, be made by the bishop. The point was reinforced in 1965 when the bishop's secretary wrote to the council stating that, since the priest had acted as the bishop's 'representative', the 'proper' procedure was to request the bishop to nominate a successor.[13] The council then proceeded to appoint the bishop's nominee.[14] When a clergyman resigned from the Limerick committee in 1974, two nominations for his replacement—a councillor and the bishop himself—were made. The impasse was broken when, following a recess, the meeting was informed by a councillor that he had just telephoned the bishop who stated that while he did not want to sit on the committee himself, he wished to have his nominee appointed. This was confirmed by the county manager who informed the council that the bishop had telephoned him with a nominee who was duly appointed.[15] In 1983, following the death of a clergyman member, another vacancy arose and the county secretary wrote to the bishop pointing to the tradition that the vacancy would be filled on his nomination.[16] The understanding between the county council and the bishop ended in 1991 when the bishop's nominee, as one of seven proposed for six committee places, had to be voted on along with the others.[17]

It would be a mistake to see such an incident as part of a general movement that might lead eventually to a complete declericalisation of committees. Old patterns, while not as clearly drawn or as pervasive as in the past, remain and continue to determine the composition of some committees. Thus, following the 1994 urban district council elections when Enniscorthy's new council met to make two nominations to the county vocational education committee, it was assumed by many of the members that the nomination of the town's senior Catholic cleric would follow precedent and go unchallenged. The clergyman in question had informed the council before the meeting that he would be available to serve as he had in the past. When a councillor attempted to challenge what appeared to him as a predictable and unfruitful deference, his appeal for support from his fellow councillors for an alternative nomination was met, it was reported, with shock and silence.[18]

The limits of representation

Like the Protestant population, female representation in the governance of vocational education remained marginal. In 1930, eighteen women were appointed to committees alongside 603 men. Subsequent elections saw the number of women decrease and reach its lowest point in 1960 when fifteen women—equivalent to 2.4 per cent of the total— were appointed. Twenty-six of the thirty-eight committees formed in 1930 were composed entirely of men, and in 1960, the number of women-less committees was twenty-two. Such patterns reflected a general absence of women from public life during the half-century after independence. Very few women stood for election and most of those who did and were successful took over a seat left vacant by a male relative. The handful who contested a seat in their own right had little success. During that period the proportion of Dáil deputies who were women varied between 1.9 per cent and 4.1 per cent, and it was not until the election of six women to the Dáil in 1977 that the benchmark established by five of their predecessors in 1923 was exceeded. The pattern was similar in local government. In 1934 thirteen women were elected to councils and corporations, and when twenty-six were elected in 1967 they held but 3.2 per cent of all seats.[19]

During the 1970s the number of women appointed to committees rose steadily but it is not possible to say conclusively if the moulds formed over the previous half-century had been broken. Fifty women were appointed in 1980, and following the formation of committees in 1991 the number of women members had increased to fifty-seven. The possibility that women were now being regarded as full committee members, equal to men in status and role, rather than as a token female presence was indicated perhaps by the election of women to the chair of three committees in 1991. Despite that achievement, the proportion of women members on vocational education committees (9.1 per cent) trailed somewhat behind the proportion in local government councils (11.4 per cent) and in the national parliament (12 per cent). Up to and including the committees formed in 1991 no woman had ever been appointed to a committee in Mayo, Drogheda, Tralee or Waterford city. No woman had ever held the post of chief executive officer of a committee, though in Leitrim a woman principal, Molly Kerrigan, acted as chief executive at various times between 1939 and 1969. The absence of women chief executives may not have been entirely for want of trying. In Clare in 1930 four candidates applied for the vacant post. When the committee met to make the appointment it decided to first exclude the sole woman candidate, on the grounds that as a women she would have lacked 'sociability', a quality it regarded as essential in a chief executive officer.[20]

It could be argued that since the bulk of committee members came from local authorities and were expected to be representative of them, a lack of female members was inevitable. Notwithstanding this, the nomination of women as added members might have facilitated their incorporation in a process where the gender-based curriculum would have benefited from their contribution as teachers, as homemakers, as trade unionists or as farmers. Nor were women's interest groups silent on the issue. During the 1950s and 1960s a few county councils, notably Carlow and Limerick, responded to pressure from the ICA and nominated a member to the local vocational education committee.[21] In general, however, the record suggests that for most of their history, neither the councils nor the committees regarded a substantial female presence as being essential to the concerns of vocational education. The notion that women might indeed have some part to play in the governance of vocational education, but not just yet, was tellingly revealed in the decision by Waterford county council in June 1945, having finalised the appointment of a completely male committee, to recommend that 'a Lady be appointed on the committee in the event of a vacancy occurring'.[22]

In terms of representation of other interests in the governance of vocational education, teachers were an obvious category for inclusion.

Table 8.2: Male and female membership of vocational education committees 1932–92

	1932	1942	1952	1962	1972	1982	1992
Male	603	604	603	606	605	571	564
Female	18	17	18	15	16	50	57
Female %		2.8%	2.7%	2.8%	2.4%	2.6%	8.1%	9.1%
Committees with no female member	26	25	23	22	21	8	8

Source: Table is based on data extracted from membership lists supplied by the respective committees and chief executive officers.

Consequently many councils looked for non-councillor members in the ranks of local primary school teachers. Thus two teachers were nominated for appointment to the Cork county committee in 1930. So also were eleven of the county's senior Catholic clergy and two university professors, making a total of fifteen nominations for six seats. Despite such august competition the two teachers were comfortably elected.[23] When Limerick county council met to elect a committee in 1930, four clergymen, five primary school teachers and a former councillor were nominated for the six added places. On the first vote the four clergymen and the former councillor were unanimously elected *en bloc* and a second vote was held to select one of the teachers.[24] The practice of electing teachers seems to have peaked at the formation of the 1950 committees when, for example, four primary school teachers were appointed in Westmeath, three each in Kerry, Tipperary north riding and Meath, and two each in Galway county, Laois and Mayo. A primary school teacher was appointed to the Limerick county committee in 1950 and reappointed in 1955, and when he died in 1960 the Irish National Teachers' Organisation (INTO) formally nominated a successor who served until 1974.[25] The practice continued, but as with the case of other bodies such as the ICA which also sought to have a member appointed, the INTO had to compete with other, often better organised, groups. In Limerick city, members of the trades council, the umbrella of the local labour movement, were effortlessly nominated up to 1967 while the Gaelic League formally nominated a member between 1942 and 1951.[26]

During the early part of the century a highly devolved form of educational governance existed in the 'school area' or local committees formed under the technical education committees. In counties such as Cork and Wexford, where technical education was relatively well established, such committees became prominent in the initiation of new courses and centres. Teachers were often active members and it was usual that the local technical school principal would act as secretary. The principle of local committees was maintained in the 1930 Act which made provision for subcommittees whose members did not have to be committee members, and in some parts of the country this was used to set up local committees. Thus at its first meeting in 1930 the Cork county committee established a subcommittee in each urban district and in the other towns of the county, sixteen in all. It decided that the parish priest—*ex officio*—should in each case be chairman.[27] Each acted as an advisory body to the parent committee. They had little authority and a power that was mainly symbolic, and they had almost ceased to function when they were superseded by new school committees in 1974.

Vocational teachers as employees of a 'local authority' were themselves excluded from membership of committees by the Local Government Act 1925. From the mid-1950s the Vocational Teachers' Association (VTA) sought the formation of 'joint bodies' composed of members of the association and members of committees in an attempt to promote effective communication. Despite a degree of hesitation on the part of the Irish Vocational Education Association (IVEA)—the central organisation of vocational education—many such committees were formed and in a parallel movement some committees welcomed the appointment of a teacher to observe meetings. The Department of Education sought the formation of school committees composed of parents and committee members following the conclusion of a dispute in Wexford in 1974, using the provisions of section 21 of the 1930 Act. In 1977 the Worker Participation (State Enterprises) Act provided for one-third worker representation on the board of state-sponsored bodies, and in 1984 the Teachers' Union of Ireland (TUI) launched a campaign to have the provisions of the Act extended to include committee employees. That year the Minister for Education's *Programme for action in education 1984–87* contained a proposal to legislate for teacher representation on committees.[28] The union's campaign—a vigorous lobbying of public representatives and departmental officials—continued through 1985 and 1986. In early 1987 the executive sought a meeting with the minister on proposed restructuring of committees and argued that the one-third worker participation provided for in 1977 be extended to vocational education. Local authority elections which would lead to a reconstituting of committees were scheduled for the summer of 1991. The congress that year called on all political parties to promote the nomination of TUI representatives to committees. A Fine Gael private member's bill to amend the legislation regulating committee membership to ensure teacher and parent representation was defeated. While the campaign continued, the minister, Mary O'Rourke, requested the local authorities to nominate one parent and one vocational teacher to the vocational education committee.[29] Of the thirty-three committees which were formed in 1991, all but Cavan, Kerry, Laois, Leitrim, Limerick and Sligo appointed union representatives.

There is then evidence that recent decades have seen an alteration in the composition of committees. Women, vocational school teachers and lay people are now more likely to be committee members and more likely to hold positions of authority within the structure than was previously the case. Nonetheless, committees remain largely as they had been conceived, a microcosm of dominant local political interests. In that they remain representative of the business, farming and professional interests that dominate the local councils and corporations and are less likely to have the less skilled manual workers, the lower paid or the unemployed as members. Committee membership is still largely drawn from the social groups whose own children attend secondary schools and who have reaped the benefit of participation in that sector. The vocational school, attended disproportionately by the children of the less advantaged, is under the immediate control of individuals whose own educational aspirations and interests lie elsewhere. As Sheelagh Drudy and Kathleen Lynch have argued, they are unlikely to want to upset the status quo or to seek a radical alteration in prevailing patterns of educational provision and outcome.[30]

Jobs from the boys

The appointment of teachers is widely regarded as a defining prerogative of a school authority, and the autonomy which the 1930 Act gave to committees is exemplified by their power to appoint teachers. Given the Act's emphasis on the local nature of the service, such freedom seemed entirely appropriate. The architects of vocational education expected that committees would shape the contours of education to local needs, thereby creating a powerful resource in a developing economy. They believed that a monolithic structure in which power was wielded centrally and hierarchically might be contrary to local economic interests and to the interests of future employees. But the adaptability of the Act, combined with the traditions of localist political brokerage, had the potential to create dissension and alienation amongst teachers and unease amongst political rivals.

Ironically it was the very democratic nature of the committees themselves which made them so vulnerable to manipulation, for while the state could control any partisan tendency in its own employees, through agencies such as the Civil Service Commission and the Local Appointments Commission, it could not so easily control the actions of elected representatives. Consequently, the aspiration to develop a meritocratic and universalistic public ethos in vocational education was continually challenged in its formative years by the clientelist culture of constituency politics.[31] This tension was particularly acute because committee members had been given a high degree of freedom in making appointments and defining conditions of service. The manner in which this freedom was used had the potential to take the highly charged and contentious issues of favouritism and undue influence to the forefront of national political life, and such a possibility became all the greater at a time of educational expansion characterised by a growing sense of professional solidarity amongst teachers.

An appointment by the Limerick city committee in April 1951 revealed the potential for conflict within the system. When the committee met to appoint a teacher of home economics the chief executive gave details of three candidates having the stipulated qualifications, and in answer to a question revealed that one was from Limerick city, another from Limerick county and the third from Mayo. In proposing the city woman for the post the chairman gave as his reason his knowledge of her late father, who between 1930 and 1951 had been the committee's chief executive officer. He stated that he would be lacking in appreciation of his great work and in his regard and friendship for him if he did not propose his daughter for the job. In seconding the proposal another committee member argued that it would be in the interests of the woman's widowed mother if her daughter were appointed and able to return home. Opposing the appointment, Councillor Michael O'Malley stated that the family of the teacher from County Limerick had been associated with the county for almost a century, and without giving any other argument he felt that 'in all the circumstances' she was the better candidate. The third candidate, the Mayo woman, was without a proposer.

At that point Dr Bourke, observing the meeting as a senior inspector of the Department of Education, intervened to state that while the committee had the right to appoint any suitably qualified candidate he was under the impression that the committee had tentatively agreed, from a sense of gratitude and loyalty, to appoint the daughter of its late chief executive, and he appealed that it proceed to do so unanimously. Councillor O'Malley pointed out that no such agreement had been made and that he considered the inspector's intervention unfair to the other candidates. The members voted with O'Malley, eight to six, thereby securing the appointment of his candidate. The incident showed the extent to which localist loyalties and friendships determined support for one or other of the local candidates. It also indicated the extent to which the inspector, despite his purely consultative role, felt that he too could intervene and allow personal sentiment rather than consideration of a candidate's personal qualities to determine his position. It may be reasonable to assume that the lack of any such local or personal connections left the third candidate, the Mayo woman, without support.[32]

Canvassing was not by any means rare among candidates or their supporters, and the belief that it might not be in the best interests of teachers generally was not uniformly shared. At the 1958 congress of the VTA the executive proposed a resolution deploring party political influence on appointments. However, when put to the delegates the motion was lost.[33] The following year, the congress passed a resolution that proposals for all new appointments and promotions should be submitted to a panel representative of the VTA, the appointing committee, the department and local industrial and commercial interests. Another resolution that the power of making recommendations for the principalship of 'important' schools should be transferred to the Local Appointments Commission also indicated growing unease with existing appointment procedures. The VTA's general secretary, Charles McCarthy, then launched a systematic attack on canvassing through the press and through direct lobbying of committees, the IVEA and the Department of Education.[34] In June 1960, he wrote to each committee expressing concern about the prevalence of political patronage and urging that all advertisements should indicate that canvassing was strictly prohibited and would lead to immediate disqualification.[35] The committees universally resented what they regarded as an intrusion into their affairs and generally responded with the dismissive gesture of marking the letter 'read'. Following its discussion by the Cork county committee one member proposed that the committee should actively discourage canvassing, but she remained without a seconder.[36]

The spectre of canvassing had been raised, however, and it would continue to haunt vocational education through the following decade. It occasionally drew nationwide attention, as in 1961 when an appointment by the Limerick city committee prompted the local Labour Party deputy, Stephen Coughlan, during Dáil question time to accuse the committee and the Department of Education of making the appointment 'because of party affiliations and for services rendered', rather than on merit.[37] The Minister for Education, Patrick Hillery, was clearly embarrassed and stoutly denied that the appointee had any political affiliations with his party, Fianna Fáil. At a subsequent committee meeting two councillors detailed how they had been canvassed. Annoyed at the suggestion that such traditional practices might be inappropriate, Councillor John Danagher told his colleagues that the first step in any appointment 'is the canvass of members'.[38] His comment would have a lengthy reverberation.

A motion at the 1962 congress of the IVEA called for the outright disqualification of any candidate who canvassed. The discussion which the motion provoked indicated that canvassing was not only widely practised but was considered acceptable by many committee members.

For Councillor Gilbert Hughes of Dublin city 'it was an undeniable fact that canvassing was rampant' and, along with several other speakers, he stressed that it did not hinder his capacity to act judiciously:

> We are all aware of letters from clergy, from politicians, from mutual friends, from various other people . . . we know the use made of the 'old school ties' and the 'political ties' but we need not be 'tied' when we are exercising our judgement.[39]

The practice had deep roots. Recalling his childhood, Gearóid Ó Broin, the chief executive officer of the Wexford county committee, commented that his home had been 'like a knocking house' as prospective candidates for jobs came to see his father, twenty years a committee member. Seán Ó Dochartaigh, the chief executive officer for Galway county, argued that the motion, if passed, could 'do a lot of harm because it would give the impression that committee members were not as trustworthy as they should be'. Resistance to the motion was such that it was withdrawn.[40] But the issue was by no means buried.

On 29 July 1966, just two weeks after being appointed Minister for Education, Donogh O'Malley attended a specially convened meeting of the Limerick city committee. The members competed to welcome and congratulate the new minister but were soon shocked into silence when O'Malley stated that he was seriously perturbed by their past behaviour. For a number of years he had been concerned by the committee's financial practices and by its appointment procedures; considerations other than relevant qualifications, he bluntly declared, were often used in the making of appointments.[41] He was requesting Seán Mac Gearailt, one of his most senior officers, to conduct a full inquiry. Mac Gearailt commenced work in November and until Christmas investigated financial irregularities. On 3 January 1967 he began consideration of five interrelated staffing issues: the manner of making appointments, the grading of posts, their assignment between schools, the designation of duties and the supervision of a teacher's duties. Each led Mac Gearailt to examine specific cases and how they were handled by the committee.

The first concerned the principalship at the Municipal Technical Institute, the case which Deputy Coughlan had raised six years before in the Dáil. The committee had created the post at its meeting on 27 September 1961, and without any notification to possible candidates, filled the post at the same meeting. When making the appointment the committee had been aware that another teacher in the school had the same grade and qualifications as the person appointed. Nonetheless, the proposition to make the appointment was adopted without dissent.[42] Subsequently, relations between the new principal and some of his colleagues worsened and on foot of complaints from teachers, a confidential report was written by the chief executive officer and an attempt was made to create better working relations in the school.[43] In October 1962 two officers of the Department of Education attended a committee meeting and informed it that applications should have been sought from suitably qualified teachers. In May 1963 the department was forced to give an assurance to three aggrieved teachers at the school that the appointment of principal did not amend or reduce their existing conditions and that their opportunities for promotion would not be affected.[44] Despite that, duties were reallocated without discussion and the teachers grew increasingly discontented. In July 1966, following more complaints from staff, the chief executive officer recommended that the department hold an inquiry.

The second case arose from the appointment of a principal at the School of Electrical Engineering in 1964. The appointment itself promoted little discussion. It was advertised, two teachers were interviewed and the post was filled on a vote of eight to four. Subsequently, a problem arose over the duties attached to the new post. The unsuccessful candidate had previously carried out administrative and organisational duties, work which was then taken over by the successful candidate and the committee established a subcommittee to formulate acceptable conditions of service for both teachers. Legal advice obtained by the VTA suggested that while the defeated candidate had not been designated principal, he had been performing the duties of principal and therefore the appointment had been 'incorrect'.[45] Friction between the two men continued and the aggrieved teacher threatened to seek a court injunction restraining anyone from interfering with his duties in the school. Two years after the appointment the subcommittee recommended that the conditions of service of both teachers be amended to clearly indicate territories of command. The recommendations were never implemented.

The third case concerned the creation of a post and the allocation of duties in the School of Art. In January 1962, the department had sanctioned the appointment of a teacher of ceramics. At the same time the committee also approved hours for another teacher although only one post had been created. Proposing the second appointment, Councillor Patrick Powell stated that a student of the school, who was 'as well, if not better qualified' than the person initially appointed, was available for work and should be accommodated. The committee agreed to appoint the second teacher, resulting in a reduction in the number of hours held by the original appointee. In supporting the appointment, Councillor Rory Liddy told the committee that the applicant had come first in Ireland in his exams and that he deserved every consideration: 'this young man', he reasoned, 'was anxious for a teaching career and the only way he could get this was by appointment to the school'.[46] At the February meeting, the chairman, Councillor P. J. Donnellan, had affirmed the committee's decision on the basis of the candidate's 'qualifications' and 'other reasons', though what these might be, he did not specify.[47] The appointment caused dissatisfaction, not least with the principal who objected to the detrimental effect it was having within the school. He sought to have the committee set up an advisory sub-committee, but despite the support of an independent councillor on the committee and the chief executive officer, his intervention was roundly rebuffed.[48] When the dispute worsened and spilled over into the local press, an incensed committee held a special meeting.

The minutes of that meeting record the committee's anger at the principal's challenge to its authority. That it came from one of its employees heightened the sense of hurt. Councillor Donnellan felt that public representatives held 'dignified' positions and that any criticism which held them up to public opprobrium 'could not be justified'. His colleague Councillor Frank Leddin wanted the principal to apologise, and following a protracted defence of its position the committee requested that he do so publicly.[49] Having, in his words, 'no option' but to do so, he instead tendered his resignation. It was received with little fuss and the process of appointing a replacement was begun.[50]

The resignation of a head of school over the relatively minor issue of the creation of extra hours for a former student may have seemed rather dramatic in the circumstances. Unless, that is, it was the act of a desperate man in an impossible situation. Councillor Donnellan was reticent when questioned about this at the inquiry: he did not find it strange that hours were taken from a physical education class to facilitate the creation of a second post in the School of Art, nor could he say why no vacancy arose when the appointee to that second post left the school the following year, or whether he had actually taught ceramics during his time there. Furthermore, he insisted that he did not know if the principal's resignation bore any relation to the appointment. Contributions from the teacher whose post was in dispute did throw some light on the situation. He told the inquiry that at the time of his appointment he had not been aware of a vacancy in the school but that he had sought work there by contacting the committee chairman and the chief executive officer.[51]

The fourth case arose from the need to appoint a new principal for the School of Art in 1962. The Limerick city committee established an expert panel consisting of its chairman, the chief executive officer, a chief inspector of the Department of Education, its art inspector and the director of the National College of Art to interview candidates and make a recommendation, which it duly did. The committee met to make the appointment and was informed by Councillor Donnellan that in fact there was 'very little difference' between the recommended candidate and another candidate. He was supported in this by Councillor Paddy O'Sullivan who stated that the unsuccessful candidate was an ex-student of the school, that he was currently a teacher there and that further 'he was a local man and merited support'. The committee then voted, eight to four, to appoint him, thus disregarding the recommendation of the expert panel.[52] It was never made clear why Donnellan in particular decided to reject the candidate which his panel had recommended. At the inquiry he repudiated the suggestion that any localism functioned in the appointment. To the contrary, he stated that while he had certainly looked at the application of the person appointed, he had no idea where he was from.[53]

In reviewing these cases the inquiry held that the committee had behaved contrary to proper procedure but went to some length to distinguish between that and the results of the appointments. For example, the inquiry concluded that had correct procedure been followed in the filling of the principalship of the Municipal Technical Institute, the same person would probably have got the job. No doubts were raised about that person's ability but the committee's decision to create and fill a post at the same meeting had placed the Department of Education in the position of having to either sanction the appointment or request that the committee conduct a fresh appointment exercise including the issue of an advertisement. The department's position was that if it had adopted the latter course it would only have 'aggravated whatever sense of grievance' members of staff already had. And while the appointment itself was a major cause of anger in the school, the inquiry concluded that it was aggravated by the committee allowing the new principal to flout its authority, for instance when he would not attend meetings which might have facilitated a resolution of some of the conflicts.

In the case of the principalship of the School of Electrical Engineering, the inquiry found that the committee had ignored the advice of its chief executive and disregarded the specialist needs of the post. The committee, it was suggested, acted to promote the needs of an individual rather than those of its school. Similarly, in the case of the School of Art, the committee had created a post specially to accommodate an individual who had canvassed for work, although the school requirements did not warrant the post. The ability of the appointee to perform his tasks was not doubted but the department believed that his Limerick origins had led the committee to make the appointment. In publicly condemning this the principal may have been both indiscreet and injudicious, but the committee, in asking him to make a public apology, treated him unfairly. It had behaved in a rigid way, and in analogous circumstances had treated other teachers with greater consideration. In the case of the appointment of a new principal at the School of Art, the inquiry did not accept the committee's view that there was little to distinguish between the two candidates or that the committee had not acted in the knowledge that one of the candidates was a local man. It was, Mac Gearailt unequivocally stated, an action which merited 'condemnation' and typified the committee's assiduity in 'having its own way'. This was revealed by its creation of higher posts to the advantage of favoured individuals and in its transfer of courses from one centre to another without due concern for the rights of the teachers thus affected. The creation of these higher posts had little to do with requirements or merit, and decisions taken about the transfer of courses 'savoured, at the very least, of establishing a position for individuals rather than catering in the best possible way for these courses'.[54]

Distilled to a single issue, much of the inquiry was occupied by the question of canvassing and the use of personal connections. When asked if it was true that his committee encouraged canvassing, Councillor Donnellan replied that any candidate was entitled to approach any member of the committee but he stubbornly refused to be drawn much further.[55] While denying that considerations of birthplace were necessarily taken into account, it would be 'natural', he said, to give 'a local man preference if he were fully qualified and competent'.[56] During a cross-examination that lasted nine hours, Donnellan, perhaps not surprisingly, denied charges of patronage. He did, however, accept that teachers had been upgraded for the purpose of rewarding 'faithful service' over a period; but, he asserted, this did not increase friction nor was it contrary to school needs. Mac Gearailt could not agree with him, however, and he concluded that the bitter disputes in the School of Art and the School of Electrical Engineering had a serious impact on school morale.

The inquiry concluded on 3 February 1967 and less than a month later the committee received a ministerial order suspending it and appointing a principal officer of the department, Pádraig Ó Cuilleanáin, to perform its duties. He travelled to Limerick once a month for the next three years to conduct the meetings of the 'ghost' committee, where he was assisted by the chief executive officer and the clerk. In every other way, proceedings continued as normal. The local press attended; the minutes summarised their discussions and recorded decisions taken. Elections for a new local authority were not due until 1974, but in 1970 the minister introduced an amendment to the Vocational Education Act which allowed Limerick corporation to appoint a new committee. Three members of the old discredited committee were reappointed but P. J. Donnellan, who had held the chair since the committee's foundation in 1930, was not among them, thus bringing to an end a remarkable reign at the Limerick Athenaeum.

Clientelism, defined by one commentator as an interdependent voluntary relationship between two partners of unequal power which benefits both and conserves the power of the dominant partner, has long been identified as a feature of national politics.[57] Irish society has, furthermore, been characterised as displaying a profound attachment to informal community loyalties above any universalistic or meritocratic values.[58] The evidence from Limerick suggested that the city provided the basis of a strong sense of 'community' within which clientelism became the norm. Locality was used by politicians in a way which enhanced the notions of community implicit in vocational education, while at the same time strengthening their local power base. The Vocational Education Act, as a piece of enabling legislation, gave autonomous rein to such behaviour. Thus the local—the known—was not only favoured above others but in fact was bestowed with special consideration. So long as relevant locals benefited, the system would continue to grind on.

In contrast, the concern voiced by the state throughout the inquiry was that only meritocratic and universal criteria should be used in the filling of positions. The inquiry forced the state to act to ensure that localist tendencies were stamped out, and shortly after the books on Limerick were closed, the Minister for Education Donogh O'Malley ordered new procedures to effect this. Distinguishing between higher and lower grade posts, he proposed the establishment of selection boards consisting of committee representatives, the chief executive officer, officers of the department and, where required, non-voting expert advisers. It was envisaged that the boards would make selections which the committee would accept and which the department would then sanction. The measures, if utilised properly, would be a significant check against the excesses of patronage. They did mean, however, a diminution of local power and increased state intervention in the distribution of one of its most tangible bounties.

The most coherent immediate response to the changes was voiced at the 1967 congress of the IVEA which devoted considerable time to the implications of the new procedures: nine motions out of a total of twenty-nine referred to them. Members rallied around tradition and railed against the minister's intervention, insisting on the fairness, efficacy and suitability to 'local needs' of the old procedures. Fr James Holloway, the chairman of the Meath committee, supported the status quo and argued that one of the successes of vocational education was its close personal contact with the local community and its first-hand knowledge of local requirements. 'The committee is the voice of the people', he reasoned, 'and it is the people, the parents, who have the first, the God-given, the inalienable right to educate their children.' Alderman Fergus Byrne of Wexford town argued that the proposals, if accepted, would lead to a 'negation of true democracy'. Though most speakers appeared to argue that the proposed selection boards would undermine the committees, no motion expressing that was put and the association agreed to support the new procedures for a one-year trial.[59] It might have seemed that the decision had spelt the end of canvassing.

The following year's congress again addressed the issue. The atmosphere was strained somewhat as a result of earlier public statements from VTA general secretary, Charles McCarthy, that canvassing still persisted. The association's president, Fr W. Breen, set a combative tone in his address. Obviously stung by McCarthy's charges, he articulated a rousing defence of the local committees in the messianic tones then typical of IVEA debates:

> Canvassing where it is prohibited is more discreditable to the canvasser than to the canvassed . . . . since 1930, a constant body of 570 men and women of all creeds, clergy and laity, of varied occupation, but all voluntary and unpaid in this particular work, have in a system of democratic control, involved themselves in every corner of the country in a purely educational process, with a lively local interest and committedness . . . that dedication and devotedness, subject as all human endeavour is, to the purely human failings of a body composed of so many varied interests, has been the hallmark and the glory of the membership of the IVEA.[60]

If the president seemed to be distancing himself somewhat from the use of canvassing, some of his fellow delegates, particularly those who were elected representatives, did not. Councillor Bernard Joyce of Mayo, for example, declared:

> I do not like the word 'canvass' but I do not see why people who elected me to serve their interests in public bodies cannot be entitled to discuss a matter with me. If parents thought fit to elect me as a member of a public body, surely they have the right to ask me to consider the merits of a son or daughter.[61]

As public representatives, acting on behalf of their constituents—their clients—committee members such as Joyce clearly saw themselves as mediators between these clients and public and impersonal institutions. This type of clarion response echoed throughout the debates at congress, though there was a significant difference between the position of the chief executive officers and that of rank-and-file committee members. Each chief executive who spoke evaluated the new procedures in a positive light. J. Healy of the Dublin city committee spoke for his fellow chief executives when he declared that his committee would have to appoint seventy new teachers within the following fortnight and that a systematic approach to making those appointments would ease his task. As chief executives in a rapidly expanding system, where time and cost effectiveness were a priority, they were quick to defend the usefulness of selection boards operating uniform procedures under their direction. If an appointment system had been moulded to the needs of political patronage, it might now be formed to respond to administrative imperatives. The potential for a conflict of interest, between managerial requirements and representational imperatives, would become all the greater as vocational education underwent rapid expansion. That reality, and the dramatic ministerial intervention in Limerick, may have led the delegates to reject the motion calling for an abandonment of the new system and to pass a more cautious motion calling for it to be kept under review.[62]

Having left his mark on the IVEA congress, McCarthy ploughed ahead with his campaign and supplied the department with evidence of the persistence of canvassing. It seemed clear to him that the minister's recommendations had not been universally adopted and that the lessons of Limerick were not being applied. He submitted details of how the Laois committee, following a complaint from the department, reinterviewed candidates but then proceeded to confirm the original appointment. The Limerick county committee had appointed a vice-principal without following the regulations and it was the belief of the VTA that substantial canvassing had taken place. The Galway county committee also appointed a vice-principal having allowed canvassing to take place.[63]

As far as the VTA was concerned, the ministerial order had not been sufficient. At its 1970 congress, Charles McCarthy reported what must have been disappointing results of his campaign to clear out canvassing. Committees had been requested by the association to include in all job advertisements the rider that canvassing would automatically disqualify. The committees in Carlow, Kildare, Westmeath, Mayo, Kerry, Kilkenny and Tralee town had agreed to do so, stating calmly and in unison that this had always been their policy. Wexford town and Meath had marked the request 'read' while the Longford and the Roscommon committees had explicitly refused to adopt the request. No response was received from any of the remaining twenty-seven committees.[64]

It might be suggested that the only people to have benefited from the practice of canvassing were the committee members whose sense of power was intensified by the pleas by prospective candidates and whose perceived status in the locality was enhanced following an appointment. Notwithstanding that, it cannot be denied that canvassing also worked for teachers well placed in the appropriate political machine, and it could be argued that the persistence of canvassing owed as much to its service to clients as to its returns to patrons. Committee members would continue to regard lobbying by the public as part of the democratic process and would argue that to approach a public representative was a citizen's democratic right. None of this is to say that all committee members abused their power, or that the democratic principle of the committee was inherently flawed, as some of its critics have argued. Rather, it may have been that the interpretation of the Vocational Education Act, an enabling more than a directional piece of legislation, led to powers being wielded widely by local forces in ways that may not have been intended in 1930. It was certainly the case that, despite the persistent and sometimes flagrant abuse of power, good decisions continued to be made and good teachers continued to be appointed.

The balance of national and local interests

The danger of political exploitation had, in fact, been adverted to at the system's inception. Speaking in the Dáil debate on the second stage of the Vocational Education Bill 1930, Ernest Alton, a Dublin University deputy, echoed the views of opposition deputies not only when he welcomed the encouragement of adaptability to local demands, but also when he questioned the advisability of using local political personnel to manage the system. The administration of vocational education would require expertise not necessarily present in a councillor, he suggested.[65] The plea to balance public accountability with professional expertise was directed to the Minister for Education, John Marcus O'Sullivan, who reasoned that the body responsible for striking the rate to fund the schools ought to control them. He felt that the local authorities would select their 'best men' but he argued that they might not necessarily constitute the best authority to administer an education scheme. However, he concluded that notwithstanding its potential for abuse, the balance in a public system had to lie with democratic control.[66]

The tipping of the balance in Limerick revealed the system's weakness. But it was also strained in another key area of the administration which the inquiry highlighted, namely financial control. From 1958 until 1966, the Limerick city committee had continued to remit fees which had been unpaid by students. In 1961, the Minister for Education had intervened and requested the chief executive officer to personally supervise fee collection. Despite his efforts, fees went uncollected and the committee continued to sanction their remittance. The inquiry was told that while a committee had the authority to remit fees it did not have the authority to write them off retroactively. In explanation, committee members told the inquiry that an explosion in student numbers had left principals overworked and unable to ensure payment. It was also suggested that the resistance was a matter of principle for parents who, it was argued, were already funding the system through their rates.[67]

It emerged in the inquiry that the committee had established its own procedures. If a student claimed inability to pay, the school chaplain was requested to inquire into the family's circumstances, generally through consultation with the parish priest. If the circumstances were considered to be mitigating, fees were waived. The role of the chaplain gave him discretionary powers, and committee members clearly felt that the interests of the church and their own interests were at one on this question. In patronage terms, the power bestowed on the clergymen on the one hand and on the committee members—some of whom were also clergymen—on the other, facilitated a perfect convergence. The committeee members had power to validate or dismiss pleas of poverty while the clergy retained the power to grant the reward of free schooling. Both performed as patrons in the system and it was evident that the state, as represented by the chief executive officer and by the Department of Education, was thereby rendered powerless.

A similar disregard for the concerns of the state was also revealed by the Limerick inquiry's investigation of overexpenditure by £33,000 on the refurbishment of a school building in 1965. The committee defended its overrun on the original tender by the need to make unanticipated but urgent alterations. The chairman of the inquiry was at pains to point out that it was not the changes themselves which were being questioned but the manner in which they occurred. It was the committee's autonomy of action and its enabling of the architect to presume approval by the committee for any extra work that the state felt it had to censure.[68] Committee members may have felt that their responsibilities gave them the discretion to commit the committee. Such independence would not have been an issue in an agency that funded its own initiatives. That may have been envisaged in 1930 but each year saw an increasing proportion of the funds for vocational education disbursed by the national exchequer through the Department of Education. In 1967, the year of the inquiry, only 20 per cent of vocational education committee income was raised locally. That reality revealed the subservient nature of the operation, not just in the regulation of income and expenditure, but ultimately in almost any sphere of importance.

In ordering an inquiry in Limerick, Donogh O'Malley had opened up a remarkable vista on the workings of vocational education. Committee proceedings in Limerick as elsewhere had been habitually reported in the local press but those accounts had rarely caught the currents underlying a committee's operation. In defence of the Limerick committee, it might be argued that its misdemeanours were not necessarily any worse than those of any other committee. Ironically, it was the localist politics which had been its norm that brought it to grief because of a combination of events, culminating in the appointment of a local man as minister. O'Malley had little respect for convention and would, if circumstances demanded it, act swiftly with the avidity of the 'new broom'.[69] The Limerick committee, unlike most others at the time, did not reflect his party's pre-eminence in national politics. Consequently a whip-like discipline, operated through the local constituency machine, could not be used to achieve compliance. As members scored off each other, public attention was drawn to the committee, conveying, perhaps correctly, an impression of perpetual disharmony and political corruption. There was an inevitability in Stephen Coughlan's 1961 Dáil condemnation of a committee decision as a piece of Fianna Fáil trickery, and if on that occasion O'Malley's predecessor had been embarrassed, he himself would want to avoid a similar fate.[70] Years of wrangling over appointments had frayed the patience of department officials and created an atmosphere of mutual suspicion, and if some of them believed that the problem could only be solved with an inquiry, O'Malley's own sense of party loyalty would be served by siding not with the committee but rather with the officials who wanted to clean up a bureaucratic mess.[71] His brother Michael had served as a member of the committee throughout the 1950s and he had been frustrated on more than one occasion by the intransigence of his follow members as they sought to have their favoured candidates appointed. Political point-scoring by O'Malley cannot be discounted as a factor, and since he had fewer party allies than political opponents on the committee, may have greased the wheels of ministerial intervention. Had O'Malley been given a different cabinet brief, the dismal proceedings of the Limerick city committee might not have raised an eyebrow beyond the readership of the local papers. He was, after all, the minister who in reply to a Dáil question on the allocation of state contracts stated that, 'everything else being equal', it would be given to a supporter of his party.[72] The findings of the inquiry were national in their impact however, for its exposure of the process of appointments was undoubtedly the catalyst for the ministerial reforms of 1967.

Conclusion

The constitution of the vocational education committees in the 1930 Act ensured that they would reflect and reproduce some of the characteristics of Irish politics. They were overwhelmingly composed of men and were controlled by the local members of the two parties which dominated national politics. The clergy were strongly represented amongst the added members, and consequently local economic and cultural interests which the legislation identified as legitimate educational agencies were less well represented than they might have been. The presence of clergymen underlined the transcendent institutional authority which religion had throughout the vocational sector despite its secular constitution, and revealed more generally the Catholic Church's power in the education system as a whole. This deference is perhaps best symbolised in the allocation of the chair to a man of the cloth. Those patterns began to change in the 1970s, however. The number of clergymen nominees began to decline, their election was less likely to be automatic, and other interest groups, particularly teachers and parents, intensified their demands for representation and achieved some success in obtaining places formerly allocated to priests.

It has been argued here that the role of local politicians in political culture and the power allocated to them as committee members ensured that their participation would be influenced by their willingness to act as local patrons. Because of its emphasis on satisfying local needs the 1930 Act enabled committee members to do so, however, to the exclusion of universalistic, meritocratic demands. The 1967 regulations governing appointments went some way to attenuating the likelihood of localist jobbery, while local government reform would ensure that single-party dominance of committees would become less common. However, a multi-party committee was not, in itself, a brake against clientelism, for its primary cause was a deeper unswerving localism.

Ultimately, however, the vocational education committee had to operate as an instrument of the state within a framework that reflected the subservience of local government to the will of the Oireachtas. This was made clear in 1930 by the powers of dismissal vested in the minister which, if rarely invoked, were no less real. Most decisions depended on finance for their implementation and the proportion of those funds coming to vocational education from local sources diminished steadily over the years. The major restructuring and expansion of vocational education in the 1960s required expenditure at a level that no local authority could ever have contemplated, and with that expansion, paradoxically, the power of the committees and of their individual members grew weaker. Nonetheless, after many decades of institutional growth, committee members could look back on a history of significant achievement knowing that it had been accomplished within structures that had set real limits on their capacity to operate autonomously. In their wiser moments, however, they might well have wondered if they had always been as effective as their limited powers allowed.

Notes

1 Vocational Education Act 1930, section 7, subsection 3.

2 Cork County Council, minutes, 30 September 1930.

3 Personal communication, Professor Michael Hillery, May 1995.

4 *The Kerryman*, 22 June 1979.

5 Department of Education, Memorandum V 53.

6 Data extracted from membership lists supplied by the respective committees and chief executive officers.

7 City of Galway VEC, minutes, 1949–59.

8 City of Dublin VEC, minutes, 19 October 1950.

9 County of Cork VEC, minutes, 5 October 1961.

10 Matt Power, *Half-a-century: Co. Clare VEC 1930–1980* (Ennis, 1980), p. 14.

11 Limerick County Council, minutes, 28 April 1956.

12 *Ibid.*, 26 May 1956.

13 *Ibid.*, 14 October 1961; Limerick County Council, correspondence, 92/9/1, Patrick J. Lee to CEO Limerick VEC, 7 October 1965.

14 Limerick County Council, minutes, 26 November 1965.

15 *Ibid.*, 22 November 1965.

16 *Ibid.*, 28 September 1983.

17 *Ibid.*, 11 July 1991.

18 *The Echo and South Leinster Advertiser*, 23 June 1994.

19 Yvonne Galligan, 'Women in Irish Politics', in John Coakley and Michael Gallagher (eds.), *Politics in the Republic of Ireland* (Galway, 1992), p. 185.

20 Power, *Half-a-century*, p. 17.

21 Personal communication, 18 May 1994, Mrs D. Foley, past-president of Carlow federation of the ICA and member of Carlow VEC 1960–7; see also Limerick County Council, minutes, 25 February 1956 and 26 May 1956.

22 Comhairle Contae Phortlairge, Oifig Runaidhe an Conntae, S. 3/19, 30 June 1945.

23 Cork County Council, minutes, 30 September 1930.

24 Limerick County Council, minutes, 27 September 1930.

25 Limerick County Council, county secretary's office, 92/9/1, M. J. McNamara, secretary, County Limerick branch, INTO to secretary, Limerick County Council, 4 July 1960.

26 City of Limerick VEC, minutes, 27 November 1951.

27 County of Cork VEC, minutes, 28 November 1930.

28 Department of Education, *Programme for action in education 1984–87* (1984), section 2.19.

29 Department of Education, circular F 37/91, C. N. Lindsay to each local authority, 6 June 1991.

30 Sheelagh Drudy and Kathleen Lynch, *Schools and society in Ireland* (Dublin, 1993), pp. 125–6.

31 Desmond Roche, *Local government in Ireland* (Dublin, 1982), especially chapter 5.

32 City of Limerick VEC, minutes, 3 April 1951.

33 VTA, *Gairm*, 1, 13 (1959), 'General Secretary's report', p. 32.

34 VTA, *Gairm*, 1, 19 (1960), 'General Secretary's report', p. 37.

35 Archives Department, University College, Dublin (hereafter, ADUCD), TUI papers, TU/10, Charles McCarthy to chief executive officers, 22 June 1960.

36 County of Cork VEC, minutes, 26 July 1960.

37 Dáil Éireann, *Debates*, cxcii (30 November 1961), col. 1186; also ADUCD, TUI papers, TU/30, Department of Education to general secretary, 12 December 1961.

38 City of Limerick VEC, minutes, 4 December 1961.

39 IVEA Annual Congress, *Report*, 1962.

40 *Ibid.*

41 City of Limerick VEC, minutes, 29 July 1966.

42 *Ibid.*, 27 September 1961.

43 *Limerick Leader*, 4 January 1967.

44 ADUCD, TUI papers, TU/30, Letter from Department of Education, 15 May 1963.

45 *Limerick Leader*, 7 January 1967.

46 City of Limerick VEC, minutes, 28 March 1962.

47 *Ibid.*, 21 February 1962.

48 City of Limerick VEC, Patrick McEvoy to P. J. Donnellan, 16 March 1962.

49 City of Limerick VEC, minutes, 28 March 1962.

50 *Limerick Leader*, 7 January 1967.

51 *Ibid.*, 14 January 1967.

52 City of Limerick VEC, minutes, 25 July 1962.

53 *Limerick Leader*, 11 January 1967.

54 Letter to Limerick VEC as printed in *Limerick Leader*, 17 December 1966.

55 *Limerick Leader*, 11 January 1967.

56 *Ibid.*, 14 January 1967.

57 Ellen Hazelkorn, 'Class, clientelism and the political process', in P. Clancy et al. (eds.), *Ireland: a sociological profile* (Dublin, 1986), pp. 326–43.

58 J. P. O'Carroll, 'Strokes, cute hoors and sneaking regarders', in *Irish Political Studies*, 2 (1987), pp. 77–90.

59 IVEA Annual Congress, *Report,* 1967.

60 IVEA Annual Congress, *Report,* 1968.

61 *Ibid.*

62 *Ibid.*

63 ADUCD, TUI papers, TU/30, Charles McCarthy to Department of Education, 24 July 1968.

64 'Report', in Cumann na nGairm Mhúinteoirí, *Annual Congress: Gairm*, 1970, pp. 7–8.

65 Dáil Éireann, *Debates*, xxxiv (14 May 1930), col. 1801.

66 *Ibid.*, cols 1809–11.

67 *Limerick Leader*, 17 December 1966.

68 Letter to Limerick VEC as printed in *Limerick Leader*, 17 December 1966.

69 See for example, Sean O'Connor, *A troubled sky: reflections on the Irish educational scene, 1957–1968* (Dublin, 1986), p. 139–41.

70 Dáil Éireann, *Debates*, cxcii (30 November 1961), col. 1186.

71 See for example, City of Limerick VEC, minutes, 27–8 July 1952.

72 Dáil Éireann, *Debates*, ccxxvi (23 February 1967), col. 1892.

9. The Modern Union: The Teachers' Union of Ireland 1973–1994

Michael McGinley and Frances Donoghue

By the standards of comparable organisations the Teachers' Union of Ireland (TUI) flourished during the 1970s and 1980s. Its membership almost doubled, it performed effectively in negotiations and it reorganised its structures against the backdrop of economic crisis and change in society and educational institutions. While pursuing its primary goals the TUI also addressed broader social issues. This chapter charts its history during the period from 1973 to 1994, focusing on a number of interrelated themes, including the economic and political contexts within which the TUI operated, its ongoing concern with organisation, conditions of service, gender equity and educational reform, and the movement for an amalgamation of teacher unions. Inevitably, it is difficult to get a clear perspective on the most recent events in the union's history: issues considered here are at the time of writing the subject of continuing negotiation with employers, the state and other unions. Important archives holding key documents remain closed, and only time will reveal which of the events of these two decades will be of greatest long-term significance. This chapter deals with issues that now appear to be of major concern to members, but the temptation to assert that recent challenges have been uniquely difficult will be resisted. Each generation has its own preoccupations, but members of the union today will admit that their successes are built on the hard-earned experience of their predecessors.

The changing economic context

By 1980 the average annual economic growth of about 4 per cent achieved in the early 1970s was slowing and showing signs of decline.[1] Then followed a deficit in four of the eight years between 1981 and 1989, resulting in an overall average growth of less than 1 per cent. The consumer price index, having risen in the 1970s, declined sharply in 1980. Unemployment hovered at about 5 per cent in the early 1970s, but registered an increase each year from the late 1970s until it reached

17.5 per cent in 1987. For most of the period from 1970 public finances followed a hazard-strewn path. By 1991 the national debt had
risen to £25.4 billion or 107 per cent of gross national product, due
mainly to a policy of deficits on the current budget designed to delay
the impact of the international financial crises of the mid-1970s and
early 1980s.[2] Welfare payments were kept ahead of price rises during
those years of inflation and the numbers dependent on them escalated
as unemployment rose. The variability of these key economic indicators
from year to year and the marked contrast between the growth of the
early 1970s and the decline of the 1980s formed an uncertain base for
educational development, not least because the state of the public finances bore directly on the strategies of public sector unions, of whom
the teacher unions were a major element. Political and economic chick-
ens came home to roost, and from the mid-1980s, following significant
reductions in gross national product, the public service unions bore the
brunt of efforts at retrenchment. The difficulty was amplified by growth
in public service employment. Between 1970 and 1983 the notion that
job creation in the public service was a useful way to beat unemployment led, in part, to over a 50 per cent rise in its personnel, as Table 9.1
indicates. The belief facilitated an expansion of educational provision
and the total employed in education rose from 33,100 in 1970 to a
peak of 54,700 in 1987. By the end of the 1980s the total had dropped
back to 51,000, and the future was uncertain. Despite that, the overall
increase during the period 1970–90 was a remarkable 54 per cent.[3]

During the 1970s population grew steadily and against a back-

Table 9.1: Growth in public service employment 1970–90

	Number employed*			Percentage change	
	1970 (000)	1980 (000)	1990 (000)	1970–80	1970–90
Civil service	20.1	34.1	28.6	+70	+42
Garda'	6.5	9.6	10.9	+48	+68
Defence	9.8	15.5	14.4	+58	+47
Health	38.8	59.5	58.4	+53	+51
Education	33.1	49.1	51.0	+48	+54
Total	108.3	167.8	163.3	+55	+51

* Part-time numbers converted to full-time equivalents.

Source: P. C. Humphreys, *Public service employment* (Dublin, 1993); Michael
McGinley, 'Pay 1970–91: climbing in the fog', in *Industrial Relations News*,
33 (September 1991).

ground of policies which sought to maximise participation in education, so too did the pupil population. In 1970 there were 506,000 pupils in first-level schools but by the end of the decade the total had risen by 9 per cent to 552,00. At second level the growth was much more remarkable: in 1970 there were 197,142 pupils enrolled but by 1980 there were 295,592, an increase of 50 per cent. The impact was enormous in terms of the number of classrooms and teachers needed and the consequent increase in public expenditure. In 1981 the annual fertility rate showed a decline for the first time since 1958 and its effect on primary schools became apparent in the 1985/6 school year when the first-time enrolment of 73,367 was 68 less than the previous year. Each subsequent year revealed continuing decline and in 1992/3 first-time enrolment was 55,291. The expected decline in first-year enrolment in second-level schools occurred in 1994 when at 69,420 it was 489 less than the previous year. Such trends underpinned much of the ongoing debate on education policy. Assuming that teacher–pupil ratios remained constant, a decline in the number of pupils would lead to a decrease in teaching jobs. If ratios worsened, as they had in the early to mid-1980s, the decrease would become even greater. In such circumstances the possibility of school closures and teacher redundancy would loom and teachers would look to their unions for advice and, when necessary, for negotiations and effective action.

The TUI sought to deliver improved conditions for its members in a climate which proved hostile both to improvement in the quality of service and to the winning of better working conditions. The effective exercise of trade union pressure was continually hampered by the state of the public finances. This difficulty was heightened by the perception that a burgeoning public service pay bill, of which teachers' pay was a significant slice, aggravated an already difficult problem. The situation was intensified by significant changes in political culture which saw many old certainties upset. Between 1932 and 1973 Fianna Fáil's enviable capacity to form a government had but two brief setbacks, when, between 1948 and 1951 and between 1954 and 1957, coalitions of smaller parties held office. In contrast, during the two decades after 1973 Fianna Fáil's time in opposition was almost as long as its time in office, and from the early 1980s its capacity to form a government was realised only with the support of independent deputies or through coalition with the Progressive Democrats or the Labour Party. Labour also joined Fine Gael in coalition governments in 1973–7, 1981–2 and 1982–7. This was a period when old moulds were broken and the early 1980s, in particular, were marked by debilitating political instability: three gen-

Figure 9.1: Total TUI membership and combined total of whole-time teachers in technological, vocational, community and comprehensive sectors 1973–94

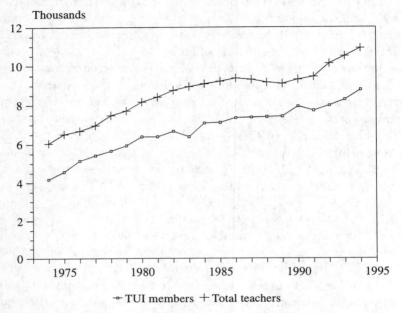

Source: Teachers' Union of Ireland, *Annual reports*, 1973–94.

eral elections were held within eighteen months and in that same period, six different people held the office of Minister for Education. Traditional patterns of political loyalty appeared less assured and the trade unions, especially the public service unions, had to exercise a high degree of political caution.

Union membership and organisation

The development of educational institutions under the control of vocational education committees provided a fertile soil for the continuing growth of the TUI, though its expansion into institutions where more than one union recruited makes it difficult to provide a simple account of membership.[4] The TUI continued to be the sole representative body for vocational teachers but from 1966 it was competing with the Association of Secondary Teachers, Ireland (ASTI) in the comprehensive schools and from 1972 in the community schools. In each of the new sectors schools were formed, in part, from existing vocational schools. In the new schools former vocational school teachers continued as mem-

Figure 9.2: Percentage distribution of TUI membership between sectors 1973–94

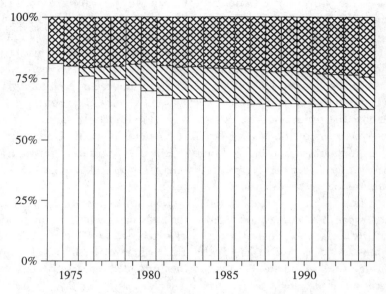

□ Vocational schools ◩ Other second level ⊠ Technological

Source: Teachers' Union of Ireland, *Annual reports,* 1973–94.

bers of the TUI whose policy it was that they should do so, while co-operating fully with their colleagues who had already been members of the ASTI.[5] The second-level sector became even more diverse following the creation of community colleges in 1982. These were all under the control of vocational education committees and the TUI had the reasonable expectation that it would thus be the sole representative body for teachers in the fledgling sector. However, the Irish Congress of Trade Unions (ICTU) ruled against that on the basis that some community colleges had been created following the closure and absorption of secondary schools whose teachers had already been represented by the ASTI.[6]

The expansion of technical education at third level from the early 1970s also contributed to diversity in TUI membership. The technical sector grew rapidly and an increasing proportion of members of the TUI were drawn from it. In 1974 one-fifth of members were employed in higher education; by 1994 the proportion had risen to a quarter. Most of these were from the regional technical colleges and the Dublin

Institute of Technology, but significant numbers were in the home economics teacher college, St Angela's, in Thomond College of Education and in the University of Limerick. Other unions were also recruiting at third level, particularly in the universities, but as a result of the expansion of the technological colleges, the majority of teachers in higher education continued to be represented by the TUI. Progress was not unhindered and some dissatisfaction over TUI effectiveness emerged in early 1984 following a dispute in Kevin Street College of Technology. A settlement was reached with the help of the Labour Court but the TUI felt that the conduct of the dispute was undermined by lecturers who were members of the Marine Port and General Workers' Union. In a subsequent arbitration ICTU found for the TUI and soon afterwards a small group of lecturers formed themselves into a breakaway group, the Dublin Colleges' Academic Staff Association.

When Charles McCarthy took leave of absence from the TUI in September 1972 he was succeeded as general secretary by a former president, Maurice Holly, who in turn was succeeded in 1975 by another former president, Kevin McCarthy. Each came to the post following distinguished presidential terms and they provided a necessary sense of continuity following Charles McCarthy's long reign. In 1976 a career trade unionist, Christy Devine, previously with the Civil and Public Service Staff Association, was appointed general secretary, and on his nomination as a workers' member of the Labour Court in 1982, the serving assistant general secretary and a former president of the union, Jim Dorney, was appointed to the post.

The expansion of the TUI led to the creation of the post of assistant general secretary in 1975. Pat Brady was appointed but left to go to the Workers' Union of Ireland. He was succeeded by John Dowling and he left in 1980 to go to the Association of Higher Civil Servants. He was replaced by Harry Connolly who resigned soon afterwards to be succeeded by Jim Dorney who served until appointed general secretary in 1982. At that point a second post of assistant general secretary was created and Mairín Ganly and Hugh Pollock were each appointed with responsibility for second-level and third-level affairs respectively. Hugh Pollock left in 1989 to go to the Irish Distributive and Administrative Trades Union (IDATU) and was replaced by Alice Prendergast and then Peter MacMenamin. That year also saw the creation of a new post, deputy general secretary, to which Mairín Ganly was appointed. On her resignation in 1994 she was succeeded by Peter MacMenamin. The vacant post of assistant general secretary was then filled by Seán MacCarthy, a former president. The post of research and education officer was created in 1984 and filled by Gráinne O'Flynn who over the next decade was responsible for a series of important research projects and publications. On her retirement in 1994 she was replaced by Rose Malone. The day-to-day administration of head office had been entrusted to Anne Hanley in 1963 and when she retired in 1986 her twenty-two years' continuous full-time service was the longest in the union's history. Mark Sherry was appointed as her successor and on his resignation in 1987 was replaced by Hilary O'Byrne. Expansion also necessitated a continuing increase in head office clerical staff: five were being employed in 1974, a sixth was added in 1979 and by 1987 there were nine.[7]

The pressures generated within a growing organisation exacted a price. In 1984 a branch passed a motion which implied that there was a need for greater efficiency amongst the clerical staff at head office. This precipitated dispute action which continued until the offending part of the motion was withdrawn.[8] In 1989 the clerical staff sought a pay increase and despite protracted negotiations by their union, IDATU, agreement could not be reached. In February 1990 dispute notice was served. The matter was referred to the conciliation service of the Labour Court, and when no agreement was reached the TUI sought the assistance of ICTU which convened a series of meetings between the parties. Settlement was eventually reached with the help of the Labour Court.[9] The dispute occurred at a time of intense activity at the union's head office at Orwell Road: a major salary negotiation had been successfully completed, a record eighteen meetings of the executive were held in one year, subcommittee meetings which had numbered fifty in 1989 jumped to eighty in 1990, and the number of seminars organised by head office increased sixfold.[10] At a time of rapidly changing work routines and increased output frustration could easily develop, and if the union had acquired the capacity to identify and resist ailments in the ranks of vocational education, it was not immune to disaffection within its own body.

Throughout the period the executive continued to devolve much of its work to subcommittees and their scope charts the expansion of TUI concerns. Committees dealing with community and comprehensive schools, second-level vocational education, union organisation and conditions of service were established and in a decision redolent of the foundation of a women's committee by the Vocational Teachers' Association (VTA) in 1959, congress agreed to set up a Women's Council in 1982. A national panel of third-level college representatives was established in 1973 to act as a forum for college views and soon after the executive established a colleges subcommittee. The national panel for colleges which was reconstituted in January 1981 as a broadly based forum representative of the various grades in each college which was to act as a bridge between the members in the individual colleges and the executive's colleges subcommittee. It was renamed the Colleges' Advisory Council in 1983.[11]

The union also continued to sponsor various self-help and voluntary organisations. The Vocational Teachers' Building Group Limited, founded in 1968, continued to operate under the guidance of former president, Liam Trundle, in the early 1970s. It acted as guarantor for the City of Dublin Local Utility Society, a friendly society which organised the building of houses for teachers. A decision to operate within head office with the general secretary as its director was implemented in January 1976 and it continued to negotiate preferential mortgages and bridging loans on behalf of members. The Credit Union formed at Orwell Road in 1967 was renamed the Teachers' Union of Ireland Credit Union Limited in April 1973 and the inaugural meeting of a revived Retired Members' Association was held on 29 June 1985.[12]

Special organisations for school principals, whether within the larger body or alongside it, had been formed during each phase of the history of technical education. Yet another group, the Headmasters' Association, or Cumann Ard Mhaistrí Éireann, was founded in the late 1960s and granted recognition by the executive in January 1971.[13] A revised constitution submitted in 1978 implied that in protecting the rights of its members the association might 'take such action as may be decided' and the union executive pointed out that this might undermine its own position. In response, the association referred to another clause in its constitution—'to maintain the closest links with the TUI and to take no action contrary to the constitution of that body'—and argued that the clause precluded it from taking independent action. Despite giving that assurance the association made a separate submission to the 1980 Review Body on Teachers' Pay. The union believed that should the association's submission be accepted by the review body it would lead to a worsening of conditions, not just for school principals, but for teachers generally. Consequently, the union withdrew recognition of the association.[14] The suspension remained through 1981 but following informal contacts with the union in early 1982, that year's congress was informed that the association now appeared more reasonable and conciliatory. Agreement was soon reached on the respective roles of the association and the union—in particular the association's acceptance of the inclusive negotiating role of the union—and as a result recognition

TUI members Barney Winston, Don Dillon, Jack Lennox, Valerie McCormick and Seán Connolly at the consultative congress, Dublin, 1986 (Jim Connolly)

TUI members Mary Healy, Elaine McElligott, Denis Magner and Anne Mahon at the annual congress, Malahide, 1990 (Tony O'Connell Europhoto)

Minister for Education Gemma Hussey in discussion with TUI President Tom Hunt, General Secretary Jim Dorney and Assistant General Secretary Mairín Ganly at the Department of Education, 1983 (Irish Times)

TUI General Secretary Jim Dorney addressing TUI members, Cork, 1986 (Patrick Redmond)

ASTI General Secretary Kieran Mulvey, ASTI President Louis O'Flaherty, INTO General Secretary Gerry Quigley, INTO President Róisín Carabine, TUI General Secretary Jim Dorney and TUI President Seán MacCarthy sign the agreement on the formation of Teachers United, 1986 (Lensmen)

INTO President John White, TUI President Billy Fitzpatrick and ASTI President Joe Costello at the inauguration of the Council of Teachers' Unions, 1990 (Lensmen)

Jim Dorney 1979–81

Tom Hunt 1981–3

Larry Kavanagh 1983–5

Seán MacCarthy 1985–7

Michael Hanly 1987–8

Peter MacMenamin 1988–90

Billy Fitzpatrick 1990–92

Ed Riordan 1991–4

Tony Deffely 1994–6

Alice Prendergast 1996–8

Joe Carolan 1998–

Art teacher Peadar McNamara with pupil Patricia Cahill, Vocational School, Ennis, 1985 (Seán Kilmartin)

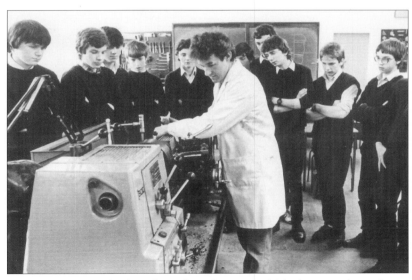

Metalwork teacher Richard Hayden with pupils, Vocational School, Maynooth, 1984 (Irish Times)

The Library, Regional Technical College, Limerick, 1994 (Mary Costelloe)

Chemical instrumentation student taking B.Sc. degree, Regional Technical College, Limerick, 1994 (Limerick Institute of Technology)

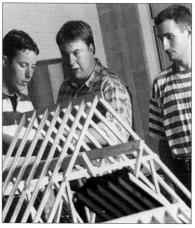

Chartered surveying students, Regional Technical College, Limerick, 1994 (Mary Costelloe)

TUI members Seamus Kilgannon, Seán Connolly and Eugene McCoy on picket duty, Leinster House, 1990 (Lensmen)

TUI members from Cork City Colleges branch on picket duty, Leinster House, 1988 (Lensmen)

as a subcommittee of the TUI was restored to the association by the executive on 22 October 1982.[15] In a somewhat analogous development the Adult Education Organisers' Association developed as an organisation within the TUI representing its members' interests and campaigning for better resources for a frequently overlooked sector.

In addition to their formal functions union officers and staff continued to participate as representative members in national organisations such as the Campaign for Nuclear Disarmament, the Irish Anti-Apartheid Movement and the National Association for Mentally Handicapped in Ireland.[16] They also served as executive members of educational agencies such as Aontas, the Irish Association for Curriculum Development, the Association of Remedial Teachers, the Institute of Guidance Counsellors, the People's College and the National Adult Literacy Association. In 1974 the union was at last granted membership of the Secondary Teachers' Registration Council and it continued to be represented on official bodies such as the Intermediate Certificate Examination Committee, the Apprenticeship Curriculum Advisory Committee and various subcommittees of An Chomhairle Oiliúna (AnCO), the industrial training authority. Officers and members were also appointed to the governing body of Thomond College of Education, the National Council for Educational Awards and the Council for the Status of Women.

Between 1957 and 1973 the VTA had been a member of the World Confederation of Organisations of the Teaching Profession, the WCOTP. In 1973 it transferred its affiliation to the International Federation of Free Trade Unions, the IFFTU. In 1978 the TUI affiliated to the European Teachers Trade Union Committee, the ETTUC, which was founded in 1971 following negotiations among the international teacher organisations to promote the 'defence, at the European level, of the interests of teacher trade union members'.[17] ETTUC was dissolved in 1981 and replaced by the European Trade Union Committee for Education, the ETUCE.[18] Its role was a matter of disagreement and while the IFFTU set up a European committee to act in its stead in 1984, the ETUCE continued to operate with TUI support.[19] The IFFTU office in Amsterdam helped to process a TUI complaint to the International Labour Organisation against the Irish government's interference in the free collective-bargaining process.[20] In 1992 the IFFTU amalgamated with the WCOTP to form Education International. The general secretary, Jim Dorney, continued to serve on its executive. The TUI also remained a member of the ETUCE which would continue as the 'authoritative' voice of education in the broader European trade union movement.[21]

For the whole of the 1970s and again from 1987, ICTU, the representative voice of Irish trade unionism, played a leading role in the centrally negotiated agreements which determined teachers' pay and conditions. If the TUI was to have an effective say nationally it had to have influence in ICTU and as a relatively small union it gained significantly in strength as its senior officers were appointed to the ICTU executive: Maurice Holly was elected for the period 1974–5, Christy Devine was elected for 1976–7 and again for 1982–3, Mairín Ganly was elected each year between 1984–5 and 1989–90, Alice Prendergast served in 1990–1 and Jim Dorney served from 1991. Pay negotiations in the public service were decisively influenced by the position adopted by ICTU's Public Services Committee and the TUI's effectiveness was greatly enhanced when the general secretary, Christy Devine, held the chair of the committee from 1976 until 1982. Members and officers have at various times served on other ICTU subcommittees dealing with issues such as trade union education, women, and new technologies.[22]

Throughout this period the TUI continued to pursue its goal of having members appointed to vocational education committees. A few vocational teachers were nominated by political parties throughout the 1970s but the union argued that such gestures were always fortuitous and usually ineffective and in 1984 it launched a campaign to have the provisions of the Worker Participation Act 1977—which provided for one-third worker representation on the boards of certain state-sponsored organisations—extended to include teachers. That year the Minister for Education's *Programme for action in education 1984–1987* proposed to provide for teacher representation on committees and to make provision for their inclusion on boards of comprehensive schools and boards of regional technical colleges.[23] The union lobbied vigorously for such measures and in early 1987 the executive met the minister and argued for an adoption of the principle enshrined in the 1977 legislation. During the late 1980s the lobbying continued and the issue was kept under review in the knowledge that proposals for a restructuring of committees were being considered by the government.

Local authority elections and a consequent reconstitution of committees were scheduled for the summer of 1991 and at that year's congress the president, Billy Fitzpatrick, characterised the continuing refusal of local authorities to appoint TUI members to committees as 'offensive' and called on all political parties to support the union's demand. Hopes had been raised and crushed shortly before when a Fine Gael private member's bill to provide for teacher and parent representation was defeated in the Dáil. While the campaign continued the minister, Mary O'Rourke, wrote to the local authorities asking that they each nominate one parent and one teacher to committees and stating that if they did not do so, she might be forced to make such appointments mandatory. As a result, of the thirty-three committees formed following the elections, twenty-seven appointed TUI representatives. Not satisfied that the appointment should remain discretionary, the union continued to lobby for legislation which would make teacher representation mandatory.[24]

Pay and working conditions

Pay, the condition which most effectively determines standard of living, is the issue by which members most readily judge their union's performance. Pay is never fixed according to a simple formula nor is it fixed in a vacuum, and the intricate web of institutional and personal pressures which attend its settlement can never be accurately anticipated nor does it provide a precedent for further action. Regardless of the circumstances of a particular claim, the TUI, no less than any other union, had to take account of changing government policy while relating effectively to the real concerns of other unions in its sector and to those in the wider labour movement.[25]

As a public service union the TUI had to be at its most effective in its negotiations with the state. Throughout the 1970s these were conducted against a sombre backdrop of parlous public finances with the goal of reaching national agreements or understandings. A feature of the period was the growing influence of the Public Services Committee of ICTU in attaining negotiated pay settlements and the TUI, as a prominent member of the committee, contributed to that process, not only when it was part of a consensus in the 1970s but also when it followed an independent line in the late 1980s. The public service unions increased their influence due to sectoral cohesiveness but even more so because the negotiating skills and personal qualities of leading figures commanded respect. In this, despite its relatively small size, the TUI played a remarkably strong hand. Some unions, particularly those with headquarters in Britain, had opposed centralised negotiation but as long as the biggest union, the Irish Transport and General Workers' Union, and the public service group of unions supported such agreements, the system continued to operate. The TUI favoured the central approach as did the Public Services Committee of ICTU and consequently teachers' pay was settled within that framework for more than a decade. The agreements of the 1970s had provision for exceptional increases subject to strict criteria. The TUI and the other teacher unions were to the fore in using those devices to their advantage and were able to obtain controversial and sometimes much-criticised 'special increases'.[26]

A decade of central bargaining ended in 1981, its demise hastened by inflation of over 20 per cent and disillusionment prompted by government ambivalence on undertakings given in the two most recent understandings. Though private sector negotiation became decentralised, a high degree of centrality remained in the public service and was characterised by two fairly uniform pay rounds—the 24th and 25th—based on civil service arbitration and conciliation settlements.[27] A report of the consultative National Economic and Social Council in 1986 provided the ideological underpinning to moves for a further and much wider national deal.[28] The return of Fianna Fáil to power the following year produced the necessary political underpinning and a draft *Programme for national recovery* was put to individual ICTU unions for consideration.[29]

The TUI took a position which differed from that of most public service unions. Its executive, dissatisfied with the modest pay increases, recommended to its members that they reject the draft programme, which they did in the proportion of three to one. The union's spirited commitment to a campaign against education cuts at the time helped firm its opposition to the proposed *Programme for national recovery*. Despite TUI opposition, ICTU adopted the draft programme by a narrow margin in November 1987. The union's independent role had a wider significance than was immediately apparent, for it revealed that the support of public service unions for central pay agreements could not be taken for granted. In 1990 there was pressure from some unions to renegotiate the *Programme for national recovery* and at a special ICTU meeting the TUI representatives, notwithstanding their earlier opposition, argued that the deal should be honoured. That position was accepted. When the *Programme for national recovery* expired, a further initiative, the *Programme for economic and social progress*, was proposed and it may be that its more attractive terms reflected the realisation that the support of unions such as the TUI could no longer be taken for granted.

The years of the *Programme for national recovery*, 1988–90, saw a transformation in a key economic indicator, the gross national product. After a lengthy period of decline and stagnation, economic growth returned and gross national product increased by about 5.5 per cent in

1989 and by 8.3 per cent in 1990.[30] Unemployment continued to escalate however, as the number of new jobs created did little to absorb the rapidly increasing workforce. While the national debt relative to gross national product began to fall, intractable problems in the public finances remained and there were many interests which sought to find a scapegoat in public service pay. Neither the cost of servicing the public debt nor the escalating welfare payments bill was similarly targeted. In such a climate it was unsurprising that the government—a centre–right coalition of Fianna Fáil and the Progressive Democrats—announced that it would not honour the public service terms of the *Programme for economic and social progress*. Instead it proposed that the basic pay increases be cut and that pending special increases be postponed.[31]

TUI reaction was understandably hostile. It took the view that the short economic boom of 1988–90 was due in some measure to the restraint of unions in accepting low increases under the *Programme for national recovery*. It had resisted pressure to reopen the programme's pay agreement before it expired and equally it now resolved to resist the government's threat to the agreed terms of the *Programme for economic and social progress*. Despite its earlier reservations, the TUI had honoured the programme, and consequently it was now in a strong moral and tactical position. Not surprisingly, it was to the fore in the campaign to defend the threatened programme. The Public Services Committee of ICTU co-ordinated the pressure on the government. In this the TUI played a central role and its profile was raised considerably when the general secretary, Jim Dorney, took part in television and radio broadcasts, explaining the unions' attitude. In the face of apparent government intransigence tension increased and detailed plans were made for a public service day of action on 27 January 1992. In the political arena too there was heightened tension as a result of rapidly changing patterns of loyalty and leadership within Fianna Fáil. Such circumstances may have weakened the government's resolve to stand firm and shortly before the day of action the Ministers for Finance and Labour met the unions and agreed a compromise. Under its terms increases would be eventually paid in full, subject to discussions to take account of the budgetary position.[32]

Whatever the vicissitudes of national politics, TUI members would continue to judge their union mainly on its record in forwarding their interests. Like members of any other union they may have been more interested in their pay relative to other workers, especially those in the same sector as themselves, rather than in absolute pay levels. The national pay agreements of the 1970s and late 1980s and the public service agreements of the mid-1980s did not change relativities in the public service greatly, despite some small degree of higher increases for the lower paid. Activity by the TUI on the general front did not, therefore, affect teachers' pay greatly, relative to other workers. Thus the general increases tell only half the story and it is in the area of special increases that evidence of how teachers fared relative to other workers may be found.

In the 1970s and 1980s, special increases, additional to the basic increases in the national agreements or whatever other agreement applied, had to satisfy increasingly stringent criteria. It was here that the TUI and the other teacher unions, usually acting in close concert, achieved some of their most significant victories. In 1978 the teacher unions went to arbitration and by proving there was a 'specific relationship' with the pay of civil service executive officers—the criterion for a special increase laid down in the prevailing national pay agreement—got a two-phase increase of 4.5 per cent and 3.3 per cent at the maximum of the common basic scale from 1 July 1978 and 1 January 1979. This brought the maximum of the teachers' common basic scale to £6,278. The unions pressed further, using political channels rather than the more orthodox industrial relations route. The Fianna Fáil government had just seen its share of the vote decline from a previous 51 per cent to 35 per cent in the June 1979 European Parliament elections. Electoral difficulties were exacerbated by the party's internal struggles and on 11 December 1979 Charles Haughey took over as Taoiseach from Jack Lynch.

Shortly afterwards a Review Body on Teachers' Pay was appointed with judge, Noel Ryan, as its chairman. On 22 September 1980 it presented an interim report recommending increases but with a delaying device whereby several years would separate the higher points of the scale.[33] The three teacher unions were dissatisfied and involved both the Minister for Education—a former president of the ASTI, John Wilson—and the new Taoiseach in negotiations. Agreement was finally reached on 24 October 1980 after an exhausting nine-hour session. Despite the recently defended executive-officer link, teachers broke away and got a rise of 34.5 per cent at their final maximum (the 26th point) and 14.6 per cent at their normal maximum (the 15th point). Increases in allowances were also agreed. In 1980 inflation stood at 18.2 per cent. The teachers' negotiators displayed industrial relations skill of a very high order but even this was outshone by their political skill in getting an improvement on the figures put forward by the review body.[34] Significantly, the review body did not present any further reports and soon disbanded.

The drama which accompanied that increase was eclipsed by the events attendant on the next special increase. From September 1980 many public service groups got special increases of about 10 per cent and the teachers presented a consequential claim in December 1982. Disagreement was recorded on the claim at conciliation in December 1983 and in January 1985 the teachers presented the claim to arbitration. In November 1985 the arbitration board recommended a 10 per cent rise, half to be paid from 1 September 1985 and half from 1 March 1986. The increase would, it was estimated, cost £10 million in 1985, £55 million in 1986 and £60 million in each subsequent year. This was a time of growing economic difficulty when the gross national product was falling and public finances were in disarray. As a result great pressure was put on the teachers to defer implementation and have the increase granted in three phases: one-third from 1 December 1986, one-third from 1 December 1987 and one-third from 1 July 1988.[35]

The teachers' unions initiated a strong campaign against the loss of arrears. The tension was dramatically heightened when during a radio interview the Fine Gael Minister for Education, Gemma Hussey, questioned the 'morality' of the teachers' claim.[36] Her intervention was bitterly resented and by heightening the sense of grievance amongst teachers would prove hugely counterproductive. Garret FitzGerald, then Taoiseach, has recorded in his memoirs that Hussey had his sympathy, 'as she met a flood of almost hysterical denunciation from indignant teachers'.[37] In her diary she too would record her disillusionment, not only with the teacher unions—'the teachers' quite vicious campaign against me continues'—but with her civil servants and government colleagues as well.[38]

On 6 February 1986 Hussey moved a motion in the Dáil to have the increase paid through a mechanism of phased implementation. If accepted, her proposal would save the exchequer £63 million in 1986 and £110 million overall. Most of the public service arbitration schemes allow the relevant minister to reject or amend an arbitration finding with Dáil approval but this power had hardly ever been used. Indeed, the conciliation and arbitration schemes had depended for their effectiveness on the assumption that arbitration would be the final stage. The only other time when the option to move a Dáil motion was used was in 1953 when Seán MacEntee got Dáil approval to defer a general pay increase for civil servants. Widespread protest followed on that occasion and may well have been a factor in the defeat of Fianna Fáil in the May 1954 general election.[39] If ghosts from that era were offering counsel, the minister remained unmoved and when her motion was put to the Dáil, it was passed by eighty-two votes to seventy.[40] Hussey's difficulties were compounded when government plans to cease funding Carysfort College of Education, a decision which would lead, inevitably, to its closure, were leaked to the president of the college. There were elements of high farce in the incident as FitzGerald recorded it, particularly in his frustrated attempts to reshuffle his government—a botched job, as he remembered it—which left Hussey 'deeply distressed' as she moved from Education to Social Welfare.[41]

On 8 February 1986 the three teachers' unions held special delegate conferences and decided to ballot for strike. The TUI ballot showed that 81 per cent of members favoured strike and the executive then decided that a series of three-day regional strikes should take place in March. Further action was contemplated but given the unwillingness of the ASTI to pursue such a strategy the TUI stopped short of preventing the holding of Department of Education language examinations.[42] Despite a personal appeal from the new Minister for Education, Paddy Cooney, the TUI annual congress authorised further industrial action, including an agreement not to participate in voluntary supervision and assessment of the summer examinations. Over 70 per cent of members endorsed that position at ballot and a ban on involvement in that summer's practical examinations was agreed. The debate intensified, with the Taoiseach passionately insisting in a television interview that compromise by the government was not possible, while the three unions countered by asking ICTU to have the issue referred to the Employer–Labour Conference. Following complicated negotiations, and just before the ban on examinations came into effect, an offer of *ex gratia* payments totalling £35 million was made. It was also agreed that further discussions could be convened later. Despite being put to the members 'without recommendation', 77 per cent of TUI members voted to accept the offer while the ASTI voted 78 per cent in favour and the INTO, 72 per cent. The plan for regional strikes was then suspended.

In his assessment of Paddy Cooney's handling of the issue, Garret FitzGerald gives a somewhat left-handed compliment to the unions while revealing the sometimes fortuitous process of dispute resolution:

> He turned out to be too easily convinced by his civil servants of the need to concede to some of the teachers' unions demands although, in fairness I should add that they ended up persuading me also, against my better judgement, to agree to these concessions on the basis that the cost would be covered by a combination of savings on the salaries of teachers who had been on strike and a claim for a graduates' allowance that was due to be settled but could be subsumed in settlement of the dispute. I subsequently came to doubt the validity of this calculation.[43]

In September 1986 the unions wrote to the political parties seeking support in a campaign to have the balance of the arbitration award, £75 million, paid. They followed this in October and November with a series of meetings with the five parties represented in the Dáil. A meeting with the Minister for Education and the Minister for Labour in October appeared to make little progress.[44]

The general election of February 1987 brought Fianna Fáil back to office, though without a clear majority. In October that year ICTU, in discussions on the *Programme for national recovery*, raised the issue of the arbitration award. It was informed that the government would not be able to consider payment during the term of the programme, though it recognised the right of the teacher unions to raise the matter again at its expiry on 31 December 1990. The unions submitted two pay claims to arbitration in 1989; one for an increase in the common basic scale, the other being a 'claim for the recovery of the £75m withheld by governments'. The claim for an increase in the basic scale was taken to arbitration and resulted in increases of 8 per cent for the 1st to 4th points; 9 per cent for the 5th to 14th points; 10 per cent on the 15th and the 18th points; 11 per cent on the 22nd point and 12 per cent on the 26th point. Qualification, responsibility and other allowances would also be increased by 10 per cent. Under the *Programme for economic and social progress* these increases were to be implemented as to 40 per cent from 1 May 1991, 30 per cent from 1 March 1992 and 30 per cent from 1 September 1992 but due to budgetary difficulties this phasing was altered, by agreement, in January 1992, the full amount, including arrears, to be paid at specified dates.[45]

The pay of teachers relative to others in the public service and elsewhere had been determined essentially by special increases: general increases which applied to all categories made little relative change. Between 1 January 1972 and 1 December 1981 there had been nine general pay rounds, the 13th to 21st postwar pay rounds, negotiated under the series of national agreements and understandings. The 22nd, 23rd, 24th and 25th rounds—1 December 1981 to 31 December 1986—were negotiated in the public service following the collapse of national bargaining. The process of national pay deals recommenced on 1 January 1987 under the *Programme for national recovery* and the *Programme for economic and social progress*, the 26th and 27th rounds in the public service. The special increases—described above—won by teachers during the two decades from 1972 to 1992 and the increases obtained by their traditional analogue grade in the civil service, that of executive officer, are set out in Table 9.2. Up to 1980 teachers got exactly the same special increases as executive officers so their relative position was unchanged. In the 1980s, however, they improved their relative position substantially by getting cumulative special increases of 39 per cent at the normal maximum (15th point) and 63 per cent at the final maximum compared with the 27 per cent granted to executive officers.

Table 9.2: Special increases for teachers and executive officers 1972–92 (%)

	Increases in the maximum of the teacher scale	Increases in the maximum of the executive officer scale
1 April 1974	–	5.0
1 January 1975	5.0	–
1 July 1978	4.5	4.5
1 January 1979	3.3	3.3
1 September 1980	14.6 (15th point—normal maximum)	8.5
	34.5 (26th point—final maximum)	
1 October 1985	–	2.4
1 December 1985	–	2.5
1 December 1986 }		
1 December 1987 }	10.0 (in three phases)	–
1 July 1988 }		
1 September 1988	–	1.0
1 July 1989* }		
1 April 1990 }	10.0 (in three phases)	–
1 October 1990 }		
1 May 1991* }		
1 March 1992 }	10.0 (in three phases—normal maximum)–	
1 September 1992 }		

* Original phasing

The TUI's success in enhancing the basic scale should not obscure its achievements in other less well-known claims. Of these the conditions of part-time teachers were of particular importance, all the more so when restrictions on the employment of whole-time teachers resulting from budgetary cuts led to an increase in part-time and temporary positions. In 1977 the union sought to have the pay of part-time teachers adjusted in line with basic rates. The Department of Education was unsympathetic and raised not only financial objections but also the plea that such teachers did not come within the scope of the conciliation and arbitration scheme, nor were they covered by general legislation on working conditions since they did not work a sufficient number of hours weekly. The TUI tackled the issue nationally as it joined ICTU's campaign on the conditions of part-time workers while at the level of the European Community it contributed to an ICTU lobby to have a directive introduced on equal rights for part-time workers. The union had some success in direct negotiations in 1982 but it was not until 1984 that significant progress was achieved.[46]

Following extensive research the TUI lodged a claim for fully proportional treatment of part-time teachers in all aspects of pay and conditions with the sector's largest employer, the Dublin city vocational education committee. It also sought full consultation before any attempt to extend the use of part-time teachers. Following the threat of a public demonstration the Dublin city committee indicated its support for the union's claim, thereby clearing the way for direct discussions with the Department of Education and as a result of heavy pressure by the union the claim was submitted to the Labour Court. It recommended *pro rata* pay and conditions comparable with those of wholetime teachers and following further detailed negotiations with the department, agreement was reached on a renewable annual contract covering all aspects of the conditions of part-time teachers including, in 1989, maternity leave. The net result was that the TUI achieved a landmark agreement of significant value to part-time members and in so doing established that these workers had, as of right, access to the Labour Court.[47] Shortly afterwards the union also had the satisfaction of seeing its pressure through ICTU contributing, however indirectly, to the passing of the Worker Protection (Regular Part-Time Employees) Act 1991.

While the high-profile activities of the TUI impinged on significant elements of national finance, on economic planning and on social policy, they did not necessarily impress any rank-and-file member who was not active in union affairs. For many such members, a 'special case' which involved direct negotiation with a vocational education committee or with the Department of Education generally proved more compelling. Most of these cases never come to national attention but it is their relentless pursuit which captures the loyalty of members. Advice and help were most usually sought— increasingly through a clinic system— when a service was being established and duties were yet undefined. Most such cases were settled quickly but less clear-cut individual cases, especially claims for incremental credit, responsibility allowances, permanent appointment and lapsed posts of responsibility, claimed a substantial portion of union resources. The uncertainty which attended the establishment and application of fair promotion procedures continued to be the most persistent cause of difficulty, at it had been at every stage of the service's history.[48]

Gender equity

By the early 1970s two significant conditions of employment, equal pay—regardless of sex or marital status—and the removal of the bar on married women obtaining permanent posts, had obtained statutory underpinning. As a consequence the general secretary could report to the 1974 congress that discussions in relation to the full implementation of equal pay were being concluded successfully and that it would be fully implemented from 31 December 1975.[49] The optimistic, egalitarian mood of the time was reinforced by the UNESCO designation of 1975 as International Women's Year, echoed by the promise of the Minister for Labour to mark the year with the introduction of anti-discrimination legislation. Such ideals were not easily translated into reality and in his presidential address to the 1977 congress Billy Webb referred to the 'hysterical' attempts by some vocational education committees to impede a married woman's teaching career. In this the right to paid maternity leave was critical, an issue the TUI was forced to pursue in a number of instances. Since the lifting of the bar on married women obtaining permanent posts, the union had also pursued their right to be paid a gratuity similar to that traditionally paid to men on marriage. The principle was finally conceded in 1979 but with the full implementation of equal pay—regardless of marital status—marriage gratuities, for either men or women, had become an anachronism.[50]

Concerns about women's issues were not confined exclusively to questions of salary or tenure. Thus two resolutions at the 1981 congress sought to have the TUI declare opposition to abortion while another condemned the restrictions in family planning legislation as being anti-woman. Progress and consensus were recorded that year, however, when the union successfully concluded negotiations it had initiated in 1978 for paid maternity leave. Continuing anxiety that women's issues were not being effectively considered within existing union structures resulted in the adoption of a resolution that a special Women's Council be established. An inaugural meeting in the Shelbourne Hotel, Dublin on 2 October 1982 adopted the aim to promote greater involvement of women in the union, to investigate their working conditions and to promote gender equality through the various levels of the education system.[51]

The Women's Council also planned a programme of affirmative action and in response to widespread concerns both within and outside the union commissioned research to establish the factors which determined the allocation of senior positions. It also produced a discussion document on sexism, considered the issue of child-care facilities for working parents and initiated debate on job-sharing and appointment procedures.[52]

Within a short period the Women's Council had done much to raise consciousness of equity issues and by 1984 was well placed to guide the union's submission to the joint Oireachtas committee on women's rights. In it the union argued for an extension of the 1977 Employment Equality Act to the education system. It attributed considerable significance to the power of teacher attitudes which wittingly or unwittingly reinforced gender stereotyping and it thus welcomed moves to promote an official examination of sex stereotyping embedded in the curriculum, whether in its allocation of subjects, the design of texts or the allocation and promotion of teachers. The union argued that the provision of a 'different' curriculum implied the acceptance of inequality and as a consequence it declared its commitment to a fully integrated co-education school system, where teachers, subjects and classes would be organised so that boys and girls would have access equally to all that a school might offer.[53]

The Women's Council developed its position further in 1985 through seminars and a series of workshops which sought to formulate strategies that might provide for a translation of principles into action. Thus it suggested alternative forms of time-tabling which would facilitate greater access to subjects, it developed strategies for the organisation of vocational preparation classes on a desegregated basis and it contributed to the setting of the agenda for meetings with the national apprenticeship authority, AnCO, to discuss the problems facing women entering non-traditional occupations.[54] The educational cutbacks of the mid-1980s had worsened the pupil–teacher ratio and hindered attempts to provide non-traditional subjects for girls. The goal of promoting a general adoption of job-sharing strategies also ran into difficulties. ICTU pronounced against it, arguing that if primarily confined to women workers it would lead to further reductions in the level of female earnings relative to those of males. An overall reduction in working hours for all employees would remain a priority, it declared, until the gap between men's and women's pay was closed.[55] Despite some setbacks the Women's Council became increasingly vigorous in the late 1980s in its support of various initiatives including the provision of créche facilities, the ICTU programme 'Equality for Women', occupational health strategies and sex-education programmes.[56]

From a varied and full agenda, the conditions of women teachers and particularly their participation in school management would remain the prime concern of the Women's Council. As a result, the union, in conjunction with the Employment Equality Agency, commissioned research on equality of opportunity in teaching. The results were published in 1990 and highlighted the extent to which attitudes within the profession reflected the attitudes of society in general, the extent to which women still carried the main responsibility for children and the degree to which men and women members alike believed that married women seeking promotion were strongly disadvantaged.[57] If the dimensions of the issue were greater than anything the union might tackle, members of the council may have found consolation in the establishment of the Second Commission on the Status of Women in 1990. Among its members was the TUI's deputy general secretary, Mairín Ganly. Its brief was to report on the means 'by which women will be able to participate on equal terms and conditions with men in economic, social, political and cultural life'.[58] The commission's report was published in 1993 and in endorsing its findings the TUI urged the Department of Education to set up a working party to devise a suitable training programme to support the implementation of relevant recommendations in the schools.[59]

At various times the Women's Council had been asked to change its name to reflect a more general concern with equality. Such proposals reflected the belief that its agenda, by focusing on women alone, was necessarily limited and that the creation of equitable conditions required a focus on all workers. A change in the conditions of one group of teachers, it was argued, would lead to changes in the conditions of the other. The council rejected that proposition on the basis that there was clear evidence that women were more disadvantaged than men in their attempts to obtain positions and promotion, and that, it argued, warranted a special focus for union action. Notwithstanding the strength of that argument, the 1990 congress adopted a resolution from the County Cork branch that the Women's Council should be renamed the Equality Council.[60]

In what would prove to be one of its final initiatives, the Women's Council recommended the setting up of a task force to examine the extent to which the union's own structures inhibited the promotion of equality and the 1991 congress adopted a report that the standing committee of the now renamed council should review participation rates by men and women at the various levels of union activity and report to the 1994 congress. When the report was duly submitted it revealed that while women made up approximately 40 per cent of the union their representation at executive level fell far short of that. While there seemed to be little prospect of a dramatic or immediate change, there was some evidence of a gradual increase in the number of women delegates to the annual congress. Greater involvement by women in union affairs might be facilitated, it was suggested, by the appointment of an equality officer in each branch.[61]

Institutional and curricular reform

The Vocational Education (Amendment) Act 1970 gave committees the power to work with other interests to provide second-level education. The way was thus cleared for them to participate in planning for local school provision, particularly the proposed community schools, and to be represented in any new management structures. Many TUI members took a literal interpretation of the name given to the new schools and argued that they should become a focus for community activity and be able to serve the needs of all, as had the vocational school, regardless of sex, class or religion. Addressing the 1973 congress, the president, Kevin McCarthy, articulated the view of a membership proud of its democratically controlled and socially unrestricted schools and argued that the vocational school had always been a community school, in the truest meaning of the term.[62]

When the community school was first proposed in 1970, Fine Gael, then in opposition, argued that teachers should be represented in the new management structures. In power it was unable to include them, however, and a draft deed of trust issued in May 1974 specifically excluded teachers from boards of management. Equally worrying to TUI members was a proposal to reserve a quota of teaching posts in each school for members of religious orders and a clause that implied restrictions on the moral and religious beliefs of a teacher. As the number of proposals for community schools grew, an increasing number of TUI members realised that their future work might be in contexts quite different from what they had experienced previously. At the 1975 congress the president, Billy Webb, outlined the TUI's objections to the proposed structure and suggested that if accepted, it would be a victory for interests that could not accept a system in which their power could be less than absolute. As long as such anxieties remained unallayed, the union would oppose acceptance of deeds of trust and employment contracts.[63]

Discussions on the control and management of community schools dragged on through 1975 and 1976 without any apparent progress, and with a growing sense of unease the TUI realised that it had been only marginally involved in critical negotiations.[64] The seriousness of the issue forced the executive to appoint a subcommittee to monitor developments and to formulate policy proposals. Pressure on the Minister for Education, John Wilson, increased and he soon indicated that he would invite the union to join discussions and would strive to get agreement from the other interests for the inclusion of teachers on boards. By September 1978 the ASTI and the TUI were able to formulate a joint approach, a unilateralism that may have increased the urgency of discussions between the unions and the religious interests. As the talks progressed it became clear that the TUI would lessen its opposition to the proposed deed of trust if the religious interests showed a willingness to accept the principle of teacher representation.[65] When a revised draft deed was issued in July 1979 it provided for an enlarged ten-person board with two places for teacher representatives while the proposal that the principal or a school chairman would have the right to dismiss a teacher had been removed. Revised 'faith and morals' provisions now seemed less threatening and as the number of religious teachers continued to decline, any provision to guarantee their employment seemed less relevant. The union convened a special congress on 3 October 1979 which agreed to ballot second-level members on the withdrawal of objections to the deed of trust. The motion was carried and the subsequent ballot revealed a divided second-level membership which on balance supported acceptance of the deed of trust document even though unsettling questions on the precise conditions of representation and the filling of posts remained unresolved.[66]

Clearly the community schools had been perceived as a threat by the vocational sector. Through the 1970s their number increased steadily while at the same time no new vocational school was sanctioned. Between late 1976 and 1980 various committees which faced the prospect of seeing community schools established in their jurisdictions argued that the Department of Education should encourage the founding of new vocational schools that would have some of the characteristics of a community school.[67] Negotiations between the department and the committees revealed that it might be possible to get Catholic Church endorsement for the project in return for the guarantee of seats on individual school boards and provisions for the employment of school chaplains. The schools, now generally referred to as community colleges, would each have a board of up to twelve members representing various interests including teachers, parents and the churches. They would thereby appeal to those parents for whom the involvement of religious had been one of the attractions of the community school, while at the same time lessening the need for the religious interests to push for a more costly involvement in a local community school. To the TUI they had many attractions, not least that as vocational education committee foundations they would afford a 'higher degree of democratic account-ability' than the community school, while their adherence to Memo-randum V 7 as the basis of a teacher's contract would ensure negotiated conditions of service.[68]

The strains exerted within an expanding and reformed second-level system promoted a concern with curriculum development which was as intense, perhaps, as those that had accompanied the introduction of continuation education in 1930 or the Group Certificate in 1947. An early response was concentrated within a pioneering voluntary group, the Irish Association for Curriculum Development, which drew much of its vigour from its association with Dublin vocational schools and teachers. The TUI was strongly supportive of its work and the presi-dent, Kevin McCarthy, asked delegates to the 1973 congress to regard it as a resource for teachers who struggled to reach learners unconvinced of the relevance of school.[69] The following year his successor, Pádraig Ó Conghaile, called for curricular alternatives for pupils from constituen-cies formerly excluded from the secondary school and for whom the secondary curriculum was now being advocated. 'Failures at what?' he asked, and he went on to demand investment in curriculum develop-ment which would seek ways to validate and cherish the intelligence and personal skills of each pupil.[70] Not surprisingly then the union's education committee reacted negatively to the report of the Intermedi-ate Examination Committee in 1975. It argued that what was being proposed would lead to an examination of a limited range of skills and aptitudes and that by making assessment school-based and certification school-specific, the divide between the two sectors would deepen.[71] By now it was becoming more obvious that the goals of educational equal-ity may have been hastily conceptualised and perhaps misunderstood in the heady and optimistic 1960s. Significant changes in the school sys-tem would not be easily accomplished and a substantial alteration in the alignment of educational success and social class would prove to be even more problematical. Such concerns caused a great deal of soul searching amongst members and intense, if inconclusive, debate at suc-cessive congresses.[72]

A major curricular reform was anticipated with the establishment of an interim Curriculum and Examinations Board in January 1984. The teacher unions together canvassed for 80 per cent of its places to be allocated to education interests while the TUI argued that at least 50 per cent of its membership should be drawn from teacher unions. Throughout 1985 and 1986 the TUI actively sought increased representation on the board and its various subcommittees, a matter of considerable importance following the passing of the Department of Education's syllabus committees to the aegis of the board, and it intensified its campaign following the publication in November 1986 of a Bill to give the board statutory power. Hopes for a representative and accountable body with real responsibility and power were dashed the following February by the formation of the non-statutory National Council for Curriculum and Assessment. The union objected to its *ad hoc* nature and low teacher representation. More fundamentally it wondered if there was a serious commitment to curriculum reform while staffing ratios in schools remained poor. Consequently, it agreed to participate only in course committees and delayed joining the council itself until December 1988. A second council was formed on 7 March 1991 and the union accepted the two places offered to it, despite continuing anger at the council's narrowly based composition and limited powers. Consequently, it continued to press for greater teacher representation, a statutory basis for the council's work and an end to the division of responsibility for curriculum content and for assessment between the council and the department.[73]

From the 1930s two different systems of second-level education had been characterised by widely differing forms of curriculum and assessment. The decision to introduce the Group Certificate in 1947 was largely in response to demands from teachers and managers within the vocational education sector for a national, centrally administered examination that would bear some degree of comparison with the examinations of the secondary sector. The extension of the secondary curriculum to the vocational schools in the late 1960s revealed that vocational teachers were in agreement on the merits of the new system and its examinations. Many argued for the retention of the Group Certificate as the sole examination of the sector's junior cycle, as a preliminary stage, perhaps, before progressing to a 'technical' Leaving Certificate. Others argued for the abolition of the Group Certificate on the basis that its continuance would only serve to reinforce social and pedagogic divisions.[74] From the late 1960s, however, the union increasingly supported policies that promoted convergence in second-level education and there was general support in 1991 for the decision to introduce a common examination, the Junior Certificate, to replace the dual system of Group and Intermediate Certificates. As had been the case on the occasion of many previous innovations, the arrival of the Junior Certificate found teachers and pupils ill-prepared. The union was engaged in vigorous negotiation with the Department of Education during the school year 1991/2 over the availability of sample papers, schemes of marks and standards, the role of external moderation and the need for additional staff allocation, while the level of remuneration for examination duties continued to be, as ever, a contentious issue.[75]

The 1980s had been punctuated by many initiatives and by proposals for structural and curricular reform. Few of these were fully realised and a government green paper published in 1985 proposed to set a framework for consensus and the basis of future policy. The TUI made its submission. When the subsequent white paper was published at Easter 1992 there was much in it that the union could welcome but serious differences emerged, particularly over what the union came to characterise as a sheepish call for an unquestioning alignment of the school to the perceived needs of the economy. The union's response was set out in detail in *Equality in education*, a reaffirmation of its belief that education could and should be the means of achieving a more just and equitable society and not merely a mechanism to supply specific forms of labour for industry.[76] That goal was articulated more fully and given a clear policy orientation in the union's submission to the National Convention on Education in October 1993. It was an opportunity to reaffirm the values detailed in many previous position papers and submissions and it reflected an evolution of ideas that had developed over the previous half-century. The TUI would remain committed to the formation of a system of education that was free, non-selective, multi-denominational and co-educational.[77]

Financial retrenchment

Education expansion and reform had led, inevitably, to greatly increased expenditure and by the early 1970s the debts incurred during the relatively free-spending 1970s pressed heavily on successive governments as did a public service pay bill swollen mainly by the rampant inflation of the 1970s. In December 1982 Gemma Hussey, Minister for Education in the newly formed Fine Gael–Labour coalition, was given the unpalatable job of cutting expenditure. Over the Christmas holidays restrictions in the school transport scheme were introduced, the pupil–teacher ratio increased and vice-principals in schools with under 250 pupils and guidance counsellors in schools with under 500 pupils were included with a school's ordinary staffing allocation. Teachers reacted with predictable anger. Meetings were sought with Dáil deputies and with the minister, a one-day strike was planned for 26 January and TUI members were instructed not to undertake the administration of duties associated with the new policies. In an impressive show of unity on strike day the three teacher unions combined to give a press conference which outlined the likely effects of the cuts, while 7,000 teachers demonstrated outside Leinster House. However, apart from the minister's promise that she would look at 'hardship' cases in the matter of school transport, the government made no concession.[78]

In his presidential address to the 1983 congress, Tom Hunt denounced what he characterised as a serious undermining of the concept of free second-level education in order to save a few 'paltry' pence. 'No president has stood before an annual congress in the last two and a half decades amid such educational devastation', he declared; the free bus scheme had revolutionised access to education and now its good would be undone by penny-pinching charges, cuts in the guidance service were indefensible at a time of high unemployment, while changes in the pupil–teacher ratio would reduce the range of subjects and choice.[79] A survey conducted by union officers revealed that many schools had begun to limit the courses they were prepared to offer and that remedial and guidance services were everywhere showing strain.[80]

Over the next two years the impact of the cuts became more apparent as teachers retired or resigned, leaving gaps in staffing which the Department of Education insisted should not be filled. Within schools, morale was slipping dangerously and material conditions worsened. The request of the chief executive officer of Sligo vocational education committee that in planning holidays meteorological forecasts might be used to identify 'heat efficient days'—a holiday at the end of December would result in greater savings than one in October—revealed the desperate nature of some retrenchment strategies. The practice of 'career breaks', not long established and providing an opportunity for teachers to appraise their work and recover from its inevitable toll, was now seriously at risk as schools grew reluctant to release a teacher whose place might not be filled. The department's firmly held position was not to replace a teacher if the school met its criteria of being 'overstaffed'. The right of return to work was also made subject to a suitable vacancy arising—an increasingly remote possibility given the unrelenting policy of rationalisation.

Following the formation of a Fianna Fáil government in February 1987 a series of cuts more severe than the first was introduced. Most critically, a higher pupil–teacher ratio of 20 : 1 was imposed. The TUI president, Michael Hanly, warned delegates at that year's congress that as a result of their sector's inability to attract private funding or parental subvention they were facing the prospect of a return to the socially stratified institutions of earlier decades. Teachers were further enraged when appointees to posts within a permanent quota were informed that their jobs were temporary. In response, the union initiated court proceedings and took limited strike action. The action resulted in a change in policy and by the following year each of 100 threatened posts had been saved.[81]

The process of retrenchment was monitored with growing dismay by the TUI's education subcommittee and in May 1988 it published an analysis of the social and educational consequences of the cuts. Its chilling title—*Death by a thousand cuts*—did not overstate the atmosphere of anger and disillusionment which had grown within the sector during the previous six years.[82] A slight thaw came when under the auspices of the *Programme for national recovery* a package was produced which included the allocation of 175 new posts for 'disadvantaged' schools. The TUI rejected the package because twenty-five of the posts went to secondary schools which it believed had suffered relatively little. The first significant halt to the decline came in 1990 with the concession that where there were teachers over the quota they could be retained by the application of a 19 : 1 pupil–teacher ratio to make available remedial and guidance services. [83] The change in government attitude, if unspectacular in its immediate effects, was a faint gleam after a long and debilitating darkness.

The expansion of higher technical education

If higher technical education had been conceived as a jewel in the crown of vocational education, its actual size, in terms of both student numbers and the deployment of resources within the system, remained minute through the 1930s, 1940s and 1950s. Industrial expansion and the subsequent reforms in education in the 1960s brought unprecedented development, however. Intake to higher education grew steadily in the 1960s and 1970s but especially so in the greatly expanded technological sector. With the development of the regional technical colleges as exclusively third-level institutions, the traditional equation of university education with higher education became untenable and the TUI was poised to become the largest third-level union.

In most cases the curriculum of the new regional colleges continued the technical education project of the vocational education committees. Thus many of the founding staff in the colleges had been long-serving committee employees, and consequently veteran members of the VTA and then of the TUI. Separate college branches were formed which from 1973 were represented at head office through an advisory panel and later by the colleges subcommittee of the executive. An assistant general secretary was given responsibility for higher education in 1982 and the following year a widely based and representative Colleges' Advisory Council was formed. As the rate of recruitment of second-level teachers began to decline, members drawn from an expanding higher education sector became an increasingly significant part of the union.

During their initial years the development of the regional technical colleges had been inhibited by inappropriate administrative and managerial structures. It had become clear that many of the tensions within the colleges sprang from the uncertainty that characterised their planning. Some vocational school teachers regarded technical education as one stream, albeit the highest stream within an ordinary vocational school, while for others, technical education always had the potential to become a vibrant second force in higher education. Ambivalence was widespread and was tellingly revealed in 1973 when Seán O'Connor, an assistant secretary at the Department of Education, noted with a degree of disquiet that the colleges now 'appeared to be assuming the roles of third-level institutions or mini-universities'. It was time to reappraise that role and as a result the department convened a seminar to discuss the issue in October 1973; it was attended by principals, chief executive officers, representatives of boards of management and the TUI. At its conclusion, Finbar O'Callaghan, the officer of the Department of Education with responsibility for the colleges, had to admit that Memorandum V 7 which had provided the basis of working conditions under the vocational education committees since 1930 was less than suitable for the new institutions and he indicated the preparedness of the department to negotiate new conditions.[84]

Government proposals for higher education reform in 1975 included the academic validation of degree-level courses in the technological sector by university institutions and a restriction on degree-level work in technical colleges. In a submission to the minister, the TUI expressed its fears and argued that the unique character of the regional technical colleges must be maintained and to this end the establishment of a significant proportion of degree work in the colleges should be regarded as a positive development and not an unnecessary academic drift.[85] The trend to diminish the higher education role of the colleges was firmly

reversed by Fianna Fáil in 1977 when it restored degree-awarding powers to the National Council for Educational Awards (NCEA), the sector's award-validating body. In July 1979, in a submission preceding
the compilation of a proposed white paper, the TUI indicated acceptance of a binary division of higher education on curricular lines but
voiced resolute opposition to any subsequent hierarchical division that
valued the technological curriculum less than that of the universities. It
welcomed the restoration of degree-awarding powers to the NCEA and
looked to a fully developed sector obtaining equal allocation of resources,
staffing and research facilities.[86]

In 1978 a series of claims on college staffing and salary structures
were submitted to conciliation, the outcome of which was accepted by
college members and by the TUI executive in 1979.[87] Nonetheless later
that year some college members complained to ICTU of lack of service,
a claim that ICTU rejected.[88] Dissatisfaction with what may have been
a hastily concluded agreement was revealed in resolutions to the 1981
congress from the Cork, Galway and Waterford branches. Members of
the colleges committee worked through 1981 and 1982 to renegotiate
the document and a satisfactory agreement was reached in 1982.[89]
Undoubtedly the union was chastened by the issue and one result was
the establishment of the Colleges' Advisory Council. Its most pressing
task was to respond to the growing sense of unease at the extent to
which the involvement of TUI members in technical education and
training was being affected by the expansion of organisations such as
AnCO and the Youth Employment Agency. Soon the council became
the informed voice of the union on third-level education. An important
point was reached at arbitration when pay relationships were established with the staffs of the national institutes for higher education and
a further important milestone was passed at arbitration in 1992 when
appropriate links and allocations were clarified for the higher lecturing
grades.[90]

The Lindsay committee (an interdepartmental committee representing the Departments of Education and Finance) reported in September
1989 on courses leading to awards by the NCEA and other bodies outside the universities. Its main recommendations included reduction of
on-campus duration of courses, reduced emphasis on degree and diploma courses in favour of certificate courses, expansion of research and
development, and measures to increase efficiency. The TUI rejected the
overall thrust of the report as an attempt to get unpaid-for productivity
and asserted that it underemphasised quality of service at the expense of
apparent cost effectiveness. In 1990 the executive committee decided

that as forthcoming legislation on the colleges would have major reference to increased research activities in the colleges, the executive should formulate union policy on pure and commissioned research. Subsequently, the terms of reference of this initiative were extended to include the administration of European Community initiatives in the colleges.[91]

The Regional Technical Colleges Act 1992 and the Dublin Institute of Technology Act 1992 took the colleges from the control of vocational education committees and from 1 January 1993 gave each independent status under the Department of Education. There may have been some in the TUI who regretted the sundering of the historic link but they drew assurance from the time-honoured commitment in the legislation that the working conditions of transferred staff would not worsen. The legislation was welcomed not least because it gave teachers in the sector rights of representation for the first time, though the authorities of the Dublin Institute of Technology—the sector's largest institution— attempted to exclude almost half of its staff from election on the basis of their part-time contracts.[92]

The TUI and teacher trade union unity

At various times in their history the representative bodies for technical and vocational teachers formed links with other labour organisations. For example, between 1923 and 1928 the Irish Agriculture and Technical Instruction Officers' Organisation sent delegates to the Irish Trade Union Congress. During the 1930s the Vocational Education Officers' Organisation proposed a council of education on which all teacher organisations would be represented, while a resolution at the 1945 congress for a conference of the three teacher organisations led to a series of meetings which considered joint action for 'common purposes'.[93] Such calls were repeated in the 1950s and 1960s, but the growing convergence in the profession, by highlighting remaining differences, especially in salary, promoted suspicion. Thus the publication of the 1969 Louden Ryan report on salaries signalled the beginning of bitter and complex disagreements, precisely because it had within it elements—a common pay structure, joint negotiation procedures and common conciliation and arbitration—which might facilitate professional unity. Following the publication of the report, the government determined to extend the logic of a common salary to the formation of a common scheme for conciliation and arbitration. The VTA and INTO began operating a joint scheme in February 1970 but it was not until October

1973 that it included the ASTI. From that point the three unions co-operated closely on pay, thereby raising again the possibility of eventual unity.

The impetus towards unity may also be considered as part of a process to reduce the number of trade unions, particularly those operating in similar sectors. Rivalry between such unions could be intense, especially if they actively competed for members. The realisation that competitiveness could result in overall loss of effectiveness had prompted ICTU to commission a study by the International Labour Organisation in 1974 on rationalisation. Its author, Johannes Schregle, pointed out what many in the Irish labour movement already knew: the fragmented state of Irish trade unionism was the 'fruit' of a struggle between strong personalities and different political and organisational traditions. History had left a futile legacy and he warned of the hazards on the road to unity.[94] The state too was keen to reduce the number of unions and hoped that the elimination of rivalry would ease the process of negotiation. To that end, legislation which might facilitate amalgamations was enacted.

At the 1972 congress the president, Kevin McCarthy, issued an invitation to the ASTI to discuss the possibility of greater co-operation. In May 1975 the ASTI accepted a TUI invitation to consider some form of federation and a working group of representatives of the two unions was convened and chaired by the general secretary of ICTU, Donal Nevin. The group quickly identified two possible alternatives, amalgamation or federation, and the advantages and disadvantages of both were tabulated. The group clearly favoured amalgamation, provided that it could be accomplished without affecting existing conditions in either sector. The group regarded federation less enthusiastically: such a structure, it suggested, might 'inhibit progress towards a merger and would not represent any real advance on the present position'.[95]

At the 1976 congress the TUI committed itself to a merger, in principle, as did the ASTI at its convention the following year. Thus endorsed, the working group produced a briefing document in early 1978. Joint meetings throughout the country were convened but practical difficulties began to appear and the hoped-for consensus was slow to emerge. Donal Nevin prepared a synthesis of the various responses and he proposed a draft outline structure for a merged union in January 1979. At that point the TUI broadened the discussion by asking the INTO and the Irish Federation of University Teachers (IFUT) for comments on a proposal to discuss unity. Both the INTO and IFUT were in favour, but the ASTI hesitated and significant strategic differences surfaced, particularly about the most appropriate means to obtain government agreement for a special pay review. Other difficulties emerged in July 1979 when the TUI made a submission to the state's Commission of Inquiry on Industrial Relations whereas at that point, neither the INTO nor the ASTI was prepared to make a submission.

Though the proposal for formal unity languished, practical co-operation continued. It was especially evident in 1980 in the approach of the unions to the Review Body on Teachers' Pay. For example, when the review body produced an interim report the three unions set up a working party with five members each to compose a joint response. This was achieved with great effect, making full use of access to the Minister for Education, John Wilson. Similarly, a joint TUI and ASTI committee on community and comprehensive schools found agreement on critical issues.[96] Union co-operation within ICTU and the teachers' conciliation council helped to provide the basis for the establishment at the end of 1981 of a Council of Education Unions. It included the TUI, ASTI, INTO, IFUT and a Northern Ireland union, the National Association of Teachers in Further and Higher Education. Its first chairman was TUI general secretary, Christy Devine. The council provided a useful point of contact and the base from which, in 1983, the TUI and IFUT would form a liaison committee to co-ordinate policies and demands at third level. At that point the IFUT had 1,300 members, all at third level, while 1,500 of the TUI's 7,000 members were at third level.[97]

The mood of amicable co-operation evaporated in November 1983 when the ICTU Disputes Committee heard a complaint from the TUI that the ASTI was seeking to recruit members in community colleges. The committee found that apart from colleges constituted solely on the basis of an existing vocational school, there should be the possibility of joint organisation and representation. This ruling would leave both unions competing for members in community colleges set up following the absorption of a secondary school into the vocational sector, in new colleges set up jointly by a vocational education committee and a religious agency and in colleges resulting from reconstitution of an existing vocational school. The TUI appealed the finding to ICTU, arguing that rationalisation of union structures was being hindered rather than helped by the Disputes Committee's report. It added, somewhat ominously, that 'in the event of an equitable solution being found the TUI will be more than willing to resume discussions with a view to union rationalisation'. In May 1984 ICTU ruled that there were no grounds for an appeal.[98]

While such a stand-off did little to foster good relations, it did not hinder continuing co-operation on critical issues. Thus the joint TUI–ASTI advisory committee on community and comprehensive schools was reconvened in January 1986, allowing both unions to object jointly to unilateral policy changes by the Department of Education. Similarly, the three teacher unions joined in insisting that the proposed Curriculum and Examinations Board should have 80 per cent representation for professional education interests and discussions were also opened with the ASTI on agreed appointment procedures in community and comprehensive schools. The three unions forged even stronger links while negotiating during the pay dispute in the late 1980s. In early 1986, the TUI proposed that joint executive meetings be held to facilitate the smooth running of the ensuing campaign. Statements and press releases were issued over the names of the three general secretaries and the umbrella organisation for the campaign, 'Teachers United', emerged as 'the strongest campaigning force in the trade union movement and as the most concrete expression ever of teacher unity'.[99] Such action reinforced existing alliances and by 1987 a tide favouring rationalisation was in full flow. In March, ICTU representatives initiated a series of meetings with the four principal education unions to promote rationalisation. Throughout the remainder of 1987 various options were explored and while it was becoming clearer that agreement would not be easily reached, joint executive meetings continued to formulate policy in areas of mutual concern.

An apparently significant step towards formal unity was taken at one such meeting on 22 March 1988 when following unanimous agreement that rationalisation was imperative it was agreed that the Minister for Labour be asked to facilitate the process. Areas for co-operation, including joint branch meetings, a common magazine and joint negotiation of benefits, were readily identified but it was also clear that each union's affinity with a different sector and the operation of the INTO in Northern Ireland might present special difficulties. In late 1988 disagreement had to be overcome in reaching a common policy on membership of the Curriculum and Examinations Board, but on the crucial issue of budget cuts the TUI and ASTI worked in harmony and together met the Taoiseach, the Minister for Education and the Minister for Labour to press for the reversal of a hastily conceived pupil–teacher ratio policy.

The momentum quickened in February 1989 when the ASTI, TUI and INTO agreed to once more ask Donal Nevin to facilitate discussion. There was general support at the annual congresses and after many sessions of careful drafting, proposals for a Council of Teachers' Unions were endorsed by the TUI in March 1990. The council's twenty-four places would be allocated amongst the three unions roughly in proportion to their respective sizes: the INTO with 24,100 members (56 per cent) would have twelve places, the ASTI with 12,000 members (28 per cent) would have seven and the TUI with 7,000 members (16 per cent) would have five. The council would act on conciliation and arbitration, pay, services, trade union education and international affairs. It would appoint an administrator and would draft a constitution for a single union for teachers in Ireland for submission to the three union congresses. The Council was not empowered to take any decision which any of the unions formally declared unacceptable.[100]

Following the agreement of each organisation, the inaugural meeting of the Council of Teachers' Unions was convened on 4 December 1990 in the Burlington Hotel in Dublin with Billy Fitzpatrick, TUI president, in the chair. Three working groups were then set up to co-ordinate day-to-day business—the recent withdrawal of the ASTI from the National Council for Curriculum and Assessment without consulting the TUI had provided a salient reminder of the need for such co-ordination. A subcommittee of the council with five representatives from each union was asked to consider the question of unity as provided for in the document establishing the council and an office was established to administer the council's affairs, subject to the authority of the three general secretaries.[101]

Throughout 1991 the tide swept towards unity with increasing vigour. Thus a joint meeting of the three executives on 27 March 1992 agreed to promote co-operation and contacts at school and regional level as well as nationally and it was agreed that a motion to each of the 1993 annual conferences would seek authorisation for the preparation of an outline constitution for a single union. In a heady mood of unprecedented comradeship arrangements were made for a Council of Teachers' Unions diary to replace individual union diaries and for the formulation of common policies on school–home relations, Irish, in-service education and entrance examinations.[102] The congenial mood soon evaporated. The motion for unity was readily accepted by the TUI and ASTI but its acceptance by the INTO was conditional on the other two supporting its demand for a change in the system whereby the points rating of a school and thus the allowances payable to its principal and vice-principal were based on the age of its pupils. By giving younger pupils a lower weighting, such a system appeared to favour second-level schools. Neither of the two second-level unions would agree to what they now described as an ultimatum by the INTO and that led to the withdrawal of the INTO from the council. The TUI executive then decided to invite the ASTI to have bilateral discussions on forming a single union and both also agreed to close down the council's offices. Joint TUI and ASTI meetings through the summer and autumn of 1993 continued to discuss a possible union while agreeing that any joint progress should not preclude a widening of the discussions at a later date.[103]

Conclusion

From the early 1970s into the 1990s, the growing complexity of educational institutions made challenging demands on the members and officers of the TUI. In this they were sustained by a commitment to the development of representative institutions, not only in education but in national life generally. While the TUI's services grew to keep pace with the rising expectations of members perhaps its main achievement was its ability to extend the influence of the union where its interests could be advanced to greatest effect. Thus its role within ICTU strengthened as did its participation in an increasing number of consultative and statutory bodies. With the advent of a concerted attempt to establish new parameters for planning by the social partners in 1987 the union was well placed for its attempts to influence the future shape of Irish education and society. In this it drew on a reservoir of progressive social ideas and its traditionally well-articulated concern for the plight of less well-off pupils gave its voice in that debate a special authority.

Consensus was less easily formed on other issues. Disagreement on the nature of the Women's Council in some ways seemed to echo the ambivalence of the 1950s and 1960s on the attainment of equal pay and the removal of the marriage bar. Women members were frequently reminded that the prevailing ethos in the vocational sector was and remained that of an institution where men predominate. Following a period of unprecedented expansion, membership grew less rapidly at second level and as this narrative ends the contraction in the pupil population has ensured that recruitment in the schools has just about kept pace with the numbers resigning on retirement. Any loss has been more than compensated for by a continuing expansion at third level that makes the TUI the biggest union by far in higher education. The overall age of its members continues to rise and, like them, the TUI has settled into an assured maturity. That sense of confidence may have encouraged the TUI to seriously pursue a more permanent partnership with its erstwhile competitor. Such a possibility had been raised in every decade of its history but in the period from 1974 onwards it became more central to its concerns. The creation of joint salary scales provided the basis for the growing belief that unity was no longer a romantic ideal but a realistic and necessary goal and it is not without significance that when unity moves faltered in 1993 it was on the issue of the points rating of schools, an issue with significant salary implications. The failure of the Council of Teachers' Unions to survive a short infancy prompted the question of whether unity would ever come about. But the answer to that and to many other topical questions will have to form part of another history.

Notes

1 For the general economic context see, Kieran A. Kennedy, Thomas Giblin and Deirdre McHugh, *The economic development of Ireland in the twentieth century* (London, 1988).

2 Organisation for Economic Co-operation and Development, *Economic surveys: Ireland* (Paris, 1989).

3 P. C. Humphreys, *Public service employment* (Dublin, 1993), pp. 53–101.

4 Membership data are published annually in TUI, *Annual report* (hereafter, *Report*).

5 *Report*, 1973, p. 9.

6 *Report*, 1985, pp. 27 and 64–70.

7 For a list of officers and staff see Appendix 2 below.

8 *Report*, 1985, pp. 40–1.

9 *Report*, 1991, p. 65.

10 *Ibid.*

11 *Report*, 1981, p. 5 and Appendix 1, p. 21.

12 *Report*, 1982, p. 10.

13 *Report*, 1981, pp. 66–70.

14 *Report*, 1982, p. 32.

15 *Report*, 1983, p. 22.

16 Details of membership of other organisations are printed in successive annual reports.

17 *Report*, 1984, p. 36.

18 *Report*, 1982, p. 33.

19 *Report*, 1986, pp. 49–50.

20 *Report*, 1987, p. 56.

21 *Report*, 1994, p. 42.

22 Details of union membership are printed in successive annual reports.

23 Department of Education, *Programme for action in education 1984–1987* (Dublin, 1984), section 2.19.

24 TUI, *News and Views*, 14, 1 (1991), pp. 1–2.

25 See Niamh Hardiman, *Pay policies and economic performance in Ireland 1970–1987* (Oxford, 1988) pp. 53–6.

26 Michael McGinley, 'Pay 1970–91: the issue of control', in *Industrial Relations News*, 30 (1989), p. 19.

27 *Ibid.*, p. 18.

28 National Economic and Social Council, *A strategy for development 1986–90* (Dublin, 1986).

29 *Programme for national recovery* (Dublin, 1987).

30 Anthony J. Leddin and Brendan M. Walsh, *The macro-economy of Ireland* (Dublin, 1995), pp. 10–20.

31 *Report*, 1991, pp. 77–83 and *Report*, 1992, pp. 14–20.

32 *Report*, 1992, p. 25.

33 Review Body on Teachers' Pay, *Interim report* (Dublin, 1980).

34 *TUI News*, 24 October 1980.

35 *Report*, 1987, pp. 25–8.

36 The comment was made initially at a Young Fine Gael meeting in Bray on 20 August 1985 and repeated the following day on RTÉ's *Morning Ireland*; see Dáil Éireann, *Debates*, cccdxiii (6 February 1986), cols 1864 and 2005–33; also Gemma Hussey, *At the cutting edge: cabinet diaries 1982–1987* (Dublin, 1990), p. 170.

37 Garret FitzGerald, *All in a life* (Dublin, 1991), pp. 621–4.

38 Hussey, *At the cutting edge*, pp. 188–97.

39 J. J. Lee, *Ireland 1912–1985: politics and society* (Cambridge, 1989), pp. 325–8.

40 Dáil Éireann, *Debates*, cccdxiii (6 February 1986), col. 2033.

41 Hussey, *At the cutting edge*, pp. 194–5.

42 *Report*, 1986, pp. 19–37.

43 FitzGerald, *All in a life*, p. 624.

44 *Report*, 1987, pp. 29–42.

45 *Report*, 1992, pp. 14–20.

46 *Report*, 1985, pp. 36–7.

47 *Report*, 1990, pp. 19–22.

48 For examples see, *Report*, 1990, pp. 38–9 and *Report*, 1980, pp. 29–30.

49 'Conciliation council for teachers, agreed report, 12/75', in *Report*, 1976, pp. 67–8.

50 'Circular letter, 72/79', in *Report*, 1980, pp. 63–5.

51 *Report*, 1983, pp. 30–1.

52 *Report*, 1984, pp. 25–6.

53 'TUI submission to Joint Oireachtas Committee on Women's Rights', in *Report*, 1985, p. 76.

54 *Report*, 1986, pp. 68–70.

55 'ICTU policy on job sharing', in *Report*, 1987, p. 92.

56 *Report*, 1989, p. 39.

57 *Report*, 1991, pp. 32 and 58–9.

58 Second Commission on the Status of Women, *Report to government* (Dublin, 1993), p. 6.

59 *Report*, 1994, p. 15.

60 *Report*, 1991, p. 53.

61 See 'TUI policy on sexual harassment', in *Report*, 1994, p. 40 and 'Equality task force: review', in *Report*, 1994, pp. 44–5.

62 *The Irish Times*, 25 April 1973.

63 *The Education Times*, 25 April 1974.

64 *Report*, 1977, p. 28; *Report*, 1979, pp. 28–31.

65 *Report*, 1979, pp. 28–30.

66 *Report*, 1980, p. 84.

67 See, Margaret Dorney, 'The concept of a community college: a case study' (MEd thesis, University of Dublin, 1988).

68 Louis O'Flaherty, *Management and control in Irish education* (Dublin, 1992), pp. 76–82.

69 *The Irish Times*, 25 April 1973.

70 *The Irish Times*, 17 April 1974.

71 Executive education subcommittee, 'Report on Intermediate Certificate Examination', printed as Appendix 7 in *Report*, 1976, pp. 75–7.

72 *Report*, 1972, p. 23.

73 *Report*, 1993, pp. 26–7.

74 For example see, *Gairm*, 1, 19 (1960), p. 41 and 6, 4 (1965), p. 13.

75 *Report*, 1994, pp. 31–3.

76 TUI, *Equality in education* (Dublin, 1992).

77 Printed as an appendix in *Report*, 1994, pp. 50–8.

78 *Report*, 1983, pp. 10–18.

79 *The Irish Times*, 6 April 1983.

80 'Press statement, 15 November 1983: the effect of the cut-backs in education', printed as appendix in *Report*, 1984, pp. 51–3.

81 *Report*, 1989, pp. 30–3.

82 TUI, *Death by a thousand cuts: public service education and the cuts in educational expenditure* (Dublin, 1988); also, 'Results of a survey undertaken by the Union into the effects of the education cuts imposed in 1988 on the school year 1988–89', in *Report*, 1989, pp. 59–62.

83 *Report*, 1989, pp. 22–6.

84 *Report*, 1974, pp. 8–9.

85 'TUI submission to the Minister on Government proposals in relation to Higher Education', in *Report*, 1976, pp. 78–9.

86 'Aontas Múinteoirí Éireann, submission to the Minister for Education for his consideration in the preparation of the white paper on education', printed as Appendix 1 in *Report*, 1980, pp. 41–2.

87 *Report*, 1980, pp. 8–20.

88 *Report*, 1981, p. 4.

89 See, 'Appendix to agreed report 5/82', in *Report*, 1983, pp. 35–40.

90 *Report*, 1993, pp. 47–8.

91 *Report*, 1990, p. 52.

92 *Report*, 1994, pp. 24–6.

93 Vocational Education Officers' Organisation, *Vocational Education Bulletin*, 1 (1934), p. 4; and 38 (1946), p. 799.

94 International Labour Organisation, *The restructuring of the Irish trade union movement* (Geneva, 1974).

95 'Interim report of ASTI/TUI working group', in *Report*, 1976, pp. 29–37.

96 *Report*, 1982, p. 34.

97 *Report*, 1984, pp. 13–14.

98 'TUI appeal in respect of Disputes Committee report 83/7, dated 28 November 1983', printed as appendix in *Report*, 1985, pp. 64–70.

99 'Teachers' pay dispute and certificate examination', in *Report*, 1987, pp. 29–42.

100 *Report*, 1990, pp. 22–4.

101 *Report*, 1991, pp. 28–30.

102 'Council of Teachers' Unions, *Report*', printed as appendix in *Report*, 1973, pp. 63–7.

103 *Report*, 1994, pp. 22–4.

10. 'All the Children': The Vocational School and Education Reform 1930–1990

John Logan

A country-wide system of free elementary schooling was one of the successes of the nineteenth-century state. It became a central element of policy—an instrument which successive governments hoped would shape the mind and character of each generation of pupils and thereby form the behaviour of its citizens. Despite its controversial origins in the 1830s, the national system proved immensely popular: each year saw an increasing proportion of children enrol and by the end of the century almost one million were in attendance at over ten thousand schools. If at some point in a barely remembered past the state had been fretful of the consequences of popular education, by the late nineteenth century it had instead come to fear that a child might pass into adulthood without the formation that its carefully regulated curriculum might impart. Similarly, if the churches had been anxious lest the state system might weaken the faith of their flocks, they soon saw the immense value of a country-wide network of schools which the state had placed under their patronage and management. The civil and religious project merged in the person of the national teacher who operated both as a valued catechising assistant to the priest-manager and as a dutiful promoter of civic values. The children of professional and gentry families may also have attended a national school, but more likely their elementary instruction took place privately, either at home or in an exclusive and selective school. While there, they followed a curriculum in most respects no different from that of the national schools but their formation would take on a distinctive focus in the select second-level schools whose advanced literary and computational curriculum was the means of promoting the values and skills required in economic, civic and religious leaders. At independence the new state saw little need to alter the system, and except for the Gaelicisation of the curriculum, it was left much as it had been conceived: the primary school was the country's instrument of secular and religious instruction for the children of working people while the secondary school prepared future members of its élite.

A bipartite second-level system 1930–65

The secondary schools inherited by the independent Irish state were small, private and exclusive. Throughout the 1920s their total enrolment never exceeded 30,000, representing no more than 10 per cent of all those between the ages of thirteen and eighteen. Pupils were concentrated in the lower years, and fewer than one-third of those who took the Intermediate Certificate examination would proceed to the Leaving Certificate. The system was predominately male: throughout the 1920s 60 per cent more boys than girls were enrolled and it would not be until the 1960s that the proportion of female pupils equalled the proportion of young females in the general population. Girls were concentrated in the lower years of the school cycle, and few took the full course. Thus, of the 1,058 pupils who sat the Leaving Certificate in 1929, only 313 were girls. Along with the core curriculum of religion, Irish, English and mathematics, the typical student took history and geography, science and another language, usually Latin in the case of boys and French in the case of girls.[1] If the schools were small and socially restricted, they were probably more than adequate for their purpose of preparing a future generation of managers, administrators and public servants as well as those who progressed to university.

The Vocational Education Act 1930 paved the way for the creation of another system of second-level schools. While the new vocational education committees inherited a total of seventy-seven technical schools, they were also given the power to establish additional schools in response to perceived local need. With the active encouragement of progressive reformers in the Department of Education, the number of schools doubled in the following four years, and by the end of the 1930s had reached an impressive 200. If a permanent building could not be provided, a committee could hire and equip temporary premises, of which there were over 600 by 1940. The extension of the network of schools and colleges was dramatic, particularly so in areas which previously had no provision for technical instruction. For example, in 1928 none of the counties Clare, Leitrim, Limerick, Roscommon, Sligo and Wexford had a single technical school, but by 1935 they had, between them, twenty-nine new vocational schools.

Against such expansion, the growth in the overall number of students from 64,606 in 1931 to 65,349 in 1941 seems less impressive, but the simple totals mask a continuing shift in the balance of enrolments from part-time to full-time students and a sustained improvement in regularity of attendance. A surer indication of growth, perhaps, is the number of teachers employed throughout the system. In 1931 a total of 585 were employed full time and by 1941 this had increased by 57 per cent to 921. During the same period the number of part-time teachers increased by 42 per cent. Following this initial period of rapid growth during which deficits accumulated in earlier periods were eliminated, the rate of increase in teacher numbers lessened. A growing impression of sluggishness was heightened when school building was all but halted during the war years and in its immediate aftermath. Thus during the 1940s, the total of whole-time teachers increased by 24 per cent and only four new schools were opened. However, in the latter part of that decade pupil numbers began to grow, and from the mid-1950s onwards, the combined effect of increased job opportunities arising from industrial development and a growth in population unprecedented in the history of the state stimulated rapidly increasing demand: in the 1950s the number of teachers increase by almost 60 per cent and an average of nine new schools were opened each year.

The expansion of second-level continuation courses was part of a continuing expansion of second-level schooling. A comparison of enrolment data reveals however that the movement of pupils from primary schools into continuation vocational schools lagged somewhat behind that of the pupil flow into secondary schools: enrolments in vocational schools increased at an average annual rate of 3.6 per cent during the 1950s while the rate for the secondary schools was 4.4 per cent. Growth of vocational schooling was greatest in areas lacking alternative forms of low-fee secondary schooling, in districts with distinctive patterns of industrial development and in sparsely populated and impoverished regions unattractive to the principal suppliers of secondary schools. In other words, the role of vocational education, in so far as it catered for pupil populations not covered by the mainstream secondary school, remained somewhat peripheral. On the other hand, in an era when not only schooling but many other aspects of everyday life were segregated by class, religion and sex, vocational education's policy of non-selection may have given it, in regions of low secondary school provision, a greater cultural and social significance.[2] In County Cavan in 1951, for example, there was but one secondary school admitting Catholic boys and another admitting Protestant boys, both located in the county town, while six vocational schools, spread through the county, admitted boys irrespective of religion. Adjacent Leitrim had one boys' secondary and one girls' secondary school, both again in the county town, but a total of six vocational schools spread through the county, each open to boys and girls regardless of religion.[3]

Figure 10.1: Pupil population 1924–64

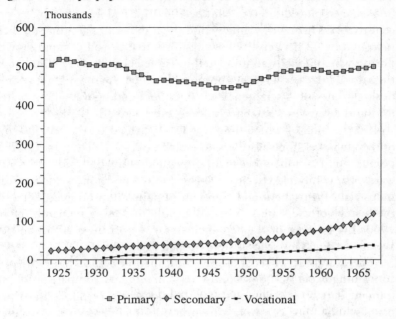

Thousands

Primary ◆ Secondary ✦ Vocational

Source: Department of Education, *Annual reports*, 1924–64.

The growth in second-level schooling is shown most dramatically in data collected in the national census from 1966 onwards. They reveal that over two-thirds of the children born in the 1920s finished their schooling in a primary school, but the proportion had dropped to just under half for those born in the 1930s. For the majority of children born in the mid-1940s and thus coming to the end of primary schooling in the late 1950s some degree of second-level schooling had become usual and for many, particularly boys, this was in a vocational school. Thus almost 60 per cent of girls leaving primary school between 1956 and 1961 continued into a second-level school, and of those 27 per cent attended a vocational school. Just 53 per cent of boys of the same cohort continued into a second-level school and 38 per cent of those attended a vocational school.[4]

The census data also reveal that the vocational school had become part of the formation of specific social groups, especially middle-size farmers and skilled manual workers.[5] By the 1950s most young people joining those occupations had attended a vocational school and it was probably the case that for many of those the opportunity of second-level schooling became possible only because of the widespread diffusion of the vocational school. While these children were regarded by some of their contemporaries as socially inferior and their school characterised as educationally second-rate, they were far from the bottom of the scale of educational advantage for there were yet some social groups, particularly the smaller farmers, the less skilled manual labourers and the unemployed, whose children would not have any chance of a second-level schooling. When the *Investment in education* team investigated the flow of children through the school system in 1963 it found that while 42 per cent of that year's primary school leavers transferred into secondary school and another 29 per cent transferred to vocational school, 29 per cent had already terminated their schooling and entered the labour market. Even less educated were the 8,000 of the cohort who had left the primary school before reaching the end of sixth class and for whom childhood, at least in educational terms, had by then come to an end.[6] If the schooling of adolescents was arranged along a social divide that had its institutional expression in the secondary and vocational schools, another, perhaps deeper, division was drawn between those still in school and those at work.

The demand for schooling reflected the efforts taken by a growing number of families to strengthen the bargaining power of their children in an economy where position was increasingly dependent on educational attainment and credentials rather than inherited position. As the occupational structure changed there was a continuing decline in the pre-eminence of agriculture and in the number of positions it could offer family members and relatives. Successive census reports revealed a continuing decline in the number of less skilled manual workers, particularly in agriculture, while the number classified as skilled manual workers and those holding educational qualifications increased. Regardless of the rhetoric—official and otherwise—that education was universally valued for its inherent worth, its economic significance remained paramount. The introduction of the Primary Certificate examinations in 1929 was justified by the need for a standard acceptable to employers, parents and teachers alike, while an important argument in its eventual removal in the 1960s was that it was no longer an appropriate standard for admission to apprenticeship.[7]

The curricular provisions in the 1930 Act rested on a fundamental distinction between the 'continuation' instruction of pupils who would probably enter manual occupations and the 'technical' instruction of those who had already finished school and now required instruction in a particular trade or craft. Both forms of curriculum could be provided in response to local demands, generally in the same school building and staffed from a common pool of teachers. Thus while the promotion of a technical curriculum would ensure the perpetuation of the project of the former technical schools, the new goal of widespread provision of continuation education—in effect another form of post-primary schooling—would be a major innovation. Together these goals ensured that the vocational school might have pupils of any age from fourteen upwards and following a curriculum chosen from a range of technical and manual-skills subjects. It was far from clear at the outset how these initiatives might develop, but the relatively low demand for advanced technical education, at a time when there was a growing demand for second-level schooling, ensured that between 1930 and 1965 the continuation second-level education of adolescents became the principal activity of most vocational schools.[8]

The vocational education legislation in 1930 required that the continuation curriculum should reflect local conditions. Nonetheless curricular guidelines formed by the inspectorate and issued as departmental memoranda ensured a measure of state-wide uniformity. Up to half of all instruction was in manual work, defined as woodwork, metalwork, rural science or construction skills in the case of boys, and domestic or secretarial skills in the case of girls. The remainder of the time was allocated to a general curriculum which included religious instruction and a continuation of the literacy and numeracy curriculum of the primary school.[9] The celebrated Memorandum V 40 issued by the Department of Education in 1942 reinforced those general patterns, and its stipulative tone, somewhat at variance with the intent of the 1930 legislation to promote regional diversity in curriculum, reflected growing demands for uniformity.[10] Despite that, some critics continued to characterise the vocational school as localist and unsystematic in contrast to the secondary school whose curriculum was propelled by the centrally organised and prestigious Intermediate Certificate and Leaving Certificate examinations. Employers and parents, it was suggested, were unable to judge a vocational school effectively while its teachers and pupils lacked the motivation which a national examination would provide. During the 1940s those and other arguments resulted in the case for school-based and regionally based schemes of curriculum design being lost; and with the support of the teachers through the Vocational Education Officers' Organisation and the central body of the vocational education committees, the Irish Vocational Education Association, the Department of Education inaugurated a national continuation syllabus and an examination for 'groups' of continuation subjects—the Day Vocational (Group) Certificate—in 1947.[11]

By the end of the 1950s up to twenty different subjects were provided for by the Department of Education as part of the Group Certificate syllabus. Few schools had every subject, but all, irrespective of size, provided a core consisting of arithmetic, commerce, domestic economy, English, Irish, mechanical drawing, religion, typewriting and woodwork. Less commonly available subjects such as art, French or German tended to be found only in the larger urban schools, thus giving them elements of a curriculum more usually identified with the secondary school.[12] The differences were greater than any similarities, however. The secondary school alone provided for Latin, a requirement for entry to many university faculties until the 1960s, and most vocational schools did not teach any language other than Irish and English, though the universities required three languages for matriculation. Another major difference was that the language curriculum of the vocational school emphasised functional communication skills, while that of the secondary school aimed to systematically introduce the basis of literary culture. Most significantly, the basic vocational school course of two years' duration was briefer than the three years of the secondary school's junior cycle, or its more commonly completed full cycle of five years whose curriculum was aligned to university entrance requirements.

Such contrasts were a consequence of differing goals. The continuation curriculum aimed to provide pupils with elementary manual skills and basic skills in literacy and numeracy which could be applied in agricultural, business, domestic or manufacturing contexts, while the secondary curriculum—vocational in all but name—aimed to provide advanced skills which could be applied in administration or business or which might provide a basis for further training in a university.[13] The continuation curriculum was an attempt to add to the available forms of second-level schooling through a curriculum that was fundamentally different from what was already available. Thus it was conceived to complement the secondary school and to buttress its role, rather than as a challenge to its prerogatives. In 1930 the Minister for Education John Marcus O'Sullivan had gone to some lengths to reassure the Dáil on that, and when the Roman Catholic bishops, as holders of a substantial interest in secondary education and as spiritual authorities, asked for a special assurance on the separate spheres of secondary and vocational schools, the minister was able to oblige.[14]

Notwithstanding its importance to the educational project of both the state and the Catholic Church, the bipartite curriculum of Irish second-level schooling did not remain unquestioned. In the late 1940s some vocational school teachers, through their representative body, the

Vocational Education Officers' Organisation, argued that the vocational school should not be precluded from being a path to higher education and the organisation petitioned the National University of Ireland to grant matriculation exemption for a handful of students who had successfully completed special courses in vocational schools. The request led to a patronising and humiliating rejection.[15] For the university to consider varying its entrance requirements it would first have had to engage in a radical reappraisal of prevailing concepts of education. Given its introversion and the caution with which it approached curricular issues at this time, it is difficult to see how it could have mustered the capacity to engage in such an analysis.[16]

A radical redefinition of entrance requirements in itself would not have led to a significant alteration in the flow of young people into university. This could occur only if the state were willing to promote more extensive and sustained participation through such measures as an increased subsidy of secondary and higher education or an extension of the period of compulsory schooling. Some such measures had been advocated during the 1920s by a few public figures, notably the Labour Party leader Thomas Johnson and his colleague T. J. O'Connell, but it had been the argument of successive education ministers, including Eoin MacNeill and John Marcus O'Sullivan, that increased state provision for the extension of secondary education was something that the country could not afford.[17] That view was echoed in 1935 by a departmental committee convened to consider the raising of the school-leaving age. Supporting the status quo, it argued that if the state extended the provision for compulsory schooling many families would be in hardship through the loss of child labour and that the state would then have to respond to calls for appropriate compensation.[18] Another committee established in 1947 was more radical and proposed raising the leaving age to sixteen and increasing the supply of second-level schools.[19] The report remained unpublished and its recommendations went unheeded.

It was against such a background that the request of the vocational teachers for the addition of history and music to their curriculum was rejected by the Department of Education in 1949, and the following year when the standing council of the Irish Vocational Education Association met representatives of the department to discuss analogous proposals, it too was disappointed. The civil servants, mindful perhaps of the assurances given to the Roman Catholic bishops in 1930, stated that official policy from the foundation of the vocational school was that it would be different from the secondary school, having a 'practical' bias and being concerned with cultural subjects only 'in so far as they related to trade, industry and art'.[20] An opportunity to undertake an examination of these issues seemed to present itself in 1950 when the Minister for Education appointed a Council of Education. One of its principal tasks would be a curriculum review of secondary education but any hopes for a thoroughgoing examination were dispelled by terms of reference which restricted the council to a circumscribed examination of the secondary school curriculum that excluded any consideration of the vocational school curriculum or of the relationship between the vocational and the secondary school.[21] When the report finally appeared in 1962 it revealed its origins in the residual corporatism of the 1940s and it offered a self-satisfied defence of the status quo. It proposed few changes in the order of things and argued trenchantly, if disingenuously, against any extension of secondary education by the state: the experience of other countries, it claimed, showed that only a minority of pupils could benefit from secondary schooling and, if freely available, the incentive to profit from it would diminish and standards would fall. Notwithstanding its self-serving strictures, the report, while noting the increasing demand for access to secondary school, supported an expansion of secondary schooling under the control of denominational interests.[22]

Despite some growth in technical education, particularly in the post-war period, continuation second-level education would remain, as it had been from the 1930s, the principal activity of the vocational school. Its content had been standardised and it remained within the substantive and pedagogical parameters which had been set down at its inauguration. Thus in 1960 most vocational schools presented a form and a curriculum which its pupils and teachers of thirty years before would have no difficulty recognising. The vocational school remained small— most pupils were in schools with less than 150 pupils—and that alone ensured that each school would have to depend on a few teachers offering a necessarily limited range of subjects. The curricular parameters ensured the alignment of the vocational school with the training and educational needs of specific social groups and classes. In this it was a school set firmly apart from the secondary school, and its experiences, ethos and curriculum would remain very different from what had been created in the secondary school for the formation of the professional, managerial and clerical élite of the new state. As long as the vocational school was unable to provide a path to higher education, it could not present itself as one of a number of alternatives for those choosing a secondary school.

If there were some educationists such as the members of the Council of Education who seemed to suggest that the basis of the difference between the two types of school was a different level of intelligence and that the children who found their way into a vocational school did so because they did not have the capacity to benefit from a secondary schooling, it was because they were not prepared to systematically examine the relationship between schooling and social class maintenance and formation. Restricted vision was not confined to the secondary school interests however, for there were moments when the leadership of the Vocational Teachers' Association appeared to have absorbed the belief that their schools and pupils were of the second class. In a 1962 submission to the Confederation of Organisations of the Teaching Professions, they repeated the characterisation of their schools as a 'dumping ground for slow learners'.[23] It was clear to more acute observers that equating the vocational school with pupils of low intellectual ability and the secondary school with the capacity of its pupils to function at a higher level was demonstrably false.[24] Wherever the 'slow' children of the professional classes were schooled in the period from 1930 to 1960, it was not at their local vocational school.

Reforming the second-level schools

The lack of economic opportunity in postwar Ireland was reflected in exceedingly high emigration which quickly reached the highest rate of any European country. Population continued to decline through the early 1950s, and the prevailing pessimism and bleak despondency were heightened as the country experienced two serious economic depressions. Nonetheless the period also saw the foundations of a national development strategy that would bring unprecedented economic growth through the 1960s and into the 1970s. A state industrial development agency was formed in 1949 and an export board and an undeveloped areas board two years later. Initiatives to promote foreign investment were undertaken based on devices such as export profits tax-relief schemes, the first of which operated in 1956. A landmark was reached in 1958 with the publication of *Economic development* in which Ken Whitaker, a radically minded secretary of the Department of Finance, proposed an integrated programme of national development including investment proposals for industries with strong export potential such as agriculture and tourism.[25]

By the goals which they had set the new policies were a success and, as J. J. Lee has suggested, the spectacular rise in living standards may have made it feasible for the number of families to increase. In 1970 marriage rates rose above seven per thousand for the first time since records began in 1864, and while the upward movement may not have been dramatic in absolute terms it reversed the trends of a century or more.[26] For educationists the new trend was of prime importance for it highlighted what had been apparent for some time: the number of children in the country was increasing, they were crowding into the primary schools and they would, in turn, add to the potential pool of second-level pupils. The demand for schooling was heightened by the continuing decline in agricultural employment. Families who once believed that their children's future was on the land now sought opportunities for them in occupations that would require higher levels of education. Educational institutions could not remain unaffected by such a transformation, but the direction of any change in their structures or curriculum was less easily predicted.

Knowledge and contact with developments elsewhere indicated possible options. The Committee of European Economic Co-operation formed in 1947 to oversee the allocation of the United States of America's aid for European postwar reconstruction directed money to Ireland, some of which filtered into curriculum development.[27] More importantly perhaps, it facilitated an exchange of experts, and though the project was formally concluded in 1952 funds continued to accrue and the exchange of viewpoints continued. Thus the secretary of the Department of Education, Tearlach Ó Raifeartaigh, spent two months in 1960 in the United States studying education systems, but especially provisions for second-level schooling.[28] The committee also established a special section, the Office for Scientific and Technical Personnel, which pioneered the study of the supply and demand for skilled scientists and engineers and the technicians who worked with them. The office was retained when the Committee of European Economic Co-operation was reconstituted as the Organisation for Economic Co-operation and Development—the OECD—in 1960 with the promotion of industry and trade and the economic development of its member countries as its goals. Believing that education was central to that process, it established committees on education, labour and social affairs and a centre for educational research and innovation. One of its principle initiatives was a study of the educational growth problems of five southern European states—the Mediterranean Regional Project —and a conference on economic growth and education investment in Washington in October 1961 agreed that the methodology and the data generated by the Mediterranean project might be used as a framework to examine other more advanced education systems. Both the Irish and Austrian representatives at the conference indicated that their governments might participate in such a project.[29]

In announcing the project to the Dáil on 3 July 1962 the Minister for Education Patrick Hillery made it clear that it was being initiated because Ireland's changing occupational structure, in which 'new occupations will evolve and old ones will die', would have significant consequences for systems of education and training.[30] The project might thus provide a conceptual framework which would link educational policies and institutions to changes in the economic and social structure and provide a range of policy options for education at all levels. A research team of economists, statisticians and educationists was appointed in October 1962, and its use of personnel seconded from the Department of Education and a steering committee chaired by the department's assistant secretary ensured that the minister would have access to data and ideas that would extend the intellectual and empirical bases of policy formulation. Technocratic expertise was being given an unprecedented attention and might now be heard alongside the political party and denominational interests which had previously dominated ministerial councils.

In general, the new experts advanced the concepts and arguments of what was then an emerging academic field, the economics of education. In particular, two of its central propositions came to dominate the discussions: first, that a non-meritocratic education system that ignored the capacity of children to perform well at any level of the school system, regardless of their social class, was wasteful of natural talent; second, that investment in the education of such talent had contributed significantly to rapid economic growth in the European postwar economies.[31] In all of this the question of educational equality—the extension of schooling and an individual's access to it as a civil and social right—was for the time being conceptualised as a secondary concern. While the issue had been given some consideration in the past, it was clear that the state had been prepared to let growth in participation rates occur by some evolutionary process—presumably one which would result from a real improvement in the material circumstances of each family —rather than as a consequence of initiative on its part.

Government policy on the expansion of school provision was revealed in October 1959, when in reply to a motion from Deputy Noel Browne that compulsory education be extended to fifteen and that scholarship schemes be augmented, the Minister for Education Patrick Hillery stated that increased provision might be preferable to any scheme for increasing the period of compulsory attendance. In support, the Taoiseach

Seán Lemass affirmed that it was the government's wish that every child would stay in school until fifteen, but that scholarships for needy children, rather than an extension of the period of compulsion, was the way to achieve that goal.[32] In the past the state had provided scholarships which covered second-level fees for a handful of the most gifted pupils and it increased the allocation of scholarship funds in 1961 so as to widen the social basis of the second-level school population.[33] However, devices which linked financial support to gaining a high place in a competitive examination could only have limited impact on the goal of keeping all children in school until fifteen, all the more so at a time when the demand for schooling was rapidly rising. When the minister was asked in November 1962 if he was considering the introduction of universal secondary education, free of fees, he replied that he was not, but that he was planning for a time when no child would be debarred from secondary education, or even higher education, by lack of means.[34]

A departmental committee formed in June that year had characterised the social and financial basis of secondary schooling as unjust and had endorsed the notion of some secondary education for all. To that end it recommended a compulsory junior cycle up to the age of fifteen that would be free of fees.[35] Despite increasing evidence of a radical shift in his department's thinking, Hillery's major policy statement in May 1963 was somewhat more cautious and equivocal.[36] He did not propose the full elimination of fees: they would be retained at a 'reasonable' level and reduced in cases of hardship. Similarly, the new transport scheme would provide for easier access for children from sparsely populated districts, but it would still charge a fare. On the other hand, Hillery stated unequivocally that it was the state's duty to provide for equality and that that 'must entail the opportunity of *some* post-primary education for *all*.[37] Educational equality was equated with equal access, and a central strategy for the achievement of that goal would be the full integration of the vocational school into a second-level school system where a newly created comprehensive curriculum—now defined as a hybrid of what was best in the traditional secondary and vocational school—would be a central feature. The bipartism which in the past had forced pupils prematurely into one stream or another was inherently unjust, he suggested, and it would be eliminated in a fully integrated secondary sector.[38]

Hillery left the Department of Education in April 1965 and it fell to his successor, George Colley, to promote the project of second-level school reform. In January 1966 he announced that from the following September the vocational schools would provide courses leading to the

Intermediate and Leaving Certificate examinations. Thus 342 more schools were added to the country's stock of 585 secondary schools and the principle of separate curricular spheres, resting since 1930 partly on the secret agreement between the state and the Catholic bishops and partly on a cautious and conservative conceptualisation of the role of schooling in social-class formation, was swept away. In July, Colley was succeeded by Donogh O'Malley, who in a decision that surprised most of his colleagues and angered more than a few, announced that from September 1967 the state would reimburse any secondary school which removed its tuition fees, a reform that would be underpinned by the introduction of free access to special transport networks for all second-level school pupils.[39] Each of these reforms extended the range of choices available to pupils and their parents and contributed significantly to the increased enrolment levels of the late 1960s. When the school-leaving age was finally raised to fifteen in 1972 it was clear that the state was now determined to ensure sustained participation at second level by all children.[40]

In the space of the ten years from 1962 to 1972 successive Fianna Fáil governments implemented a series of reforms which transformed the structure of secondary education so that it became a part of every child's formation. The policy of increasing access was immensely popular and its apparent egalitarianism contrasted with the cautious, conservative and sometimes obstructionist responses which Fianna Fáil had made to earlier proposals to extend participation. Such proposals had become more frequent from the late 1950s, and the support they drew from the opposition parties increased the urgency for reform. A re-energised Labour Party, rising from a slumber that seemed to stretch back into the 1930s, had set up a committee which produced a policy document *Challenge and change in education* in February 1963. It repeated the traditional call for the raising of the school-leaving age, some free secondary schooling and the full integration of vocational education into the secondary school system so that its graduates could proceed without hazard to university education. Fine Gael too began to chant these refrains and its most striking manifesto, *Fine Gael policy for a just society: education*, sought to place education reform in a wider social and economic context: if modern principles of social justice or old-fashioned egalitarianism were yet to find wholehearted support, there were now compelling economic and electoral arguments for a reform of schooling.[41]

Fianna Fáil Ministers for Education responded to and helped fashion the optimistic mood of the times. Each was anxious to take the doctrine of *Economic development* into his own department and to soar on the winds of economic and social change. Rather than being based on an intellectual commitment to egalitarianism, their conversion to the creed of increased access and expanded provision was thus an imaginative and pragmatic response to the new economics of education and a shrewd reaction to the demands of a changing electorate. Séamas Ó Buachalla has suggested that for many of those young ministers the expanding education budget may also have provided an ideal vehicle for political advancement.[42] His assessment converges with that of Paul Bew and Henry Patterson who have argued convincingly that Fianna Fáil under Lemass pragmatically developed a set of populist policies to counteract the social democratic reformism of Fine Gael and to keep the growing ranks of the urban, skilled manual workers from the clutches of a reinvigorated Labour Party.[43]

The reconstituted vocational school, with the Leaving Certificate as its academic apex, could now present itself as the long-sought conduit to higher education. The change was not easily effected nor was it without controversy, however. Some influential voices within vocational education cautioned against a lack of faith in its traditional curriculum. The leadership of the Vocational Teachers' Association, for example, wanted the state to provide access to higher education, but through a restructured vocational sector with its own distinctive syllabus and examination system rather than through a replication of the secondary curriculum and its Leaving Certificate.[44] The secondary teachers—at that point fighting a losing battle to maintain their higher salary scales—predictably enough objected to any policy which might lead to a homogeneous second-level system.[45] The owners of some secondary schools also remained loftily apart from the push for reform and retained their policy of charging tuition fees. Most secondary schools, however, seemed glad to accept the state's promise to reimburse them for fees forgone, though many of them, contrary to a Department of Education regulation, retained a selective admissions policy and as demand for places increased they became more ingenious in devising strategies intended to maintain the social exclusiveness of their schools.[46]

The immediate adoption of the Intermediate Certificate and then the Leaving Certificate course by vocational schools paved the way for a high degree of convergence in the second-level curriculum. This was supported by a series of policy decisions, and when the report of a review committee on the Leaving Certificate was completed in 1967, it did not endorse proposals for a long-promised 'technical' Leaving Certificate.[47] Nearly every vocational school adopted subjects such as history and geography which had long been the exclusive domain of the secondary school, and in a parallel movement some secondary schools began to offer technical subjects such as woodwork and mechanical drawing. The state's goal of a broader comprehensive curriculum found its clearest expression in the sixteen comprehensive schools established between 1966 and 1973, and thereafter in a growing number of community schools. The Department of Education urged that the curriculum of these schools might act as a prototype for the whole second-level system, but while a substantial minority followed that path, many would retain characteristics that indicated their diverse origins in either the secondary or vocational sectors.[48] Thus most vocational schools continued to provide the full range of technical subjects and to orient their pupils—disproportionately the children of less skilled manual workers, small farmers and the unemployed—towards whatever opportunities were available to them. Compared with secondary school pupils, more vocational school pupils were forced to complete their schooling earlier and to enter the lower end of the labour market where they bargained less effectively with fewer and lower level educational credentials.[49] That pattern was accentuated by the capacity of the secondary school to continue selective entry policies. By carefully and deliberately regulating the composition of the flow into their own schools, the secondary authorities played a decisive role in determining the social profile of the vocational school.

Reforming higher education

Throughout the first half of the century, higher education was largely equated with university education. This was conducted in four colleges of the National University of Ireland—Cork, Dublin, Galway and Maynooth—and in Dublin University's Trinity College. The Royal College of Surgeons, somewhat incongruously not having a university designation, completed the finely etched picture. These were all relatively small, socially exclusive institutions. In 1930 total enrolment was approximately 5,000 and it moved slowly upwards, reaching 7,000 in 1950, a trend that represented an increase from approximately 2 per cent of the relevant age cohort to approximately 4 per cent. A network of religious seminaries and teacher-training colleges could justify a claim to be higher education institutions, and while they admitted some of the highest achievers of the secondary schools their accomplishments were only grudgingly admitted. Their rigid regimes—often narrowly conceived and authoritarian—provided a 'formation' and 'training' which underlined the dependent and sometimes servile status of their students.

At the same time technical education courses, of an introductory or elementary nature, were provided in technical and vocational schools for mostly part-time adult students in evening classes. Enrolments were impressive, and if the exigencies of the workplace resulted sometimes in erratic or unsustained participation, these courses nonetheless ensured that an increasing proportion of the population, particularly in agricultural areas and smaller towns, became part of an expanding educational constituency on whom the lessons of educational investment were not being lost. Many of the courses were conducted through association with self-help groups such as the Irish Countrywomen's Association, the National Farmers' Association and Muintir na Tíre and became an important focus for personal and social development in what might otherwise have been a depressed and introspective landscape. Vocational education committees were also empowered to make provision for higher technical education courses of advanced content and longer duration and generally leading to a professional qualification, but only a few large urban centres did so. Thus in 1963 out of 1,607 students enrolled on full-time technical courses, 1,383 were in the technical schools and colleges of the major cities of Dublin, Cork and Limerick.[50] They experienced some growth—a major extension to the college at Bolton Street, Dublin opened in 1962—but it was in the universities that most of the new enrolments in higher education occurred. By the 1960s, higher technical courses were being distinguished from the bulk of technical instruction by the designation 'third level', which implied that their students had already progressed successfully through two lower levels of schooling. The growing use of the term indicated a system that had become more complex and whose components were being increasingly differentiated and compartmentalised.

In the 1959 presidential address to the Vocational Teachers' Association, Liam McGrenera argued for increased investment in technical education and for the provision of a higher technological college in each county.[51] In so doing he used an 'equal opportunity of access' argument which eloquently made the case for increasing the supply of technical education and the raising of participation rates, especially amongst those without the means to enter university. His view was widely shared not just amongst those who sought a fairer allocation of educational resources, but also amongst those in an industrial sector increasingly attuned to the potential role of education in economic development. As a consequence in 1960 the Commission on Higher Education was required to examine and report on the provision of technical education.[52] In its investigation the commission heard the claim that the technical education sector was able to meet the demands made of it; however in noting that there was a significant shortage of trained technicians, it felt forced to conclude that the technical colleges of the vocational education committees were generally 'backward'.[53] It also drew attention to a regional imbalance in provision of courses and proposed the creation of new colleges in Limerick and Dublin which would offer pass degrees and industry-based courses in technology and business.[54] It suggested that a college in Limerick might develop into a university if it 'were necessary in the national interest'.[55]

While the commission continued its deliberations, a major survey on the training of technicians was being completed for the Organisation for Economic Co-operation and Development. At a final 'confrontation' meeting in January 1963 the investigating team asked the representatives of the Irish government to consider new ways through which higher technical education might be provided. In particular they were asked how they would view the possibility of improving the facilities for higher technical education in centres outside the capital, particularly in the south and west of the country. In reply, the Minister for Education Patrick Hillery stated that he was open to change and eager for advice on the form which an expanded technological sector should take.[56] Soon afterwards, he admitted that provision for higher technical education was indeed inadequate and he suggested that rapid industrial expansion necessitated the foundation of a number of technological colleges with regional status.[57] Speaking in the Dáil some time later, he stated that the main role of such colleges would be the provision of the new 'technical' Leaving Certificate, apprenticeship training and higher level technician training. He envisaged colleges based on the existing facilities in Dublin, Cork and Limerick, and six new colleges in smaller regional centres.[58] Within a year the planning of the Carlow college, 'a blueprint', had begun, and in September 1969 regional technical colleges were opened at Athlone, Carlow, Dundalk, Sligo and Waterford. At the same time planning commenced for the creation of two national institutes for higher education to provide advanced technical courses; the first opened in Limerick in 1972 and a second followed in Dublin in 1979.

While most of the courses offered by the new institutions were an innovative response to the labour requirements of an industrialising country, a few had previously been provided in some shape or form in the technical colleges of Dublin, Cork or Limerick. Thus the new colleges and institutes facilitated the further development of a project that stretched back to voluntary and philanthrophic beginnings in the mechanics' institutes and the technical schools of the previous century. Technological education might now fan out from the cities into the new regional centres, and the new colleges, like their precursors, were expected to facilitate the state's policy of economic development through providing utilitarian courses with a high degree of vocational relevance. To that end the Department of Education carefully monitored their proposals for course provision and the appointment of appropriate teaching staff. The goal of creating a unified and nationally integrated technological sector was further advanced when, following recommendations by the Commission on Higher Education and by the Steering Committee on Technical Education, the National Council for Educational Awards was established in 1972.[59] It would provide academic validation and act as the examining and awards body for the sector. The technological institutions now formed a rapidly growing second force in higher education and it was possible that they might develop as the lower, less esteemed stream of a binary system, just as the second-level vocational school had during the period from 1930 to 1965. Alarms were sounded when a Higher Education Authority review of the regional technical colleges was forced to note deficiencies in their physical resources.[60] The divide was accentuated when the government agreed that the funding and scrutiny of the universities would be the responsibility of the Higher Education Authority while the regional technical colleges, like the second-level vocational schools, would continue to operate under the vocational education committees. The government may have been moving to create a unitary system in 1974 when it proposed to transfer degree validation for the technological sector to the universities and to transfer the validation of certificates and diplomas to

Table 10.1: Whole-time higher education students 1961–91

	1961 No. %	1971 No. %	1981 No. %	1991 No. %
Universities	9,083 (80)	20,348 (78)	26,779 (60)	43,273(58)
Teacher-training colleges	987 (9)	1,744 (7)	2,871 (6)	1,061(1)
NIHEs	– –	– –	2,200 (5)	—
Technical colleges	1,201 (11)	2,128 (8)	5,384 (12)	11,745(16)
Regional technical colleges	– –	1,940 (7)	7,119 (16)	17,903 (24)
Total	11,271(100)	26,160 (100)	44,353(100)	73,982(100)

Source: Department of Education, Annual report, 1961/2, Statistical reports, 1971/2–1991/2; Higher Education Authority, Annual reports, 1971/2–1991/2.

a special council for technological education. The strategy was reversed in 1978; in retrospect, if it had been implemented it would have done little to modify the binary nature of higher education. Rather, by accentuating the distinction between degree-awarding institutions and those awarding diplomas and certificates, the policy could only have served to further reinforce the division, though one that would now be within institutions as well as between them.

Throughout the 1980s the technological colleges and institutes grew rapidly and, as Table 10.1 shows, they took a growing share of those entering higher education to the point where it seemed that the technological sector might soon equal the university sector in size of student population. That trend was halted somewhat in 1989, when the long-sought designation of the two national institutes for higher education as universities reduced the proportion of students in the technological sector. This transformation once again prompted the question of what, if any, was the difference between a technological college or institute and a university college. Many differences were cited, including a commitment to research by the universities, their claim to a historic role as guardians of intellectual freedom, and their traditional commitment to education as opposed to utilitarian training. Those in the technological institutions were increasingly prepared to make similar claims, and for many the most tangible difference between the universities and the technological colleges was the extent to which the universities had maintained a greater capacity to determine their own policies and an ability to create more favourable working conditions for their members.

Such distinctions became even more blurred during the late 1980s. The supervisory and policy-making power of the Higher Education Authority increased, and the ability of the universities to act independently in planning their courses, their staffing and salary levels and the size of their student intake was no longer assured.[61] Notwithstanding the power devolved to the Higher Education Authority, the state, through the Minister for Education, also sought to directly influence the workings of individual university institutions, particularly in relation to budgetary issues. As the autonomy of the universities lessened, the technological sector lobbied for greater independence and sought an end to the connection with the vocational education committees: such localist structures, it was argued, attempting to deal at once with local second-level schools and with regional if not national institutions, lacked an appropriate vision and inhibited institutional initiative. Structural reform was signalled in the 1985 green paper *Partners in education*, and in 1992 the regional technical colleges and the Dublin technical colleges—

since 1978 federated into the Dublin Institute of Technology—were released from the control of the vocational education committees.[62] The college governing bodies, like those of the new universities, would in future be appointed by the Minister for Education and their budgets allocated and scrutinised by the Department of Education. If the technical colleges were being freed from the rule of the vocational education committees, greater independence would not necessarily follow, for they, like the universities, would now operate under converging policies which aimed to make all higher education institutions more immediately responsive to the state.

They continued to differ in the social composition of their intake, however. Patrick Clancy's national survey carried out in 1986 showed that farm families contributed a higher proportion of the entrants to the regional technical colleges (28 per cent) and to the teacher-training colleges (32 per cent) than to the universities (16 per cent), while children from the higher professional families were disproportionately underrepresented in the regional technical colleges. Students from the skilled manual group formed a higher percentage of entrants to the regional technical colleges (18 per cent) and to the Dublin Institute of Technology (16 per cent) than to the universities (8 per cent). A relatively minute number of children of the unemployed and the less skilled manual workers scraped into the universities and slightly more entered the technical colleges: mostly they did not participate in higher education at all, having performed badly at first and second level.[63] Thus the universities remained, as they had been conceived, places of formation and training for the old professions and increasingly for the higher managerial members of the emerging services and information technology sectors.

Apprenticeship: training or education?

In 1927 the Commission on Technical Education advocated a formalised relationship between the schooling of apprenticed craft workers and the demands of their employers. It proposed systems of day-release courses and evening classes, the certification of journeymen and apprentices and the introduction of legislation which would provide for statutory regulatory committees for each trade. When the Apprenticeship Act was passed in 1931 its provisions disappointed those who had hoped for an officially regulated country-wide system of compulsory instruction. Instead, it provided for the voluntary formation of committees for designated trades but only following joint representation by workers and employers.

The success of such a scheme would depend to a large extent on the co-operation of organised labour and on the willingness of employers to release apprentices to whatever courses were offered by the vocational education committees. Some observers believed that an idealistic faith in voluntary action would be self-defeating. For example, Seán Lemass, then an opposition deputy, argued that employers were unlikely to willingly allow their apprentices to be absent from the workplace to attend technical courses and consequently it was unlikely that the Act would be utilised in the trades in which regulation and training were most urgently needed.[64] Such prescience was soon vindicated and it became clear that not many trades would follow the example of the few such as furniture-making, house-painting and decorating which had applied for training courses. Outside Dublin the absence of adequate school provision inhibited such initiatives but gradually links were forged between local vocational schools and some industries, not all of them designated.

Radical new approaches to industrial development in the late 1950s led to a review of provisions for training. It resulted in the repeal of the 1931 Act and new legislative provisions, including the setting up of a national apprenticeship board, An Cheard Chomhairle, in 1959. Vocational teachers were active in the new body and they continued to urge that, notwithstanding their status as employees, apprentices should be recipients of education as well as training. New reforms, including a national apprenticeship curriculum for each of the various trades and crafts and the designation of the Group Certificate as the basic entrance level qualification, were soon proposed. These provided the basis for uniform training standards, but it soon became clear that even though industrial employment was expanding rapidly, most apprentices would remain without the benefits that such training might provide. The 1961 census revealed that there were over 15,232 apprentices in the state, but the following year a survey by An Cheard Chomhairle showed that only 10,490 were registered for training and of these only 5,774 were attending classes. In a few trades training courses were the norm—94 per cent of apprentice fitters and turners were attending courses at vocational schools—but in others, such as baking where only 13 per cent attended classes, the traditional reliance on workplace training persisted. Not surprisingly, apprenticeship education accounted for only 6 per cent of all vocational education course provision, a minute increase on the 5 per cent attained in the mid-1930s.[65] The new national apprenticeship agency, like its precursors under the 1931 Act, had been constituted without effective regulatory power, and the central dilemma—whether the apprentice was to be regarded as an employee whose work-rate would be lessened, albeit temporarily, by participation in vocational education, or as a student whose future productivity would be enhanced by a formal, if relatively costly, training course—remained unresolved.

While the structure of technical education was being transformed in the 1960s it became clear that apprenticeship training had become a diminishing part in the work of the vocational school. Despite the setting up of a new apprenticeship authority in 1959, most craft workers, artisans and technicians continued to receive their training 'on the job', and as the state intensified its promotion of industrial expansion it would be increasingly suggested that these frequently *ad hoc* arrangements were insufficient to ensure an appropriate labour supply. Influential international bodies, including the Organisation for Economic Co-operation and Development and the International Labour Organisation, were critical of provisions under the 1959 Apprenticeship Act. So also were the central organisation of vocational education committees, the Irish Vocational Education Association, and the teachers' organisation, the Vocational Teachers' Association, and in 1967 a new regulatory body, An Chomhairle Oiliúna, which became generally known as AnCO, was formed under the Industrial Training Act. Like its predecessors, AnCO had the power to make regulations for apprenticeship; however, in a sharp break with the past, the Act gave it the power to set up and manage its own centres which would provide special training, not just for registered craft apprentices, but for an expanding range of manual, business and managerial occupations. The new body was invigorated by its power to raise funds through a levy on employers and grants from the Department of Labour. Following accession to the European Economic Community in 1973, funds for training would flow in an apparently ever-swelling stream from the European Social Fund.[66]

AnCO retained the historical link between apprenticeship training and vocational education, and members of the Vocational Teachers' Association and later the Teachers' Union of Ireland were active in its various committees. Special block-release and part-time training courses continued to be offered in vocational schools and regional technical colleges and new courses were added, but the primary focus of non-workplace training for craft apprentices was gradually shifting to facilities under the direct control of AnCO. As a consequence, the number of apprentices registered at technical colleges went into decline from 1981, and while the colleges continued to expand, apprenticeship training became a relatively small part of their work. From the late 1970s, state policies formulated and pursued by agencies such as the National Manpower Service, the Youth Employment Agency and AnCO increasingly sought to promote the integration and co-ordination of industrial training with employment policy. These agencies were merged under the Labour Services Act 1987 to form a national training agency, An Foras Áiseanna Saothair, more generally known as FÁS. In future, craft-apprentice training schemes would be pursued within the framework of the state's employment and training strategies, and the young apprentice would be regarded unequivocally as an employee, more properly the object of labour legislation and regulation than of education policy.

Conclusion

A system of second-level schooling with two sharply divergent sectors reflected the prevailing class structure of Irish society between the 1930s and the 1950s. The secondary school operated to furnish the children of the élite with the skills and values necessary in managerial, administrative and supervisory positions or with the qualifications required for university entrance. In contrast, the vocational school was created to teach manual and technical skills appropriate to local economic needs to the children of manual workers and small farmers. Continuation schooling became the main activity of the vocational school, which provided relatively cheap, accessible courses for a growing number of children, many of whom would otherwise not have obtained any second-level schooling.

Changing occupational opportunities in the industrialising economy of the postwar period brought pressure to that bipartite structure. Viewed in purely instrumental terms, relatively low school-participation rates were sufficient for a predominately agricultural society, but if that were to change significantly, expansion would be required and in such a way as would ensure a greater use of dormant talent. What was required was a transformation that would greatly increase the numbers at secondary school which, by being more socially inclusive, would replicate the egalitarian school systems of advanced western societies. Consequently, a series of structural and curricular reforms implemented between 1962 and 1972 transformed the vocational school; this transformation, along with the introduction of the new comprehensive and community schools, helped the state to realise its goal of some secondary schooling for all. The changes were encouraged by reformers who had long decried the absence of a pathway from the vocational school to higher education, by those whose social conscience was offended by the division in the school system and by those who shuddered as they contemplated the annual wastage of unrealised talent. As a result, from 1970 onwards an increasing number of vocational pupils obtained places in university and substantially greater numbers were admitted to the technological colleges. However, a disproportionate amount of vocational school pupils would continue to find their way into poorly rewarded, low-skilled occupations. The vocational school had quickly demonstrated a capacity to prepare pupils for higher education but that, in itself, would not always override stronger and more pervasive factors within families, households and neighbourhoods that influence the formation and reproduction of cultural perspectives and occupational aspirations.

The technical curriculum—whether in part-time, whole-time or apprenticeship courses—had traditionally been a relatively small part of the work of the vocational teacher and it remained so until industrial expansion created a vastly increased demand for labour with technical skills. These would not be supplied in the ordinary vocational schools however, but primarily in the new regional technical colleges, in new national institutes for higher education and, to a lesser extent, in the universities. The regional technical colleges grew rapidly and began to play an increasingly important role in the state's project of forming a higher education system more immediately responsive to its industrial and employment policies. To that end the state removed the colleges from the controls which the vocational education authorities had developed in a more leisurely era and placed them within the increasingly homogeneous managerial framework being developed for the higher education sector. Notwithstanding their enhanced status the technical colleges would remain, for the time being, a second force in higher education. Despite their proven capacity to attain high standards in teaching and research and growing internal pressure to develop as university institutions, they are directed to confine most of their resources to courses whose sub-degree designation keeps them apart and in second place.

If the work of the vocational school remained relatively unchanged during its first thirty years, the following thirty years saw it transformed. With technical education removed to the regional technical colleges, the vocational school was left to develop exclusively as a second-level school. When the regional colleges themselves were removed from vocational education, the vocational education committees were reduced to overseeing a network of second-level schools whose curriculum, as part of an integrated second-level school system, differed in fundamental ways from what had been stipulated in 1930. In its formative decades the carefully defined curriculum of the vocational school had set it very far apart from the secondary school. Within real constraints its teachers realised the promise to provide a continuation curriculum to the highest standards. Its capacity to perform at a high level remains undiminished, but despite reforms which have sought to eliminate the cleavages that have long characterised Irish society and its schools, it remains, in some respects, a less esteemed sector in second-level education.

Notes

1 This and subsequent yearly data on pupils, teachers and schools are taken from the annual reports of the Department of Education.

2 *Investment in education: report of the survey team appointed by the Minister for Education in October 1962* (Dublin, n.d.), pp. 283–4.

3 Data supplied by Cavan and Leitrim vocational education committees.

4 Central Statistics Office, *Census of population of Ireland 1966*, vii (Dublin, 1970) and *Census of population of Ireland 1971*, xii (Dublin, 1978).

5 R. C. Geary and E. W. Henry, 'Education and socio-economic class: a statistical analysis of 1971 Irish census data' in *Irish Journal of Education*, 13, 1 (1989), pp. 5–23.

6 *Investment in education*, pp. 138–68; Séamas Ó Buachalla, *Education policy in twentieth-century Ireland* (Dublin, 1988), p. 340.

7 T. J. O'Connell, *History of the Irish National Teachers' Organisation 1868–1968* (Dublin, 1968), pp. 421–31.

8 *Investment in education*, p. 283.

9 Department of Education, 'Vocational continuation schools and classes, memorandum for the information of committees' (Dublin, 1931).

10 Department of Education, 'Organisation of whole-time continuation courses in borough, urban and county areas' (Memorandum V 40) (Dublin, 1942).

11 See VEOO, *The Vocational Education Bulletin* (hereafter, *Bulletin*), 31 (May 1944), p. 631; 33 (November 1944), p. 669; and 38 (July 1946), p. 799; see also ITEA Annual Congress, *Report*, 1943, pp. 57–8; IVEA Annual Congress, *Report*, 1945, p. 56.

12 *Investment in education*, pp. 292–4.

13 See Department of Education, *Secondary schools programme* (1933/4); *Clár na meadhan scol* (1934/5–1942/3); *Rialacha do leith meadhan scol* (1944/5) and *Rialacha agus clár do leith meadhan scol* (1945/6–1990/1).

14 See Dáil Éireann, *Debates*, xxxiv (14 May 1930), col. 954; John Marcus O'Sullivan to David Keane, 31 October 1930 as transcribed in Ó Buachalla, *Education policy*, pp. 399–403.

15 *Bulletin*, 20 (July 1948), p. 1033.

16 For the university mindset see, J. J. Lee, *Ireland 1912–1985: politics and society* (Cambridge, 1989), pp. 394–5.

17 O'Sullivan to Keane, 31 October 1930, in î Buachalla, *Education policy*, p. 399.

18 Department of Education, *Report of the departmental committee on the raising of the school leaving age* (Dublin, 1935).

19 'Report of the departmental committee on educational provision' (unpublished, 1947), pp. 18–23.

20 IVEA Annual Congress, *Report*, 1956, p. 52.

21 Department of Education, *Terms of reference to the Council of Education and inaugural addresses* (Dublin, 1950).

22 *Report of the Council of Education on the curriculum of the secondary school* (Dublin, 1962), paras 428–9.

23 *Gairm*, 2, 1 (January 1962), pp. 15–16.

24 See for example, John J. O'Meara, *Reform in education* (Dublin, 1958); *Investment in education*, pp. 133 and 168–76.

25 K. A. Kennedy, Thomas Giblin and Deirdre McHugh, *The economic development of Ireland in the twentieth century* (London, 1988), pp. 55–65.

26 Lee, *Ireland*, p. 360.

27 Bernadette Whelan, 'Ireland and the Marshall Plan 1945–51' (PhD thesis, University College Cork, 1989), pp. 260–5.

28 T. Ó Raifeartaigh, 'Education in the USA', in *Studies*, 1 (Spring 1961), pp. 57–74.

29 John Vaizey, in review of *Investment in education*, in *Irish Journal of Education*, 1, 1 (Summer 1967), pp. 71–4.

30 Dáil Éireann, *Debates*, cxcvi (3 July 1962), col. 1303.

31 Richard Breen, Damian Hannan, David Rottman and Christopher Whelan, *Understanding contemporary Ireland: state, class and development in the Republic of Ireland* (Dublin, 1990), pp. 127–8.

32 Dáil Éireann, *Debates*, clxxvii (21 October 1959), col. 202.

33 Local Authorities (Education Scholarships) (Amendment) Bill 1961.

34 Dáil Éireann, *Debates,* cxcvii (15 November 1962), col. 1389.

35 'Tuarascáil shealadach ón choiste a chuireadh i mbun scrúdú a dhéanamh ar oideachas iarbhunscoile' (unpublished, 1962), para. 6.

36 'Statement by the Minister for Education P. J. Hillery in regard to post-primary education 20 May 1963', as printed in Eileen Randles, *Post-primary education in Ireland* (Dublin, 1975), pp. 328–37.

37 *Ibid.*, para. 12; Hillery's italics.

38 *Ibid.*, para. 13.

39 National Archives, Department of an Taoiseach, 96/6/357.

40 For the relative impact of the various reforms see, R. Dale Tussing, *Irish educational expenditures: past, present, future* (Dublin, 1978), pp. 34–6.

41 Ó Buachalla, *Education policy*, pp. 171–204.

42 *Ibid.*, pp. 190–202.

43 Paul Bew and Henry Patterson, *Sean Lemass and the making of modern Ireland 1945–66* (Dublin, 1982), pp. 145–90.

44 Liam McGrenera, *Gairm*, 2, 4 (1961), pp. 23–9; Charles McCarthy, *Irish Press*, 22 May 1963 and 'The changing patterns of technical and vocational education', in *Tuairim*, 8 (May 1962).

45 John Coolahan, *The ASTI and post-primary education in Ireland 1909-1984* (Dublin, 1984), pp. 256–9.

46 For an acknowledgement by secondary school authorities of the social divisiveness of those strategies see, Conference of Major Religious Superiors, *Inequality in schooling in Ireland* (Dublin, 1988) and *Inequality in schooling in Ireland: the role of selective entry and placement* (Dublin, 1989).

47 'Structure of Leaving Certificate course and examination', unpublished report as printed in Randles, *Post-primary education*, p. 279.

48 Kathleen Lynch, *The hidden curriculum: reproduction in education—an appraisal* (London, 1989), pp. 46–8.

49 Damian Hannan, Richard Breen, Barbara Murray, Niamh Hardiman, Dorothy Watson and Kathleen O' Higgins, *Schooling and sex roles: sex differences in subject provision and student choice in Irish post-primary schools* (Dublin, 1982), pp. 156–97; Richard Breen, *Education and the labour market* (Dublin, 1984), pp. 106–21; Patrick Clancy, *Who goes to college?* (Dublin, 1988), pp. 31–5.

50 *Investment in education*, pp. 143–4 and 295–301.

51 *Gairm*, 1, 12 (1959), pp. 23–4.

52 Commission on Higher Education, *Presentation and summary report*, i (Dublin, 1967), p. 1.

53 *Ibid.*, p. 102.

54 *Ibid.*, p. 138.

55 *Ibid.*

56 Organisation for Economic Co-operation and Development, *Training of technicians in Ireland* (Paris, 1964), pp. 95–102.

57 Press conference statement 20 May 1963; see note 36 above.

58 Dáil Éireann, *Debates*, ccvii (5 February 1964), cols 379–80.

59 Commission on Higher Education, *Presentation and summary report*, i, p. 96. Steering Committee on Technical Education, *Report to the Minister for Education on regional technical colleges* (Dublin, 1967), p. 41.

60 Higher Education Authority, *Progress report, 1974* (Dublin, 1974), pp. 57–61.

61 Patrick Clancy, 'The evolution of policy in third-level education', in D. G. Mulcahy and Denis O'Sullivan (eds.), *Irish educational policy: process and substance* (Dublin, 1989), pp. 99–132.

62 Department of Education, *Partners in education: serving community needs* (Dublin, 1985); Regional Technical Colleges Act 1992.

63 Clancy, *Who goes to college?*, p. 25.

64 Dáil Éireann, *Debates*, xxxviii (29 April 1931), col. 436; ITEA Annual Congress, *Report*, 1941, p. 70.

65 *Investment in education*, p. 22.

66 National Economic and Social Council, *Manpower policy in Ireland* (Dublin, 1985), pp. 47–56 and 91–131.

Appendix 1: Chronology

1893   Founding of the Technical Education Association of Ireland
1894   Founding of Irish Trade Union Congress in Dublin
1895   Local Government Act
1899   Agriculture and Technical Instruction Act
1900   Founding of the Department of Agriculture and Technical Instruction
1902   Founding of the Irish Technical Instruction Association
1903   Founding of the Association of Principals of Institutions of Technical Instruction in Ireland, the first sectional association in the country
1917   Founding of Representative Council of Associations of Officers of Agriculture and Technical Instruction Committees in Ireland
1920   Government of Ireland Act
1921   Signing of Anglo-Irish Treaty
1922   Dáil Éireann approves constitution of Irish Free State (Saorstát Éireann)
1923   Founding of Irish Agriculture and Technical Instruction Officers' Organisation
1925   Local Government Act precludes teachers from vocational education committees
1926   Appointment of Commission on Technical Education
1927   Submission of Commission on Technical Education's Report to Minister for Education
1929   Irish Technical Instruction Association becomes Irish Technical Education Association
1930   Vocational Education Act provides for election of vocational education committees
          Founding of Vocational Education Officers' Organisation
1931   First memorandum on continuation education from Department of Education
          Apprenticeship Act
1932   Formation of first Fianna Fáil government
1941   Trade Union Act provides for licensing of trade unions
1942   Memorandum V 40 on continuation education from Department of Education
1944   Irish Technical Education Association becomes Irish Vocational Education Association
1945   Split in Irish Trade Union Congress: formation of Congress of Irish Unions
1947   Day Vocational (Group) Certificate examinations instituted
1948   First 'national wage agreement' between trade union and employer organisations. Organisation for European Economic Development established; Ireland a member
1949   Appointment of committee on teachers' salaries
1950   Establishment of Council of Education
1951   Proposal to join WUI debated by Dublin city branch of VEOO
1952   VEOO executive committee appoints Billy McNamara general secretary

Resignation of Gerry Lovett from presidency of VEOO

1953   Founding of Cumann Mhúinteoirí Gairm-Oideachais
Final congress of VEOO, 1 May

1954   Founding of Eagraíocht na nGairm-Mhúinteoirí, 1 December

1955   Eagraíocht na nGairm-Mhúinteoirí renamed Cumann na nGairm-Mhúinteoirí, or Vocational Teachers' Association

1956   Appointment of Charles McCarthy as general secretary of VTA
Founding of Provisional United Trade Union Organisation

1957   Establishment of conciliation council for vocational teachers

1958   Teachers' Salaries Committee set up

1959   First meeting of Irish Congress of Trade Unions
Apprenticeship Act provides for establishment of An Cheard Chomhairle

1960   Commission on Higher Education set up
Publication of Report by Teachers' Salaries Committee

1961   OECD conference, 'Economic growth and investment in education', Washington

1962   Appointment of 'Investment in Education' study team by Minister for Education

1963   Statement of proposed educational reforms by Minister for Education
Appointment of study team on technological education

1965   Publication of *Investment in education*

1966   Opening of comprehensive schools at Carraroe, Cootehill and Shannon
'Free' second-level schooling promised by Minister for Education
Appointment of Committee on Technical Education to plan regional technical colleges

1967   Industrial Training Act provides for establishment of AnCO
'Free' second-level schooling and transport scheme implemented
Appointment of Tribunal on Teachers' Salaries by Minister for Education
Publication of Report of Commission on Higher Education

1968   Report of Tribunal on Teachers' Salaries presented to Minister for Education
Announcement of common salary scales for teachers

1969   Secondary teachers engage in three-week strike
Opening of regional technical colleges at Athlone, Carlow, Dundalk, Sligo and Waterford

1970   VTA members in Wexford strike over working conditions
Issue of 'community school' document by Department of Education to Catholic bishops. INTO and VTA join common scheme of conciliation and arbitration.

1971   Commission on the Status of Women, *Interim report on equal pay*

1972   School leaving age raised from fourteen to fifteen
Appointment of National Council for Educational Awards
Opening of first community schools at Blanchardstown and Tallaght

1973   ASTI joins the common scheme of conciliation and arbitration
VTA changes its name to Aontas Mhúinteoirí Éireann, or Teachers' Union of Ireland

1978   Formation of Dublin Institute of Technology from existing third-level technical colleges in the city

1980   Appointment of Review Body on Teachers' Pay

Formation of first community college

1982 TUI establishes Women's Council

1983 TUI establishes Colleges' Advisory Council

1984 Appointment of Curriculum and Examinations Board by the Minister for Education

1986 Formation of Teachers United by ASTI, INTO and TUI

1989 Establishment of University of Limerick and Dublin City University

1990 Inaugural meeting of Council of Teachers' Unions

1991 Appointment of National Council for Vocational Awards

1992 Regional Technical Colleges Act removes regional technical colleges from vocational education committee control and Dublin Institute of Technology Act removes the institute from vocational education committee control

1993 National Education Convention meets in Dublin

1994 Withdrawal of INTO from Council of Teachers' Unions

Discussions on unity between TUI and ASTI continue

Appendix 2: Officers, Executive Committee Members and Officials

The sporadic rate of organisational publication and the complete absence of official minutes for the period prior to 1934 preclude the compilation of a comprehensive listing for that period. For the period from 1934 lists are based on those published in the *Vocational Education Bulletin* and from 1954 on those printed in executive committee minutes.

Officers

Representative Council of Associations of Officers of Agriculture and Technical Instruction Committees in Ireland

	Chairman	Honorary secretary	Honorary treasurer
1917	W. E. Roche	J. J. O'Connor	R. MacDonald

Irish Agriculture and Technical Instruction Officers' Organisation

	President	Honorary secretary	Honorary treasurer
1923	George Russell (Æ)	Frank McNamara	J. J. O'Connor

Cumann na nOifigeach Gairm-Oideachais: Vocational Education Officers' Organisation

	Chairman	Honorary secretary	Honorary treasurer
1934–5	Gus Weldon	Edward Daly	J. J. O'Connor
1935–6	Gus Weldon	Edward Daly	J. J. O'Connor
1936–7	Barney O'Neill	Edward Daly	J. J. O'Connor
1937–8	Barney O'Neill	Michael Cryan	J. J. O'Connor
1938–9	Michael Cryan	Michael Hickey	J. J. O'Connor
1939–40	Michael Cryan	Michael Hickey	J. J. O'Connor
1940–1	Fred Cronin	Michael Hickey	J. J. O'Connor
1941–2	Fred Cronin	Michael Hickey	J. J. O'Connor
1942–3	J. A. McDonell	Michael Hickey	J. J. O'Connor
1943–4	J. A. McDonell	Michael Hickey	J. J. O'Connor
1944–5	William Cleary	Michael Hickey	Michael Cryan
	President		
1945–6	William Cleary	Michael Hickey	Michael Cryan
1946–7	Paddy Tarpey	Michael Hickey	Michael Cryan

1947–8	Paddy Tarpey	Michael Hickey	Michael Cryan
1948–9	Paddy Tarpey	Michael Hickey	Michael Cryan
1949–50	Paddy Parfrey	Michael Hickey	Paddy Tarpey
1950–1	Paddy Parfrey	Michael Hickey	Paddy Tarpey
1951–2	Paddy Parfrey	Michael Hickey	Paddy Tarpey
1952	Gerry Lovett	Michael Hickey	Paddy Tarpey
1953	Liam Trundle	Michael Hickey	Paddy Tarpey
1953–4	Liam Trundle	Maura Egan	Liam McGrenera

Cumann Mhúinteoirí Gairm-Oideachais

1953–4	Eileen Quinlan	V. Farrington	Paddy Parfrey

Eagraíocht na nGairm-Mhúinteoirí

1954–5	Liam Trundle and Eileen Quinlan

Cumann na nGairm-Mhúinteoirí: Vocational Teachers' Association

President	Vice-president	Hon. secretary	Chairman, finance cttee
1955–6			
Tom Carney	Maura Egan	D. MacConfhaola	D. MacConfhaola
1956–7			
Tom Carney	Maura Egan	Liam McGrenera	Liam McGrenera
1957–8			
Liam McGrenera	Maura Egan	John McDonald	P. J. Lane
1958–9			
Liam McGrenera	Martin Phillips	L. McDonnell	P. J. Murtagh
1959–60			
John McDonald	W. O'Brien-Crowley	L. McDonnell	Tom Bridgeman
1960–1			
John McDonald	T. McDonnell	Seán Ó Conaill	Tom Bridgeman
1961–2			
T. McDonnell	Gerry Lovett	Joseph Earlie	Tom Bridgeman
1962–3			
T. McDonnell	T. Bridgeman	P. O'Callaghan	W. H. Finch
1963–4			
Gerry Lovett	Seamus Peyton	P. O'Callaghan	Peadar Murtagh
1964–5			
Gerry Lovett	Seamus Peyton	P. O'Callaghan	George Latchford
1965–6			
Seamus Peyton	Seán Cooney	Kevin O'Regan	George Latchford
1966–7			
Seamus Peyton	George Latchford	Kevin McBrien	Michael Slattery

1967–8

Seán Cooney	Michael Slattery	Kevin McBrien	Seán Ó Glaisin

1968–9

Seán Cooney	Kevin McBrien	Kevin McCarthy	James Doran

1969–70

Maurice Holly	Brendan Conway	Kevin McCarthy	Mary Hughes

1970–1

Maurice Holly	Brendan Conway	Patricia Hurley	John Calnan

1971–2

Kevin McCarthy	Patricia Hurley	Maurice Holly	John Calnan

1972–3

Kevin McCarthy	Patricia Hurley	Maurice Holly	Billy Webb

Aontas Múinteoirí Éireann: Teachers' Union of Ireland

1973–4

P. Ó Conghaile	Billy Webb	Joe Rooney	Declan McDonnell

1974–5

P. Ó Conghaile	Billy Webb	Joe Rooney	Dennis Harley

1975–6

Billy Webb	Moya Corry	Kevin McCarthy	Paddy O'Doherty

1976–7

Billy Webb	Joe Rooney	Jim Dorney	Kevin McCarthy

1977–8

Joe Rooney	Jim Dorney	Fachtna O'Reilly	Kevin McCarthy

1978–9

Joe Rooney	Jim Dorney	Tom Hunt	Margaret Dorney

1979–80

Jim Dorney	Tom Hunt	Fachtna O'Reilly	Frank Buckley

1980–1

Jim Dorney	Tom Hunt	Larry Kavanagh	Frank Buckley

1981–2

Tom Hunt	Larry Kavanagh	Tony Rice	John Daffy

1982–3

Tom Hunt	Larry Kavanagh	Tony Rice	Michael O'Brien

1983–4

Larry Kavanagh	Seán P. McCarthy	Larry Duffy	Gerry Mulhern

1984–5

Larry Kavanagh	Seán P. McCarthy	Alice Prendergast	Michael Hanly

1985–6

Seán P. McCarthy	Michael Hanly	Eamonn Kinch	P. J. Mitchell

1986–7

Seán P. McCarthy	Michael Hanly	Tom Creedon	P. J. Mitchell

1987–8

Mick Hanly	P. MacMenamin	Kevin McCarthy	P. J. Mitchell

1988–9

P. MacMenamin	Billy Fitzpatrick	Tom Fennell	Joe Carolan

1989–90

P. MacMenamin	Billy Fitzpatrick	Ed Riordan	P. J. Hayes

1990

Billy Fitzpatrick	D. J. O'Connor	Ed Riordan	P. J. Hayes

1990–1

Billy Fitzpatrick	Ed Riordan	Richard Walsh	Seamus Kilgannon

1991–2

Billy Fitzpatrick	Ed Riordan	Tony Deffely	Michael Clarke

1992–3

Ed Riordan	Tony Deffely	Eugene McCoy	Alice Prendergast

1993–4

Ed Riordan	Tony Deffely	John Twohig	Martin Hoye

1994–5

Tony Deffely	Alice Prendergast	Derek Dunne	Joe Carolan

1995–6

Tony Deffely	Alice Prendergast	Mary Higgins	Joe Carolan

1996–7

Alice Prendergast	Joe Carolan	Paddy Healy	Dympna Reilly

Executive Committee Members

Liam Arrigan (1978–80)

Angela Barden (1990–2), Michael Birmingham (1952–4, 1964–6), Anthony Bradley (1995–7), T. J. Brady (1958–9), B. Brennan (1978–80), Vincent Breslin (1990–5), Tom Bridgeman (1955–63, 1967–9), Frank Buckley (1977–81), Bernard Burke (1977–9)

John Calnan (1970–2, 1975–6), Frank Carney (1969–70), Tom Carney (1955–8), Joe Carolan (1985–9, 1994–7), Michael Casserly (1973–4, 1975–7), Richard Chute (1971–2), Gabriel Clancy (1973–4), Michael Clarke (1988–92), Larry Cleary (1971–2), William Cleary (1943–50, 1951–2), Michael Coghlan (1952–3), Gabriel Colleran (1992–6), Jim Connolly (1984–6), Seán Connolly (1988–9), Kevin Conry (1987–91), Brendan Conway (1969–71), Pat Conway (1983–7, 1995–7), Seán Cooney (1964–70), Austen Corcoran (1980–2), Denis Corcoran (1971–4), Pat Corcoran (1983–5), Moya Corry (1972–4, 1975–6), Tom Creedon

(1983–7, 1991–5), Fred Cronin (1937–42), Peadar Crowley (1958–60), Michael Cryan (1937–49)

John Daffy (1980–4), Tom Dalton (1970–2), Brendan Daly (1981–3), Edward Daly (1934–7), Liam Damery (1954–5), Eric Deacon (1969–71), Tomás de Bhilliers (1967–8), Tony Deffely (1988–97), Don Dillon (1995–7), Paul Dolan (1986–90), P. J. Donoghue (1969–71), Michael Dooher (1973–4, 1975–6), James Doran (1967–9), Jim Dorney (1973–4, 1975–82), Margaret Dorney (1975–9), John Duffe (1972, 1973–4), Larry Duffy (1980–4), Derek Dunne (1991–5)

Joseph Earlie (1960–2), Seán Edwards (1995–7), Maura Egan (1952–8), Mary Enright (1995–7)

Vincent Farrington (1954–5), Mary Feeney (1945–50), Tom Fennell (1985–9), W. H. Finch (1961–3), Billy Fitzpatrick (1985–94), Vincent Forde (1970–2)

Pádraig Gallagher (1952–3), Pádraig Gallagher (1987–8), Mairín Ganly (1979–82), Finbar Geaney (1989–93), Declan Glynn (1992–4)

Michael Hanly (1981–92), Dennis Harley (1971–4, 1981–3), John Harnett (1955–6), Nicholas P. Hartnett (1946–50, 1955–9), P. J. Hayes (1986–90), Paddy Healy (1993–7), Jim Hickey (1973), Michael Hickey (1934–54), Mary Higgins (1992–5), P. Higgins (1976–90), Desmond Hogan (1966–8), Paddy Hogan (1994–7), Maurice Holly (1969–73), Maisie Hopkins (1955–6), Danny Howley (1994–6), Martin Hoye (1990–4), Barry Hughes (1975–8), Mary Hughes (1968–70, 1978–82), Tom Hunt (1975–85), Patricia Hurley (1970–2), T. J. Hurley (1934–6), Brian Hyland (1977–9, 1985–7, 1995–7)

Larry Kavanagh (1978–87), Michael Kelleher (1953–4), M. J. Kennedy (1941–6), Frank Kielty (1977–81), Ted Kiely (1968–70), J. G. Kiernan (1957–8), Seamus Kilgannon (1987–91), Eamonn Kinch (1983–7), Gerry King (1996–7), Colm Kirwan (1984–8)

P. J. Lane (1956–8, 1962–4), Joe Langan (1970–2), Jim Lanigan (1936–40), George Latchford (1963–7), Mary Leahy (1996–7), Maura Leahy (1943–4), Michael Lee (1952–4), Liam Lenihan (1983–6, 1990–2, 1996–7), Maureen Levey (1985–7), Mary Lonergan (1983–5), Gerry Lovett (1951–2, 1960–6), Kieran Lucas (1988–92), Anne Lucey (1984–6)

Kevin McBrien (1965–9), Jim McCafferty (1975–6), P. J. McCafferty (1976–7), Jim McCarthy (1983–6), Kevin McCarthy (1968–78, 1980–4, 1986–90, 1992–4), Seán P. MacCarthy (1980–8, 1992–6), Darach Mac Confhaola (1954–6), Oliver McCormack (1983–5), Valerie McCormick (1990–4), Eugene McCoy (1989–93, 1996–7), Brendan McDermott (1956–8), Catherine McDermott (1986–7), Seamus McDermott (1972–3), John S. McDonald (1955–63), J. A. McDonell (1935–6, 1948–54), Declan McDonnell (1972–3), Laurence McDonnell (1958–60), Thomas McDonnell (1955–6, 1959–64), Hughie McFadden (1991–5), John Mac Gabhann (1994–7), Frank McGinn (1988–91, 1994–7), Liam McGrenera (1952–4, 1956–60), Phil McHugh (1981–3), John McKeever (1972–4), Peter

MacMenamin (1978–80, 1986–9), Peadar McNamara (1984–6)

Gerard Mackle (1972–4), John Maher (1973–4), Helen Mahony (1994–5), Patrick Mitchell (1996–7), P. J. Mitchell (1976–8, 1984–8), Teresa Molloy (1956–7), Michael Moore (1975–6), M. Moran (1934–6), Mary Moylan (1941–2), Gerry Mulhern (1980–4), Madge Mullany (1947–52), Peadar Mulligan (1994–7), Kevin Murnane (1979–81), Brigid Murphy (1938–40), George Murphy (1975–7), Thomas Murphy (1949–52, 1960–2), Peadar Murtagh (1961–4), P. J. Murtagh (1958–9)

Geoffey Naughton (1992–4)

Antoin Ó Brian (1972–4, 1975–6), Donough O'Brien (1991–5), Hugh O'Brien (1975–8), Michael O'Brien (1979–83), William O'Brien-Crowley (1953–61), Patrick O'Callaghan (1961–5), Mícheál Ó Conaill (1963–7), Seán Ó Conaill (1958–61), Pádraig Ó Conghaile (1967–9, 1973–4, 1975–6), D. J. O'Connor (1986–90, 1994–5), J. J. O'Connor (1930–52), Paddy O'Doherty (1972–4, 1975–6), J. A. O'Donnell (1936–47, 1952–3), Michael O'Donnell (1996–7), Tom O'Donnell (1935–8), John O'Donoghue (1990–4), Domhnall Ó Faolain (1965–7), Marcus Ó Flaithbheartaigh (1954–5), Seán Ó Glaisin (1957–9, 1966–8), Labhrás Ó Gotharaigh (1959–61), Pat O'Halloran (1977–80), Pádraig Ó Loingse (1966–7), Seán Ó Lonagain (1954–5), Tim O'Meara (1980–2, 1987–91), Barney O'Neill (1936–40), Ray O'Neill (1977–9), Kevin O'Regan (1964–6), Fachtna O'Reilly (1976–80), Patrick O'Reilly (1971–2), Des O'Shea (1969–71), Ed O'Toole (1962–4), Seán Ó Tuama (1948–50), R. Ó Tuathail (1978–80)

Paddy Parfrey (1943–52), Seamus Peyton (1961–8), Martin Philips (1956–60, 1962–6), Tom Powell (1934–7), Joseph Power (1981–6), S. Power (1946–8), Alice Prendergast (1982–5, 1989–97)

Eileen Quinlan (1954–6)

Dympna Reilly (1994–7), Tony Rice (1979–83), Ed Riordan (1986–96), Gatrick Rohan (1975–6), Joe Rooney (1972–3, 1976–9), Bride Rosney (1987–90), Anne Ryan (1937–8)

Michael Slattery (1966–8), Liam Spring (1945–6, 1953–4)

Patrick Taafe (1952–3), Paddy Tarpey (1941–53), Buach Toibín (1970–2), Liam Trundle (1951–5), Eamonn Tuttle (1975–8, 1982–6), John Twohig (1990–3)

Seán Ua Ceallaigh (1939–40), Pádraigín Uí Riordáin (1994–6)

James Walsh (1973–4), Richard Walsh (1987–91), Billy Webb (1971–3, 1975–6, 1979–81), Gus Weldon (1934–42), Owen Wims (1981–4), Barney Winston (1987–8)

Officials

General secretary

Cumann na nOifigeach Gairm-Oideachais: Vocational Education Officers' Organisation

1930–52	Frank McNamara
1952–4	Billy McNamara

Eagraíocht na nGairm-Mhúinteoirí

1954–5	Henry Sexton

Cumann na nGairm-Mhúinteoirí: Vocational Teachers' Association

1955–6	Tom Donaghy
1956–72	Charles McCarthy
1972–3	Maurice Holly

Aontas Mhúinteoirí Éireann: Teachers' Union of Ireland

General secretary

1973–5	Maurice Holly	1982–9	Hugh Pollock
1975–6	Kevin McCarthy	1989–90	Alice Prendergast
1976–82	Christy Devine	1990–4	Peter MacMenamin
1982–	Jim Dorney	1994–5	Seán P. MacCarthy

Deputy general secretary

1989–94	Mairín Ganly	1996–	Declan Glynn
1994–	Peter MacMenamin		

Education and research officer

1984–94	Gráinne O'Flynn
1994–	Rose Malone

Assistant general secretary

Training and information officer

1975–7	Pat Brady	1995–	Jerry Fitzpatrick
1977–80	John Dowling		

Administrator

1981	Harry Connolly	1963–86	Anne Hanley
1981–2	Jim Dorney	1986–7	Mark Sherry
1982–9	Mairín Ganly	1987–	Hilary O'Byrne

Administrative staff

Bernadette Clancy (1969–70), Angela Curran (1973–9), Susan Curran (1988–), Liz Daly (1983–), Angie Davis (1996–), Teresa Dodd (1979–), Sarah Dooley (1975–9), Mary Earls (1972–3), Mary Flanagan (1963–72), Breda Hall (1977-), Noeleen Harrison (1991–), Mercedes Hogan (1970–2), Carole Kealy (1970–1), Pauline Kelly (1966–72), Sandra Leddy (1996–), Anne Lowther (1980–96), Maureen McGill (1974–), Eilis McNamara (1967–8), Carmel Madden (1975–9), çine Maher (1986–93), Terry Malloy (1956–63), Joan Mooney (1970–2), Mary Morrissey (1971–3), Madeline Roche (1986–8), Carol Ryan (1979–), Maria Tobin (1993–), Cecilia Tubbert (1969–70)

Sources

Interviews

Michael Birmingham, Tom Carney, Anne Hanley, Muriel McCarthy, Billy McNamara, Noel Power, Eileen Quinlan, Liam Trundle

Unpublished sources

Cork
Cork County Council
Minute books, 1930–91
County of Cork Vocational Education Committee
Minute books, 1930–91
Dublin
Archives Department, University College Dublin
    Teachers' Union of Ireland papers
    William McNamara papers
    Richard Mulcahy papers
    John Marcus O'Sullivan papers
National Archives
    Department of the Taoiseach (Cabinet) papers
    Department of Agriculture papers
    Department of Education papers
    Department of Finance papers
National Library of Ireland
    Commission on Technical Education: typescripts of evidence
City of Dublin Vocational Education Committee
    Minute books, 1930–91
Ennis
County of Clare Vocational Education Committee
    Minute books, 1930–91
Galway
County of Galway Vocational Education Committee
    Minute books, 1930–91
Limerick
City of Limerick Vocational Education Committee
    Minute books, 1930–91
    Correspondence files, 1950–91

Official inquiry files, 1967
County of Limerick Vocational Education Committee
Minute books, 1930–91
Limerick County Council
Minute books, 1929–91
Tralee
Town of Tralee Vocational Education Committee
Minute books, 1930–91

Publications of the TUI and of other labour and education organisations

Irish Technical Journal: a record of agricultural and technical education in Ireland
(1903–5)
Representative Council of Associations of Officers of Committees of Agriculture and
Technical Instruction in Ireland, *Agriculture and Technical Education* (1918–20)
Vocational Education Officers' Organisation, *The Vocational Education Bulletin* (1934
–53)
— *Constitution* (25 July 1945)
Vocational Teachers' Association, *Gairm* (1956–68)
— *Congress Magazine* (1956–73)
— *News Sheet* (1962)
— *Rulebook*, 1973, 1976, 1992
Teachers' Union of Ireland, *Views and News* (1973–8).
— *Congress Magazine* (1974–94)
— *TUI News* (1978–)
— *1976 Handbook* (1976)
— *1978–79 Handbook* (1978)
— *Remedial education* (1987)
— *Death by a thousand cuts* (1988)
— *TUI policy on remedial education and guidance counselling* (1988)
— *A positive approach to health through education* (1990)
— *Apprenticeship education: a new approach* (1990)
— *Vocational education: our future?* (1990)
— *Equality in education* (1993)
Council of Teachers' Unions, *Stress and teachers* (1991)
— *Education conference* (1992)
— *Entrance examinations for post-primary schools* (1992)
— *In-service education and training* (1992)
Irish Trades Union Congress, *Report* (1894)
Irish Trades Congress, *Report* (1895)
Irish Trades Union Congress, *Report* (1896–1914)

Irish Trades Union Congress and Labour Party, *Report* (1916–17)

Irish Labour Party and Trade Union Congress, *Report* (1918–29)

Irish Trade Union Congress, *Report* (1930–59)

Congress of Irish Unions, *Report* (1945–59)

Irish Congress of Trade Unions, *Report of the executive committee* (1959–)

Irish Technical Instruction Association, *Congress: official report* (1902–29)

Irish Technical Education Association, *Congress: official report* (1930–43)

Irish Vocational Education Association, *Congress: official report* (1944–94)

Official publications

Report of the select committee appointed to inquire into the administration of the Royal Dublin Society with a view to the wider extension of the advantages of the annual parliamentary grant to that institution and to whom the return of the charter rules and regulations of the Dublin Society was referred, H.C. 1836 (445) xiii. 355

Report from the select committee on scientific institutions (Dublin); with the proceedings, minutes of evidence, appendix and index, H.C. 1864 (495) xiii.477

Report of the commission on the science and art department in Ireland, i: H.C. 1868–9 [4103] xxiv.1

— ii, *minutes of evidence, appendix and index*, H.C. 1868–9 [4103–I] xxiv.43

Royal commission, primary education I, part I, report of the commissioners [C 6] H.C. 1870 xxviii part i

Royal commission on technical instruction, first report, (C.3171) H.C. 1881 xxvii.153

Royal commission on manual and practical instruction in primary schools under the board of national education in Ireland: first report of the commissioners and minutes of evidence taken at the first seven public sittings, [C.8383] H.C. 1897 xliii.1

— *Second report of the commissioners*, [C.8531] H.C. 1897 xliii.109

— *Second volume of evidence, comprising that taken in England between March 18 and April 9, 1897, being a supplement to the second report of the commissioners*, [C.8532] H.C. 1897 xliii.109

— *Third report of the commissioners*, [C.8618] H.C. 1897 xliii.401

— *Third volume of minutes of evidence, comprising that taken between April 29 and July 21, 1898, being a supplement to the third report of the commissioners*, [C.8619] H.C. 1897 xliii.405

— *Final report of the commissioners*, [C.8923] H.C. 1898 vliv.1

— *Fourth volume of minutes of evidence, comprising that taken between September 29 and December 17, 1897, being a supplement to the final report of the commissioners*, [C.8924] H.C. 1898 xliv.77

— *Appendices to the reports of the commissioners*, [C.8925] H.C. 1898 xliv.531

Report from standing committee on trade (including agriculture and fishing), shipping and manufactures, on the Agricultural and Technical Instruction (Ireland) Bill; with

proceedings of the committee, H.C.1899 (284) viii.497

Report of the departmental committee of inquiry into the provisions of the Agriculture and Technical Instruction Act, 1899, [Cd 3572], H.C. 1907 xvii and xviii

Report showing the names of the permanent officials of the department on the 1st day of May, 1903; description of office; salary and travelling expenses; date of appointment and previous employment; tenure of office; and similar returns of officials employed by the various county councils in Ireland in carrying out the provisions of the Agriculture and Technical Instruction (Ireland) Act, H.C. 1905 (40) lx.513

Department of Agriculture and Technical Instruction (Ireland), *Annual general report* (1901/2–1918/19)

— *Journal (*1900/1–1923/4)

Department of Education, *Annual report* (1924/5–1965/6)

— *Tuarascáil, táblaí staitistic* (1966/7–1971/2)

— *Tuarascáil staitisticœil* (1972–3–1990/1)

— *Statistical report* (1991/2–1993/4)

Dáil Éireann, *Debates,* 1922–94

Seanad Éireann, *Debates,* 1922–94

Commission on Technical Education, *Report* (1927)

Report presented to the Minister for Education by the inter-departmental committee on the raising of the school-leaving age P.2086 (1936)

Report of the Commission on Vocational Organisation, 1943 P.6743 (1944)

Reports and appendices of the Committee on National Teachers' Salaries P.9634 (1949)

Terms of reference to the Council of Education and inaugural addresses (1950)

Report of the Commission on Youth Unemployment Pr.709 (1951)

Department of Education, *Report of the Council of Education as presented to the Minister for Education: (1) the function of the primary school; (2) the curriculum to be pursued in the primary school from the infant age up to 12 years of age* Pr.2583 (1954)

Economic development Pr.4796 (1958)

Programme for economic expansion P.4796 (1958)

Teachers' Salaries Committee, *Reports and appendices presented to the Minister for Education, 29th July, 1960* Pr.5694 (1960)

Report of the Council of Education as presented to the Minister for Education on the curriculum of the secondary school Pr.5996 (1962)

Second programme for economic expansion Prl.7670 (1963)

Investment in education: report of the survey team appointed by the Minister for Education in October, 1962 Pr.8311 (1966)

National Industrial Economic Council, *Comments on Investment in education* Pr.8886 (1966)

Investment in education: annexes and appendices (1967)

Commission on Higher Education, *Presentation and summary of the report*

Pr.9326 (1967)

— *Report,* i Pr.9389 (1967)

— *Report,* ii Pr.9588 (1968)

Tribunal on Teacher Salaries, *Report presented to the Minister for Education* Prl.87 (1968)

Steering Committee on Technical Education, *Report to the Minister for Education on regional technical colleges* Prl.371 (1969)

Department of Education, *Ár ndaltaí uile—all our children* (1969)

Higher Education Authority, *Initial recommendation on the question of establishing a body which would award national qualifications at technician and technological levels; recommendation on the provision of third–level educational facilities at Limerick* Prl.586 (1969)

— *Report on teacher education* (1970)

— *Report on the Ballymun project* (1972)

Committee on the Form and Function of the Intermediate Certificate Examination, *The I.C.E.* Prl.4429 (1975)

Review Body on Teachers' Pay, *Interim report* Prl.9232 (1980)

White paper on educational development Prl.9373 (1980)

Report of the Pupil Transfer Committee Pl.686 (1981)

The way forward: national economic plan, 1983–87 Prl.1061 (1982)

Programme for action in education, 1984–87 Prl.2153 (1984)

Building on reality 1985–87 Prl.2648 (1984)

Partners in education: serving community needs; green paper Pl.3598 (1985)

Programme for national recovery Pl.5213 (1987)

Technological education: report of the international study group appointed by the Minister for Education (1987)

Programme for economic and social progress Pl.7827 (1991)

Science, technology and innovation: the white paper Pn.2361 (1996)

Acts, bills and parliamentary orders

A bill to amend the law relating to technical education in Ireland, 1895 (15) VI.325

A bill for the establishment of a department and a board for the purpose of promoting agriculture and other industries in Ireland, 1897 (204) I.29

A bill for the establishing of a department of agriculture and other industries and technical instruction in Ireland and for other purposes connected therewith, 1899 (180) I.55

A bill (as amended by the standing committee on trade etc.) for the establishing of a department of agriculture and other industries and technical instruction in Ireland and for other purposes connected therewith, 1899 (280) I.73

Lords amendment to the Agricultural and Technical Instruction (Ireland) Bill, 1899 (300) I.93

Ministers and Secretaries Act 1924 [16]

Intermediate Education (Amendment) Act 1924 [47]

Local Government Act 1925 [5]

School Attendance Act 1926 [17]

Local Authorities (Officers and Employees) Act 1926 [39]

Vocational Education Act 1930 [29]

Apprenticeship Act 1931 [56]

Vocational Education (Amendment) Act 1936 [50]

Bunreacht na hÉireann (1937)

Trade Union Act 1941 [22]

Vocational Education (Amendment) Act 1944 [9]

Industrial Relations Act 1946 [26]

Vocational Education (Amendment) Act 1947 [1]

Vocational Education (Amendment) Act 1950 [33]

Vocational Education (Amendment) Act 1953 [37]

Apprenticeship Act 1959 [39]

Vocational Education (Amendment) Act 1962 [28]

Industrial Training Act 1967 [5]

Vocational Education (Amendment) Act 1970 [15]

Higher Education Authority Act 1971 [22]

Unfair Dismissals Act 1977 [10]

National Council for Educational Awards Act 1979 [30]

National Institute for Higher Education, Limerick, Act 1980 [25]

National Institute for Higher Education, Dublin, Act 1980 [30]

Thomond College of Education, Limerick, Act 1980 [34]

Worker Participation (State Enterprises) Act 1988 [13]

Dublin City University Act 1989 [15]

University of Limerick Act 1989 [14]

University of Limerick (Dissolution of Thomond College) Act 1991 [16]

Dublin Institute of Technology Act 1992 [15]

Regional Technical Colleges Act 1992 [16]

Limited circulation papers of the Department of Education

Vocational continuation schools and classes, memorandum for the information of committees [Memorandum V 7] (1931)

Programme containing general regulations and syllabuses for examinations in technical and commercial subjects, domestic science and art [Memorandum V 16] (1935; revised 1941)

Organisation of whole–time continuation courses in borough, urban and county areas [Memorandum V 40] (1942)

Report of the departmental committee on educational provision (1947)

Revocation of rule 72/1 of department's rule [circular 11/58] (1958)

Tuarascáil shealadach —n choiste a chuireadh i mbun scrúdú a dhéanamh ar oideachas iarbhunscoile (1962)

Statement by the Minister for Education, Dr P.J. Hillery, in regard to post-primary education (1963)

Letter from George Colley, TD, Minister for Education, to the authorities of secondary and vocational schools (1966)

Community school (1970)

Establishment of boards of management of vocational schools [circular 73/74] (1974)

Report to the Minister for Education on the establishment of An Comhairle Mhuinteoireachta (1974)

Full-time courses in the VEC colleges: report of a committee established to examine third-level courses which lead to awards by NCEA and other bodies outside the universities (1989)

Policy documents of political parties

Irish Labour Party and Trade Union Congress, *Policy on education* (1925)

Irish Labour Party, *The nation organised: Labour's constructive policy and programme* (n.d., c. 1933)

— *Labour's programme for a better Ireland* (1943)

— *Labour's constructive programme* (1952)

— *Challenge and change in education* (1963)

Fine Gael, *Policy towards a just society, no. 3, education* (1966)

Labour Party, *Labour Party outline policy* (1969)

Fianna Fáil, *Action plan for national reconstruction* (1977)

Fine Gael, *Policy document on education: action programme for education in the '80s* (1980)

Fianna Fáil, *The way forward* (1982)

Labour Party, *Socialist principles in education policy: discussion paper* (1986)

Articles and books

Akenson, D. H., *The Irish education experiment: the national system of education in the nineteenth century* (London and Toronto, 1970)

— *Education and enmity: the control of schooling in Northern Ireland 1920–50* (Belfast, 1973)

— *A mirror to Kathleen's face: education in independent Ireland, 1922–1960* (Montreal, 1975)

Allen, Kieran, *Fianna Fáil and Irish labour: 1926 to the present* (London, 1997)

Archdiocese of Dublin, *Community schools and community colleges in the archdiocese of Dublin* (Dublin, 1982)

Archer, M. and Vaughan, M., *Social conflict and educational change 1780–1850* (Cambridge, 1973)

Barry, David, 'The involvement and impact of a professional interest group', in D. G. Mulcahy and Denis O'Sullivan (eds.), *Irish educational policy* (Dublin, 1989), pp. 133–62

Bew, P. and Patterson, H., *Sean Lemass and the making of modern Ireland, 1945–66* (Dublin, 1982)

Brayden, W.H. (ed.), *Royal Dublin Society bi-centenary souvenir 1731–1931* (Dublin, 1931)

Breen, Richard, 'Irish educational performance: past performance and future prospects', in *Public social expenditure: value for money?* (Dublin, 1984)

— *Education and the labour market: work and unemployment among recent cohorts of Irish school leavers* (Dublin, 1984)

Breen, Richard, Hannan, Damian, Rottman, David B. and Whelan, Christopher T., *Understanding contemporary Ireland* (Dublin and London, 1990)

Brenan, Martin, 'The Catholic school system in Ireland', in *Irish Ecclesiastical Record*, lii (1938), pp. 257–72

— 'The vocational schools', in *Irish Ecclesiastical Record*, lvii (1941), pp. 13–27

— 'Rural education: the principles', in *Christus Rex: an Irish Quarterly Journal of Sociology*, vii (1953), pp. 387–99

Browne, Michael, 'Why Catholic priests should concern themselves with social and economic questions', in *Christus Rex: an Irish Quarterly Journal of Sociology*, i (1947) pp. 3–9

Clancy, Patrick, *Participation in higher education: a national survey* (Dublin, 1982)

— *Who goes to college? A second national survey of participation in higher education* (Dublin, 1988)

— 'The evolution of policy in third-level education', in D. G. Mulcahy and Denis O'Sullivan (eds.), *Irish educational policy* (Dublin, 1989), pp. 99–132

Coates, R., *Teachers' unions and interest group politics* (Cambridge, 1972)

Cooke, Jim, *Technical education and the foundation of the Dublin United Trades Council 1886–1986* (Dublin, 1987)

Coolahan, John, *The ASTI and post-primary education in Ireland 1909–1984* (Dublin, 1984)

Coombes, J. and Hewitt, N., *Two hundred and fifty years of technical education in Ross diocese* (Skibbereen, 1984)

Coyne, W. P., *Ireland: industrial and agricultural* (Dublin, 1902)

Daly, M. E., *Industrial development and Irish national identity* (Dublin, 1992)

— *The buffer state: the historical roots of the Department of the Environment* (Dublin, 1997)

Devane, Richard, 'Adolescence and the Vocational Education Bill', in *Irish Ecclesiastical Record*, xxxvi (1930), pp. 20–36

Dooge, J. C., *Technicians* (Dublin, 1962)

Dowling, P. J., 'A plea for continuation education', in *Irish Ecclesiastical Record*, xxvi (1909), pp. 146–52

Duffy, P. J., *The lay teacher in Ireland* (Dublin, 1967)

Duffy, Seamus S., '"Treasures open to the wise": a survey of early mechanics' institutes and similar organisations', in *Saothar*, 15 (1990), pp. 39–47

Educator, 'The Vocational Education Bill', in *Irish Rosary* (1930), pp. 433–7

Fanning, Ronan, *The Irish Department of Finance 1922–58* (Dublin, 1978)

FitzGerald, Garret, *All in a life* (Dublin, 1991)

Gill, T. P., *Education and citizenship with special reference to the labour problem* (Dublin, 1914)

Girvin, Brian, *Between two worlds: politics and economy in independent Ireland* (Dublin, 1989)

Gray, William, *Science and art in Belfast* (Belfast, 1904)

Greaney, V. and Kellaghan, T., *Equality of opportunity in Irish schools: a longitudinal study of 500 students* (Dublin, 1984)

Griffith, Arthur (ed.), *Thomas Davis: thinker and teacher* (Dublin, 1914)

Hackett, J. P., 'Vocational groups and vocational education', in *Irish Monthly*, lxvi (1938), pp. 743–55

Hannan, Damian F. and Boyle, M., *Schooling decisions: the origins and consequences of selection and streaming in Irish post-primary schools* (Dublin, 1987)

Hannan, Damian F., Breen, R., Murray, B., Watson, D., Hardiman, N. and O'Higgins, K., *Schooling and sex roles: sex differences in subject provision and student choice in Irish post-primary schools* (Dublin, 1983)

Hardiman, Niamh, *Pay, politics and economic performance in Ireland 1970–1987* (Oxford, 1988)

Hoctor, Daniel, *The department's story: a history of the Department of Agriculture* (Dublin, 1971)

Holland, J. J., *The Bannow Farm School 1821–1827* (Dublin, 1932)

Hoppen, K. Theodore, *The common scientist in the seventeenth century* (London, 1970)

Humphreys, P. C., *Public service employment* (Dublin, 1993)

Huson, J. M., *The history of adult education* (London, 1851)

Hussey, Gemma, *At the cutting edge: cabinet diaries 1982–1987* (Dublin, 1990)

Hyland, J. P. and Harbinson, J. H., *Meeting the demand* (Dublin, 1964)

International Labour Organisation, *The restructuring of the Irish trade union movement* (Geneva, 1974)

Irish Marketing Surveys Ltd, *A survey of equality of opportunity in teaching carried out by Irish Marketing Surveys Ltd on behalf of the Teachers' Union of Ireland in conjunction with the Employment Equality Agency* (Dublin, 1986)

Irish National Teachers' Organisation, *A plan for education* (Dublin, 1947)

Jones, Mary, *These obstreperous lassies: a history of the Irish Women Workers' Union* (Dublin,

1988)

Kane, Robert, *The industrial resources of Ireland* (Dublin, 1844)

Keating, Patrick, 'Sir Robert Kane and the Museum of Irish Industry', in *Proceedings of the Educational Studies Association of Ireland Conference* (Dublin, 1997), pp. 276–86

Kellaghan, T. and Greaney, V., 'Factors related to choice of post-primary school in Ireland', in *Irish Journal of Education*, 4.2 (1970), pp. 69–83

Kennedy, Finola, 'Industrial training and further education of young people', in *Administration*, 16.2 (1968), pp. 160–6

Keogh, Dermot F., *The Vatican, the bishops and Irish politics 1919–39* (Cambridge, 1986)

— 'The Irish constitutional revolution: analysis of the making of the constitution', in *Administration*, 35 (1987), pp. 4–84

Lee, Joseph J., *Ireland 1912–1985: politics and society* (Cambridge, 1989)

Lucey, Cornelius, 'A guild for education', in *Irish Ecclesiastical Record*, li (June 1938), pp. 584–92

— 'Making the school system of Ireland Catholic', in *Irish Ecclesiastical Record*, lii (October 1938), pp. 405–17

McCarthy, Charles, *The decade of upheaval: Irish trade unions in the nineteen sixties* (Dublin, 1973)

— *Trade unions in Ireland 1894–1960* (Dublin, 1977)

McGinley, Michael, 'Pay 1970–91: the issue of control', in *Industrial Relations News*, 30 (1989), pp. 17–24

— 'Pay 1970–91: climbing in the fog', in *Industrial Relations News*, 33 (1991), pp. 12–18

McKenna, Lambert, 'State rights in Irish education', in *Studies*, xvi (1927), pp. 115–30

McKeown, Michael, 'Professional status as an operational and aspirational characteristic of the teaching force in the Republic of Ireland', in *Irish Educational Studies*, ii (1982), pp. 109–24

McLoughlin, Seamus, 'The vocational school in the rural community', in *Christus Rex: an Irish Quarterly Journal of Sociology*, vii (1953), pp. 428–41

MacNeill, Eoin, 'A view of the state in relation to education' in *Irish Review*, i (October 1922), pp. 3–4

— 'Education: the idea of the state', in *Irish Review*, ii (November 1922), pp. 28–9

Mapstone, Richard, 'Trade union and government relations; a case study of influence on the Stormont government', in *Saothar*, 12 (1987), pp. 35–46

Moody, T. W. and Beckett, J. C., *Queen's Belfast, 1845–1949: the history of a university*, i (London, 1959)

Morton, R. G., 'Mechanics' institutes and the attempted diffusion of useful knowledge in Ireland', in *Irish Booklore*, ii (1972), pp. 67–9

Ó Buachalla, Séamas, *Education policy in twentieth-century Ireland* (Dublin, 1988)

Ó Cathain, Seán, 'Secondary education in Ireland: i', in *Studies*, xliv (1955), pp. 385–400

— 'Secondary education in Ireland: ii', in *Studies*, xlv (1956), pp. 50–66

O'Conallain, Donal, 'Education: free for all', in *The Secondary Teacher* (1966), pp. 6–9

O'Connell, T. J., *A 100 years of progress: a history of the Irish National Teachers' Organisation, 1868–1968* (Dublin, 1969)

O'Connor, Emmet, *Syndicalism in Ireland 1917–23* (Cork, 1989)

— *A labour history of Ireland 1824–1960* (Dublin, 1992)

O'Connor, Seán, 'Post-primary education: now and in the future', in *Studies*, lviii (1968), pp. 233–49

— *A troubled sky: reflections on the Irish educational scene, 1957–1968* (Dublin, 1986)

O'Flaherty, Louis, *Management and control in Irish education* (Dublin, 1992)

O'Flynn, Gráinne, 'Our age of innocence', in Mary Cullen (ed.), *Girls don't do honours: Irish women in education in the 19th and 20th centuries* (Dublin, 1987), pp. 79–99.

O'Hara, B., *Regional Technical College Galway: the first twenty-one years* (Galway, 1993)

O'Leary, Eoin, 'The Irish National Teachers' Organisation and the marriage bar of women national teachers 1933–1958', in *Saothar*, 12 (1987), pp. 47–53

O'Meara, J. J., *Reform in education* (Dublin, 1958)

O'Neill, Joseph, 'Department of Education: church and state', in *Studies*, xxxviii (1949), pp. 419–29

Ó Raifeartaigh, T., 'The state's administration of education', in *Administration*, 2.4 (1954–5), pp. 67–77

— 'Changes and trends in our education system since 1922', in *Journal of the Statistical and Social Inquiry Society of Ireland*, xx (1957–8), pp. 42–51

— 'Education in the USA', in *Studies*, l (1961), pp. 57–74

O'Reilly, Barney, 'Issues in the development of vocational education', in *Administration*, 37.2 (1989), pp. 152–70

Organisation for Economic Co-operation and Development, *Training of technicians in Ireland* (Paris, 1964)

— *Economic surveys: Ireland* (Paris, 1989).

Ó Riordáin, Muiris, 'Technical and vocational education, 1922–52: the cultural emphasis', in *Proceedings of the Educational Studies Association* (1977), pp. 194–200

O'Riordan, Michael, *Catholicity and progress in Ireland* (London, 1905)

O'Sullivan, Denis, 'Cultural strangers and educational change: the OECD report *Investment in education* and Irish education policy', in *Journal of Education Policy*, 7.5 (1992), pp. 445–69

Owens, Timothy J., 'Central initiatives and local realities: curriculum change in the County Cork VEC schools, 1963–1983', in D. G. Mulcahy and Denis O'Sullivan (eds.), *Irish educational policy* (Dublin, 1989), pp. 163–89

Parkes, Susan, 'George Fletcher and technical education in Ireland 1900–1927', in *Irish Education Studies*, 9.1 (1990), pp. 13–29

Pettit, S. F., 'The Royal Cork Institution: a reflection of the cultural life of the city', in *Journal of the Cork Historical and Archaeological* Society, lxxxi (1976), pp. 70–90

Plunkett, Horace, *Ireland in the new century* (London, 1904)

Power, Matt, *Half a century: County Clare VEC 1930–1980* (Ennis, 1980)

Randles, Eileen, *Post-primary education in Ireland 1957–1970* (Dublin, 1975)

[Recess Committee] *Report of the Recess Committee on the establishment of a department of agriculture and industries for Ireland* (Dublin, 1896)

Rogan, Edward, *Synods and cathecesis in Ireland, c. 445–1962* (Rome, 1987)

— *Irish cathecesis: a juridico-historical study of the five plenary synods, 1850–1956* (Rome, 1987)

Ryan, Liam, 'Social dynamite: a study of early school leavers', in *Christus Rex: an Irish Quarterly Journal of Sociology*, xxi (1967), pp. 7–44

Sheehan, J., 'Education and society in Ireland', in J. J. Lee (ed.), *Ireland 1945–70* (Dublin, 1979), pp. 61–72

Tierney, Michael, *Education in a free Ireland* (Dublin, 1919)

Titley, E. Brian, *Church, state and the control of schooling in Ireland, 1900–44* (Toronto, 1983)

Troddyn, Peter M., 'Community schools', in *Studies*, lix (1970), pp. 341–76

Turpin, John, *A school of art in Dublin since the eighteenth century: a history of the National College of Art and Design* (Dublin, 1995)

Tussing, Dale, 'Labour force effects of 1967–8 changes in education policy in the Irish republic', in *Economic and Social Review*, 7.3 (1976), pp. 289–304

— *Irish educational expenditure: past, present and future* (Dublin, 1978)

Waterford City Vocational Education Committee, *Diamond jubilee of technical education in Waterford City, 1906–1981* (Waterford, 1981)

Weiner, Martin, *English culture and the decline of the industrial spirit 1850–1980* (Cambridge, 1981)

Whyte, John H., *Church and state in modern Ireland, 1923–1970*, 2nd edn (Dublin, 1980)

Unpublished theses

Byrne, Kieran, 'The origins and growth of technical education in Ireland, 1731–1922' (PhD, University College Cork, National University of Ireland, 1982)

Carton, J. J., 'The development of technical education in Ireland, 1889–1930' (MEd, Trinity College, Dublin University, 1972)

Clune, Michael, 'Horace Plunkett and the Department of Agriculture and Technical Instruction' (MEd, Trinity College, Dublin University, 1978)

Cooke, James J., 'The movement for a separate department for technical instruction, with particular reference to the role of Dublin Corporation 1867–1902' (MLitt, Trinity College, Dublin University, 1984)

Dolan, Paul, 'The origins of vocational education in Ireland and changing conceptions of it, 1930–78' (MEd, University College Dublin, National University of Ireland, 1980)

Dorney, Margaret, 'The concept of a community college: a case study' (MEd, Trinity College, Dublin University, 1988)

Farry, M. J., 'The structure and the law of vocational education in Ireland' (MLitt, Trinity College, Dublin University, 1984)

Hennessy, M., 'A reassessment of vocational education in Ireland, 1930–1987, including a case study of vocational schooling in a rural area' (MEd, University College Cork, National University of Ireland, 1987)

Kennedy, B., 'The origin and development of vocational education in County Meath: a case study' (MEd, Trinity College, Dublin University, 1981)

MacEoin, S., 'Forbairt an Ghairmoideachais i gCondae na Gaillimh' (MEd, University College Galway, National University of Ireland, 1981)

Moriarity, Gerard A., 'Some aspects of the development of vocational teachers' organisations in Ireland, 1913–59, (MEd, University College Cork, National University of Ireland, 1984)

O'Leary, Patrick Kevin, 'The development of post-primary education in Éire since 1922 with special reference to vocational education' (PhD, Queen's University of Belfast, 1962)

O'Reilly, Barney, 'Vocational education and society in Ireland 1930–90: a case study in the politics of education' (PhD, University of Edinburgh, 1998)

O'Shea, Finbarr, 'Government and trade unions in Ireland 1939–46: the formulation of labour legislation' (MA, University College Cork, National University of Ireland, 1988)

Index

abortion, 254
academic education, 5–8
Adult Education Organisers' Association, 243
Agricultural and Technical Education, 48–9
Agricultural Overseers' Association, 45
agriculture, 67, 73–4, 131, 145, 280, 286
  education for, 79–80
Agriculture, Department of, 33, 50, 54, 140, 143
Agriculture and Technical Instruction, Department of, 4, 28–30, 31, 32, 39–51, 109
  RCO, 43–51
  sectional associations, 39–43
Agriculture and Technical Instruction (Ireland) Act 1899, 17, 28, 39, 40, 41, 131–2, 204
Albert College, Glasnevin, 22, 28, 38, 39, 54, 162
allowances, 112, 174, 175–6
Aloysius, Fr, 157
Alton, Ernest, 228
An Chomhairle Oiliuna (AnCO), 9, 197, 243, 255, 265, 298–9
Anti-Discrimination (Pay) Act 1974, 183
Aontas, 243
Apothecaries' Hall, 1
apprenticeship, 8, 9, 79, 105–7, 154, 162, 196–7, 280, 293
  gender equity, 255
  reform, 296–9
  and VECs, 143–5
Apprenticeship Act 1931, 105, 144, 296–7
Apprenticeship Act 1959, 145, 197, 297–8
Apprenticeship Curriculum Advisory Committee, 243
Arklow, Co. Wicklow, 105
Arklow Technical School, 98
Armagh, County, 20
Army Air Corps, 105
Association of Chief Executive Officers of VECs (ACEOVEC), 189
Association of Comprehensive School Teachers, 168
Association of Higher Civil Servants, 240
Association of Principals of Institutions of Technical Instruction in Ireland

(APITII), 41
Association of Principals of Technical Institutes, 53
Association of Remedial Teachers, 243
Association of Science and Engineering Technical Teachers, 46
Association of Secondary Teachers, Ireland (ASTI), 47, 48, 49, 86, 100, 248
  and INTO, 52
  allowances, 175–9
  boards of management, 258–9
  salaries, 172, 250
  strikes, 177, 178–9
  and TUI, 238–9, 267–71
  and VTA, 166, 168
Athenaeum Society, Limerick, 23, 37
Athlone RTC, 293

Balfour, Arthur, 27
Barrie, Hugh T., 50
Belfast, 5–6, 19–20, 26, 29, 31, 37
  art school, 23, 24
Belfast Academical Institution, 19
Belfast Mechanics' Institute, 22
Belmore commissioners, 133
benevolent fund, 100
Bernard, Mother, 4
Bew, Paul, 290
Bianconi, Charles, 37
Birkbeck, George, 20
Blair, Robert, 29
Blanchardstown community school, 168, 195
Bloxham, Elizabeth, 49–50
boards of management, 257–9
Bolton Street Technical Institute, 105, 157, 292
Botanic Gardens, 39
Bourke, Dr, 218
Bowe, J.J., 189
Brady, Pat, 240
Brady, Tom, 158
Bray VEC, 139, 205
Breen, Fr W., 226
Brenan, Fr Martin, 76–7, 135
Brenan, James, 23–4
Britain, 7–8, 148, 175

higher, 263–6
planning, 197
reform, 296–9
trade unionism in, 37–57
Technical Education Association of Ireland, 27, 38
technical education committees, 215–16
Technical Instruction Act 1889, 26, 38
technical instruction committees, 100
technical schools, 83, 277
third level education, 241–2, 263–4, 271, 283
  reform, 264–5, 291–6
  and vocational education, 7, 9, 191, 282–3, 290
Thomond College of Education, 240, 243
Tipperary, County, 104, 195, 205, 215
trade preparatory schools, 134–5
Trade Union Bill 1941, 114–15
trade unions, 44, 157, 199, 237–8, 240, 243–4
  apprenticeship, 106
  mergers, 267–8
  RCO as, 47–8
teachers' unity, 266–71
  and technical education, 37–57
  and VECs, 216
trades councils, 215
trainee teachers, 167
Tralee Technical School, 49–50
Tralee VEC, 205, 214, 228
Tribunal on Teachers' Salaries, 168
Trinity College, Dublin, 1, 7, 17, 162, 173, 198, 228, 240, 291
Trundle, Liam, 126–7, 157, 158, 242
  VEOO split, 159–61

Ulster Unionist Council, 30
UNESCO, 254
UNICEF, 164
United Nations, 182
Universal Declaration of Human Rights, 181
universities, 101, 295–6
  and RTCs, 180
  and vocational education, 7, 9, 191, 282–3
University College Cork, 54
University College Dublin, 54, 133
University College Galway, 160
University of Limerick, 240
Urrus na nGairm-Mhúinteoirí, 162

Vaughan, Canon P. J., 209
vocational education, 62–89, 276–301. *see also* curriculum; technical education

certification, 149–53
economic context, 235–8, 246–7, 261–3
examinations, 103–4
under Fianna Fail, 73–7
funding, 85
under interparty government, 85–8
in *Investment in education*, 153–4
Memo V 40, 83, 84–5, 102
non-denominational, 70–2, 76, 77–8, 87–8, 194–5, 204, 278
pupil numbers, 279
and rural life, 140–2
statistics, 81, 83
and universities, 282–3
Vocational Education Act 1930, 8, 53, 55–6, 70–2, 85, 101, 108–9, 116, 133, 148, 217, 277
  agriculture, 140, 145
  curriculum, 280–1
  salaries, 111
  section 99, 113, 117
  subcommittees, 215
  technical education, 142
  VEC appointments, 225, 228, 231–2
  VECs, 204–8
Vocational Education (Amendment) Act 1970, 89, 257
Vocational Education Amendment Bill 1943, 115–17
Vocational Education Bulletin, The, 42–3, 93–6, 98, 100, 101, 116, 124
  apprenticeships, 105–6
  on CMGO, 159
  and Education dept, 117, 118
  equality of opportunity, 102, 103
  final edition, 126
  first edition, 109
  qualifications, 112, 113, 150
  requirements of office, 115
  salaries, 119, 121, 122–3
Vocational Education Committees (VECs), 74, 86, 266. *see also* Memorandum V 40
  1930-92, 204–32
  appointments by, 217–28
  canvassing, 220–8
  clerical involvement, 77, 208–13
  conciliation council, 170
  constitution of, 204–8
  established, 56
  finances, 229–30
  limits of representation, 213–17
  national and local interests, 228–31
  open competition, 110
  and RTCs, 263–4
  salaries, 111–12